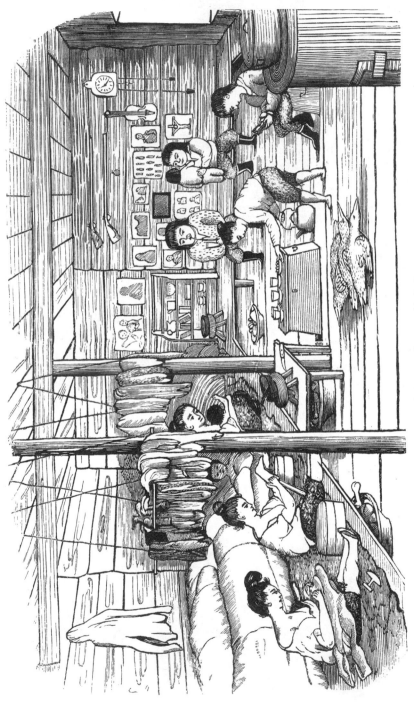

*Interior of the house of a very rich family.*

# TALES AND TRADITIONS
## OF THE
# ESKIMO
### WITH A SKETCH OF THEIR HABITS, RELIGION,
### LANGUAGE AND OTHER PECULIARITIES

## Hinrich Rink

Introduction by
## Janet Catherine Berlo
*Susan B. Anthony Chair of Gender Studies and Art
History at the University of Rochester in New York.*

# DOVER PUBLICATIONS, INC.
## Mineola, New York

Published in Canada by General Publishing Company, Ltd.,
30 Lesmill Road, Don Mills, Toronto, Ontario.
Published in the United Kingdom by Constable and Company,
Ltd., 3 The Lanchesters, 162–164 Fulham Palace Road, London
W6 9ER.

*Bibliographical Note*

This Dover edition, first published in 1997, is an unabridged
republication of the volume first published by William Blackwood and Sons, Edinburgh and London, in 1875. A new Introduction has been prepared specially for this edition.

*Library of Congress Cataloging-in-Publication Data*

Rink, H. (Hinrich), 1819–1893.
 [Eskimoiske eventyr og sagn. English]
 Tales and traditions of the Eskimo : with a sketch of their
habits, religion, language and other peculiarities / Hinrich
Rink ; introduction by Janet Catherine Berlo.
  p.  cm.
 This Dover edition is an unabridged republication of Tales
and traditions of the Eskimo: Edinburgh and London : William
Blackwood and Sons, 1875. A new introduction has been pre-
pared specially for this edition.
 Includes bibliographical references.
 ISBN 0-486-29966-X (pbk.)
 1. Eskimos—Greenland—Folklore.  2. Tales—Greenland.
I. Title.
E99.E7R5413   1997
398.2'089971—dc21                    97-24234
                                      CIP

Manufactured in the United States of America
Dover Publications, Inc., 31 East 2nd Street, Mineola, N. Y. 11501

# INTRODUCTION
# TO THE DOVER EDITION.

*Tales and Traditions of the Eskimo* is a classic in the vast
literature on Arctic peoples. One of the very first books
on Eskimo culture to be published for the general
reader,[1] it drew upon more than twenty years of its
author's experience, principally in Western Greenland,
and remains a fine and unique contribution to the literature. Like many scholars of his generation, the Danish
writer Hinrich Johannes Rink[2] (1819–1893) was trained
in the natural sciences, earning his Ph.D. from the University of Kiel in 1844. Shortly thereafter he sailed to Greenland to conduct geological research. It was the people he
found there who would transform his life. His ethnological
and folkloric research were only a sideline, however, for
Rink became a colonial administrator, eventually directing the Royal Greenland Board of Trade, the Danish
governmental corporation that controlled commerce
between Greenland and the rest of the world.[3]

---

[1] The other was Charles Hall, *Arctic Researches and Life Among the Esquimaux*
(New York: Harper Publishers, 1865).
[2] Rink chose to anglicize his first name when he translated his own book
into English.
[3] The most detailed biographical discussion on Rink can be found in
*Dansk Biografisk Leksikon*, ed. by Povl Engelstoft and Svend Dahl (Copenhagen: J. H. Schultz Forlag, 1940), vol. 19, pp. 560–564. See also George
Nellemann, "Applied Anthropology in Greenland in the 1860s: H. J. Rink's
Administration and View of Culture," *Folk: Dansk Ethnografisk Tidskrift*,
vol. 8–9 (1966-67): 221–241.

Mid-nineteenth century Greenland was quite different from other parts of the Arctic, many of which were still essentially unexplored. After a period of Norse settlement beginning in the late tenth century, Western Greenland was "rediscovered" for Europe by Martin Frobisher on his expedition of 1575–78. Dutch and Danish-Norwegian trade occurred throughout the seventeenth and eighteenth centuries, and the first missionaries arrived in 1721. By the end of the eighteenth century, most West Greenlanders were at least nominally Christian. There was a great deal of intermarriage between successive generations of traders and Greenlandic women. The missionaries established a written language, and in 1861 Rink himself founded the first newspaper written in Greenlandic, *Atuagagdliutit*.

Considering how little was known in the 1860s about the central and western Arctic (Canada and Alaska), Rink's generalizations about Eskimoan peoples in his introduction to this volume were surprisingly not far off the mark. He did, however, overstate their general reliance on the sea and sea animals, for little was then known about inland Eskimos of the central Canadian Arctic, whose world revolved around caribou.

Rink worked in the north earlier than Edward Nelson in the Bering Strait region of Alaska (1877–81), John Murdock in Point Barrow, Alaska, on the Arctic Ocean (1881–83), or Franz Boas in the central Canadian Arctic (1888–84).[4] Yet because he worked in an area that had

---

[4] See Edward W. Nelson, *The Eskimo About Bering Strait*, 18th Annual Report of the Bureau of American Ethnology, Part I (Washington: Government Printing Office, 1899); John Murdock, *Ethnological Results of the Point Barrow Expedition*, 9th Annual Report of the Bureau of American Ethnology (Washington: Government Printing Office, 1892); and Franz Boas, *The Central Eskimo*, 6th Annual Report of the Bureau of American Ethnology (Washington: Government Printing Office, 1888).

had such early and prolonged contact with outsiders, he did not find the rich material culture that they documented so fully. Indeed, he noted that in Greenland "scarcely any traces of the arts of drawing and sculpture belonging to earlier times remain" (p. 69). While the panoply of material culture—masks, clothing, hunting equipment, ivory carving, and architecture—would preoccupy the anthropologists and scientists who studied Alaskan and Canadian Eskimos in the following decades, Rink astutely recognized that in Greenland only language and folklore remained as "the two national treasures" (p. 78) of the aboriginal Greenlandic peoples. Although Christian missionaries had worked relentlessly in West Greenland since the early eighteenth century, Rink saw that in traditional tales could be found vestiges of "the whole national store of intellectual or moral property—religion, science, and poetry at once" (p. 86).

Rink was surely one of the first to recognize the essential cultural unity of all Eskimoan peoples.[5] Many of the social customs he describes are evident, in their general parameters, across Arctic America. His work was an important source of ethnological and folkloric information for those who conducted fieldwork in the generations that followed. Boas recognized that there were pan-arctic elements in Rink's Greenlandic stories. Knud Rasmussen, the most famous and prolific of all scholars of the north (who was himself of mixed Danish and Greenlandic parentage), followed in Rink's footsteps, studying Eskimo

[5] A note on terminology: while the term Eskimo is still used across the Arctic, in Canada the term Inuit has official recognition as the proper term for this ethnic group. In Alaska, the term Eskimo as well as two more specialized cultural names, Yupik and Inupiaq, are used. In Greenland, the word Eskimo is less often used today, being replaced by the generalized term Inuit or the specifically Greenlandic term Kalaallit.

cultures from Alaska to Greenland from 1912 to 1933. His work on the Fifth Thule Expedition, in particular, confirmed that many of the traditions Rink documented were firmly entrenched in oral literatures across the Arctic.[6]

The tale of the origin of the sun and the moon, a story of brother-sister incest (p. 236), is well known across the north and is today given new life in many prints and drawings made by Canadian Inuit artists, as well as in stories. Giviok (p. 157) is the Greenlandic version of the pan-arctic Odysseus-like character known elsewhere by the similar names Kivioq or Quiviuq, who roams far and wide and has many adventures. As a central Canadian Inuit storyteller asked of Knud Rasmussen in 1923, "have you seen Kivioq? You must have met him in your travels! For like you he has been in all countries, and the most wonderful things are told about him!"[7] Similarly, the modern reader will recognize age-old human types in these stories collected in Greenland and Labrador, and perhaps discover some new versions of human foibles and frailties as well.

[6] See, for example, Knud Rasmussen, *Intellectual Culture of the Caribou Eskimos*, Reports of the Fifth Thule Expedition, vol. 7, part 2 (Copenhagen: Gyldendalske Boghandel, 1930); *Iglulik and Caribou Eskimo Texts*, Reports of the Fifth Thule Expedition, vol. 7, part 3 (Copenhagen: Gyldendalske Boghandel, 1930); *The Netsilik Eskimos: Social Life and Spiritual Culture*, Reports of the Fifth Thule Expedition, vol. 8, parts 1 and 2 (Copenhagen: Gyldendalske Boghandel, 1931); and *Intellectual Culture of the Copper Eskimos*, Reports of the Fifth Thule Expedition, vol. 9 (Copenhagen: Gyldendalske Boghandel, 1932).

[7] Rasmussen, *The Netsilik Eskimos*, p. 365.

# PREFACE.

THE author of this work has partly resided, partly been travelling about, on the shores of Davis Strait, from the southernmost point of Greenland up to 73° north latitude, for sixteen winters and twenty-two summers ; first as a scientific explorer, afterwards as Royal Inspector or Governor of the Southern Danish establishments in Greenland. The first series of tales was published by him in 1866 ; but as this field of ethnological investigation was at that time almost uncultivated, much new material came to hand after that publication, and, moreover, the author had then only acquired such a degree of familiarity with the language, as made it possible for him to understand his native informants sufficiently well to write down their verbal communications. In 1871 he determined to publish a new series of tales as a supplement to the former, in which he has also described the general habits, religion, and other peculiarities of the Eskimo, having by that time been enabled to give a more comprehensive account of these subjects, and to make some farther improvements on the first publication.

Besides the translation into English, a twofold object has been aimed at in this edition : first, that of incorporating the two parts into one ; and second, of partly abbreviating their contents. The principal aim of this abridgment has been to make these accounts more available to readers engaged in archæological studies, or investigations of the earliest history of mankind by comparison of the traditional tales, languages, and religious opinions of the more primitive nations, in which respect the Eskimo, and specially the Greenlanders, have been studied more minutely, perhaps, than any other similar people. Keeping this object in view, some of the tales, as well as a certain part of the original work, seemed to be of special interest only to the Danish colonies, and have therefore been wholly omitted, or only given in an abridged form, in the present publication.

The wholly modern study of " prehistoric man," which in our time is making such progress, has hitherto almost exclusively been founded upon the study of the ornaments, weapons, and other remains of primitive peoples, which for this purpose have become greatly valued, and are searched for in the bowels of the earth, and drawn forth to light in nearly every part of the globe. But the time will certainly come when any relics of spiritual life brought down to us from prehistoric mankind, which may still be found in the folklore of the more isolated and primitive nations, will be valued as highly as those material remains. In this respect the Eskimo may be considered among the most interesting, both as having been almost entirely cut off from other nations and very little influenced by foreign intercourse, and also as representing a kind of link between the aboriginals of the New and the Old World.

Some illustrations, designed as well as drawn and engraved on wood by natives of Greenland, are given, the author having supplied the original blocks to be used in this edition for this purpose.

As to the spelling of Greenland words and names, we have to draw a distinction between those which are more properly used as representing the foreign expressions themselves, and those which have been wholly embodied in the Danish or English language of the text, and thereby subject to the orthography of these languages. In the first instance, the words distinguished by a different type, are spelt in exact accordance with the orthography now adopted in the native schools of Greenland. In the preliminary sketch, where this orthography is explained, it will be seen that all the sounds may be expressed by our usual Latin characters, with the exception only of a deep guttural *k*, for which the character к has been formed; the other more peculiar sounds having been substituted by double consonants or expressed by accents. The other letters are pronounced almost identically with those of the German and Scandinavian languages. In the second instance we have, as far as possible, accommodated the mode of spelling to the English pronunciation of the letters, in some instances using *y* for j, *gh* for g, *k*, or in some more peculiar cases, *k'* for к, &c.; as, for instance, *anghiak* (ångiaк), *kayak* (кajaк), *k'ivigtok* (кivigtoк).

The personal and geographical names are given with fewer alterations of the kind mentioned, and nearly agree with the Danish orthography.

To prevent, as far as possible, misunderstanding and farther corruption of the original Greenland words, we have added, wherever it appeared necessary, in parentheses, how the word is most nearly to be pronounced (pron. . . .), in other instances how it is to be correctly spelt in Greenlandish (cor. sp. . . .); as, for instance, *Kulange* (pron. *Koolanghee*), *angakok* (cor. sp. **angåkoк**).

The following general rules may be laid down : The letter *e* at the end of a word is never mute, but always to be pronounced ; *ai* is pronounced like *y* in *by;* *i*, like *i* in *it;* *g*, like *g* in *good;* *u*, like *oo*.

In some instances we have used the Greenland plural, formed by substituting a *t* at the end of the word, such as *angakut* instead of *angakoks*.

As to uncommon words or expressions in general, those peculiar to Eskimo life will be found explained in the preliminary sketch. But in order to make the stories more readable, as well as better understood, we have, without paying particular attention to this, inserted the most necessary explanations in parentheses or in notes, in different places of the text itself, where it appeared most useful ; especially in the earlier pages, where the expressions are first met with.

Dr Robert Brown, who at the author's request has been good enough to revise the manuscript and make such corrections or emendations in the style and construction of the collection as in his judgment were advisable, has had in his travels in the northern regions of America, as well as in Greenland and on the western shores of Davis Strait and Baffin Bay, an opportunity of visiting the aborigines of these countries in their own homes ; and these advantages, coupled with his long personal acquaintance with the author, and his experience as a writer on Ethnology, have rendered him peculiarly fitted for this friendly editorial task.

H. R.

KONGL, GRÖNDLANDSKE HANDEL,
COPENHAGEN, *Sept.* 1875.

# CONTENTS.

## THE ESKIMO.

## TALES AND TRADITIONS.

# THE ESKIMO.

———◆———

## INTRODUCTORY REMARKS.

WITH the exception of a few small and scattered
tribes who may be considered as the only link
between the coast people and the inlanders, the Eskimo
always have their habitations close to the sea, or on the
banks of rivers in the immediate vicinity of their outlets
into the sea. Even on their hunting and trading expeditions they seldom withdraw more than twenty, and
only in very rare cases more than eighty miles, from the
sea-shore. Save a slight intermixture of European settlers, the Eskimo are the only inhabitants of the shores
of Arctic America, and of both sides of Davis Strait and
Baffin Bay, including Greenland, as well as a tract of
about four hundred miles on the Behring Strait coast of
Asia. Southward they extend as far as about 50° N.L.
on the eastern side, and 60° on the western side of
America, and from 55° to 60° on the shores of Hudson
Bay. Only on the west the Eskimo near their frontier
are interrupted on two small spots of the coast by the
Indians, named Kennayans and Ugalenzes, who have
there advanced to the sea-shore for the sake of fishing.
These coasts of Arctic America, of course, also comprise
all the surrounding islands. Of these the Aleutian

Islands form an exceptional group ; the inhabitants of these on the one hand distinctly differing from the coast people here mentioned, while on the other they show a closer relationship to the Eskimo than any other nation. The Aleutians, therefore, may be considered as only an abnormal branch of the Eskimo nation. The Aleutian language, though differing completely from the Eskimo with regard to the sound of the words, shows a great similarity to it in structure ; and otherwise the Aleutians only seem to differ from the Eskimo inasmuch as some institutions have been slightly more developed among them. On the other hand, all over the eastern and widest parts of their territories the Eskimo are very distinctly severed from the adjoining nations. In the western part some slight transitions may be traced : namely, in the case of the inland Eskimo by the different situation of their dwelling-places ; in that of the Aleutians by their language and social institutions. Finally, it may be mentioned that a few small Indian tribes have adopted somewhat of the Eskimo mode of life, which has also been the case with some of their neighbours on the Asiatic side.

As regards their northern limits, the Eskimo people, or at least remains of their habitations, have been found nearly as far north as any Arctic explorers have hitherto advanced ; and very possibly bands of them may live still farther to the north, as yet quite unknown to us.

From the north-western to the southernmost point the Eskimo territories in a straight line measure about 3200 miles. If we consider their extreme western range to be Behring Strait, and their extreme eastern one to be Labrador and Greenland, the natives from either of these points would have to travel about 5000 miles along the coast in order to reach the others. Strictly speaking, these journeys might still be performed by the natives with their own means of conveyance ; but there are certain boundaries which, in our days at least, are scarcely ever passed—partly on account of natural obstacles, partly because the nation at those points has been broken up into tribes, whose mutual intercourse for the purpose of barter has been frequently interrupted by hostilities. For these reasons the Eskimo might now be divided into many smaller tribes. But from our point of view the following principal divisions will be sufficient :—

1. *The East Greenlanders*, along the whole of the east coast of Greenland down to Cape Farewell, the southernmost of whom every year make bartering excursions to the Danish settlement nearest the Cape, and have intercourse with the next section.

2. *The West Greenlanders*, or inhabitants of the Danish trading districts from the Cape upwards to 74° N.L. In conformity with the administrative division of the colonies, they are generally divided into North and South Greenlanders—only the latter are not to be confounded with the next, with whom they seem to have had no intercourse whatever since these regions have been known to Europeans.

3. *The Northernmost Greenlanders*, or inhabitants of the west coast to the north of Melville Bay, or what Sir John Ross called the " Arctic Highlanders."

4. *The Labrador Eskimo.*

5. *The Eskimo of the middle regions*, occupying all the coasts from Baffin and Hudson Bays to Barter Island near Mackenzie River. This division is the most widely spread of them all—its territories representing an extent of land, traversed and intercepted in many directions by the sea, measuring 2000 miles in length and 800 miles in breadth. Perhaps there may be reasons for establishing subdivisions of this section, but they do not appear anywhere to exhibit such mutual differences as those separating them from the next tribe, with whom they have regular meetings on Barter Island.

6. *The Western Eskimo*, inhabiting the remaining

coast of America from Barter Island to the west and
south. They seem to deviate from all the former in
respect of certain habits, such as the labial ornaments
of the men and the head-dress of the women. They
must also be considered as the nearest akin to the Aleutians and the inland Eskimo, and in the vicinity of
Alaska they show traces of intermingled Indian blood.
This may be owing to the Indian women captured in
war with the Eskimo having been married into the
nation.

7. *The Asiatic Eskimo.*

As regards their development when they first became
known to modern Europeans, the Eskimo may be
classed with the prehistoric races of the age of the
ground stone tools with the exceptional use of metals.
It has been usual to designate all nations of this kind
as "savages;" some authors have even described them
as being totally destitute of those mental qualities
through which any kind of culture is manifested, such
as social order, laws, sciences, arts, and even religion.
That those opinions find utterance can scarcely be
wondered at when we observe the carelessness with
which such important questions are discussed, and see
travellers who merely go on shore from a ship and
spend a couple of hours with the inhabitants proceed to
make inquiries as to their ideas of God and the origin
of the world; and also how European settlers among
natives whose language they are quite unconversant
with pretend to have found them altogether without
religion. Such views, however, resting upon the prejudice of race and on superficial observation, are now
being abandoned. We have gradually been finding out
that manifestations of culture must be supposed to exist
in every nation, although they may not assume the same
form as those we observe among more advanced races.
We think it a great mistake to suppose any people devoid of religion; and it seems to us equally unreason-

able to fancy a community of men living altogether without laws, if by laws we understand bonds or restrictions by which the community voluntarily limits the free actions of its members. In the lower stages of development, the laws, being principally represented by habits and customs, leave the individual perhaps even less free than in a more civilised state, inasmuch as they dictate his mode of life, and not even in his most private and domestic affairs is he left to act at liberty. These habits and customs are closely allied to the religious opinions, by which they are still more powerfully influenced. When laws and religion were asserted to be wanting, there was still less likelihood of art and science being observed. In these introductory remarks we shall endeavour to explain how these utterances of culture are for the most part embodied in the traditional tales.

It is in accordance with the views here stated that the author has been guided in attempting to divide and arrange the subject-matter of the following remarks. It has already been mentioned, and will, moreover, become evident from the traditions, that the Eskimo exhibit great conformity and similarity, notwithstanding their being spread over such vast territories. An examination of one of the principal divisions or tribes named above will therefore more or less illustrate the others. For this reason the Greenlanders, who are by far the best known of all, may here be considered to represent the Eskimo in general ; though it must not be forgotten that, as there can scarcely have existed any absolute stability with regard to culture lasting for many centuries, there is also no absolute or actual identity between the different tribes. It must therefore be kept in mind that wherever no other particulars are specially brought forward, the following descriptions refer to the West Greenlanders, such as their state is supposed to have been when Europeans came to settle among them during last century—viz., in 1721.

## I.—SUBSISTENCE AND MODE OF LIFE.

The sustenance of the Eskimo is entirely derived from the capture of seals and cetaceous animals, which has made them inhabitants of the sea-shore. Both kinds of animals enable them, especially by means of their blubber, and the seals also by their skins, to brave the severity of climate, and, independent of any vegetable resources, to settle and procure the means of life as far north as any explorers have hitherto found human inhabitants. The seals are sufficient, and at the same time indispensable, for this purpose. They are caught partly from kayaks, or shuttle-shaped boats, and partly from the ice and the shore. Among their more or less peculiar hunting contrivances we may mention: (1) *Their kayaks, or boats, which consist of a framework of wood*, joined together principally by strings, and provided *with a cover of skins* impenetrable to the water. (2) *The adjustment of the kayak itself and the kayak-coverings*, with a view to provide *an entire shelter for the kayaker*, or seal-hunter, with the exception only of the face, to protect him against the water. Only a small number of Eskimo have kayaks fitted for more than a single man ;[1] and still more exceptionally, in the farthest north some are found who have no kayaks at all, from the sea being almost constantly frozen. (3) *The adaptation of a bladder filled with air to the harpoons or javelins*, in order, by retarding the animals, to prevent them escaping after being struck, and to prevent the harpoon sinking, should the hunter miss his aim. (4) *The very ingenious way in which the point of these weapons*, and of the spears with which the animals are finally killed, *are fitted into the shaft*, so that having penetrated

[1] Such kayaks, suited for two people—one sitting behind the other —are the "baidars" of the Eskimo of Behring Strait.

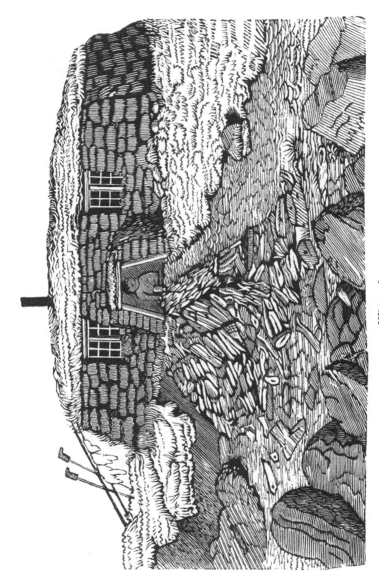

*Winter house.*

the skin of the animal, the point is bent out of the shaft, which is either entirely loosened, while only the point with the line and the bladder remains attached to the animal, or keeps hanging at the point. Without this precaution, the animal in its struggles would break the shaft or make the barbs slip out of its body again. (5) *The sledge with the dogs* trained for drawing it. In speaking of these complex contrivances as characteristic of the Eskimo, we do not claim any of them as their exclusive property or invention, or as having been unknown among other nations now or in former ages. It would, however, be perhaps difficult to find anything at all like their kayaks in any other part of the globe.

*Their dwellings* are always of two kinds—namely, tents for the summer, and houses or huts for winter use. The tents, generally adapted for less than ten and rarely for more than twenty individuals, consist of from ten to fourteen poles, with one end raised high and leaning on the frame which forms the entrance, and the whole covered over with a double layer of skins. The tents seem to be constructed in the same way everywhere, and to differ from those of neighbouring nations in having their highest point at the entrance in front, from which the roof inclines towards the sides, resting all round upon a low wall of stones and turf; while the neighbouring tribes generally construct their tents of a conical form, with the top in the centre. The winter-houses are far more varied in structure. Generally they are built of stones and turf, the roof-spars and the pillars which support the middle of the roof being of wood. Only the Eskimo of the middle regions have vaults of snow for their habitations ; whilst the western Eskimo build their houses chiefly of planks, merely covered on the outside with green turf. Some of the very far northern Eskimo are obliged to use bones or stones instead of wood. As to the form of the houses, the passage leading into them is long and very narrow, and

elevated towards both ends—viz., the outer and the inner
entrances ; so that on entering the house one has first
to descend, and afterwards again to ascend before reaching the interior.    This consists of a single apartment,
only the ledge or bench for resting and sleeping on is
divided into separate portions for the different families.
In Greenland the ledge or bench—the "brix," as the
Danes call it—only occupies one side of the house, its
length being proportioned to the number of the families,
whose rooms or stalls are separated by low screens, each
of these rooms having its lamp standing on the floor in
front of it.    The snow-huts, from their circular form,
are of course arranged differently ; and this is also the
case with the plank-houses in western Eskimo-Land,
which have a cooking-place in the centre of the floor,
with a smoke-hole in the roof, like the houses of the
neighbouring Indians.    But the house-passage has
generally everywhere a small side-room with a cooking-
place.    The provisions are sometimes kept in rooms
connected with the house or house-passage ; in other
places in separate storehouses, or in caves or holes of
the rocks covered with stones.    In former times it
seems to have been the custom at the more populous
places to have a public building for meetings, especially
for solemn occasions.    Such buildings are still in common use among the western Eskimo : they are also
spoken of in Labrador ; and in Greenland they are well
known by tradition, and were called ᴋagsse; while in
.other districts they are termed *kagge, karrigi*, and
*kashim*.    Though the dwelling-houses are nearly always
built for more than one family, the number of these is
seldom found to exceed three or four.    In south Greenland, however, houses have been met with more than
sixty feet in length, and containing stalls for ten families.
At Point Barrow, Simpson found nearly fifty houses
with two *karrigi*, for 309 inhabitants.

*The dress* for men and women is much alike, consist-

*Woman with a child in the amowt (after present fashion).*    *Godthaab.*

*A girl in holiday costume (present fashion).  Godthaab.*

ing of trousers, and a jacket with a hood to be drawn
up to cover the head (at least for men), and otherwise
fitting tightly round the body, leaving no opening excepting for the face and the hands. The same shape
is adopted for the kayak-jacket, the inside border of
which is pressed closely round the rim encircling the
opening in which the man sits, and the hands are protected by a pair of waterproof leather mittens. The
foot-gear consists of different kinds of boots, exceedingly
well made, and in preparing the skins for the manufacture of which a considerable degree of care and in-
genuity is displayed.

*The Eskimo may more properly be classed among the
people having fixed dwellings than among the wandering
nations*, because they generally winter in the same place
through even more than one generation, so that love of
their birthplace is a rather predominating feature in their
character. During the rest of the year, however, they
are constantly on the move, carrying their tents and all
their furniture with them from one place to another,
choosing their route with different objects, generally
preferring that of reindeer-hunting, but also having an
eye to seal-hunting, fishery, or trade. When travelling
in this manner for very distant places, they are sometimes arrested on their route and obliged to take up
winter quarters before reaching their proper destination.
An Eskimo from the northern shores of Hudson Bay,
who accompanied Franklin as interpreter, is said to
have reported that people in his house resided during
the winter on the borders of the lakes in the interior,
and in summer at the sea-shore. If this be true, it would
form a remarkable exception to the general rule.

*The mode of life* of the Eskimo being mainly that of
hunters and fishers, they must, in comparison with other
nations, be regarded—speaking broadly—as having no
regular property. They only possess the most necessary
utensils and furniture, with a stock of provisions for less

than one year; and these belongings never exceed certain limits fixed upon by tradition or custom. On account of these limits, which are of great importance as regards their social order, and the laws which will be discussed hereafter, the properties may be thus classified:—

1. Property owned by an association of generally more than one family—*e.g.*, the winter-house, which, however, is only of any real value as regards the timber employed in raising it, the rest of it being built of such materials as are to be found everywhere, by the work of women's hands.

2. Property the common possession of one, or at most of three families of kindred—viz., a tent and everything belonging to the household, such as lamps, tubs, dishes of wood, soapstone pots; a boat, or *umiak*, which can carry all these articles along with the tent; one or two sledges with the dogs attached to them; the latter, however, are wanting in South Greenland. To this must be added the stock of winter provisions, representing as much as, used exclusively, will be sufficient for two or three months' consumption; and lastly, a varying but always very small store of articles for barter.

3. As regards personal property—*i.e.*, owned by every individual—cognisance must be taken of clothes, consisting of, at least for the principal members of the family, two suits, but rarely more; the sewing implements of the women; the kayaks of the men, with tools and weapons belonging to these; a few other tools for working in wood; and weapons for the land-chase. Only a very few first-rate seal-hunters own two kayaks, but several of them have two suits of the appertaining implements,—namely, the *large harpoon* (**tukak,** the point; and **ernangnak,** the shaft of it), with its bladder and line; the *bladder-arrow* or javelin (**agdligak**), a smaller harpoon with the bladder attached to its shaft; the *bird-arrow* or bird-spear (**nugfit**); the *lance* or spear (**anguvigak**), the point of which is without barbs; *fishing-lines*, and various smaller articles.

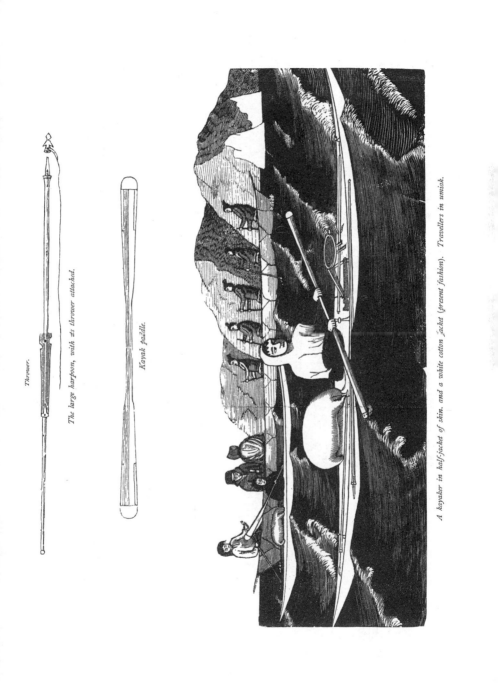

*Thrower.*

*The large harpoon, with its thrower attached.*

*Kayak paddle.*

*A kayaker in half-jacket of skin, and a white cotton jacket (present fashion). Travellers in umiak.*

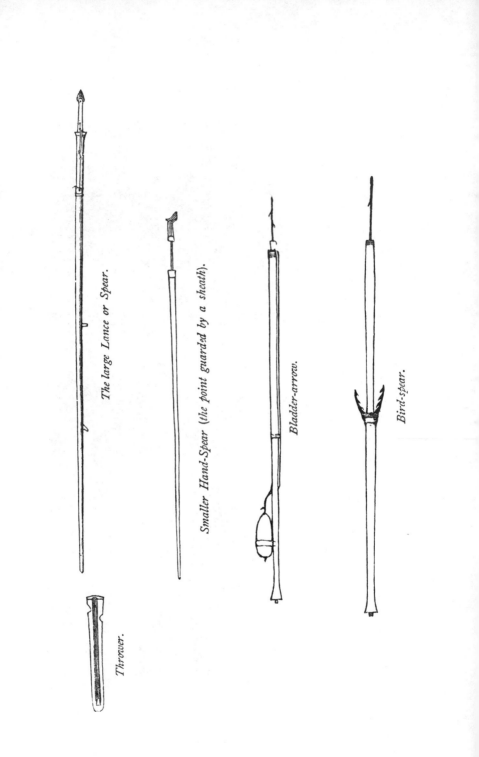

The large Lance or Spear.

Smaller Hand-Spear (the point guarded by a sheath).

Bladder-arrow.

Bird-spear.

Thrower.

Excepting the houses of the western Eskimo, which, being composed of timber, are of more value, the conditions of property seem to be nearly alike everywhere. With a few exceptions, the natives carry all their movable goods along with them in the boat on their summer travels, and on arriving at some narrow strip of land which has to be crossed, everything is brought over along with the boat.

Notwithstanding their very limited feeling as to accumulating property, the Eskimos have kept up a kind of *trade* among themselves, and it is for this purpose that some of their most distant journeys are undertaken. But the mere desire to travel may perhaps have urged them quite as much as the prospect of gain. The objects for barter have been such as were produced or were only to be found in certain localities, and which nevertheless might to a certain degree be considered almost indispensable—such as soapstone, and the lamps and vessels manufactured from it, whalebone, narwal and walrus teeth, certain kinds of skin, sometimes even finished boats and kayaks, but rarely articles of food. The articles looked upon as most precious were, however, any objects made of metal, or other materials more exclusively possessed by foreign nations. In the most remote ages the Eskimo on those trading expeditions appear to have overpassed their present southern limits. This may be gathered partly from pure Eskimo words being found in the language of more southern tribes, partly from the sagas of the old Scandinavians, who seem to have met travelling Eskimo even to the south of Newfoundland. In more modern times, a regular trading communication has been discovered, by means of which certain articles from Asia have reached the Eskimo of the middle territories, perhaps even sometimes the shores of Davis Strait or Hudson Bay; and others, on the other hand, have travelled from there to Behring Strait,—all through internal trading carried on among the natives themselves. No communication of this kind seemed to have existed between the tracts last named and Greenland; but the inhabitants of different parts of Greenland, with the exception of the northernmost tribes, have always maintained an intercommunication. The European settlements have, of course, entirely altered or annihilated this intercourse; but even while it existed, the mutual trade among the natives has scarcely given rise to any organisation of labour, or furthered any kind of industry which might have been of some consequence for the development of certain manufactures. Every community of kindred being in possession of a boat and a tent, must be able to provide what is necessary to secure themselves a comfortable life, except the few articles mentioned as among the principal articles of trade.

------

## II.—LANGUAGE.

Of all the original American languages, perhaps none has been so minutely scrutinised, both lexicographically and grammatically, as that of the Greenlanders. The Labrador dialect also belongs to the better known amongst them. But as regards the dialect spoken by the western Eskimo on the shores of Behring Strait, our only source of information is a few lists of words given by travellers of different nations, partly modified by translation. Such exist in Russian, English, and German. There are also a few very scanty grammatical remarks given by a single author. These lists are inevitably exceedingly imperfect copies of the original words. They have been procured by questioning natives, which has been partly done by gestures and

through interpreters of little intelligence; and then the
structure is so widely different from that of European
languages, that a single word in most cases has no corresponding word in these, but requires several for its
complete expression. The sounds, too, may make a
different impression on different hearers—may be imperfectly expressed in Russian, English, and German writing, and this also may not be free from errors of tran-
scription. All this may cause any amount of misunderstanding. Let us first take up the question of a variety
of dialects, where closer examination will perhaps show
the contrary. These authors alluded to mention about
eight different Eskimo dialects round Behring Strait.
Some examples will explain how the supposed differences between the words here and in Greenland may
have originated. For instance, wife is called *nulijak* and
*ahanak;* man, *uika* and *nuhelpach;* baby, *mukisskok;*
shoulders, *tuichka* and *tuik;* hand, *tatlichka* and *aigeil;*
dying, *tukko* and *tukoeuchtuk;* cold, *ninhlichtu* and *paz-
nachtuk;* heat, *matschachtuk* and *uknachtuk;* fire, *eknek*
and *knk* (!). Let us now take what we find in the
Greenlandish dictionary and grammar: **nuliaĸ,** wife (of a
man); **arnaĸ,** woman; **uviga,** my husband; **nukagpiaĸ,**
unmarried man; **mikissoĸ,** small; **tuvîka,** my shoulders;
**tuvik,** shoulders; **tatdlıka,** my arms; **agssait,** fingers or
hand; **toĸo,** death; **toĸussoĸ,** dead; **nigdlertoĸ,** cool;
**panertoĸ,** dry; **masagtoĸ,** wet; **ûnartoĸ,** hot; **ingneĸ,**
fire. The apparent differences between these two lists
seem evidently to have arisen from mere misunderstanding, without any real variation between the languages.
On comparing, in the same manner, the rest of the lists
of words from Behring Strait, two-thirds or three-
fourths of the words are found to be more or less Greenlandish. Moreover, taking into consideration the manner
in which travellers have been enabled to communicate
with one tribe of Eskimo, by interpreters taken from
another, and that the difference between the Greenland

and the Labrador is smaller than, for instance, between Swedish and Danish, one is induced to assume an affinity of language among all the real Eskimo sufficient to allow mutual intercourse everywhere. On the other hand, it cannot be denied that the language of the Eskimo to the west of the Mackenzie is considerably different from that of the eastern tribes.

Taking it for granted that Greenlandish may be held to represent the Eskimo tongue in general, we shall endeavour to give an idea of its remarkable construction. Its most striking general peculiarity is the length of its words; and this, in fact, expresses its chief dissimilarity from all languages, except the American. What in other tongues may demand a whole sentence, and even additional dependent sentences, in Greenlandish may sometimes be expressed by a single verb. Consequently, Greenlandish grammar has both to construct words and to fix them in the sentence. This construction is effected by the help of additional elements or imperfect words, having no meaning by themselves, but expressive as additions to the main word, with which they can be combined in varieties of number and order, every combination altering or modifying the sense of the radical or adding a certain complexity of notions to it. Composition is completed by flexion, and particularly by conjugation, which not only, as in several other dialects, can make the verb include a pronoun as subject, but also as object, and in this way can form a sentence by itself, whereby these additional elements may render the sentence compound, or even include other sentences. The following abstract of Samuel Kleinschmidt's Greenlandish grammar will give a sufficient idea of this process :—

*Writing and pronunciation.*—The language is written with the same letters as the German, only omitting some, and with the addition of the following :—

ĸ, differing from **k** by its being formed in the remotest

part of the mouth, and sounding as something between gh, rk, and rkr.

r, sounding like a very guttural German ch.

ss, like the French j.

ng and rng, nasal sounds.

The pronunciation of the vowels is often modified by the next consonants. The letter *a* is often heard as in the English word *at*. The accents ′∧ ⌣ , which show whether the syllable is to be pronounced sharp, long, or long combined with sharp, are of the greatest importance as to the sense of a word. Otherwise, the letters have mostly the same power as in German and the Scandinavian tongues.

Greenlandish likes simplicity in its syllables, preferring those composed of one vowel and one consonant. More than one consonant in a syllable is allowed, if any harshness should arise. No word can end with other consonants than ĸ, k, p, and t, nor begin with others than these, and m, n, and s. All the combinations of consonants possible in the structure of words are limited to thirty.

*Parts of speech.*—The words are composed of the *stem* and the *enclitic for flexion*. The stem can be changed, even abbreviated to the root, which is the part always remaining.

*The stems* are divided into (1) *primitive*, as igdlo, house ; (2) *added*, as ssuaĸ, great or large ; lik, having or endowed with. The latter can never be used alone, but must be appended to the former singly, or followed by more, as igdlorssuaĸ, a large house; igdlorssualiĸ, one who has a large house. These added stems, which perhaps originally were words, are numerous as well as completely movable, and can be embodied in the word as required by the meaning. Affixes of this kind are of course not wanting in our better-known European languages, but are by no means so numerous or serviceable as in Greenlandish. On the other hand, the forma-

tion of compound words by simply joining other real
words, is completely unknown in Greenlandish.

With regard to their endings, both kinds of stems are
divided   into  (1)  *nominal*,  having   of  themselves  the
meaning of nouns ; (2) *verbal*, which, with their proper
endings,  are  only  used  exceptionally  in  phrases,  or with
the  sense  of  interjections,  but  for  the  verbal  purpose
require  a  particular  addition, which  is  the  part  altered
through  the  conjugation—for  instance,  ajoᴋ  and  pisuk
are  incomplete  words, giving  the  notions  of  illness  and
going,  but  with  the  verbal  ending  they  give  ajorpoᴋ,
he  is  bad;  pisugpoᴋ,  he  goes.   By  help  of  the  same
ending  also, nouns  can  be  converted  into verbs, but  only
a  few  of  them, and  then  they  comprise  some  peculiar
additional  signification, such  as  that  of  acquiring  or getting,  as  âtâᴋ, a  seal ;  âtârpoᴋ,  he  caught  a  seal.

In  the  way  here  described,  the  stems  give  rise  to
*nouns and verbs;*  and in reality these are *nearly the only
elements  of  speech*  in  this  tongue,  which  otherwise  has
only  some  particles  or  inflexible  words,  and  even  these
seem  to  have  had  the  same  source,  whereas  all  the  other
parts  of  speech  are  more  or  less  directly  to  be  looked
for  in  the  nouns  and  verbs,  the  pronouns  especially  in
the latter.

*The grammatical forms.*—Flexion is obtained by help
of  some  additional  endings,  combined  with  more  or  less
modification  of  the  word.   It  comprises  the  *number*—
viz.,  singular,  dual,  and  plural ; and  as  to  the  verbs,  also
persons,  as  igdlo,  a  house ;  igdluk,  two  houses ;  igdlut,
several  houses;  takuvoᴋ,  he  sees ;  takuvugut,  we  see.
Next,  the  flexions  express  something  *relating  to  another*
thing,  either  as  a  property  or  as  an  object ; and  in  these
cases  they  have  obtained  the  name  of  *suffixes*,  as
igdlua,  his  house ;  igdluvut,  our  houses ;  takuvâ,  he  sees
it ;  takuvavut, we  see  them.   Moreover,  the  nouns,  besides  their  simple  form,  in  which  they  are  used  as  objects,
and  which  on  this  account  is  called  objective,  also

have a subjective form given to them, either in case of
their being possessors (corresponding to genitive) or
subjects in a transitive sentence, as **teriangniaκ,** the
fox; **teriangniap,** the fox's; **teriangniaκ takuvâ,** he sees
the fox; **teriangniap takuvâ,** the fox sees him. In
nouns flexion also takes the *place of prepositions,* by
help of cases answering to the questions *where, in what
way, whereto, in what manner,*—as **nuna,** land; **nuname,**
on the land; **nunavtinut,** to our land. Lastly, in verbs
the flexion comprises *seven moods*—viz., indicative, inter-
rogative, optative, conjunctive, subjunctive, infinitive,
and participle.

While end-flexion thus expresses the relations in a
remarkable manner, on the other hand it has no form
for sex and tense. The context must show whether
the verb has the sense of present or past, and otherwise
time is expressed more distinctly by help of additional
stems containing the notions of begins to, has finished,
is going to, joined to the original verb.

As regards nouns particularly, they all in their objective form end in a vowel, or in **κ, k,** and **t,** the subjective taking **p,** the dual **k,** and the plural **t.** There are two
kinds of suffixes expressing the relation to the sentence
itself, or to another; and besides this, every suffix has its
peculiar form for number, subjective, objective, and the
local cases. But in order to add the above flexional
letters, the nouns themselves, in certain cases, must be
somewhat modified; and the rules for this transformation are nearly the only complicated part of Greenlandish
grammar. Yet the natives would seem sometimes not
to consider this transformation absolutely necessary in
correct speaking, saying **igdlo,** house; **igdlut,** houses;
but **tupeκ,** tent; **tovκit,** or also **tupit,** tents. Excepting
these transformations, the numerous forms may be represented by help of a scheme which can be written on
a quarto page.

The verbs are divided, according to the mark of the

third person indicative, into five classes, with endings as
follow : **poκ, rpoκ, gpoκ, voκ,** and **aoκ,** but each still to
be conjugated according to the same scheme, which comprises all the numerous combinations of these forms—
viz., numbers, persons, suffixes, and moods—and still, on
account of its regularity, can be written on one folio
page. Negation is expressed by the additional stem
**ngilaκ,** which is conjugated in a somewhat peculiar
manner.

In consequence of what has just been explained, personal pronouns generally are of no use. Still, some
words of pronominal signification exist, used when the
person must be expressed more distinctly ; but even
those words seem to have been formed by help of
suffixes, such as **uvanga,** I, which perhaps originally
signified, my being here. However, of demonstrative
roots twelve are found corresponding to the notions
here (**ma**), north, south, there, above, &c. Without any
addition or flexion, they only occur as interjections, but
otherwise always as nouns, answering to the questions
—*where, whence, which way,* and *whereto.* Of these roots,
pronouns for the third person are formed by adding **na,**
with the sense of, *this here* (**mána**), he there in the
north, &c.

The real numerals only run from 1 to 5, like the
fingers on one hand, then the fingers on the other are
enumerated, and afterwards, if necessary, the toes on the
feet. For this reason 20 is called "the man finished."
The rest are expressed by some partitive word showing the number counted, as **atauseκ,** 1 ; **mardluk,** 2 ;
**pingasut,** 3 ; **sisamat,** 4 ; **tatdlimat,** 5 ; but **arfineκ pingasut,** 8 (or 3 upon the other hand) ; 24 is called 4 upon
the second man, and 80, finishing 4 men.

*Construction of words.*—We have already mentioned
the signification of the stems. These are derived from
roots, and it must be supposed that either several stems
have a common root, or that several roots have been

related to each other, as, for example, ᴋôᴋ, urine; and
kûk, a river.  But the grammar does not explain the
origin of the stems, whose formation is considered as
accomplished and fixed; and here we shall only try to
give an idea of their further application in constructing
words.  With the exception only of the verbal ending,
necessary for the formation of real verbs, words are
always composed or formed by help of the *additional
stems*, also called *affixes*.  These are divided into (1) the
transforming class, by which verbs can be converted into
nouns, or nouns into verbs; (2) the formative class, by
which the word remains unchanged in this respect.

*A selection of the most remarkable additional stems or
affixes.*

I. Added Nouns or Nominal Affixes.

### 1. *Transforming.*

ʼtoᴋ or ssoᴋ, being or doing so, consequently a sort of nominal participle, as ajorpoᴋ, he is bad; ajortok, a bad one;
autdlarpoᴋ, he goes away; autdlartoᴋ, he who is departed.

taᴋ, ssaᴋ or gaᴋ, representing a kind of passive participle,
as tûniûpâ, he gives it; tûniûssaᴋ, what is given, a present.

fik, the time or place, when or where the action has passed.

ut or t, the means or reason for the action, as agdlagpoᴋ,
he writes; agdlaut, a thing to write with, pen, ink, and also
the object described.

### 2. *Formative.*

*a. Adjective-like* or neutral, which alter the stem-word in no essential way.

gssaᴋ, destined for or future, as pôᴋ, a bag; pûgssaᴋ,
a cloth or skin for making a bag.

ssuaᴋ, large or very, as idglorssuaᴋ, a large house;
ajortorssuaᴋ, very bad.

nguaᴋ, small or little.

tsiaᴋ or atsiaᴋ, tolerable or somewhat.

*b. Substantive-like*, which make the stem-word totally subordinate.

**lik,** provided with.

**mio,** inhabitant of.

**ussaᴋ,** like or similar, as **sioraᴋ,** sand; **sioraussaᴋ,** something like sand, among other meanings used for raw sugar.

## II. Additional Verbs or Verbal Affixes.

### 1. *Transforming.*

**gâ** or **râ,** has for, uses as, regards—as **erneᴋ,** son; **ernerâ,** he has him for a son.

**ᴋarpoᴋ,** has or there is, as **savik,** a knife; **saaveᴋarpoᴋ,** he has a knife, or there is a knife.

**liorpoᴋ,** makes, builds.

**liarpoᴋ,** travels or goes to.

**uvoᴋ,** is; **savik,** a knife; **saviuvoᴋ,** it is a knife.

**sivoᴋ,** gains or acquires.

### 2. *Formative.*

*a. Neutral*, with a meaning partly as auxiliary verbs, partly as adverbs.

**savoᴋ,** will or shall; **saveᴋâsavoᴋ,** he shall have or will get a knife.

**niarpoᴋ,** endeavours to.

**dluarpoᴋ,** well, sufficiently; **ingerdlavoᴋ,** it moves; **ingerdlavdluarpoᴋ,** it goes quick.

**ngârpoᴋ,** highly; **angivoᴋ,** it is large; **angingârpoᴋ,** is very large.

**tarpoᴋ,** repeatedly or using to.

*b. Intransitive.*

**juîpoᴋ,** never.

**gajugpoᴋ,** is bending to, likes to.

**narpoᴋ,** is to make one; **masagpoᴋ,** is wet; **masangnarpoᴋ,** is to grow wet from.

*c. Transitive.*

**típâ,** causes him to; **autdlarpoᴋ,** goes away; **autdlartípâ** he sends him away.

**rᴋuvâ,** commands or wishes that he.

**serpâ,** waits till he; **tikipoᴋ,** he comes; **tikitserpâ,** is waiting till he comes.

It is by combining a series of these added stems to the principal stem, that such an extraordinary complexity of ideas can be conveyed in a single word. Only the more intelligent, however, are perfectly skilled in this operation, and the number of affixes attached to one primitive stem seldom amounts to ten. The order in which they are linked to one another depends on the meaning, besides certain particular rules for each of them; but they are always put after the primitive stem, and the flexion always ends the word. The total number of affixes is about two hundred. As a sample, we shall try here to compose a word of some of the stems given above—

**igdlor-ssua-tsia-lior-fi-gssa-liar-ĸu-gamiuk.**

This word consists of a primitive stem, seven affixes, and lastly the flexion for the third person conjunctive with the suffix for him. It signifies—as he commanded (or wished) him to go to the place, where the tolerably large house shall be built.

**igdlu-gssar-si-ni-uti-ger-ĸu-vara.**

This word is constructed of one primitive and six additional stems, with the flexion for the first person indicative, and the suffix for him or it, and signifies—I ordered him to use it as a means for buying (endeavouring to get) house-materials (a future house).

*Syntax.*—In consequence of what has been explained above, much of what in other dialects belongs to syntax, in Greenland is represented by composing words and by flexion. There is a very sharp distinction between the verbs as transitive, intransitive, or having both qualities at once. The exclusively transitive verbs always require a suffix; where this is wanting they grow *reflective* —for instance, **toĸupâ,** he killed him; but **toĸûpoĸ,** he killed, always supposes himself.

Among the seven moods of the verb, the infinitive and the participle do not exactly correspond to what are

so called in other languages.   The infinitive is very
often used like the participle in a run of sentences, to
express what in other tongues is obtained by help of
while, then, as, during, &c.   The participle exhibits the
peculiarity of only *in some degree corresponding to a noun*,
on which account it has been called a verbal participle.
It can become the object, but not the subject of a sentence.   On the other hand, even in this mood the verb
includes at once its own subject and its object, for which
reason the participle is used for subordinate sentences,
as **takugâ**, he who sees him; **takugingma**, thou who seest
me; **takugivкit**, I who see thee; **nalugavkit** (of **naluvâ**,
he does not know it), **takugingma**, as I did not know
thee, thee who saw me—viz., as I did not know that
thou sawest me; **naluvarma takugivkit**, thou didst not
know that I saw thee.

Lastly, it must be remembered that in agreement
with what has already been explained, if even a sentence
has its subject and object expressed by particular nouns,
its verb nevertheless must indicate both by aid of the
suffix in its ending, as **inûp igdlo takuvâ**, the man (s)—
the house—he saw it,—viz., the man saw the house.

---

## III.—SOCIAL ORDER, CUSTOMS, AND LAWS.

As a matter of course, what we have now to treat on is
closely connected with what has already been said regarding the sustenance and mode of life peculiar to the Eskimo, because the life of a hunting people appears to require
or give rise to a certain natural partnership or joint possession of goods confined to wider or smaller circles of
the inhabitants, and directed by certain laws or customs.
What one individual gains by his own labour being, in

consequence of this partnership, made accessible to others, this restriction of his right of property must necessarily be counterbalanced by certain obligations on the part of others ; or, in other words, the right of property being in a peculiar way restricted with all the hunting nations, the personal rights and duties must have their corresponding peculiarities. In dealing with this part of our subject, we shall first treat of the division of the inhabitants into smaller communities ; second, of the mutual rights and obligations of the individuals and of those communities as regards persons as well as property ; and lastly, of the larger or smaller public meetings, which at once represent the national rejoicings and the courts of justice, by which the laws were maintained.

*The smaller communities or subdivisions which were based upon a certain partnership*, we have already alluded to as falling under the three following classes — the family, the inhabitants of a house, and the inhabitants of a wintering place or hamlet. But scarcely any further connection of this kind can be traced between the different wintering places.

*Firstly, regarding the family*. Scarcely anywhere did more than a very few of the men appear to have more than one wife, but the right of divorce and of taking another wife seems to have been tolerated without any definite restriction. Divorce, however, as well as polygamy and the exchange of wives, which is also mentioned as having existed, was only approved of by public opinion in so far as it aimed at propagation, especially of male descendants. The betrothal was managed in three ways—by mediators, as being fixed on from childhood, and by compulsion. But the wedding itself seems rarely to have taken place without some degree of force having been practised upon the bride—a custom of very universal use among barbarous and savage races. It also seems that the engagement had first to be settled with the bride's parents and

brothers, and that their consent in every case was re-
quisite. A girl having many and eligible suitors, but
the parents and brothers being unwilling to part with
her, is a very common theme in the traditional tales.
The wedding was performed without any special ceremony, and without imposing any peculiar obligations.
The bride brought along with her her clothes, an " oolo,"
or semicircular knife, and generally a lamp. The family
in a narrower sense comprised foster-children, as well as
widows and other helpless persons, who were adopted
into it on the ground of relationship, and more or less
occupied the place of servants. We are inclined to
believe that the so-called slaves or war-prisoners of the
western Eskimo live under conditions similar to those
held by the latter. The use of slaves as an article for
barter is not so contrary to the ideas of social order in
general as one would at first incline to believe. We
only need to call attention to a tale in which a company
of brothers are spoken of as being unwilling to allow
their sister to marry till one of them happened to acquire
a good friend, whom he persuaded to take her solely
with the view of making him his brother-in-law. This
story is in no way offensive to the feelings of the Greenlanders. But, on the other hand, their mode of life and
of housekeeping hardly seems to allow of these slaves
being treated otherwise than as subordinate members of
the family. In a wider sense the family comprised
married children, where these did not found a separate
household by acquiring a separate boat and a tent for
summer-travels. The joint ownership and use of these
belongings, and the common labour and toil in obtaining
the means of support by their aid, seems consequently
to define the real community of family or kindred. The
right of being adopted into the family may also be
claimed by the parents-in-law. The new-married
couple used to join the parents of one party, and as
soon as the parents of the other were no longer able to

support themselves, they also took up their abode with the children. Besides these, brothers or sisters without providers, and widows of brothers, were also adopted by the family, as circumstances might require it. Where a mother-in-law was a member of the family, the daughter-in-law or wife of the master of the house was subordinate to her. The husband also had the right of punishing his wife by striking her in the face with just sufficient force to leave visible traces. But the children were never, and still less the servants, subjected to any corporeal punishment. If a man had two wives, the last was always considered as a concubine only, but succeeded the first in case of death. In cases of divorce the son always followed the mother. As a result of these arrangements every family generally had more than one provider. Widows or unmarried women with children rarely set up housekeeping by themselves, and were generally provided for by their housemates or kindred. If there was more than one son, the subsequent ones sometimes, on acquiring a boat and tent, left home and established a separate family or household. The owner of a boat or a tent was thus considered the chief or head of the family, and it was principally he who was called the **igtuat** of the others. Simpson mentions the chiefs on Point Barrow as *Oomeliks*, which no doubt must be the Greenlandish **umialik**, signifying *owner of a boat*, and thus is in strict accordance with what has just been said. When a man died, the oldest son inherited the boat and tent, along with the duties incumbent on the provider. If no such grown-up son existed, the nearest relative took his place and adopted the children of the deceased as his foster-children. But when these were grown up, and had themselves become providers, their widowed mother was at liberty to establish a separate household with them, without any further obligation to the foster-father. As regards inheritance in general, it must be remembered, that among the Greenlanders it represented a question of obligations and burdens rather than of personal gain. Moreover, the only real hereditary goods—viz., the boat and tent—required annual repair and covering with new skins, almost as many as one hunter on an average could procure during the whole year. Lastly, it must be noticed that, even if the family were divided by removing to distant winter-quarters, the ties of relationship were always respected whenever mutual assistance was required.

*The next kind of community was that of the housemates,* where more than one family agreed to inhabit the same house. This, as a general custom, has perhaps only existed in Greenland, where often three or four, sometimes even more, families housed together. Each of these families, however, in the main maintained their own household; every family in the narrower sense— viz., the married couple with their children—having its own room on the main ledge with its lamp standing in front of it, while the unmarried people and the guests slept on the window and side ledges. As the house was built and repaired by joint labour, it could scarcely be said to have any particular owner; or if there happened to be one, he would only have all the burdens and obligations without any real rights as to possession. But among the heads of the several families one was generally found who was held in greater esteem than the rest by all the housemates, though not in the same degree as the members of a family respected their so-called *igtuat.*

*The third kind of community is what we may call place-fellows*—viz., inhabitants of the same hamlet or wintering place. Only in exceptional cases might a single house be found at such a place. When it is considered how widely the population was spread, and how distant the hamlets were from each other, it will be understood as a matter of course that the inhabitants living together on such a sequestered spot must continually come into contact with each other in the hamlet itself, as well as in their common hunting-places, which made them form a band or community separated from the rest of the population. But still less than among the housemates was any one belonging to such a place to be considered as chief, or as endowed with any authority to command his place-mates. The folk-lore in many cases shows how men who had succeeded in acquiring such a power were considered as usurpers of undue authority, and vanquishing or killing them ranked as a benefit to the community in general. However, it was a standing rule that nobody from a distance could settle down for good at the place without the general consent of its inhabitants.

## THE PRINCIPAL LAWS WITH REGARD TO PROPERTY AND GAIN WERE AS FOLLOWS :—

*Of every seal caught at a winter station* during the whole season of their dwelling in the winter-houses, small pieces of flesh, with a proportionate share of the blubber, were distributed among all the inhabitants ; or if insufficient for so many, the housemates first got their share. Nobody was omitted on these occasions, and in this way not the very poorest could want food and lamp-oil so long as the usual capture of seals did not fail. Besides this general distribution, every man who had taken a seal used to invite the rest to partake of a meal with him. It must, however, be understood, that where the population of a place exceeded a certain number, or at times when the seals were very plentiful, this sharing of flesh and blubber, either by distribution or by feasting, would probably be limited, in the first case, to perhaps some of the nearest houses or relatives.

*Beyond the confines of such places* as were already inhabited, *every one was at liberty to put up his house*

*and go hunting and fishing* whenever he chose. Not
even where others had first established a fishing-place,
by making weirs across a river, would any objection be
made to other parties making use of these, or even
injuring them.

*Any one picking up pieces of driftwood or goods lost at
sea* or on land was considered rightful owner of them ;
and to make good his possession, he had only to carry
them up above high-water mark and put stones upon
them, no matter where his homestead might be.

*If a seal was harpooned and got off* with the harpoon
sticking in it, the first striker lost his right to it as soon
as the hunting - bladder became detached. It then
became the property of whoever found and finally
killed it. This would take place when the animal had
been hit with the large harpoon and the hunting-line
snapped, while the small harpoon or bladder-arrow has
the bladder attached to it. But if the animal ran far
away with the bladder-arrow, the first hunter also lost
his claim, just as if the bladder had been wanting. The
weapons attached to the animal were restored to the
proper owner when he announced himself.

*Any other kind of goods found* were considered the
property of the finder.

*If two hunters at the same time hit* a bird or a seal, it
was divided into equal parts with the skin attached.
But if this happened with a reindeer, the animal belonged to the one whose arrow had reached nearest the
heart, the other only getting part of the flesh.

*All kinds of game or animals which happened to be rare*,
on account of their size or other unusual circumstances,
were more than ordinary species considered common
property. Of walrus and the smaller cetaceous animals,
in localities where they were rarely found, the killer only
took the head and tail, the remainder being given up to
public use. This was also the case on the first capture
of such animals as only appeared at certain seasons, or

with any animal caught during times of long want and bad luck to the hunters. But if *an animal of the largest size, more especially a whale, was captured, it was considered common property*, and as indiscriminately belonging to every one who might come and assist in flensing it, whatever place he belonged to, and whether he had any share in capturing the animal or not. The flensing was also managed without any order or control ; and if any one happened to wound another on such an occasion, he was not held answerable for it.

In South Greenland, where bears are rarely seen, it is said that, *on a bear being killed*, it belongs to whoever first discovered it, setting aside altogether the person who killed it.

*When no seals or other larger animals were brought home to a house*, those families who were best off for provisions generally invited the other housemates, but not the place-fellows, to partake of the principal daily meal with them ; or one or two families went joint shares in this, each contributing something.

*If a man had borrowed* the tools or weapons of another, and lost or injured them, he was not bound to give the owner any compensation for the loss or damage. Moreover, if any one neglected to make use of his fox-traps, and another went and had them set and looked after, the latter became owner of the game captured.

*If a man repented of a bargain*, he had a right to retract it. Nothing was sold on credit, at least not without being paid for very soon.

Looking at what has been said regarding the rights of property and the division of the people into certain communities, in connection with the division of property into the classes just given, we are led to the conclusion that the right of any individual to hold more than a certain amount of property was, if not regulated by law, at least jealously watched by the rest of the community; and

that, virtually, the surplus of any individual or community—fixed by the arbitrary rate which tradition or
custom had assigned—was made over to those who had
less. From this point of view, the first class of goods
would be what belonged to a single person—viz., his
clothes, weapons, and tools, or whatever was specially
used by himself. These things were even regarded as
having a kind of supernatural relation to the owner,
reminding us of that between the body and the soul.
Lending them to others was not customary; but if a
person owned more suits than usual, public opinion
would doubtless compel him to allow others to make
use of them. The custom just mentioned, that a borrowed article which was lost or damaged need not
necessarily be returned or compensated to the owner,
strikingly shows that if a man had anything to spare or
lend, it was considered superfluous to him, and not held
with the same right of possession as his more necessary
belongings, but to be ranked among those goods which
were possessed in common with others. The consequence was, that superfluous garments or implements
rarely existed. Only a few first-rate hunters possessed
two kayaks, one fitted for the open sea and another for
the sheltered inlets; but if he did happen to have three
kayaks, he would at times be obliged to lend one of
them to some relative or housemate, and sooner or later
would lose it. The next class of property was what
belonged to the whole family—the boat and tent, the
provisions collected during the summer season, and
lastly, a small store of skins and other articles intended
either for family use or for bartering purposes. The
third class consisted of what belonged to the housemates in common—viz., the house itself, the supply of
victuals sufficient for certain meals, &c. A fourth class
we may make comprise what was shared with the inhabitants of the same hamlet, such as the flesh and
blubber derived from all the seals caught during the

stay in winter-quarters. A fifth and last class might be added, comprising those spoils which, either on account of the size of the captured animal, or sometimes owing to great scarcity and famine, were shared with the inhabitants of the neighbouring hamlets.

Some of the laws or customs above described concerning property—as, for instance, those that relate to things found—which at first sight may appear very strange, will find their explanation on closer inspection, and with due consideration of the peculiar localities, the long distances, and the scanty population, on account of which any article lost could hardly be expected to be recovered in a state still fit for use. But as to the principal peculiarities, it naturally follows that the members of the different communities, in profiting by the gains of so dangerous and toilsome a trade as that of the seal-hunter, could not be exempted from certain mutual obligations. *The principal of these obligations were as follows :—*

*The duty of providing*, and the right of being *adopted into a family*, have already been described in connection with the mutual relationship of its members. In order *to become housemates*, an agreement between the families in question was of course required. So also, if a *new family wished to settle at an inhabited place*, the newcomers had to wait the consent of the people already settled there, which was given by means of certain signs of civility or welcome, the strangers having meanwhile put their boat ashore, but not yet begun bringing up their goods. If those signs were not given, they put off again, and went on to look for another place.

It might be considered a law that *every man, as far as he was able to do it, should practise the trade of a hunter on the sea*, until he was either disabled by old age or had a son to succeed him. This duty neglected, he brought upon himself the reprehensions not only of the other members of his own family, but also of the wider community.   So also he was in duty bound to bring up his sons to the same business from their early childhood.

From their living together in small habitations, *a friendly way of conversing* was necessary; and all high words or quarrelling are considered as unlawful.   The Greenlandish language is therefore devoid of any real words for scolding.   The general mode of uttering annoyance at an offence is by silence; whereas the slightest harshness in speaking, even to younger or subordinate persons, is considered as an offence in so far that it may give rise to violent quarrels and ruptures.

In what has now been said, as in general, we have mainly had in view the Greenlanders under ordinary conditions.   We have, however, also noted, that the rules of property were necessarily subjected to several modifications, according to the size of the houses, the hamlets, and other local circumstances.   Where among the western Eskimo one place is said to contain 50 houses and 300 inhabitants, the housemates here must have represented the family as well, and the population have been too numerous to allow of any general distribution of flesh and blubber during the winter.   In such cases it would be reasonable to suppose that the inmates of a certain number of houses were united, and made a community by themselves, like that of a whole hamlet in Greenland.   Nobody being able to acquire and accumulate property beyond certain limits, and the state and conditions of the different households being all alike even there, the principles of social institutions among the western Eskimo can hardly be supposed to have differed much from those of the Greenlanders.

*No court of justice was established as a special authority* to secure the maintenance of the laws.   With exception of the part which the angakoks, or the relatives of an offended person, took in inflicting punishment upon the delinquent, public opinion formed the judgment-seat, the general punishment consisting in the offenders being shamed in the eye of the people ; and *the only regular courts were the public meetings or parties*, which at the same time supplied the national sports and entertainments, and greatly contributed to strengthen and maintain the national life.

*The first kind of meetings* were those which daily occurred when the men returned from their seal-hunt and invited each other to partake of whatever they had brought home. The men alone partook of those meals, the females getting their share afterwards. During these meals the events of the day were told and commented on, several matters of common interest discussed, and the bad behaviour, or perhaps vices, of some individuals censured and blamed.

*The other kind of meetings* consisted of the real festivals, which were most commonly held in the middle of the winter; though they also took place during summer, when, of course, the guests could be more numerous. Besides eating and talking, the principal entertainments on those occasions consisted in (1) different games and matches of strength and agility ; (2) singing and drum-playing, with dancing and declamation ; (3) satirical songs, or nith-songs, which, properly speaking, represented the court of justice.

Playing at ball was the favourite game, and managed in two different ways,—either by throwing the ball from one person to the other among the same partners while the opposite party was trying to get hold of it ; or each of the sides had its mark, at a distance of 300 to 400 paces, which they tried to hit with the ball, kicking it along with the foot from either side. The athletic exercises or matches consisted in wrestling with arms and fingers, different exercises on lines stretched beneath the roof, kayak-races, boxing on level ground, and several other games.

The songs and declamations were at times performed in the open air, but generally at the feast, immediately after the meal, and by the men alternately. The singer stood forth on the floor with his drum—a ring 1½ foot in diameter with a skin stretched on it—beating it with a stick in accompaniment to his song, adding gesticulations, and dancing at intervals. The nith-songs just mentioned were of a peculiar kind, used for settling all kinds of quarrels, and punishing any sort of crime, or breach of public order or custom, with the exception of those which could only be expiated by death, in the shape of the blood-revenge. If a person had a complaint against another, he forthwith composed a song about it, and invited his opponent to meet him, announcing the time and place where he would sing against him. Generally, and always in cases of importance, both sides had their assistants, who, having prepared themselves for this task, could act their parts if their principals happened to be exhausted. These songs also were accompanied by drum-playing and dancing. The cheering or dissent of the assembly at once represented the judgment as well as the punishment.

*As regards real crimes,* those in violation of the rights of property, as a matter of course, can only have been trifling ; on the other hand, the passions of the people tending to ambition, domineering, or the mere fancy for making themselves feared, sometimes gave rise to violence and murder. The practice of witchcraft must also be ranked among this class—those who believed, or even confessed themselves able to practise it, being stimulated by almost the same passions, and punished in the same way if suspected. When the witches, on being threatened with death, did not deny their guilt, the only passion which can have incited them seems to have been a kind of ambition ; and this is quite in accordance with the angakoks being their principal adversaries, de-

nouncing them, and inflicting punishment upon them.
Murder, and under certain circumstances witchcraft,
were, as a rule, punished with death, which was carried
out in two different ways—either as revenge of blood, or
being duly deliberated upon by the inhabitants of one
or more stations. To fulfil the blood-revenge was the
duty of the nearest relative; and having performed
it, he had to denounce himself to the relatives of him
whom he had killed. Capital punishment, as the
result of deliberation and decree, was inflicted upon
witches, and upon such individuals as were obviously
dangerous to the whole community, or at least suspected
of being so. Lastly, some cases of manslaughter occurred which were considered neither decidedly admissible nor altogether unlawful. These were as follow:
The killing of an infant that, from the loss of its mother,
would be liable to die from starvation; the killing of
insane persons; threatening the life of the housemates;
and lastly, the continued blood - revenge or this revenge carried out on some kindred or place-fellow of
the murderer.

---

## IV.—RELIGION.

The following account of the religious belief of the
Eskimo is principally founded upon the traditions—the
author having made inquiries among the natives as to
all that appeared doubtful and obscure, and lastly, com-
pleting this information with the help of the oldest
authors. The whole information thus brought together
has been divided and arranged with a view to making it
as convenient and intelligible to the reader as possible:
a more complete understanding of several portions of it
must be sought in the tales themselves.

I. General Ideas concerning the Existence of the World, the Supreme Powers, and the Conception of Good and Evil.

Only very scanty traces have been found of any kind of ideas having been formed as to the origin and early history of the world, and the ruling powers or deities, which seems sufficiently to show that such mythological speculations have been, in respect to other nations, also the product of a later stage of culture. Existence in general is accepted as a fact, without any speculation as to its primitive origin. Only the still acting powers concealed in nature, and to which human life is subordinated, are taken into consideration.

Men, as well as animals, have both *soul and body*. The soul performs the breathing, with which it is closely allied. It is quite independent of the body, and even able to leave it temporarily and return to it. It is not to be perceived by the common senses, but only by help of a special sense belonging to persons in a peculiar state of mind, or endowed with peculiar qualities. When viewed by these persons, the soul exhibits the same shape as the body it belongs to, but is of a more subtle and ethereal nature. The human soul continues to live after death precisely in the same manner as before. The souls of animals also, to a certain degree, seem to have been considered as having an existence independent of the body, and continuing after its death. Here and there traces have also been found of a belief in the migration of souls, both between dead and living men, and between men and animals; but it remains uncertain whether this ought not rather to be explained as having an allegorical sense. Lastly, they say that the human soul may be hurt, and even destroyed; but on the other hand, it may also be fitted together again and repaired. We sometimes find it mentioned that the migration may be partial—viz., that some parts of the soul of a deceased person may pass into another man and cause in him a likeness to the first.

The whole visible world is ruled by supernatural powers, or "*owners*," taken in a higher sense, each of whom holds his sway within certain limits, and is called **inua** (viz., *its* or *his* **inuk**, which word signifies "*man*," and also *owner* or *inhabitant*). Strictly speaking, scarcely any object, or combination of objects, existing either in a physical or a spiritual point of view, may not be conceived to have its inua, if only, in some way or other, it can be said to form a separate idea. Generally, however, the notion of an inua is limited to a locality, or to the human qualities and passions—*e.g.*, the inua of certain mountains or lakes, of strength, of eating. The appellation, therefore, quite corresponds to what other nations have understood by such expressions as spirits, or inferior deities. An owner or ruler conveys the idea of a person or soul, but it appears not necessarily that of a body. The soul of the dead seems to have been considered as the inua of the bodily remains.

*The earth, with the sea* supported by it, rests upon pillars, and covers an *under world*, accessible by various entrances from the sea, as well as from mountain clefts. Above the earth an upper world is found, beyond which the blue sky, being of a solid consistence, vaults itself like an outer shell, and, as some say, revolves around some high mountain-top in the far north. The *upper world* exhibits a real land with mountains, valleys, and lakes. After death, human souls either go to the upper or to the under world. The latter is decidedly to be preferred, as being warm and rich in food. There are the dwellings of the happy dead called **arsissut** — viz., those who live in abundance. On the contrary, those who go to the upper world will suffer from cold and famine ; and these are called the **arssartut**, or ball-players, on account of their playing at ball with a walrus-head, which gives rise to the aurora borealis, or Northern

lights.  Further, the upper world must be considered a
continuation of the earth in the direction of height, although those individuals, or at least those souls temporarily delivered from the body, that are said to have
visited it, for the most part passed through the air.  The
upper world, it would seem, may be considered identical
with the mountain round the top of which the vaulted
sky is for ever circling—the proper road leading to it
from the foot of the mountain upwards being itself
either too far off or too steep.  One of the tales also
mentions a man going in his kayak to the border of the
ocean, where the sky comes down to meet it.

The invisible rulers by which the earth is governed
can scarely be imagined without regarding them in some
relation of dependency one on another.  Inasmuch as
we are allowed to consider almost every spot or supposed object a special dominion with its special inua
ruling within certain limits, we might also be led to
imagine several of those dominions as united, and
made subordinate to one common ruler, by which
means we would have a general government of the
world under one supreme head ready organised.  The
mythology of the Greenlanders, however, does not contain any direct doctrine with such a tendency.  Very
scanty traces also have been found of any attempts
towards explaining the origin of the world, as well as of
things existing and their qualities, as, e.g., regarding
some species of animals, besides the moon and several
stars.  Though it has been asserted the Greenlanders
believe that the first of our race arose from the earth,
and that the first man, called Kallak, created the first
woman out of a tuft of sod, and also that some tradition
exists about the Deluge, yet these statements cannot be
accepted without doubt and reservation, because they may
have partly originated from the questioners themselves,
who pretend to have heard them from the Greenlanders,
but have probably involuntarily acted upon the latter by

their prepossessed mode of questioning. Still, on looking at the whole religious views of the natives, they do
seem to presuppose a single power by which the world
is ruled. Certain means were believed to exist by which
man was not only enabled to enter into communion
with the invisible rulers, but could also make them his
helpers and servants. Such supernatural assistance
might be acquired in a more or less direct way—viz.,
either through men endowed with the peculiar gift called
*angakoonek* (cor. spelling **angákûneκ**, signifying *angakok-
wisdom* or *-power*, or the state of *being angakok*). But
these men only acquired this gift by applying to and
calling on a yet more exalted power, which made these
rulers become their *helping* or *guardian spirits*, or *tornat*
(plural of **tôrnaκ**). This supreme ruler was termed
*tornarsuk ;* and in his being thus enabled to dispose at
will of all the minor powers, forcing them to serve the
angakut, and in the same degree making the whole
nature subordinate to mankind, some idea surely of the
godhead must be connected with him. It also seems to
have been ascertained that the Greenlanders have imagined him as having his abode in company with the
happy deceased in the under world; but to this vague
belief the whole doctrine concerning his existence seems
to have been limited. The early authors on Grèenland,
indeed, have given utterance to different opinions concerning tornarsuk which they have gathered from the
natives, some of them representing him as the size of a
finger, others of a bear, and so on ; but all these statements seem to rest upon error and superficial inquiry.
As far as the traditions are concerned, the name of tornarsuk is very rarely mentioned in any of them.

Among the supernatural powers was another constituting the source of nourishment, supplying the physical
wants of mankind. These being almost exclusively got
from the sea, we cannot wonder that this power had its
abode in the depths of the ocean ; and its being repre-

sented as a female is probably emblematical of the con-
tinual regeneration of life in nature, as well as of economy
and household management, generally devolving on women.   This being is named *arnarkuagsak* (cor. sp. **arnar-
ᴋuagssâᴋ,** also signifying old woman in general) ; but the
common opinion among the older authors, describing
her as a demon of evil, is quite erroneous.   She sits in
her dwelling in front of a lamp, beneath which is placed
a vessel receiving the oil that keeps flowing down from
the lamp.   From this vessel, or from the dark interior
of her house, she sends out all the animals which serve
for food ; but in certain cases she withholds the supply,
thus causing want and famine.   Her retaining them
was ascribed to a kind of filthy and noxious parasites
(**agdlerutit,** which also signifies abortions or dead-born
children), which had fastened themselves around her
head ; and it was the task of the angakok to deliver her
from these, and to induce her again to send out the
animals for the benefit of man.   In going to her he first
had to pass the *arsissut,* and then to cross an abyss, in
which, according to the earliest authors, a wheel was
constantly turning round as slippery as ice ; and then
having safely got past a boiling kettle with seals in it,
he arrived at the house, in front of which a watch was
kept by terrible animals, sometimes described as seals,
sometimes as dogs ; and lastly, within the house-passage itself he had to cross an abyss by means of a bridge
as narrow as a knife's edge.

According to the religious notions just given, there
must have existed a generally established belief in the
presence of some ruling power to which mankind and
nature were alike subjected, as well as in certain modes
of obtaining assistance from this power.   This supernatural aid, as well as all the actions of men with a view
to call it forth, were in social estimation considered
as being good and proper.   But besides this, there existed another supernatural influence, which was wholly

opposed to that which had its source from tornarsuk;
and the art of summoning it was practised and taught
from mouth to mouth by people not acknowledged or
authorised by the community. It was always invoked
in secret, and always with the object of injuring others,
and wholly in favour of the practiser. This art was
called *kusuinek* or *iliseenek* (cor. sp. ilisînek), corresponding very exactly to *witchcraft*, and representing
the worst form of evil, both with regard to the help
obtained and the means of procuring it. The essence
of it was selfishness in the narrowest sense, being alike
adverse to the interest of the community and to the
supreme rule of things existing in which the people
believed. When we look at these ideas, as very strongly
discerned and maintained by the Greenlanders, certain
opinions not unfrequently professed by authors as to
the religious creeds of the more primitive nations are
shown to be utterly erroneous,—viz., first as regards con-
founding the practice of witchcraft with their calling to
their aid supernatural powers, authorised and acknowledged by their religious beliefs; and secondly, the
maintaining that those nations on a lower stage of civilisation were wholly without any conception of moral
good and evil, and limited their regards to physical evil.

In the practice of iliseenek, or witchcraft, a power was
applied to which was superior to mankind; and we might
thus be led to suppose that this power represented an evil
being or ruler in opposition to tornarsuk. Some mystical
tradition is related by Egede, mentioning two men engaged in dispute, one desiring man to be subjected to
death, and the other insisting upon his becoming immor-
tal. The words spoken by them may perhaps be considered as magic spells, and the one of them is represented
as having made death enter into the world. This legend
is rather obscure, both with regard to its authenticity
and its meaning; but the idea of death was closely connected with that of witchcraft, this latter always more

or less having death for its aim.   Sickness or death
coming about in an unexpected manner was always
ascribed to witchcraft ; and it remains a question whether death on the whole was not originally accounted
for as resulting from it.  The fact that witches were
punished as transgressors of human laws, and were persecuted by the angakut, makes it possible that they represent the last remains of a still more primitive faith,
which prevailed before the angakut sprang up and
made themselves acknowledged as the only mediators
between mankind and the invisible rulers of the world.
These primitive religious notions may in that case have
amounted to a belief in certain means being capable of
acting on the occult powers of nature, and through them
on the conditions of human life.   Traces of the same
belief were perhaps also preserved among the people in
the shape of some slight acquaintance with the medical
art, and superstitions regarding amulets, the knowledge
of which was likewise peculiar to women.   And allowing this supposition, we shall find the most striking analogy between the persecution of witches by the angakut and the persecution of the angakut by the Christian
settlers, with this exception, that the Christian faith
exhibits a personification of the evil principle which enabled the missionaries to vanquish for ever the authority of tornarsuk as the supreme ruler and source of
benefits, by transforming him into the Christian devil,
who for this reason henceforth was termed tornarsuk.

   In the folk-lore of the Greenlanders, as well as of other
nations, divine justice principally manifests itself in the
present life. According to the older authors, they had also
some faint ideas of punishment and reward after death.
We learn from these that witches and bad people went
to the upper world ; whereas those who had achieved any
great and heroic actions, or suffered severely in this life,
such as men who had perished at sea, or women who
had died in child-birth, went to the world below.   At

the same time, some tales seem to hint at a belief that the manner in which the body of the deceased is treated by the survivors influences the condition of his soul. When closely examined, this belief is akin to the idea of punishment and reward corresponding to the actions performed in this life.

2 ON THE SUPERNATURAL AGENCIES BY WHICH HUMAN LIFE IS INFLUENCED.

By supernatural we understand such agencies as do not work according to the usual laws of nature, and accomplish their deeds in a manner imperceptible to the common organs of sense, except in a few rare instances, but only manifest themselves to certain individuals peculiarly gifted, or in some cases to animals, also endowed with a peculiar sense. This sense is generally called *nalussaerunek*, and the individual possessing it *nalussaerutok*, signifying, " not being unconscious of anything," consequently nearly the same as *clairvoyant*. Such agencies may be divided into those which are performed by the *inue* (plural of *inua*) of nature in general, and those belonging to witchcraft.

## (1.) *The Supernatural Rulers, or Inue.*

These have already been mentioned. As far as they may be perceived by the common senses, they generally have the appearance of a fire or a bright light; and to see them is in every case very dangerous, partly by causing *tatamingnek*—viz., frightening to death—partly as foreshadowing the death of a relative (**nâsârnek**). Moreover, some of these powers are able, even at a distance, to *sever the soul from the body* (**tarnêrutok**, he who is bereft of his soul; and perhaps also signifying, the soul in this way temporarily separated from the body). Heavy grief often produced a state of mind called **suilârkinek**, in which the sufferer deliberately

went out in search of horrors and dangers, in order to
deafen grief by means of *excitement.*

Although all the supernatural rulers may be considered as the inue each of their special domains, they
also lead an independent existence as individual beings
wholly apart from these. In the first place, it is possible
even for man, and in certain cases animals, to practise a
supernatural power from some motive or other; and
secondly, some of the supernatural beings must no
doubt be considered as having originated from real
beings, only transfigured through the traditional tales.

*As to men,* they are invariably free *after death to
reappear as ghosts;* but certain persons are in this
respect more dangerous than others : and besides, some
persons or people in a peculiar state of existence
are even in life endowed with superhuman properties.
Individuals belonging to this class in general are
commonly called **imáinaĸ íngitsut,** which signifies, *who
are not only such,*—meaning, *as others;* or, *not of common kind.* The dead man is considered as the inua of
his grave, and of the personal properties he left. It
is no doubt for this reason that things belonging to
absent persons can by certain signs announce the death
of their owners or their being in distress. The soul
even appears to remain in the grave during the first
days. The most harmless way in which a ghost can
manifest himself is by whistling, the next by a singing
in the ears (**aviuiartorneĸ**), by which performance he
simply asks for food ; and generally when singing in
the ear is perceived, it is the custom to say : "Take as
thou likest"—viz., of my stores. But more dangerous
are the ghosts that appear in a true bodily shape, especially those of delirious people and of angakut. The
deceased must also be considered fully able to recompense the benefits bestowed upon them during their
lifetime, being a kind of guardian spirits to their children and grandchildren, especially to those who are

named after them. But a slain man is said to have power to avenge himself upon the murderer by *rushing into him,* which can only be prevented by eating a piece of his liver. Danger is more or less connected with everything appertaining to, or having been in any contact with, dead bodies, or used at funerals, the invisible rulers in some cases being apt to take offence, or *have smoke or fog of it*—viz., causing bad weather and bad hunting on this account.

*Persons in an extraordinary state were as follow :—*

A *kivigtok* (correct spelling, ĸivigtoĸ), or a man who fled mankind and led a solitary life alone with nature, generally in the interior of the country, obtained an enormous agility, and became nalussaerutok, learned to understand the speech of animals, and acquired information about the state of the world-pillars. The reasons which led men to become kivigtok, were being unjustly treated, or being merely scolded by kindred or housemates, who in this case were always in danger of vengeance from the hand of the fugitive.

An *anghiak* (correct spelling, ángiaĸ) was an abortion, or a child born under concealment, which became transformed into an evil spirit, purposely to revenge himself upon his relatives. Akin to the anghiak were those who, either when new-born or at a maturer age, were converted into monsters, devouring their former housemates.

An *angherdlartugsiak* (correct spelling, angerdlartug-siaĸ) was a man brought up in a peculiar manner, with a view to acquiring a certain faculty, by means of which he might be called to life again and returned to land in case he should ever be drowned while kayaking (also called anginiartoĸ). For this purpose the mother had to keep a strict fast, and the child to be accustomed to the smell of urine, and be taught never to hurt a dog. Lastly, when placing him in the kayak for exercise, the father mumbled a prayer, beseeching his deceased parents or grandparents to take the child under their protection. On coming back to shore certain things might scare him, whereas the dogs protected and took care of him.

*As to animals,* if in the tales they are represented as speaking, or in the shape of men, this is not always to be understood as analogous to fable. Partly it is in the power of beasts to show themselves in a supernatural shape, partly they may appear as ghosts, or in some state akin to that. Probably they must also be considered as the inue of their own kind, having the power of avenging their destruction. The so-called *umiarissat* (plural of **umiariak**) is a supernatural "umiak," or women's boat and its crew, who are, in some cases at least, represented to be seals transformed into rowers.

Among *the purely supernatural or fabulous beings,* the following must be particularly mentioned :—

The *ingnersuit* (plural of **ingnerssuak**, properly, great fire) have their abodes beneath the surface of the earth, in the cliffs along the sea-shore, where the ordinarily invisible entrances to them are found. They have also been noticed entering through mounds of turf. Probably these abodes have some connection with the real under world itself. They are divided into two classes, the upper and the lower ingnersuit. The former, called *mersugkat* or *kutdlit,* are benevolent spirits, protecting the kayakers. They have the shape of men, but a white skin, small noses, and reddish eyes. Their mode of life is like that of the Greenlanders themselves, only their houses and furniture are finer and richer. They often accompany the kayaker, assisting and taking care of him, but invisible to himself, and only to be seen by others at some distance. The lower ingnersuit, called *atdlit,* have no noses at all ; they persecute the kayakers, especially the most skilled whom they know, dragging them down to their home in the deep, where they keep them in painful captivity.

The *kayarissat* (plural of ᴋajariaᴋ) are kayakmen of an extraordinary size, who always seem to be met with at a distance from land beyond the usual hunting-grounds. They were skilled in different arts of sorcery, particularly in the way of raising storms and bringing bad weather. Like the umiarissat, they use one-bladed paddles, like those of the Indians. Pieces of bark from American canoes, which are sometimes brought ashore on the coast of Greenland, are named after both kinds.

The *kungusutarissat* (plural of ᴋungusutariaᴋ), or mermen, are considered as the proper inue of the sea. They are very fond of fox-flesh and fox-tails, which therefore are sacrificed to them in order to secure a good hunting. They are also declared enemies to petulant and disobedient children.

The *inugpait* are giants inhabiting a country beyond the sea, where all things have a size proportionate to them, and where also one-eyed people are found.

The *tornit* (plural of tuneᴋ) are the most eminent among the inue of the interior. Their dwellings are partly situated in the tracts visited by men, but the entrance to them is hidden by vegetation and soil. They are twice the size of men, or even more, but lead the same kind of life. They also go hunting at sea, but only in foggy weather and without kayaks, sitting on the surface of the water. They are wise men, and know the thoughts of men before they are spoken.

The *igaligdlit* (plural of igalilik) are inlanders, who wander about with a pot on their shoulders, cooking their meat in it at the same time.

The *isserkat* (plural of isseraᴋ) are inlanders also, called tukimut uisorersartut, those who twinkle or blink with their eyes longwise or in the direction of length.

The *erkigdlit* (plural of erᴋileᴋ) have the shape of man in the upper part of their body, but of dogs as to their lower limbs.

The *inuarutligkat* (plural of inuarutdligaᴋ) are a kind

of dwarf, possessing a shooting-weapon, with which they are able to kill a creature by merely aiming or pointing at it.

Among the inlanders are also to be included the. *tarrayarsuit*, or shadows, and the *narrayout*, or big-bellies. Several monsters reside at the bottom of lakes and inside certain rocks, and are named the inue of these places. Among these are to be ranked the *amarsiniook* and the *kuinasarinook*, referred to in the tales.

The *amarok*, which in other Eskimo countries signifies a wolf, in Greenland represents a fabulous animal of enormous size, also repeatedly referred to in the tales.

The *kiliopak*, also called **kukoriaĸ, kukiopâgâĸ, ataliĸ,** is an animal with six or even ten feet.

The *kugdlughiak* (correct spelling, **ĸugdlugiaĸ**) is a worm, sometimes of enormous size, with a number of feet, and extraordinary speed.

Other similar monsters mentioned in the tales are: The *kukigsook, agshik, avarkiarsuk;* the *monster-foxes, hares,* and *birds,* and the *ice-covered bears.*

The upper world is also inhabited by several rulers besides the souls of the deceased. Among these are the owners or inhabitants of celestial bodies, who, having once been men, were removed in their lifetime from the earth, but are still attached to it in different ways, and pay occasional visits to it. They have also been represented as the celestial bodies themselves, and not their inue only, the tales mentioning them in both ways. The owner of the moon originally was a man, called Aningaut, and the inua of the sun was his sister, a woman beautiful in front, but like a skeleton at her back. The moon is principally referred to in the tales.

The *erdlaveersissok*—viz., the entrail-seizer—is a woman residing on the way to the moon, who takes out the entrails of every person whom she can tempt to laughter.

The *siagtut*, or the three stars in Orion's belt, were

men who were lost in going out to hunt on the ice
These are mentioned in the tales in the same way as
the *igdlokoks*, who have the shape of a man cleft in two
lengthwise.

Among the rulers who are named only according to
special domains, and whose number appears almost
unlimited, are the inua of the air, the inua of appetite
or eating, and the inerterrissok or the prohibitor—viz.,
he who lays down the rules for abstinence.

### (2.) *Witchcraft.*

The practice of witchcraft has already been explained
in the preceding pages as representing the principal
source from which all the evils to which mankind is subject have their origin—viz., death, and what will more or
less immediately lead to death, as sickness and famine.
Generally, it is called *kusuinek*, and its performance may
be limited to a single act ; but those who have practised
it to a certain degree are called *iliseetsut* (plural of
ilisîtsoᴋ), witches or wizards. It appears to have been
also practised by supernatural beings as well as by
mankind. Witches, however, in part acquired the
powers of these—their souls being able to leave the
body, and to approach those whom they intended to
injure without being visible to any but the nalussaerutut
or clairvoyants, to whom the witches themselves appeared as breathing fire, and with their hands and the
lower parts of their arm blackened.

In practising witchcraft some magic words were
spoken, but it remains uncertain if words were thought
necessary in every case, or if words alone sufficed ; and
lastly, whether witches were able to work their wicked
ends by merely touching. Generally, different materials
were considered necessary for the performance of sorcery, such as (1) parts of human bodies, or objects that
had been in some way connected with dead bodies, as
if some remnant of that power which had caused death

still attached to them. (2) Worms and insects, perhaps
on account of their apparent annual coming out of the
soil, the common grave of all that lives and breathes, or
possibly on account of their mysterious nature and destination ; spiders were used for creating sickness ; and
insects swallowed in drinking water could be made to
eat the entrails, kill the man, and reappear from out his
body enlarged in size. (3) Parts of the animals caught
by the person to whom mischief was intended. In most
cases this was done by cutting a small round piece out
of the skin. This, when put down into graves, caused
the total failure of the owner's hunt from that time.
From this kind of witchcraft the name of kusuinek is
derived, signifying, taking away from, or diminishing
something. In all cases witchcraft was an art handed
down by tradition, but taught as well as practised in
perfect secrecy.

### 3. Of the Manner in which Man by Supernatural Assist-<br>ance can avert Evil and obtain Benefit.

Certain agents or means are given to mankind by
which they are enabled to avert impending misfortune
and obtain prosperity, in a manner deviating from the
ordinary laws of nature. These means are gained by
aid of a knowledge the highest stage of which is called
*angakoonek*. But an angakok being not only able himself directly to procure specially desired advantages, but
also acting as the leading authority in all matters of religion, the angakoonek will be separately treated of
hereafter. The fair and righteous means to which mankind in general may have recourse are thus to be considered as having their source in tornarsuk, with the
angakut as mediators. Their general aim may be said
to be the counteracting and defeating of witchcraft, at
the same time serving to appease and influence the inue
of nature, partly for the purpose of averting the danger

arising from these powers, especially that of being frightened to death, partly in order to obtain what may be desired. Moreover, they may be divided into two classes: first, the general religious means to be used by people in general for certain purposes or in certain cases; secondly, some peculiar faculties, which are possessed only by certain individuals.

### (1.) *The General Religious Means.*

*The general religious means* may again be divided into three separate classes, the first consisting of words to be spoken—viz., prayer and invocation; the second, in the possession and application of certain material objects called amulets; and the third, of certain actions, such as the following out certain rules as to the mode of life, sacrifices, and different other observances for appeasing the ruling powers and defeating witchcraft.

*In the prayer or serranek,* as far as we know, only the desired object is pronounced, without any direct mention being made of the fulfiller; whereas the *invocation* (κernaineκ) is merely an appeal for aid to some special owner of power (κernarpâ, he invokes him). It is not known whether in any of these cases words of the pronouncer's own choice could be employed. The general custom, at all events, was to use distinct spells with peculiar tunes belonging to them. Such a prayer was called *serrat* (in the tales translated by *spell, magic lay,* or *song*), and might have reference to health, hunting, assistance against enemies or dangers—in short, whatever purpose might be desired within the limits of what was deemed right and proper. A serrat was supposed to have a power by itself, independent of the person who happened to know or make use of it. It was therefore considered an object of possession and barter; but it had also a deeper significance, in so far as a man in using it applied to a certain power, or had his thoughts fixed upon the fulfiller or the original giver of the spell, these persons being generally identical—viz., the nearest deceased kindred of the user. The serrats were in some cases expressly directed to the invoker's ancestors, and are also known to have been the hereditary property of the same family. In the same way, invocations were generally addressed to the souls of the grandparents, and were principally employed as a preventive against being frightened to death. A serrat had to be originally acquired by a revelation to some individual who possessed a certain degree of angakok-wisdom, and in most cases they probably dated from very remote ages. The serranek was chiefly practised by old men, who, while performing it, partly uncovered the head.

The *amulets*, or *arnuat* (plural of **arnuaк**), were small articles which either permanently belonged to the individual, and in this case were always carried about his person or worn on the body or inserted in his weapons, or were sometimes only acquired for certain special occurrences. The efficacy of an amulet depends firstly on the nature of the original thing or matter from whence it has been derived. To serve this purpose, certain animals or things which had belonged to or been in contact with certain persons or supernatural beings were chiefly chosen ; and sometimes, but more rarely, also objects which merely by their appearance recalled the effect expected from the amulet, such as figures of various objects. Undoubtedly the original inua of the objects was believed to be still acting by means of them. Those in most esteem were objects pretended to have belonged to the ingnersuit and the inuarutligkat. Very precious amulets were got from the *avingak*, which in Labrador signifies a kind of weasel, but in Greenland a fabulous animal, and the application of which in a tale from both countries exhibits a most striking similarity. It is also said to serve the western Eskimo for amulets. Probably the choice and appreciation of things most useful and appropriate for amulets was

akin to their faith in different medicines, both kinds of
knowledge being principally professed by old women,
and was perhaps, like witchcraft, a remnant of the
older religion which was tolerated by the angakut.
Although the articles thus used had a power of their
own because of their origin, they still required the application of a serrat, which was pronounced by him who
gave the amulet to its final proprietor. If it was only
to be used in particular cases, a special serrat was also
required in order to make it work ; and in some cases,
when the owner happened not to have the amulet at
hand, he might have recourse to invocation. Among
the amulets probably we should also include what was
called **pôᴋ**, or bag, signifying the skin of some animal,
enabling a man to acquire its shape. Amulets were ordinarily acquired from the parents during early childhood.

It remains somewhat doubtful how to class the art of
making *artificial animals,* which were sent out for the
purpose of destroying enemies. In the tales we meet
with bears and reindeers of this description ; but most
common is the belief in the **tupilak,** composed of various
parts of different animals, and enabled to act in the
shape of any of those animals which was wished.
The tupilak differed from the amulet in being the work
of its own user, and being secretly fashioned by himself.
It therefore might seem to belong to witchcraft ; but
according to the opinion of the present Greenlanders, it
is considered as having been a just and proper remedy,
made by help of a serrat. It must always be remembered that its secret origin and traditional teaching, and
not the immediate intention of it in every single case,
constituted the evil of witchcraft. The serrat and
arnuak might be used with a good intention, though at
the same time pernicious to their immediate objects—
viz., the enemies. On the other hand, they could certainly also be used with evil designs : and moreover, even
angakoks were known to have practised witchcraft ;

but all such cases were condemned by public opinion as evil abnormities and abuses.

*The rules concerning their mode of life* were principally concerned with *fasting* and *abstinence*, but also included certain regulations as to clothing, out-of-door life, and daily occupations in general. They partly referred to the ordinary routine of daily life, particularly that of the wife, the child, and the mourners after death ; partly to special or accidental occurrences, such as sickness. The powers worshipped through these observances appear to have been, besides the *inerterrissok*, the inue of the air, the moon, and other domains, supposed to influence the weather and the chase, and also the souls of the deceased. The lying-in woman was not allowed to work, nor to eat any flesh excepting from the produce of her husband's chase, and of which the entrails had not been wounded ; but fish was allowed. Two weeks subsequent to her delivery she might eat flesh, but the bones of it were not to be carried outside the house. In the first child-birth they were not allowed to partake of the head or the liver. They were permitted neither to eat nor drink in the open air. They had their separate water-tubs ; and if any one else should happen to drink out of these, what remained was thrown outside. The husbands likewise were not permitted to work or do any barter for some weeks. They also used to pull off one boot and put it beneath the dish they were eating, in order to make the son grow up a good hunter. During the first few days of the child's life no fire must be lighted at their stall, and nothing be cooked over their lamp. Bartering was likewise not customary where there was a person sick. Immediately after birth, a name was given to the child ; and it was always a matter of great importance to have it called by the name of some deceased relation, one of the grandparents being generally preferred. But, on the other hand, names belonging to persons recently dead must not be pronounced, for which reason a second name was generally given for daily use, and even this, for the same reason, was apt to be afterwards changed. The navel-string of the child must not be cut with a knife, but with a mussel-shell, if not bitten off, and was often used as an amulet. A urine-tub was held above the head of a woman in labour, in order to ward off all manner of evil influences. When the child was a year old, the mother licked it all over its body, in order to make it healthy. If any one happened to die in a house, everything belonging to the deceased was brought outside to avoid infecting the living. All the housemates likewise had to bring out their belongings, and take them in at night after they had been well aired. The persons who had assisted in carrying the corpse to the grave, for a time were considered to be infected, and had to abstain from taking part in certain occupations. All the kindred and housemates of the deceased for some time had also to abstain from certain kinds of food and occupation. During the time of mourning, the women had to abstain from washing themselves, and were not allowed in any way to make themselves smart or even dress their hair ; and when going out they wore a peculiar dress. The bodies of those who died in a house were carried out through the window, or if in a tent, underneath the back part. According to an account from Labrador, a small child must not eat the entrails nor blubber kept in stomach-bladders, nor the flesh on the inner side of the ribs, nor the upper part of the shoulder-blade. At the birth of a child, some of the heart, lung, liver, intestine, and stomach was provided ; and the child having been licked all over, the mother ate a dish of the mixture as a means of procuring health and long life to the baby.

To the customs just enumerated may be added various regulations regarding the chase, especially that of the whale—this animal being easily scared away by various kinds of impurity or disorder. As to all kinds

of hunting, the belief was general that liberality in dis-
posing of what had been taken secured future success.
If a person who used to have ill-luck visited a successful
hunter when an angakok was present, the latter used to
cut a piece out of the liver of a seal caught by the lucky
hunter and give it to the unlucky one, who chewed and
swallowed it slowly.

*Sacrifices* (**mingulerterrinek** or **aitsuinek**) were not
much used. Besides the fox-flesh to the *kungusotarissat*,
gifts were offered to the inue of certain rocks, capes, and
ice-firths, principally when travelling and passing those
places. Certain marks of homage were, moreover, observed towards the inue of various localities, such as
abstaining from laughing, from pointing at them, &c.

The expelling, capturing, and destroying of evil and
dangerous spirits was ordinarily incumbent upon the
angakut. The traditions, however, mention similar operations as practised also by other people; and even in
our own day, there are cases of this among the Christian inhabitants, such as shooting at tupilaks and umiarissat. Several fetid and stinking matters, such as
old urine, are excellent means for keeping away all
kinds of evil-intentioned spirits and ghosts.

### (2.) *Men gifted with Special Endowments.*

The persons now to be spoken of belong to the class
we have already referred to as **imáinak ingitsut**, or *not
of common kind*—not like other people. They may be
regarded as much the same as *canny folk* of the Scottish
peasant, wise men or clairvoyants.

*Tarneerunek*, the act of taking the soul out of the
body, may be achieved either by external means, or by
dreams or several states of the soul. When delivered
in this way, especially by the power of the moon or by
dreams, the soul is enabled to roam all over the universe,
and return with news from thence.

*Pivdlingayak* means a fool or " natural;" and *pivdler-*

*ortok*, a mad or delirious person. By degrees as madness increases, disturbing the operation of the senses, and clouding the judgment and insight into things present, the absent or concealed things, and the events of the future, unfold themselves to the inner sight of the soul. A pivdlerortok was even gifted with a faculty of walking upon the water, besides the highest perfection in divining, but was at the same time greatly feared ; whereas the pivdlingayak, being also clairvoyant, was esteemed a useful companion to the inhabitants of a hamlet.

*Piarkusiak* was a child born after several others had died off at a tender age. It was considered specially proof against all kinds of death-bringing influences, especially witchcraft, and therefore employed in persecuting witches. A child like this was even more than ordinarily petted, and had all its wishes complied with.

*Agdlerutig(h)issak*—viz., having been the cause of **agdlerneĸ,** or of certain rules of abstinence observed by the mother—was a child fostered in a manner similar to the angherdlartugsiak, and also considered to have a peculiar faculty for resisting witchcraft.

*Kiligtisiak* was a man brought up by an angakok with the purpose of training him for a clairvoyant, which on the part of the angakok was performed by taking him on his knee during his conjurations.

*Kilaumassok* and *nerfalassok* were people who, having failed in becoming angakok, had nevertheless acquired a faculty for detecting hidden things and causes. In cases of sickness, the head of the invalid was made fast by a thong to the end of a stick, and on lifting it up (**ĸilauneĸ**), the nature of the sickness was discovered.

#### 4. Angakoonek or Priesthood.

With regard to the name **angákoĸ** (plural, **angákut**), it cannot be traced back in the usual way to any positive root, but it appears to be closely akin to **angivoĸ,** he is great ; **angajoĸ,** the older one ; **angajorĸat,** the parents.

In a vocabulary of the language spoken by the inland
Eskimo on the borders of the river Kuskokwim, or the
tribe farthest from the Greenlanders, the "*Shamans*"
are called *tungalik* and *analchtuk*, which words afford a
striking instance of similarity, showing the unity of
all the Eskimo tribes, the latter sounding somewhat
akin to angakok, the first corresponding to the Greenlandish word **tôrnalik**—viz., *one who owns tornaks*, a
quality that constitutes the real definition of an angakok.
Another tribe nearer to Behring Strait, denominated
by the rather curious name of *Tschnagmiut* (probably a
corruption of a word like the Greenlandish **sinamiut,**
coast people), is also said to use the word *tungalik* for a
"*Shaman*," and a third tribe in the same district to use
the word *angaigok* for a "*chief.*"

Women as well as men might become angakut; and
this profession appears to have two, or even more, different stages. But the highest of these, described by
the older authors as that of an *angakok poolik*, is not
confirmed as being known by the present Greenlanders.
The "studies" necessary before becoming an angakok
were in most cases begun in infancy, an angakok edu-
cating the child as kiligtisiak. Afterwards, self-applica-
tion was required, consisting in strict fasting and invoking *tornarsuk* while staying alone in solitary places. In
this way the soul became partly independent of the
body and of the external world; finally, tornarsuk
appeared and provided the novice with a *tornak*—viz., a
helping or guardian spirit, whom he might call to his
aid by taking certain measures any time he chose.
While this revelation was being made, the apprentice
or pupil-angakok fell into a state of unconsciousness,
and on regaining his senses, he was supposed to have
returned to mankind. Some of the old people speak of
*angakussarfiks*, or caves, containing a stone with an even
surface and a smaller one, the angakok apprentice
having to grind the first with the second until tornarsuk

announced himself in a voice arising from the depths of the earth. Others maintain that only the inferior angakut perfected themselves in these caves, while the higher grade was obtained by allowing vermin to suck the blood of the apprentice in a dried-up lake, until the unconsciousness just referred to came on.

On returning to men subsequent to this meeting with tornarsuk, before he became an acknowledged angakok, he had still to show his power by calling forth his tornak. During this interval, his state would sometimes be revealed by the fact of his feet sinking in the rocky ground just as in snow; and according to others, he was liable to die if he did not manifest himself within a certain time. The clairvoyants could detect the angakut from their breathing fire like the witches; they had not, however, black arms like these. If an incipient angakok failed ten times in succession to call forth his tornak, he had to give up his claims to become an angakok, but still remained a *canny* or peculiarly gifted individual.

An angakok had more than one tornak, and most of the inue of land and sea could be made such, and also the souls of kivigtut, of the dead, and of animals. As to the services rendered by these, some of them were only advising and informing spirits, others assistant ones in danger, and others, again, revenging and destructive powers. The first kind, called eĸungassoĸ, were indispensable on account of their skill, but were without strength, though they boasted of their bravery, and were therefore ridiculed. According to the early authors, an angakok was raised to a higher grade, becoming *poolik*, by being able to invoke or conjure a bear and a walrus. The bear at once seizing him, throws him into the sea; and the walrus, devouring them both, afterwards throws up his bones again on the beach, from which he comes to life again. The word *poolik* has already been mentioned.

The angakut were acknowledged or authorised teachers and judges on all questions concerning religious belief;

and this belief in many ways acting upon the customs and social life of the people, the angakut necessarily became a kind of civil magistrate : and lastly, they had not only to teach their fellow-men how to obtain supernatural help, but also to give such assistance directly themselves.

With regard to the mode of practising their art, it has to be remarked that they partly made use of the same medical appliances or remedies which are accessible to mankind in general, partly that they had recourse to a means peculiar to the angakut—viz., summoning their tornaks. The first kind of acts may more or less be ranked among those explained in the preceding section, only distinguished by being still more marvellous than those performed by ordinary people. Of course the art often degenerated into mere imposture, with a view to impress the credulous with awe. To the acts of this kind belonged the *angmainek*, or taking out the entrails of a sick person, and returning them to their place after having them cleaned, the *repairing of a soul*, or from a tub of water divining information as to persons lost or missing articles. The other kind of deeds were performed by means of what is termed **tôrnineᴋ**, or *conjuring*, the angakok either merely summoning a tornak and asking counsel of him, or himself starting for an **ilimarneᴋ**, or *spirit-flight*, for the purpose of examining or accomplishing what was required, or finally calling forth evil spirits, such as witches and anghiaks, in order to defeat and destroy them. The art of *torninek* ordinarily had to be performed before a company of auditors in a house, this being made completely dark, while the angakok was tied with the hands behind his back, and his head between the legs, and thus placed on the floor beside a drum and a suspended skin, the rattling of which was to accompany the playing of the drum. The auditors then began a song, which being finished, the angakok proceeded to invoke the tornak, accompanying

his voice by the skin and the drum. The arrival of the
tornak was known by a peculiar sound and the appearance of a light or fire. If only information or counsel were
required, the question was heard, as well as the answering voice from without, the latter generally being somewhat ambiguous, in some cases also said to proceed from
tornarsuk himself. If, on the other hand, the angakok
had to make a flight, he started through an opening
which appeared of itself in the roof. Whether his flight
was supposed to be a bodily one, or by his spirit alone,
for the time severed from its mortal frame, is a question
which, like many others connected with religious matters,
has to be answered differently, according to the intelligence of the individuals applied to for information. Not
until the torninek had been finished was the house allowed
to be lighted as before, on which the angakok showed
himself released from his bands. During the following
days no work was allowed to go on in the house. Evil
spirits could exceptionally be summoned at daylight and
in the open air, in the same way as the angakok at any
time could invoke his tornaks, in case he himself required
their assistance.

Witchcraft, as well as certain other influences, such as
the presence of a woman having an anghiak, could
make the conjuration fail, and even become fatal to the
conjuror as well as to his audience.

As regards their objects, the different branches of the
craft consisted of the following :—

That of giving counsel in all cases connected with
supernatural help.

That of discovering the cause of accidental disasters,
including a certain judicial authority—viz., that of de-
nouncing certain individuals as guilty either as regards
witchcraft or any other violation of customs or rules.

Especially was their art exercised in discovering the
whereabouts and the fate of persons who had disappeared,
and in tracing out and defeating enemies in general, as

well as those who, like the anghiaks, could only be perceived and caught by the angakut.

Their other functions consisted in giving counsel and instructions as to the rules of abstinence and the mode of life, travels, hunting, and means of sustenance in general, as far as necessary on account of supernatural influence;

In procuring favourable weather (silagigsainеᴋ) ;

In procuring success in hunting (angussorsaineᴋ or pilersaineᴋ), either by conciliating the *arnarkuagsa* or by invoking a tornak in the shape of an iceberg called *kivingak*.

An angakok called to a sick person of any renown, if he saw his state was hopeless, used to console him in a solemn manner, if possible in company with others, praising the happiness of the life to come in low-keyed song accompanied by drum-playing.

The angakut used a peculiar official language, chiefly made up of allegorical expressions and transformations of ordinary Greenlandish words.

The death of an angakok was believed to be generally attended by various strange phenomena. His soul, it appeared, had more than ordinary difficulty in disengaging itself from the body ; and he might thus happen to lie in a half-dead state, reviving at intervals. Death having finally taken place, after five days had elapsed, he was apt to reappear in the shape of a ghost.

### 5. Their Religious Belief as influencing Life, Habits, and Customs.

The nation being so widely spread, its traditions, and especially the religious element in them, formed the only connecting-link between the scattered tribes ; just as the supporters of that belief, the angakut, in their persons afforded the means of connection between smaller communities. From this cause religion, more than could reasonably be the case with nations in higher stages of culture, became the standard by which

social and private life was alike regulated ; and this circumstance also very likely accounts for the marked dis-
inclination of the people to any change in their habits.
It must be observed that, the angakut being the only
authority who were acknowledged to derive their
power from the supernatural world, naturally make
the religious belief a governing principle in their actions. Their influence, of course, at the same time,
rested upon their greater intelligence and talent. The
unshaken faith with which the population regarded
their marvellous deeds cannot be explained except by
supposing them to have had a more profound knowledge
of the laws of nature, enabling them to form a more
accurate conception than others of what was likely to
happen as regards weather, hunting, sickness, and everything depending upon physical laws ; while as to their
own belief, their skill in divination most probably was
confounded in their own fancy with imagined revelations
from superior beings. No doubt they themselves relied
upon the reality of their supernatural performances, notwithstanding the necessity which, on the other hand,
often caused them to act with the sole aim of more or
less consciously deceiving others as well as themselves.

The rules and customs concerning property, position,
and what represented the administration of justice,
evidently bore a close relation to their religious belief.
The customs according to which an individual became
member of a family, partaking of its reputation as well
as its means of subsistence, were supported and confirmed by the belief that the souls of ancestors remained
guardian spirits to their descendants, having left them
their amulets and serrats as a kind of pledges. The
same ideas must be regarded as having formed the
principal foundation for the avenging of blood.

The social institutions in connection with the local
conditions leaving still ample room for arbitrary acts of
violence, the fear of vengeance by ghosts, kivigtoks,

anghiaks, serrats, amulets, and tupilaks, must have powerfully contributed to prevent weak and helpless persons being wronged.

By the custom of naming a child after a deceased person, it was intended to secure rest in his grave for the latter. The child, when grown up, was bound to brave the influences which had caused his death. If, for instance, the deceased had perished at sea, his successor had only so much greater an inducement for striving to grow a skilful kayaker.

The education of children was apparently managed without any corporal punishment ; but threatening them with the vengeance of malevolent spirits, principally the kungusotarissat, was one of the means employed to keep unruly urchins in check.

The various rules for abstinence in many instances certainly had a direct relation to health.

As to the funeral rites, the treatment of the body being considered in some way to influence the state of the soul after death, it was generally placed on the floor, for the purpose of guiding the soul on its road to the under world ; but in the case of malefactors, the body was dismembered, and the separate limbs were thrown apart. Otherwise the funeral rites differed extremely, the Asiatic Eskimo, it is said, burning their dead, the East Greenlanders throwing them into the sea ; whereas the rest and greater part of the nation buried them beneath a heap of stones, or in a kind of stone cell.

---

## V.—Traditional Tales, Science, and Arts.

In the Introduction to the Tales and Traditions which precedes them we shall endeavour to explain the probable origin and the significance of the tales, as representing the science, poetry, and religious doctrines of the nation. While these three elements are generally more or less associated, there are many tales in which one of them may be said to predominate, so that these might with propriety be called either religious, historical, or merely amusing tales.    Anything traditional, apart from the tales, which could in any sense be called science, is only to be found in the anga-kok-wisdom, in addition to some trifling knowledge of medicine, of astronomy, and of dividing the year into seasons in conformity with the wanderings of animals, the position of the sun, moon, and stars, and other scanty observations derived from experience.    Art, on the contrary, we may properly consider to be separately represented by songs, already mentioned as an entertainment at the festive meetings.    In being recited or intoned, it will be remembered that they combined mimicry and music with poetry.    To be properly appreciated, even the tales must be heard in Greenland, related by a native *racontour* in his own language; but the songs are still more unfit for rendering by writing or translation, the words themselves being rather trifling, the sentences abrupt, and the author evidently presuming the audience to be familiar with the whole subject or gist of the song, and able to guess the greater part of it. Every strophe makes such an abrupt sentence, or consists of single and even abbreviated words, followed by some interjectional words only used for songs and without any particular signification.    The gesticulations and declamation, accompanied by the drum, are said to have been very expressive, while the melody itself was rather monotonous and dull.    The old mode of singing is now nearly extinct in the Danish districts of Greenland.    The author, however, succeeded in collecting several songs which were still remembered, of which the following may serve as samples.    The first is given for this purpose in the original language, with the interjectional burden complete as it is said by the natives to have been sung.

A NITH-SONG OF KUKOOK,

who was a bad hunter, but anxious to acquire the friendship of the Europeans ; sung about sixty years ago at a large meeting in the southernmost part of Greenland.

Kukôrssuanguaк imaкaja haijâ
    imaкaja ha
haijâ oкalulerângame imaкaja haijâ
    imaкaja ha
haijâ avalagkumârpunga imaкaja haijâ
    imaкaja ha
haijâ umiarssuarssuarmik imaкaja haijâ
    imaкaja ha
haijâ ivnarssuangussaк imaкaja haijâ
    imaкaja ha
haijâ sapangarsiniúkuvko imaкaja haijâ
    imaкaja ha
haijâ ûsŭssarssuarnik imaкaja haijâ
    imaкaja haijâ
haijâ avalagsimasínardlunga imaкaja haijâ
    imaкaja ha
haijâ nunaligkumârpunga imaкaja haijâ
    imaкaja ha
haijâ erкardlerssuanguáka imaкaja haijâ
    imaкaja ha
haijâ кârкuvdlarsínardlugit imaкaja haijâ
    imaкaja ha
haijâ unatâlerumârpáка imaкaja haijâ
    imaкaja ha
haijâ agdlunaussarssuarmik imaкaja haijâ
    imaкaja ha
haijâ nuliarumârpunga imaкaja haijâ
    imaкaja ha
haijâ erngînaк mardlungordlugit imaкaja haijâ
    imaкaja ha
haijâ ivnarssuangussaк imaкaja haijâ
    imaкaja ha

haijâ ᴋassigiáinarnik atortugssaᴋ imaᴋaja haijâ
    imaᴋaja ha
haijâ aiparssuangussâ imaᴋaja haijâ
    imaᴋaja ha
haijâ natserssuaralingussaᴋ imaᴋaja haijâ
    imaᴋaja ha

## Translation.

The wicked little Kukook imakayah hayah, imakayah hah—hayah uses to say,  . . . . I am going
to leave the country . . . . in a large ship
. . . . for that sweet little woman. . . . . I'll
try to get some beads . . . . of those that look
like boiled ones. . . . . Then when I've gone
abroad, . . . . I shall return again. . . . . My
nasty little relatives . . . . I'll call them all to me
. . . . and give them a good thrashing . . . .
with a big rope's end. . . . . Then I'll go to
marry, . . . . taking two at once. . . . . That
darling little creature . . . . shall only wear
clothes of the spotted seal-skins, . . . . and the
other little pet . . . . shall have clothes of the
young hooded seals. . . . .

## MUTUAL NITH-SONG BETWEEN SAVDLADT AND PULANGITSISSOK.

### (*From East Greenland.*)

*Savdlat.* The south, the south, oh the south yonder.
. . When settling on the midland coast I met
Pulangitsissok, . . . who had grown stout and fat
with eating halibut. . . . Those people from the
midland coast they don't know speaking, . . . because they are ashamed of their speech. . . . Stupid

they are besides. . . . Their speech is not alike,
. . . some speak like the northern, some like the
southern ; . . . therefore we can't make out their
talk.

*Pulangitsissok.* There was a time when Savdlat
wished that I should be a good kayaker, . . . that
I could take a good load on my kayak. . . . Many
years ago some day he wanted me to put a heavy load
on my kayak. . . . (This happened at the time)
when Savdlat had his kayak tied to mine (for fear of
being capsized). . . . Then he could carry plenty
upon his kayak. . . . When I had to tow thee, and
thou didst cry most pitiful, . . . and thou didst
grow afeared, . . . and nearly wast upset, . . .
and hadst to keep thy hold by help of my kayak
strings.

### A SONG FRON SANERUT.

#### (*South Greenland.*)

I behold yon land of Nunarsuit ; . . the mountain-
tops on its south side are wrapped in clouds ; . .  it
slopes towards the south, . .  towards Usuarsuk.
. . What couldst thou expect in such a miserable
place ? . .  All its surroundings being shrouded with
ice, . .  not before late in the spring can people
from there go travelling.

### A SONG FROM ARSUT.

#### (*South Greenland.*)

The great Koonak mount yonder south, . .  I do
behold it ; . .  the great Koonak mount yonder south,
. .  I regard it ; . .  the shining brightness (clouds ?)
yonder south, . .  I contemplate. . .  Outside of

Koonak . . it is expanding, . . the same that
Koonak towards the seaside . . doth quite encom-
pass. . . Behold how in the south . they
(clouds ?) shift and change. . . Behold how yonder
south . . they tend to beautify each other, . .
while from the seaside it (the mountain-top) is enveloped . . in sheets still changing, . . from the
seaside enveloped, . . to mutual embellishment.

## ANOTHER SONG FROM ARSUT.

Towards the south I ever turn my gaze, . . for at
the point of Isua land, . . for near the strand of
Isua, . . yonder from the south he will appear ; . .
that way he certainly will come. . . Korsarak is
sure to clear the point, . . no doubt Korsarak will
be equal to it (in his kayak). . . But if still he did
not happen to come, . . not until the season of the
halibuts, . . not before the halibut-fishing begins,
. . not until the men are hauling up the halibuts.

---

These latter songs, of course, like the first, have
different interjectional burdens added to the strophes,
here only separated by breaks.

Lastly, it must be noticed that though the present
Greenlanders appear to have a pretty fair talent for
drawing and writing, scarcely any traces of the arts of
drawing and sculpture belonging to earlier times remain, with the exception of a few small images cut out
in wood or bone, which have probably served children
as playthings. The western Eskimo, on the other
hand, displayed great skill in carving bone ornaments
principally on their weapons and tools.

## VI.—PROBABLE ORIGIN AND HISTORY.

If we suppose the physical conditions and the climate of the Eskimo regions not to have altered in any remarkable way since they were first inhabited, their inhabitants of course must originally have come from more southern latitudes, and, after their arrival in those regions, have made the inventions and adopted the mode of life which constitute their character as Eskimo. When we consider how uniformly this character now manifests itself, notwithstanding the great separation of the tribes for upwards of a thousand years or more, it seems probable, firstly, that the nation during such a period of development must have lived in closer connection, allowing of concurrence in making the necessary inventions, as well as in bringing about a general adoption of the same mode of life; and secondly, that the development of their culture during that period must have been active and rapid in comparison with the time of separation which followed, during which the tribes have been leading a very stationary existence, almost without any perceptible change. Passing on to the next question—where this development or this change of a migrating tribe from the south into a polar coast people has taken place—it appears evident on many grounds that such a southern tribe has not been a coast people migrating along the sea-shore, and turning into Eskimo on passing beyond a certain latitude, but that they have more probably emerged from some interior country, following the river-banks towards the shores of the polar sea, having reached which they became a coast people, and, moreover, a polar coast people. The Eskimo most evidently representing the polar coast people of North America, the first question which arises seems to be whether their development can be conjectured with any probability to have taken place in that part of the world. Other geographical conditions appear greatly to favour such a supposition. It has been stated (principally by Lewis Morgan) that the primitive hunting nations of North America have obtained their principal means of subsistence from the rivers, especially by the salmon-fishery. The north-west angle of America, from California to the Coppermine river, contains several large rivers very rich in fish. The general tendency of all the primitive nations to expand by driving out one another must have almost necessarily compelled those of them who occupied the extreme confines to go onward till they reached the sea-shore. If this happened to be that of the polar seas, the new settlers would at once in its animals find a rich source of sustenance, at the same time as the country which they had passed through and left behind had gradually grown more barren and destitute of the means of supporting human life. This almost sudden change in their whole mode of life is also very likely to have given rise to the general sharp separation of this coast people from the inland tribes, and the position of hostility in which they stood to each other. The North-West Indians might be considered as forming an intermediate link between them. These derive about one-half of their supplies from the sea by whale-fishery. The rivers taking their course to the sea between Alaska and the Coppermine river, seem well adapted to lead such a migrating people onwards to the polar sea. While still resident on the river-banks in the interior, they may be supposed to have had the same language, and to have been able to communicate overland from one river to the other. This intercourse we may assume to have been still maintained while those of the bands most in advance had already settled down on the sea-shore and begun catching seals and whales, covering their boats with skins instead of birch-bark, and making the prin-

cipal inventions with regard to seal-hunting peculiar to
the Eskimo; and while the whole nation in this way
gradually settled down on the sea-shore, it also maintained the unity necessary for the purpose of defending
itself against the hostile inland people. If, in accordance with what has been above stated, we likewise
suppose the principal part of the folk-lore to have
originated about this period, the subjects mentioned
in the tales would constitute a means for guiding us in
search of the locality where the first settling on the
sea-shore is likely to have taken place. For this purpose it will be sufficient to call to mind the tales treating
of the following subjects :—

1. An expedition to the inlanders for the purpose of
procuring metal knives.

2. A man descended both from the coast people and
the inlanders, and his deeds among both.

3. The brothers visiting their sister, who had been
married into a tribe of cannibals.

4. An onslaught on the coast people, from which
only a couple of children were saved, who went off
roaming far and wide, and performed great deeds.

5. A woman living alternately among the coast people
and the inlanders, persuading them to wage war against
each other.

6. Women who from different causes went and settled
down among the inlanders.

7. A man taming wild animals for the purpose of
crossing the frozen sea.

8. Different travels to Akilinek.

On comparing these subjects of the tales with the
present geographical conditions, we will find that in all
respects they suggest America and not Asia. The probable identity of the "inlanders" with the Indians has
already been remarked on. When the new coast people
began to spread along the Arctic shores, some bands of
them may very probably have crossed Behring Strait

and settled on the opposite shore, which is perhaps identical with the fabulous country of Akilinek. On the other hand, there is very little probability that a people can have moved from interior Asia to settle on its polar sea-shore, at the same time turning Eskimo, and afterwards almost wholly emigrated to America.

On comparing the Eskimo with the neighbouring nations, their physical complexion certainly seems to point at an Asiatic origin ; but, as far as we know, the latest investigations have also shown a transitional link to exist between the Eskimo and the other American nations, which would sufficiently indicate the possibility of a common origin from the same continent. As to their mode of life, the Eskimo decidedly resemble their American neighbours ; whereas all the northernmost nations of the Old World, with the exception of the Kamtskadales, are pastoral tribes, regarding fishing on their rivers as only a secondary occupation ; and when some of them have settled on the river-sides, or even on the sea-shore, given up their reindeer, and made fishing and hunting their main means of subsistence, these have still been families originally belonging to the pastoral tribes, who have changed their mode of life chiefly on account of poverty. In the Old World we nowhere find anything at all like a coast race as opposed to an inland people, with the exception of the Asiatic Eskimo on the coast (Tschoukschees), who are quite different from, but still live in friendly relations with, the pastoral Tschoukschees. As to religion, the Eskimo are also allied to the Americans, and differ from the Asiatic nations, who have a more perfect system of deities, worship idols, and with whom sacrifices form the principal part of their religious rites. With regard to their language, the Eskimo also appear akin to the American nations in regard to its decidedly polysynthetic structure. Here, however, on the other hand, we meet with some very remarkable similarities between the Eskimo idiom and the language of Siberia, belonging to the Altaic· or Finnish group: first, as to the rule of joining the affixes to the end and not the beginning of the primitive word; and second, the very characteristic mode of forming the dual by *k* and the plural by *t.*

At all events, it must be granted that the origin of the Eskimo people remains very obscure; and that, possibly, early intercourse and subsequent mutual influence may once have existed between the northernmost nations of the two continents, which future researches may yet reveal.

As regards their numbers, the Eskimo must also be supposed to have increased considerably in early periods beyond what has been the case in later times; and the feuds between the single families, or larger bands, must probably have accelerated their being dispersed to the far east of Greenland and Labrador. According to the sagas of the Icelanders, they were already met with on the east coast of Greenland about the year 1000, and almost at the same time on the east coast of the American continent, on the so-called Vinland, probably Massachusetts or Rhode Island. Thorvald, the son of Erik the Red, was killed in a fight which ensued at this meeting; but later travellers in Vinland engaged in barter with the same natives, and brought two young Eskimo back with them, who were subsequently baptised, and stated that their mother's name was Vatheldi, and that of their father Uvœge (probably the Greenlandish *uvia*, signifying her husband). Between the years 1000 and 1300, they do not seem to have occupied the land south of 65° N.L., on the west coast of Greenland, where the Scandinavian colonies were then situated. But the colonists seem to have been aware of their existence in higher latitudes, and to have lived in fear of an attack by them, since, in the year 1266, an expedition was sent out for the purpose of exploring the abodes of the *Skrælings,* as they were called by the colonists. In 1379, the northernmost settlement was attacked by them, eighteen men being killed and two boys carried off as prisoners. About the year 1450, the last accounts were received from the colonies, and the way to Greenland was entirely forgotten in the mother country. It must be supposed that the colonists, on being thus cut off from the world abroad, retired into the interior of the fiords and creeks; while the Eskimo gradually settled on the islands,—and that the latter defeated and partly destroyed the remains of the former. The features of the natives in the southern part of Greenland indicate a mixed descent from Scandinavians and Eskimo, the former, however, not having left the slightest sign of any influence on the nationality or culture of the present natives. In the year 1585, Greenland was discovered anew by John Davis, and found inhabited exclusively by Eskimo. After a series of exploring and fishing expeditions, during which many acts of violence and cruelty were perpetrated on the natives, the present colonies were founded by Egede in the year 1721; and since then the whole west coast, upwards to 74° N.L., has been brought into complete and regular connection with Denmark. I have spoken of the habits of the Greenlanders chiefly in the past tense, simply for the reason that though their hunting habits, ways of life, and methods of thought are still much as they always were, the influence of the Danish officials, who conduct the trading monopoly, and of the missionaries, has been such that they have within the bounds of the Danish possessions abandoned many of their ancient customs along with their paganism, which change we shall endeavour to explain in the following section.

## VII.—INFLUENCE OF CONTACT WITH EUROPEANS.

The natives of the Danish districts, whose numbers during last century seem to have been greatly on the decrease, were afterwards, for a long period, again increasing ; while, since 1855, they have remained almost stationary between 9400 and 9700 souls. They have long been Christianised, and brought into a regular state of subjection to the Danish Government, by means of the monopolised trade, the missionaries and schools, as well as several other administrative institutions. The introduction of intoxicating liquors, as well as those acts of violence and oppression which in other countries have destroyed the primitive races, especially those who live by hunting, have been here unknown. Scarcely any other country will be found where the Europeans have shown so much consideration for, and been so careful of, the uncivilised natives as in this case. From the very beginning of the monopolised trade, it has been carried on with a view to introduce and make accessible to them such articles as were judged to be most necessary and useful to them ; and not without much hesitation have such articles of luxury as bread, coffee, and sugar, besides tobacco, been sold to them. By help of native schoolmasters, instruction is given to the children in all the wintering places, except a few where the number of inhabitants is too small. Attempts have been made to provide the natives with necessary medicines, along with some medical aid, although the latter remains, of course, very insufficient and illusory, on account of the extreme distances ; and finally, the Government has endeavoured to establish regular institutions for the relief of the poor, and likewise taken measures for the administration of justice and laws, as far as circumstances would admit. Still, the general destructive influence of nations at a far more advanced stage of culture upon those on a lower stage may here be traced—poverty, combined with predisposition to certain diseases, having sensibly increased. Greenland must be considered peculiarly adapted for making closer inquiries as to the nature of this influence.

From the earliest times of the colonisation, Europeans of the working classes have intermarried with native women, and formed their household after the Greenland model, with merely a few European improvements. These marriages have generally been rich in offspring; and have probably become a concurring means of temporarily increasing the population, the children, for the most part, growing up as complete Greenlanders. This mixed offspring being now very numerous, and its individuals representing the mixture of European and native blood in almost every possible proportion, any marked distinction between the Europeans and the natives might be supposed to have gradually disappeared. But the real difference of nationality depending on education, not on physical constitution, there are still sufficiently sharp distinctions to indicate what we mean by Europeans and natives. The average number of Europeans in the country, excepting at the time of existence of some temporary establishments peculiarly European, has varied between 200 and 300.

When the natives saw the first Europeans approaching their country from the sea in great ships, furnished with things all wonderful to them, they can hardly have failed to combine the idea of something supernatural with them. The Europeans, on their part, on settling down in the country, in order to make their existence more secure, were involuntarily led to abolish all native authority, especially that of the angakut, and to suppress all kinds of national meetings. Religious zeal—here of course, as everywhere else, combined with worldly and social aims—and national prejudice tended to make them despise and indiscriminately denounce all the native

customs and institutions as heathenish ; and in time,
European authority more and more became the principal law among them.   From this abolition of native
laws and authority, and a kind of self-abasement and
disheartening consequently arising among them, the
real or principal source of the national evils must be
considered to proceed.

Two national treasures yet remain to the natives, by
means of which they still maintain a kind of independence and national feeling—viz., their language and their
folk-lore.   Through the tales, they also still preserve a
knowledge of their ancient religious opinions, combined
somewhat systematically with the Christian faith.   Tornarsuk, in being converted into the devil by the first
missionaries, was only degraded, getting in the meantime, on the other hand, his real existence confirmed for
ever.   In consequence of this acknowledgment in part
of tornarsuk, the whole company of inue or spirits were
also considered as still existing.   The ingnersuit were
expressly charged by Egede as being the devil's servants.   The Christian heaven coming into collision with
the upper world of their ancestors, the natives very
ingeniously placed it above the latter, or, more strictly,
beyond the blue sky.   By making tornarsuk the principle of evil, a total revolution was caused with regard
to the general notions of good and evil, the result of
which was to identify the idea of good with what was
conformable to European authority ; but, unhappily,
the rules and laws given by the Europeans often varied
with the individuals who successively arrived from
Europe quite ignorant of the natives.   In the same
way as the ancient belief in the world of spirits has been
kept up, the Greenlanders also maintain their old faith
respecting the aid to be got from it, and have habitually
recourse to it.   The kayakers, in their troublesome and
hazardous occupation, still believe themselves taken
care of by invisible ingnersuit.   Although the natives

are aware that the aid required from the spirit-world of
the angakut is opposed to Christianity, they still discern
as clearly as formerly between that and witchcraft.
Only in rare instances have some of the natives attempted to form a Christian community independent
of the Europeans, and founded on alleged immediate
revelations from heaven; but these efforts have been soon
suppressed.    No attempts have ever been made to
re-establish the ancient authority of the angakut.

Excepting the introduction of firearms, no essential
change has taken place in the hunting operations of the
natives.    The principal means of subsistence are still
procured in the same way as they were a thousand years
ago.    It will also be evident that a consumption of from
thirty to forty pounds of bread annually per individual,
besides coffee, sugar, and tobacco, cannot have essentially contributed to change the habitual food of the
population.    As to the rules regarding property, and
the distribution of the daily gains from hunting and
fishing, some changes must of course have arisen from
the settling of Europeans among the natives; besides,
a great portion of the produce of the chase is now turned
into articles of trade.    But still, the ancient principle
of mutual assistance and semi-communism, out of the
feeling of clanship it may be, still predominates among
the Eskimo. When, however, the lazy and the active,
the skilled and the unskilled, fared the same, owing to
this division of the produce of the hunt, personal energy
and activity necessarily abated.    As to the body of persons constituting the family, the Europeans from the
first made a practice of interfering with the discipline
exercised by the head member, and even with the choice
of husband or wife; while, at the same time, the children were not, as before, invariably brought up to the
national occupation of hunters and fishers, and accordingly a temptation to waste the proceeds of the good
man's labour increased.    As to the communities com-

prising the inhabitants of the same house or the same
hamlet, their mutual relations have also necessarily been
essentially altered, partly in having members added to
their band who did not contribute to the common
household, and also by their being enabled to barter
away their seal-oil, and even the flesh, for European
articles, principally such as would serve to improve their
meals.   On the other hand, in cases of any particular
want, public opinion still requires the neighbouring seal-
hunter to proffer his aid, if he had anything left beyond
his own needs for the day.   In fact, the Europeans, and
perhaps those who are in their service, are now considered the only persons really entitled to possess property to any extent, the native sooner or later finding
too much trouble in keeping what he may have saved
up.   Probably, by way of lessening the demands made
on a provider by his house-fellows, a growing tendency
has been observed in Greenland to make the houses
smaller ; but still it is extraordinary how many persons
are entirely supported by a single man.   All this taken
into consideration, the security for person and property,
which ought to have been one of the first advantages of
the social order introduced by the Europeans, though
prospering on the whole, on closer investigation still
shows itself in some respects illusory as far as concerns
the natives.

Although the general economical conditions of the
Greenlanders now present a somewhat disheartening
picture, there remain various circumstances which leave
some ground for hope that they may regain their former
prosperity, and that contact with a people in a higher
stage of civilisation will prove no absolute hindrance to
their existence and welfare.   Firstly, in many places we
meet with pure natives who have been able to combine
the industry of their ancestors with the advantage to be
derived from the use of European articles which are now
for sale, and by means of these have established a house-

hold undoubtedly preferable to that which formed the
highest stage of comfortable life among the ancient
Greenlanders.  Next, it must be noticed that in many
families the children even of European fathers, who are
more exposed than other natives to the influence of
European habits, and also to the use of European
articles, have often become the most able kayakers and
industrious seal-hunters.  Next, it must be remarked
that the natives show a great aptitude for learning, and
are anxious to profit by the instruction imparted at
schools, regular school attendance being perhaps in no
country more popular than in Greenland ; and lastly, it
has been proved by experience that the natives themselves are acquiring a notion of the benefit arising from
suitable laws and social institutions, which are necessary
for the bringing about a more regulated way of making
those habits which are inseparable from their trade and
mode of life conformable to their relation with the
Europeans.

# INTRODUCTION

TO

# THE TALES AND TRADITIONS.

———————◆———————

THE tales and traditions, the relation of which forms one of the principal amusements and entertainments of the Greenlanders, appear to be instructive, and not without signification in regard to the study of the origin and development of traditions in general.

Firstly, it must be observed that the natives themselves divide their tales into two classes—the ancient tales, called oᴋalugtuat (plural of oᴋalugtuaᴋ), and the more recent ones, called oᴋalualârutit (plural of oᴋalualârut). The first kind may be more or less considered the property of the whole nation, at least of the greater part of its tribes; while the tales included under the second are, on the other hand, limited to certain parts of the country, or even to certain people related to each other, thus presenting the character of family records. The Eskimo are, more than any other nation, spread over a wide extent of country, only occupied by themselves, and thus are little acted upon by alien settlers. The inhabitants of their extreme western bounds, with their native means of transport, would have to traverse somewhere about five thousand miles before reaching the dwellings of their countrymen in the farthest east,

and in this journey would meet only with scanty little
bands of their own tribes settled here and there, generally consisting of less than a hundred souls. Their
little hamlets are severed from each other by desolate
tracts of ten to twenty—nay, even hundreds of miles.
Though there is every probability that the various tribes
of these vast regions have originated from one common
home, their present intercourse is very limited ; and it
may without exaggeration be asserted that the inhabitants of Greenland and Labrador, and those of the
shores of Behring Strait, cannot in any likelihood
have communicated with each other for a thousand
years or more, nor have they any idea of their mutual
existence.[1]  In accordance with this isolation, a closer
study of the traditions will also show how wide a space
of time must be supposed to exist between the origin of
the two classes of tales.  The greater part of the ancient
tales probably date from a far remoter period than one
thousand years ; the invention of the more recent traditions, on the other hand, must be supposed in most cases
not even to go back so far as two hundred years, and they
chiefly comprise events concerning families living in the
very district where they are told.  It may, however, be
taken for granted, that in days of yore such new tales
may have appeared at any time; but after a short
existence they were gradually forgotten, giving place to
others, and so on, continuously alternating during the
lapse of ages : while the ancient tales have been preserved unchanged, like some precious heirlooms which it
would have been sacrilege to have touched.  The definition we have here tried to give of the two classes is,
however, by no means exhaustive, nor without exceptions.  In our collection will be found stories which
undoubtedly must have originated between the two

[1] When Dr Kane first visited the small tribe of Eskimo living in
Smith's Sound, they were astonished to find that they were not the only
people on the face of the earth.

periods described, and therefore should form an intermediate or exceptional class, if the division were to be
complete and fully carried out. There are, moreover,
many others which we are at a loss how to classify.

The art of story-telling is in Greenland practised by
certain persons specially gifted in this respect; and
among a hundred people there may generally be
found one or two particularly favoured with the art of
the *raconteur*, besides several less tolerable narrators.
The art requires the ancient tales to be related as nearly
as possible in the words of the original version, with
only a few arbitrary reiterations, and otherwise only
varied according to the individual talents of the narrator,
as to the mode of recitation, gesture, &c. The only
real discretionary power allowed by the audience to the
narrator is the insertion of a few peculiar passages from
some shorter traditions; but even in that case no altera-
tion of these original or elementary materials used in
the composition of tales is admissible. Generally, even
the smallest deviation from the original version will be
taken notice of and corrected, if any intelligent person
happens to be present. This circumstance accounts for
their existence in an unaltered shape through ages; for
had there been the slightest tendency to variation on
the part of the narrator, or relish for it on that of the
audience, every similarity of these tales, told in such
widely-separated countries, would certainly have been
lost in the course of centuries. It would also appear
that it is the same narrators who compose the more
recent stories by picking up the occurrences and adventures of their latest ancestors, handed down occasionally
by some old members of the family, and connecting and
embellishing them by a large addition of the supernatural, for which purpose resort is always had to the
same traditional and mystical elements of the ancient
folk-lore. Undoubtedly the ancient tales have originally
been invented in a similar way, but at a time when the

different tribes were living in closer connection with each other and perhaps endowed with greater originality. It is to be supposed that the real or principal traditions, with the power of continuance through many centuries, are only produced after long intervals, and at certain periods peculiarly qualified for their production. As regards the Greenlanders, probably a new era of this kind may have arisen from the time of their being Christianised, many of the recent tales exhibiting considerable similarity to Christian legends. The elementary parts used in composing all kinds of tales being very numerous, it may be seen from the collection itself that, notwithstanding the stability and limited number of the ancient tales, the narrators, by help of the interpolations mentioned, and by their power of manufacturing modern tales, possess means for an almost unlimited variety at their story-telling entertainments.

The traditional tales, or rather the traditional elements of the ancient as well as the more recent tales, would never have been able to withstand the influence of centuries among these scattered and isolated bands if they had not been one of the most important means of maintaining their national life. Generally, all sorts of mythical traditions are looked upon chiefly as materials to aid in the search for historical facts. But with regard to a stage of culture like that of the Greenland Eskimo before their conversion to Christianity,[1] the traditions in reality may be said to comprise the whole national store of intellectual or moral property—viz., religion, science, and poetry at once, these manifestations of culture being but very imperfectly represented separately in a more specialised form.

In the first place, the traditions are to be considered as including a system of religion and morals as well as of laws and rules for social life. Such knowledge as

[1] The last pagan died in Danish Greenland only a few years ago.

they convey is unconsciously imbibed by the native
from his earliest childhood through listening to the
story-tellers, exactly as a child learns to speak. And
when the Greenlander nowadays is in doubt about any
question regarding the superstitions or customs of his
ancestors, he will try to find an answer by looking for
some sample out of his tales, ancient or modern, the
latter also containing elementary parts of ancient origin
kept up in this manner by succeeding generations. The
information used for our introductory remarks has also
been chiefly derived from this source.

Ethnologists and travellers will find themselves mistaken if they expect to discover traditions that might
supply direct information regarding the origin and history of the Eskimo. The more recent tales only may be
said to include such real historical material, and that
merely relating to family matters and events going back
as far as four or six generations. The author has often
made inquiries among the natives about events that have
taken place two or three hundred years ago, and more
especially about such occurrences as might be supposed
to have impressed themselves deepest upon the memory
of the population,—as, for instance, the first arrival of
European ships, or even the terrible smallpox epidemic
of comparatively recent date—viz., 1733-34. But these
attempts have been almost entirely without result; and,
as already said, the tales dating from an intermediate
period are either very scanty, or at least must be supposed devoid of any historical interest. It may be
considered certain that the present tribes of the nation
have not the remotest idea of their common original
home, nor of the migrations and rovings by which their
ancestors have peopled the territories now occupied by
them. Still, it may be supposed that at least a part
of their oldest tales have originated in true historical
events—are, in a word, "myths of observation;" but
in order to extract any reliable historical information

from this source, the following precautions have to be observed:—

Firstly, it not unfrequently seems that a series of occurrences happening within a limited period of time, and bearing some resemblance to each other, have in various cases been reduced to a single record which, so to speak, represents them all in one. This is confirmed by one of the few stories which undoubtedly dates from a period intermediate between ancient and modern times. When the Eskimo invaded the southern part of Greenland, they soon commenced hostilities with the ancient Scandinavian settlers, who were at length defeated, or totally disappeared. Among the generations immediately succeeding these events, there must doubtless have existed several traditions about the numerous feuds which must be supposed to have occurred between the parties; but by-and-by they were forgotten, with the exception of one or two which had perhaps been preferred to the rest, and listened to with most satisfaction. Of these, two tales still remain. The most remarkable one is now claimed as belonging to both the districts in which the ruins of the old colonies are found, each of which claims to be the homestead of the heroes mentioned in the tale. Among the older and most widely-spread tales, we need only refer to one treating of a man who wished to cross the frozen ocean, and for this purpose caught different wild beasts, which he trained to pull his sledge. It is not improbable that this story represents a whole series of similar tales, originating from the period when the Eskimo got their first dogs by domesticating some species of wild animal, such as the wolf.

Next, it must be remembered that no tale could maintain its existence unless it was entertaining to the audiences to whom it was related from time to time, and especially unless it was easy to comprehend without any elaborate explanation. For this purpose the tales had to be localised, or adapted to the different countries in which the tribes in course of time came to settle down, carrying their original traditions with them—as, for instance, when told in Greenland, their heroes were described as inhabitants not only of Greenland, but even of various districts of the country, according to the location of the narrator and his listeners. And, moreover, when foreign nations and animals unknown in Greenland happened to be mentioned in the ancient tales, they were generally, as time went on, transformed into supernatural beings, with which the imagination of the Greenlanders forthwith peopled the vast interior of their land, as well as the adjacent sea.

Besides religion and history, these traditional tales also represent the poetry of the inhabitants of the frozen North ; and this element has mainly inspired their listeners with that love for them which still continues. They present a true picture of what is likely to have formed the principal objects of the people's imagination, of what is considered great and delightful on one side, and hateful and dreadful on the other, in human life as well as in nature. They continually picture to us the great struggle for existence, which has caused personal courage and strength to be acknowledged and admired as the first condition of happiness ; and *per contra*, the idea of improving and securing the comforts of life by the aid of property is only very scantily developed in them. Not even to the almost universal sentiment of love do we find the poetry of Greenland affording much room. No wonder that such a scarcity of objects, and such simplicity of passions and feelings in these details of human life, render them uniform and rather fatiguing to us ; but, on the other hand, we cannot but admit that their inventors have exhibited a peculiar skill in producing effect and variety with the help of such very scanty materials. Closer examination will scarcely fail to discover real poetical feeling in their way of causing the highest perfection to be developed from the very smallest beginnings, as well as in their art of holding forth the dangers on one side and the means of over-coming them on the other, just as it might suit the narrator's object of arresting the attention of their audience. The poetical elements are also closely connected with the religious contents, and many religious opinions may further be regarded as emblematical or poetical. Such, for example, are expressions for certain ideas—such as, for instance, certain human qualities, the voice of conscience, an invisible ruling justice, and several powers of nature in their relation to mankind. A tendency to figurative expression is also shown in their habit of representing mankind in different stages of sexes and ages as personifications of certain common human qualities. For instance, the old bachelors always represent some ridiculous oddity; the wife is in general represented as with no care but of providing for her household, or how best she can economise; the poor widow is represented as especially excelling in benevolence and mercy; a band of five brothers, generally called "a lot of" brothers or men, represent haughtiness and brutality, and "the middlemost" of them, moreover, means envy.

The materials upon which the author has founded this collection have been written down partly by natives, partly by Europeans, from the verbal recital of the natives, and in the latter case to a large extent by the author himself. The manuscripts collected in this manner amounted to upwards of five hundred sheets or two thousand pages, and could be referred to about fifty native narrators or story-tellers. Several difficulties were met with in collecting these materials. The mode most generally adopted by travellers when making inquiries among a barbarous or foreign people about their traditions is that of selecting certain facts as subjects for questioning them upon, such as how their country was originally peopled, if their first ancestors came from the West or from the East, if they happened to know anything about a great deluge, &c. By this mode of inquiry the natives most likely, finding that they have no real information to offer, in order to satisfy the questioner and get rid of the trouble he causes them, will be influenced in their answers chiefly by what they think the questioner would best like to hear. The only way to acquire the information wanted is simply to make the natives relate what forms the principal subject of the stories told at their own assemblies. To make them understand that this was all we desired caused, however, the first difficulty. The next arose from their fear of being accused of heathenish superstition by revealing those superstitious tales to strangers. In consequence of these hindrances, several Europeans whom the author had specially requested to make investigations among the natives with whom they lived, came to the erroneous conclusion that no traditions at all, or only the most trifling ones, existed in the country. Lastly, it may easily be imagined that part of the manuscripts forwarded to him were in an incomplete and exceedingly illegible condition — some of them, indeed, conveying no meaning whatever.

The principal tales have for the most part been collated from more than one version, and all the variations have been most carefully examined and compared for the purpose of composing a text such as might agree best with the supposed original and most popular mode of telling the same story. In the first and principal part of the collection, the tales are in general to be considered as a nearly literal rendering of the verbal narratives, with only the omission of the more arbitrary reiterations and interpolations already referred to.

The natives who have contributed to this collection

were inhabitants of the following parts of Eskimo-
land :—

South Greenland, or the west coast of Greenland up
to 67° N.L.

North Greenland, or the same coast from 67° up to
74° N.L.

East Greenland, and

Labrador.

Of these regions South Greenland, in which the
author chiefly resided, has supplied the lion's share;
while, on the contrary, the east coast has furnished us
with only a few tales, which are not even written down
in that part of the country, but were picked up on the
west coast from east-coast people who had wandered
round Cape Farewell into the Danish settlement. From
Labrador only sixteen tales have been obtained, from
materials written down by Moravian missionaries resident in that country in the years 1861-63, and one half
of those are undoubtedly identical with Greenland tales,
some passages of them even exhibiting the most striking verbal conformity. Besides the tales written down
in North Greenland in 1861-63, the author was furnished
with a very valuable collection written down by natives
there in the years 1823-28, but never published.

It has generally been an easy task to make out
whether the written relations had the character of true
folk-lore, or might have been of foreign origin—*i. e.,* either
from European sources or to be traced to mere individual invention. Only a few instances of this still
remain doubtful.

The entire collection of manuscripts consisted of more
than five hundred tales, which, however, by uniting
those which were judged to be identical, have been
diminished to less than three hundred. Of that number,
in this edition a great many have been omitted or given
in an abridged form, as being more or less of only local
interest.

# TALES AND TRADITIONS.

———◆———

## 1.

## KAGSAGSUK.

[The following tale has been constructed from nine different copies, received partly from various places in Greenland, and partly from Labrador, all, however, agreeing upon every principal point. It does not appear to rest upon any historical basis, but merely to have a moral tendency, bringing before us the idea of a superior power protecting the helpless, and avenging mercilessness and cruelty.]

THERE was once a poor orphan boy who lived among a lot of uncharitable men. His name was Kagsagsuk, and his foster-mother was a miserable old woman. These poor people had a wretched little shed adjoining the *house-passage*,[1] and they were not allowed to enter the main room. Kagsagsuk did not even venture to enter the shed, but lay in the passage, seeking to warm himself among the dogs. In the morning, when the men were rousing their sledge-dogs with their whips, they often hit the poor boy as well as the dogs. He then would cry out, "*Na-ah! Na-ah!*"

---

[1] Or *doorway*, a long and very narrow, sometimes half-subterranean, tunnel, leading by an upward step to the main, or rather the only, room of the winter hut, and adapted to keeping out the cold air. Its ends we have called the outer and the inner entrance.

mocking himself in imitating the dogs. When the men were feasting upon various frozen dishes, such as the hide of the walrus and frozen meat, the little Kagsagsuk used to peep over the threshold, and sometimes the men lifted him up above it, but only by putting their fingers into his nostrils ; these accordingly enlarged, but otherwise he did not grow at all. They would give the poor wretch frozen meat, without allowing him a knife to cut it with, saying his teeth might do instead ; and sometimes they pulled out a couple of teeth, complaining of his eating too much. His poor foster-mother procured him boots and a small beard-spear, in order to enable him to go outside the house and play with the other children ; but they would turn him over and roll him in the snow, filling his clothes with it, and treating him most cruelly in various ways : the girls sometimes covered him all over with filth. Thus the little boy was always tormented and mocked, and did not grow except about the nostrils. At length he ventured out among the mountains by himself, choosing solitary places, and meditating how to get strength. His foster-mother had taught him how to manage this. Once, standing between two high mountains, he called out : "Lord of strength, come forth ! Lord of strength, come to me !" A large animal now appeared in the shape of an *amarok* (now a fabulous animal, originally a wolf), and Kagsagsuk got very terrified, and was on the point of taking to his heels ; but the beast soon overtook him, and, twisting its tail round his body, threw him down. Totally unable to rise, he heard the while a rustling sound, and saw a number of seal-bones, like small toys, falling from his own body. The amarok now said : "It is because of these bones that thy growth has been stopped." Again it wound its tail round the boy, and again they fell down, but the little bones were fewer this time ; and when the beast threw him down the third time, the last bones fell off. The fourth time he did not quite fall, and at the fifth he did not fall at all, but jumped along the ground. The amarok now said: "If it be thy wish to become strong and vigorous, thou mayst come every day to me." On his way home, Kagsagsuk felt very much lighter, and could even run home, meanwhile kicking and striking the stones on his way. Approaching the house, the girls who nursed the babies met him, and shouted, "Kagsagsuk is coming —let us pelt him with mud;" and the boys beat him and tormented him as before: but he made no opposition, and following his old habits, he went to sleep among the dogs. Afterwards, he met the amarok every day, and always underwent the same process. The boy felt stronger every day, and on his way home he kicked the very rocks, and rolling himself on the ground, made the stones fly about him. At last the beast was not able to overthrow him, and then it spoke: "Now, that will do; human beings will not be able to conquer thee any more. Still, thou hast better stick to thy old habits. When winter sets in, and the sea is frozen, then is thy time to show thyself; three great bears will then appear, and they shall be killed by thy hand." That day Kagsagsuk ran all the way back, kicking the stones right and left, as was his wont. But at home he went on as usual, and the people tormented him more than ever. One day, in the autumn, the kayakers [1] returned home with a large piece of driftwood, which they only made fast to some large stones on the beach, finding it too heavy to be carried up to the house at once. At nightfall, Kagsagsuk said to his mother, "Let me have thy boots, mother, that I too may go down and have a look at the large piece of timber." When all had gone to rest, he slipped out of the house, and having reached the beach, and loosened the moorings, he flung the piece of timber on his shoulders and carried it up behind the house, where

---

[1] Men in their kayaks, or skin canoes, made for the purpose of seal-hunting, with room only for a single person.

he buried it deep in the ground. In the morning, when the first of the men came out, he cried, "The driftwood is gone!" and when he was joined by the rest, and they saw the strings cut, they wondered how it could possibly have drifted away, there being neither wind nor tide. But an old woman, who happened to go behind the house, cried, "Just look! here is the spar!" whereat they all rushed to the spot, making a fearful noise, shouting, "Who can have done this? there surely must be a man of extraordinary strength among us!" and the young men all gave themselves great airs, that each might be believed to be the great unknown strong man—the impostors!

In the beginning of the winter, the housemates of Kagsaguk ill-treated him even worse than before; but he stuck to his old habits, and did not let them suspect anything. At last the sea was quite frozen over, and seal-hunting out of the question. But when the days began to lengthen, the men one day came running in to report that three bears were seen climbing an iceberg. Nobody, however, ventured to go out and attack them. Now was Kagsagsuk's time to be up and doing. "Mother," he said, "let me have thy boots, that I too may go out and have a look at the bears!" She did not like it much, but, however, she threw her boots to him, at the same time mocking him, saying, "Then fetch me a skin for my couch, and another for my coverlet, in return." He took the boots, fastened his ragged clothes around him, and then was off for the bears. Those who were standing outside cried, "Well, if that is not Kagsagsuk! What can he be about? Kick him away!" and the girls went on, "He must surely be out of his wits!" But Kagsagsuk came running right through the crowd, as if they had been a shoal of small fish; his heels seemed almost to be touching his neck, while the snow, foaming about, sparkled in rainbow colours. He ascended the iceberg

by taking hold with his hands, and instantly the largest
bear lifted his paw, but Kagsagsuk turned round to
make himself *hard* (viz., invulnerable by charm), and
seizing hold of the animal by the fore-paws, flung it
against the iceberg, so that the haunches were severed
from the body, and then threw it down on the ice to
the bystanders, crying, "This was my first catch ; now,
flense away[1] and divide !" The others now thought,
" The next bear will be sure to kill him." The former
process, however, was repeated, and the beast thrown
down on the ice ; but the third bear he merely caught hold
of by the fore-paws, and, swinging it above his head, he
hurled it at the bystanders, crying, "This fellow behaved
shamefully towards me !" and then, smiting another,
" That one treated me still worse !" until they all fled
before him, making for the house in great consternation. On entering it himself he went straight to his
foster-mother with the two bear-skins, crying, " There
is one for thy couch, and another for thy coverlet !"
after which he ordered the flesh of the bears to be
dressed and cooked. Kagsagsuk was now requested
to enter the main room ; in answer to which request
he, as was his wont, only peeped above the threshold,
saying, " I really can't get across, unless some one will
lift me up by the nostrils ;" but nobody else venturing
to do so now, his old foster-mother came and lifted him
up as he desired. All the men had now become very
civil to him. One would say, " Step forward ;" another,
" Come and sit down, friend." " No, not there where
the *ledge*[2] has no cover," cried another ; "here is a nice
seat for Kagsagsuk." But rejecting their offers, he sat
down, as usual, on the *side-ledge*. Some of them went

---

[1] Take off the skin and blubber.

[2] The main ledge or bench ; a low and broad bench for sitting and sleeping places, occupying the whole length of the wall opposite to the windows,
the narrower side-ledge and window-ledge bordering the other walls. It
is generally known in Greenland as the "brix."

on, "We have got boots for Kagsagsuk ;" and others, "Here are breeches for him!" and the girls rivalled each other in offering to make clothes for him. After supper, one of the inmates of the house told a girl to go and fetch some water for "dear Kagsagsuk." When she had returned and he had taken a drink, he drew her tenderly towards him, praising her for being so smart for fetching water; but, all of a sudden, he squeezed her so hard that the blood rushed out of her mouth. But he only remarked, "Why, I think she is burst!" The parents, however, quite meekly rejoined, "Never mind, she was good for nothing but fetching water." Later on, when the boys came in, he called out to them, "What great seal-hunters ye will make!" at the same time seizing hold of them and crushing them to death ; others he killed by tearing their limbs asunder. But the parents only said, "It does not signify—he was a good-for-nothing; he only played a little at shooting." Thus Kagsagsuk went on attacking and putting to death all the inmates of the house, never stopping until the whole of them had perished by his hand. Only the poor people who had been kind to him he spared, and lived with them upon the provisions that had been set by as stores for the winter. Taking also the best of the kayaks left, he trained himself to the use of it, at first keeping close to the shore; but after some time he ventured farther out to sea, and soon went south and northwards in his kayak. In the pride of his heart he roamed all over the country to show off his strength ; therefore, even nowadays he is known all along the coast, and on many places there are marks of his great deeds still shown, and this is why the history of Kagsagsuk is supposed to be true.

NOTE.—In the Labrador tale, the name of the champion is called *Kau jakjuk*, and in different copies from Greenland, *Kausaksuk, Kassaksuk, Kausasuk*, and *Kauksaksuk*. Several parts of Greenland claim the honour of pointing out the ruins of his house. A remarkable ruin on cape *Noogsuak*, of a very doubtful origin, is supposed to have been his bear-trap. In one of the writings, the relater, hinting at the European fancy for curiosities, observes : "I wonder why the masters, or even the king himself, who all seem so very fond of collecting rare things, if they really believe in the tale, have not taken one of the stones from this trap to be brought away with some ship, if possible."

---

## 2.

## THE BLIND MAN WHO RECOVERED HIS SIGHT.

[The text of this story has been collated from eight copies, among which two have been received from Labrador, the rest from different parts of Greenland, three of them having been written down before 1828. Like the former, it seems to have no historical, but only a moral or mythological reference.]

A WIDOW had a son and a daughter. When the son grew up, he made himself useful in different ways, and also commenced seal-hunting. One day in the beginning of winter he caught a *thong-seal* (a very large species, *Phoca barbata*[1]). On bringing it home, his mother wanted the skin for a ledge-cover, but he insisted on having it for making *hunting-lines*.[2] The mother grew angry, and in preparing the skin and removing the hairs, she practised some witchcraft on it, and spoke thus : "When he cuts thee into thongs, when he cuts thee asunder, then thou shalt snap and smite his face ;" and she rejoiced in the thought that it would hit him. When she had finished her prepar-

---

[1] Or bearded seal — "the ground - seal" of the English sealers : also called a "thong-seal," because the Eskimo cut their thongs and lines out of its hide. See Robert Brown's 'Seals of Greenland ;' Proc. Zoological Society of London (1868) ; and the Admiralty Manual of the Natural History of Greenland (1875).

[2] Line or thong attached with one end to the harpoon, with the other to the *hunting-bladder*, an inflated entire seal-skin, which prevents the harpooned seals running away.

ations, and he had cut out the first thong, he stretched and strained it; but in scraping it with a shell, a small blister burst, and hitting both his eyes, blinded him.

The winter coming on, they were destitute of their main provisions, and had to live entirely upon mussels (*Mytilus edulis*); and the blind boy took his place on the ledge, unable to go out hunting any more. Thus he passed the first half of the winter. A great bear then appeared, which began to eat away their (skin [1]) window-pane, and next thrust its head into the room. The mother and the sister fled in great terror to the inmost retired part of the ledge; but the blind man said to his sister, "Please bring my bow;" and she having given it to him, he bent it, and asked her to take the right aim for him. Levelling it at the animal, she gave him the signal, whereon he shot, and the arrow struck the bear so that it fell to the ground. The mother said, "Thou hitst the window instead of the beast;" but his sister whispered, "Thou hast killed a bear." They had now provisions for the coming days; but the mother never gave her son any of the boiled bear-flesh, but only a few shell-fish instead, and never let him taste a meal from his own hunting, but, in order to starve him, concealed her having any flesh. His sister, however, gave him his portion when the mother was absent, and he swallowed it in haste before her return. In this manner the greater part of the winter passed away. At last the days lengthened; and one day, in the spring, the sister said, "Dost thou remember how very delightful the time was when thou hadst still got thy sight, and wast able to go out hunting, and how we used to roam about the country?" The brother answered, "To be sure; let us be off again. I can take hold of thee." And the next morning at daybreak they went out together, he taking

---

[1] In modern times, most of the Eskimo huts in Danish Greenland have got glass window-panes; but through Eskimo-land generally, the semi-transparent entrail of some animal serves this purpose.

hold of her garments; and all day long they wandered about, the sister occupied in gathering shrubs [1] for fuel. One day they came to a large plain beside a lake, and the brother then said, "I think I will lie down a little, while thou goest away to find more fuel;" and accordingly she left him. Whilst he was thus resting himself, he heard some wild geese flying in the air above him, and when they were right over his head, he heard one of them crying out, "Look at the poor young man down there; he is blind: would we could make him see." When the birds approached him he never stirred, but lay quietly on his back. At this moment he had a sense of something warm falling down on his eyes, one of the wild geese having dropped its excrement upon them, and heard a voice saying, "Keep thy eyes shut till the sound of our wings has altogether passed away, then thou mayst try to open them." Again he lay down motionless; while the wild goose, sweeping its wings across his face, repeated, "Mind thou dost not open thy eyes." The sound of their wings now dying away, he already observed a certain brightness; but when the noise had altogether passed away, he opened his eyes wide, and had his sight restored to him. He now called out, "*Nayagta!*" (so he called his sister). But she did not return till evening, when she was seen coming across the country, moody and downhearted, with one arm drawn out of the sleeve of her jacket, and her chin hidden in the fur collar. Perceiving her, he again called out, "Nayagta, now thou needst not be in want of food or anything else; I shall give thee clothes, for now I have my sight again." But she only gainsaid him, and would not believe him until she looked into his reopened eyes, and saw their sound and healthy appearance. They both agreed not to let their mother know what had happened. In descending the hills, and approach-

---

[1] Such as the crowberry (*Empetrum*), the blaeberry (*Vaccinium*), the dwarf birch (*Betula nana*), &c.

ing the house, he caught sight of his bear-skin stretched
out to dry, and in front of the entrance its bones, and on
entering the main room he got a glimpse of its paws.
Shutting his eyes, he now took his usual place on the
ledge, and feigning to have been asleep, he started up,
saying, "I dreamt I saw a bear-skin stretched out behind the house;" but the old woman merely replied,
"Thou must surely have been thinking about somebody
who happened to hurt thee some time ago."   Again the
son feigned sleeping, and starting up, he said, "Methinks
I also saw a lot of bear-bones outside the entrance."
The old woman repeated her first answer; but the third
time, on seeming to awake, the son said, "I dreamt I saw
two bear's paws here underneath the couch;" and the
mother again giving the same answer, suddenly opening
his eyes, he said, "Mother, I mean these;" and then
she knew that he had regained the use of his eyes, and
she exclaimed, "Eat them, just eat them!"   He now
took up his old habits, and again commenced seal-hunting; but, after some time, the idea grew upon him to
take revenge on his detestable old mother.   The season
was at hand when the *white whales*[1] began to appear
along the ice-bound shore, and he used to catch them in
the following manner: he went out on the ice with his
sister, and having fastened his hunting-line round her
waist, he threw the harpoon which was attached to the
line into the fish, thus making her serve him instead of
a hunting-bladder.[2]   After which, they hauled together
till they had safely landed the fish on the ice, where
they afterwards killed it.

One day, returning home, he asked his sister, "Dost
thou like our old mother?"   She made no answer; but
on his repeating the question she only answered, "I am

---

[1] "White fish,"—a large sort of dolphin—the *Beluga* or *Delphinus albi-
cans* of zoologists.   It is captured in great abundance in Greenland.

[2] The inflated skin or bladder attached to the line to bring up the animal,
as well as the weapon when it has missed its mark and fallen into the sea.

more fond of thee than of her; thou art the only one I do love." "Well, then, to-morrow she shall serve us for a bladder. I'll pay her off for having made me blind." They both agreed upon the plan; and returning to the house where they found the mother busy mending boots, he said, "Oh dear, how tired we are with hauling in the fish! Now let my sister have a rest to-morrow; meantime thou mightst serve me as a hunting-bladder. I suppose thou canst keep thy footing when the fish pull the line." The mother declaring herself willing, they all went down to the open sea the next morning; but when the white whales appeared, and he was preparing to harpoon them, she said: "Take one of the smallest, and not the large ones;" and perceiving some very little fish coming up, she cried, "Look out and try for one of these;" but he answered, "They are still too big." At the same instant, however, one of the very largest fishes rose to the surface; and harpooning it, he let go his hold of the line, and when the animal had drawn his mother pretty close to the water, he cried out, "Dost thou remember the time thou madest me blind?" and while she endeavoured to hold back, he pushed her on, saying, "That fellow will give me my revenge." When she was close to the very edge of the water, she cried, "My *ullo!*" (woman's knife)—"it was I who nursed thee;" and with these words she was plunged into the sea, which soon covered her. Still she reappeared on the surface, crying, "My *ullo*, my *ullo;* I nursed thee!" but then disappeared for ever. It is said that she was afterwards transformed into a fish, and that her spreading hair turned into long horny teeth, from which the narwals[1] are said to have their origin. The white whales having all disappeared, brother and sister returned to the house, and lamented the loss of their mother, feeling conscious that she had nursed them, and taken care of them.

---

[1] Monodon monoceros.

They now began to be terrified at their deed, and
dared not stay in their little house; they therefore
fled on eastward, far away to the large continent,
roaming about the interior parts of the country.[1] At
first he would not even kill a bird, feeling pity towards them for having restored the use of his eyes to
him; but at last he killed a swan, because his sister
wanted to have it, and it is said that this was the only
bird he caught for the remainder of his life. Far away
from the coast they built their house; they grew to be
immensely old, and were always without friends. At
length they determined to show themselves among other
people, and he resolved upon going to some place which
had an *angakok* (priest of the heathens). After a while
he found such people, and decided to await the time
when the angakok was going to conjure his spirits. He
then went up to the house; but ere he reached it, the
angakok began to complain, and cried, " I am going to
let a spirit out upon you; a large fire is just outside "
(viz., the *kivigtok*, supernatural beings in general making
their appearance like a flame or brightness). The man
who was standing outside now made his inquiry : " Do
you not know me ?—have ye heard of him who used his
mother for a hunting-bladder?" and as no one answered
him, he repeated the same question over again. An old
woman now rejoined : " I remember to have heard in
my childhood that many many years ago there lived a
brother and a sister who fastened their poor mother as a
bladder to a white whale." The stranger outside then
said : " I am that very man; I have come to denounce
myself : do come out and see what I am like." The angakok went out, followed by his auditors, and they saw
him standing erect in the bright moonlight beside the
boat. The hair of his head was snowy white, as if he

---

[1] People who fled from mankind in order to live in the desolate interior
of Greenland were called *kivigtoks*, and believed to acquire supernatural
qualities—such as clairvoyance, immense swiftness, and longevity.

had been covered with a hood of white hare-skins ; but his face was black, and his clothes were made of rein-deer-skins, and he told them that his sister was not able to move from old age, and that they had their hut far away in the interior of the country, and that their house-

fellows were terrible beings with heads like seals ; and lastly he added : "After this, I will not show myself any more to human creatures ; those to whom I wanted to denounce myself I have done it to." After having said these words he turned away, and has never been seen afterwards.

NOTE.—The son's name has in Greenland been called Tutigak ; in Labrador, Kemongak. According to the Labrador tale, the birds make him dive into the lake ; according to the Greenland readings, the mother cried, "It was I who *cleared away thy urine*"—instead of "*nursed thee.*"

## 3.

## IGIMARASUGSUK.

[This somewhat trifling but still curious story is well known to every child
   in Greenland; and one tale has also been got from Labrador, and is undoubtedly another reading of the same original, though much abridged
   and altered.]

IT was said of Igimarasugsuk that he always lost his
   wives in a very short time, and always as quickly
married again; but nobody knew that he always killed
and ate his wives, as well as his little children.   At last
he married a girl who had a younger brother, and many
relatives besides.   Entering the house on his return from
a reindeer-hunt, he one day said to his brother-in-law:
"Pray go and fetch me my axe—thou wilt find it lying
underneath the boat-pillars" (viz., pillars upon which
the boat is laid during the winter); and at the same time
Igimarasugsuk got up and followed him.   On hearing
the shrieks of her brother, the wife of Igimarasugsuk
peeped out, and beheld him pursuing the former, and
shortly after striking him on the head, so that he fell
down dead on the spot.   After this he ordered his wife
to dress and boil some parts of the body of her brother.
Igimarasugsuk now commenced eating, and offered a
piece of an arm to his wife, insisting upon her eating
with him; but she only feigned to do so, and concealed
her portion under the ashes of the fire.   Then the husband exclaimed, "I actually think thou art crying!"
"No," she said; "I am only a little shy."   After having
devoured his brother-in-law, the husband now began to
fatten his wife; and to this end ordered her to eat nothing
but reindeer-tallow, and only drink as much as a small
shell would hold.   At last she grew so fat that she was
not able to move about at all.   One day he went away,
after having securely shut the entrance to the summer-

tent, fastening it with strong cords. When he had
been gone a considerable time she took her knife, let herself fall down from the bench, and rolled herself as far
as to the entry. By great efforts she crossed the threshold, and was now in the fore-room, where she cut the
strings fastening the outer curtain. She then rolled herself down to a muddy pool and drank a great deal of
water; after which she felt less heavy, and was able to
get up and walk back. She re-entered the tent, stuffed
out her jacket, put it on the bench with its back turned
outward; and fastening the entrance well, she went away.
But being convinced that her husband would shortly
pursue her, she took her way down to a very large piece
of drift-wood that had been hauled ashore, and she then
worked a spell upon it, singing thus: "kissugssuaĸ pin-
gerssuaĸ, ia-ha-ha, arape, ĸupe, sipe, sipe sisaria." And
forthwith the timber opened midways, and she entered
it, again singing, "kissugssuaĸ . . . . . . arape, mame,
mamesisaria." Then it closed around her, leaving her
in darkness. In the meantime she heard her husband
coming on towards the spot. He had entered the tent,
and seeing the stuffed jacket, he thrust his lance into it;
but on discovering what it really was, he ran out, and
following the footprints of his wife all the way to the
timber, he stopped there, and she plainly heard him say:
"Oh what a pity I waited so long in killing her! oh poor
miserable me!" Then she heard him turn away and
return several times; but every trace ending at the large
timber, he at last went away, and she again sang kissugssuaĸ, &c. &c., and instantly the drift-wood opening,
she crept out and ran farther on. But lest he should
overtake and discover her, she hid herself in a fox-hole.
Every trace again ending here, she heard him digging
the very earth with his hands; but he soon grew tired,
and went away, returning and again going away as
before, bemoaning himself in the same manner: "Oh
what a pity, poor miserable man that I am!" &c. &c.

Perceiving him to be gone, she again set off on her journey. Still, however, fearing him, she next took refuge
behind some bushes. Again she heard him come and
repeat his old lament: "What a pity I put off eating
her so long!" and again going away, he immediately
returned, saying, "Here every trace of her ends." Proceeding on her way, she now had a faint hope of reaching some inhabited place ere he could get up with her
again. At length she caught sight of some people
gathering berries in the country; but on perceiving her
they were on the point of taking fright, when she cried
out, "I am the wife of Igimarasugsuk." They now approached her, and taking hold of her hands, brought her
to their home. Having arrived there she said: "Igimarasugsuk, who has the habit of eating his wives, has
also eaten his brother-in-law; and if he really wants to
get hold of me too, he will be sure to come and fetch me;
and as he is very fond of entertainment, ye had better
treat him civilly and politely." Soon after, he arrived;
but she hid herself behind a skin curtain. The rest rose
up and went out to welcome him, saying: "We trust thy
people at home are quite well." "Yes, they are very
well indeed," he answered. When he had entered they
served a meal before him, and afterwards offered him a
drum, saying, "Now let us have a little of thy performance." He took hold of the drum, but soon returned
it to one of the others, saying, "Ye ought rather to en-
tertain me;" and the other man, seizing the drum, began to sing: "Igimarasugsuk—the cruel man—who ate
his wives." . . . At these words Igimarasugsuk
blushed all over his face and down his throat; but when
the singer continued, "and she was forced to eat of her
own brother's arm," the wife came forward, saying,
"No, indeed, I did not; I concealed my share beneath
the ashes." They now caught hold of him, and the wife
killed him with a lance, saying, "Dost thou remember
thrusting thy lance into my stuffed jacket?"

## 4.

## KUMAGDLAT AND ASALOK.

[This story, also well known in all parts of Greenland, has been derived
from five copies, written in different parts of that country. Unlike the
preceding tales, it exhibits a more historical appearance, apparently
referring to certain occurrences which must have taken place during the
stay of the primeval Eskimo on the shores of the American continent,
and have been repeated until our day. It indicates the first appear-
ances of culture in attempts to provide tools or weapons from sea-
shells, stones, and metal, as well as conflicts and meetings of the Eskimo with the Indians, which in recent times have still taken place on
the banks of the Mackenzie and Coppermine Rivers.]

THREE cousins named Kumagdlat, Asalok, and
Merak were very fond of one another. Kumag-
dlat occupied a house by himself, and had his own boat.[1]
The other two kept a house and a boat in partnership; but
they all assisted each other early and late, and amused
themselves in exercising and exhibiting their mutual
strength. When they went out kayaking, they always
accompanied each other in a friendly and amicable
manner, and were on the whole much attached to one
another. Kumagdlat had an old crone living with him,
and she used to be very cross-tempered; and one day
he accosted her as follows: "I won't have cross old
women living in my house, and I shall certainly put
thee to death some day or other." The old hag now
behaved peacefully and quietly, until one day she exclaimed: "I can tell thee, it is not without reason that
I am so quiet and low-spirited; from the first day thou
began to maintain and support me I have been very
sorry for thee, and this has made me silent and downhearted." "How so?" asked Kumagdlat; and she answered: "Is it not that thy cousins love thee so very

---

[1] umiak, the larger skin-boat, fit for one to three families travelling.
with their tents, and all the other necessaries, for the summer season.

dearly? Nevertheless they now intend to put an end to thy life." However, she had invented this lie, being so ill-natured and resentful that she could not even sleep at night. But from that time Kumagdlat began to fear his cousins; and though he never used to be parted from them all day long, he now began to shun them. One day in the spring they entered his house, saying, "Art thou not going out in thy kayak to-day?" But he answered, "No, I can't go; I must leave my kayak time to dry,"—and accordingly they set out without him. In their absence he dug up his tent-poles from the snow, and had just finished when they returned. Next morning they again entered with the same question, but he answered as before: "No, I must have my kayak perfectly dry before I can use it." They would have liked him to go with them; but as he would not be persuaded, they again went out by themselves. As soon as they were out of sight he prepared everything for leaving his old quarters: he had his boat put in the water, and as soon as it was loaded he pushed off; but at parting he said to the people on shore: "Tell them to follow as soon as possible; we intend to go out to sea to our usual reserves" (depots for provisions): and so saying, he started. Asalok and Merak at last returned, and when they discovered that Kumagdlat was gone, they made inquiries, and received the answer, "They have newly departed, and left word that they intended to go out seaward to their usual reserves, and that they wanted you to follow them as soon as possible." They at once determined to do so; and early the next morning the boat was put right, loaded, and away they went, taking the usual direction: but they did not find him, nor any marks or traces of him along the shore. It is said that Kumagdlat had the skull of a seal for an amulet, and that now every time when he had to pass inhabited places he fixed his amulet on the prow of his boat, that the people of the places might think it to be nothing but a spotted seal diving up and down. But in one of the settlements he thus passed there happened to be a fool, who (fools or naturals being considered as clairvoyants) always had a presentiment of whatever was to take place, and being aware of the boat passing by, he cried out, "A boat! a boat!" But when the others went out to look for it, they could only see a spotted seal diving up and down, and after a while totally disappearing. When Asalok with his company came to this place and heard these news, they knew that Kumagdlat must have passed by, because they knew of his having such an amulet. Meantime Kumagdlat travelled on night and day without going ashore; when the rowing-girls got too tired, they only made fast the boat a short time to take rest, and then continuing their voyage, until they at last stopped at a well-peopled place, where they resolved to take up their quarters. In this place they met with a very old man busily employed in making a boat. His hair was as white as the side of an iceberg, and beside him stood a bearded young man. Some time after the arrival of Kumagdlat, the old man said to him, "Before this young man here was born I commenced building that boat, and by this time I have only just finished the hull." But right and left heaps of shells were seen piled together, these being the only tools he had had to work with. "Here we have not got so much as a single knife," rejoined the old man; "but yonder, in the interior of the country, live people who have knives in abundance." And when Kumagdlat went on asking, he continued, "Farther inland numerous *erkileks* [1] have their abodes, and they are immensely rich. However, when any of the coast people go there they never return, being mostly

---

[1] A sort of fabulous beings—half men, half beasts. All sorts of *inlanders* in the Greenlandish tales represent fabulous or supernatural beings. The most common kind, and probably the inlanders in general, are called *tornit* (plural of *tunek*), which is what in the following pages we have translated by *inlanders*.

killed, I suppose." Kumagdlat now said, "I have a
great mind to go out in search of them myself;" but the
old man replied, "I am afeared thou wilt not be able to
do aught by thyself, as even several of our people going
together have always been put to death. The erkileks
are rare people, and neither to be matched in swiftness
nor agility." But Kumagdlat returned to his tent and
set about making a small bow and arrows—the quiver
he formed out of seal-skin ; and having finished these, he
started on his journey to the erkileks, all by himself.

When, meanwhile, the brothers Asalok and Merak
likewise had wandered about the country for a long
time, they at length discovered an extensive plain below
them, where the erkileks lived in many tents, and only
had a lake for their sea. They now hid themselves,
awaiting the fall of night, and watching the return of the
erkileks from their day's hunting. Beneath the rays
of the setting sun they espied a very tall man carrying a burden on his back. They were just in the act
of discharging their arrows at him, when both exclaimed, "Why, is not that man like Kumagdlat?" and
when he answered, "Yes, so it is," they said to each
other, "Well, since we have so happily met, one of the
hateful erkileks shall fall." Having thus again met and
recognised each other, Kumagdlat told his cousins how
the old hag had calumniated them to him. When it
had grown quite dark, and all was silent in the camp of
the erkileks, the cousins rose up and first set out in
search of some place of security for themselves. At the
further side of the lake the erkileks had pitched their
tents, and right opposite was a small island, which
they fixed upon as a place of refuge. On arriving
at the spot they observed that the distance of the island
might be about a stone's-throw. Kumagdlat, with the
burden on his back, was the first to venture the leap, and
succeeded in gaining the island ; Asalok, too, reached
the opposite shore; but Merak exclaimed, "I really can-

not do it." When, however, the others prevailed upon
him to try the leap, he, too, reached the island, though
not without touching the water in crossing. In this
place they now deposited their arrows, each providing
himself with only two, after which they returned to the
mainland, Merak, as before, almost touching the water.
They now advanced towards the tents, where the inmates had all retired to rest. Having reached the
largest, Kumagdlat said to his companions, " I'll jump
up on the cross-beam above the entrance, while ye pass
through the fore-room." Having passed the entrance,
and peeping through the skin curtain of the main room,
they beheld an old married couple inside, who were still
awake. The woman, who was in the family way, was
sitting upright, whilst the man was leaning forward, resting his head on his hands. All of a sudden the man
gave a howl like a dog, at which the woman arose to
her feet. He then commenced licking her belly, and
she handed him some reindeer-tallow. Kumagdlat now
said, " Next time he begins to lick her, I'll take aim and
shoot her." When the old man had finished eating he
gave a howl as before, and the woman again got up ; but
just as he was in the act of licking her, Kumagdlat shot
her right through the body. A fearful yell was now
heard, and Kumagdlat jumping quickly down, they all
hurried across to their hiding-place, while the erkileks
in great crowds issued out of their tents. The cousins,
meantime, reached the island in the same manner as
before. Having safely arrived there, they at once lay
down in a row on the ground, each behind the other,
Kumagdlat in front, then Asalok, and Merak hindmost.
The erkileks began to arm and discharge their arrows
at them, which they carried in quivers at their backs ;
but the women pulling out the arrows from above, were
enabled to discharge them much quicker than the men,
who pulled them out sideways. While the cousins were
watching the archers on shore, always diving down be-

fore their arrows, they noted one whistling through the
air, and having slightly touched the two, they heard it
strike behind them; and looking round, they saw that
Merak had been dangerously hit in the throat through
venturing to raise his head.   Then Asalok said to Kumagdlat, "Dost not thou know any spell for restoring
life?"    He answered, "Yes, I believe I do;" whereupon he began to murmur some words.   When he had
finished, they looked round and observed that the arrow
had already gone half-way out of Merak's throat, and
when Kumagdlat spoke the third time, Merak was alive
and unhurt.   The erkileks continued shooting; but
when they had used up all their arrows, Kumagdlat had
only the skin of his temple grazed a little, and the
cousins now arose to pay them back with their bows.
When a great number of the erkileks had been shot,
they pursued the rest along a river, until they reached
a waterfall, where they had a hiding-place; but there
Kumagdlat killed them all by throwing stones at them,
as they issued forth one by one.   Afterwards the friends
returned to the tents, where the children had remained
immovable, and stunned with terror, feigning to be dead;
but the cousins caught hold of them nevertheless, and
having pierced them through the ears, they quickly
killed them—only one boy and a girl being left alive.
They examined the furniture of the erkileks, and found
pots of copper, with copper handles to them, and no requisites of any kind wanting.   On opening the boxes,
the covers unlocked of themselves, because of the great
quantity of clothes they contained.   These boxes
they again closed, but opened others containing knives
with beautiful handles, of which they took as many away
with them as they could possibly carry, and then again
made their way towards the coast.   In the meantime
the people with whom Kumagdlat had left his family
often used to mock them, saying, " Look ye, those who
go to the erkileks won't fail to bring back many fine

things, such as beautiful knives, with pretty hafts to
them." On hearing this, Kumagdlat's wife would run
outside, believing her husband to be coming; but they
only said so because they believed him to have been
killed. An old bachelor had taken her into his house
and provided for her, considering her to be a widow.
At the time when Kumagdlat was actually returning to
the coast, the people were again ridiculing his family,
crying out as before. But at the same moment the old
boat-builder turned round and beheld Kumagdlat descending the hill, and carrying great loads on his back;
and on his approach he discovered his burden to consist
of knives with beautiful hafts. On entering the tent
Kumagdlat found his mother and wife mourning his
absence, and he said, "I expected to have found you
with the lamps extinguished" (viz., at the point of starvation). They made answer, "The old bachelor has
provided for us, that we might not perish from hunger."
Kumagdlat rejoined, "Many thanks to him, then, and let
him come and choose himself a knife." But the old bachelor would not enter, but wanted the knife to be brought
to him; whereupon Kumagdlat said, "Having such
great cause to be thankful towards him, I must have him
come in." But the old man, fearing some mischief (viz.,
suspecting jealousy), insisted on having the knife brought
out to him. Kumagdlat, however, continued calling
from within; and now at last the old man just crossed
the threshold, saying, "Well, then, let me have the
knife:" but Kumagdlat still entreated him to come
further into the room; and having at length made him
sit down, said, "Thou hast provided well for these poor
creatures; I thank thee very much, and hope thou wilt
accept of these knives," and he offered him two with
beautiful handles. It is said that the cousins afterwards
returned to their old home, and that they grew very renowned for their vigour and dexterity, and killed bears
as well as *kilivfaks* (fabulous beasts).

## 5.

## AKIGSIAK.

[Of this tale six different copies have been received.  It seems in a very remarkable way to refer to certain historical facts in regard to the intercourse between the Indians and the Eskimo, and is in some measure analogous to the folk-lore of several other nations, ascribing certain great actions, especially such as the defeating of some monstrous and dreadful animal, to one special hero.  The text, however, is here given in an abridged form, the story itself not being very interesting.]

IN days of yore it once happened that some people went far into a firth to fish for salmon, and at the time one of the women was carried off by an inlander, and was taken by him to a very remote place.  She belonged to the coast people, but afterwards married the man who carried her off, and they begat a son, who was named Akigsiak.  In his boyhood two of his father's nephews were his constant playfellows.  They often used to box and fight each other, but Akigsiak soon outdid them completely; even in swiftness his friends did not surpass him.  As his mother belonged to the coast people, while his father was from the interior of the country, he was smaller of growth; but notwithstanding, he was respected and feared by the other inlanders, and had a great reputation for strength and ability in hunting.  Akigsiak used to seek intercourse with the coast people in order to gain information concerning his mother's relatives; and at such a meeting he once told them as follows: "When my father grew older he was incapable of providing for us.  One winter we had a great famine, and every day I went out in search of provisions; and meanwhile my father watched me from the tops of the highest mountains, at the same time taking note of any change in the weather, and as soon as the sky darkened he made me a signal that I could hear far

and wide, after which I took my way homewards. He
also gave me several instructions, and said I might go
anywhere excepting to the north, because of a monstrous reptile that was reported to ravage those parts.
One day my father gave me the signal; but not even
having had a chance of killing any game, I did not obey
his call. Afterwards, when I was going to return home,
the storm overtook me, and I could hardly see anything
on account of the wind and the snow-drifts, and consequently lost my way. Wandering about in this manner,
I at length discovered something that appeared to me
like two large windows of a house; then I saw that the
other parts were like a hill; and finally I saw that this
was the terrible reptile against which my father had
warned me. I at once took to flight. However, he had
already seen me, and pursued me; but whenever he
came up I leapt across him, and striking him with my
lance, I continued running. At last, however, turning
round to look for him, and noticing that he was quite
close upon me, I cried aloud with fatigue, and falling to
the ground, I lost my senses. I was soon awakened by
a cool touch upon my face, and at once remembered the
monster reptile. Looking about for him, I beheld him
lying close to my feet. With my eyes constantly fixed
upon him, I very cautiously crept away; and as he did
not even move, I rose to my feet and walked on: but I
did not reach my home until the fourth day, and had
been given up for lost. On entering the house my
father said, ' Our housemates have got nothing to help
thee with.' But I told him that I had barely escaped
from the reptile, and that apparently I had left him
dead; and then my father said, ' The body of the reptile is said to consist of nothing but fat;' and he added,
' our house-fellows are almost starving.' These were now
informed of what had happened, and they went out in
search of the monster; but many of them died before
they reached the spot—some just outside their houses

others farther away, till the whole road was covered
with dead bodies. But those who reached the reptile
flensed away at him, and found him to consist principally
of fat, mixed with a little lean flesh. They afterwards
had it for food the whole winter." This was Akigsiak's
report at his first meeting with the coast people.

The next time he told how he had once been away
on an excursion with his father, and that on approaching the sea-shore they observed a whale close outside,
and a number of coast people standing on the beach.
By his father's orders he ran down and made an old
man teach him a magic lay for luring the whale up the
river. As soon as the whale had entered the river a
crowd of inlanders appeared ; but before they had been
able to penetrate the skin of the whale with their harpoons, Akigsiak ran off home in order to fetch his
weapons. Though he had to round three large bays on
his way, he was still in good time to despatch the whale
after his return, and then proceeded to give everybody
his share of it, not forgetting the old coast man, whom
he protected against the inlanders. At the third meeting he went on to tell how, having once heard that some
other inlanders had caught an immense fish the shape
of a salmon, he hurried down to the river-side and
threw his harpoon also into the fish, but that his companions being too few, the other inlanders stationed on
the opposite side succeeded in hauling it from them.
He then hastened on to a place where the river was
somewhat narrower, and in jumping across hurled himself round, head over heels, before he alighted on his
feet at the opposite shore. There he soon frightened
away the other inlanders, took his share of the fish—
which he threw across to his own people on the other
side—and then jumped back in the same way he had
come. At his fourth meeting with the coast people,
Akigsiak told them about a quarrel he once had with
an *igalilik* (viz., "pot-bearer," certain fabulous inlanders

carrying boiling pots on their shoulders), whom he had pushed down a precipice, crushing him to death against the rocks. At last, Akigsiak met with an *inorusek* (another kind of gigantic inlanders) on the high banks of a river. While they were amusing themselves with throwing stones, the inorusek persuaded him to try to hit a kayaker just passing by below, whom he did not fail to kill on the spot. Akigsiak, repenting himself of his deed, afterwards slew the inorusek, but is said never from this time to have ventured himself among the coast people again, because of the murder he had committed. Only once, they say, did he go to visit a certain coast man, who lived on the banks of a river, in order to try a boxing-match and a race with him. Although he was said to be a smaller man than the other inlanders, he was at all events larger than our people; his back was as broad as that of two others put together, and his height very little less than two people on top of each other.

---

## 6.

## THE FRIENDS.

[This is a very famous Greenland story, and is, in its present form, compiled from three copies.]

TWO friends loved each other very dearly. From childhood they had been constant companions. One lived at one of the outermost islands, and the other had his abode far up, at the head of a fiord. They very often visited each other, and when they had been parted for some days, they felt a mutual longing to meet again. In the summer the man from the fiord used to go out reindeer-hunting in the interior; but before he went back to the place where he lived, he always took a whole reindeer, choosing one of those with velvety horns and leaving all the tallow in it, to regale his friend with. The islander, on his part, saved and laid by large quantities of seals: and when the reindeer-hunter returned, he immediately visited his friend and was regaled with nicely-dried seal-flesh; but in the evening, when the room grew heated, the frozen meat was produced and set before his friend as a cold dish. The guest then praised it very much, and they gossiped till late in the evening. The next day the reindeer-hunter usually had a visit from his friend, but now they only ate reindeer-flesh, and especially the tallow. The friend found it extremely delicious, and ate till he was ready to burst; and at his departure next day he was presented with some dried meat and tallow.

One autumn the hunter lingered in the interior longer than usual. At length the earth was quite frozen over, and still he did not return. At first the friend longed very much for him, but after a while he grew angry with him; and when the first of the preserved seals began to spoil, they commenced to eat away at the whole lot. Later on, when he heard that the hunter had returned, he went out to a grave and cut a bit of fat from a dead body, and with this he rubbed certain parts of a seal he intended to treat his friend with, in order to do him an evil turn on his arrival. Shortly afterwards he came to pay his visit. The meeting was very pleasant, and as usual he was regaled with various delicacies; and the hunter now told that he had had small luck in getting the reindeer with velvety horns, and this was the reason why he had stayed away so long; and his friend answered, "I was expecting thee very anxiously for some time, but when my first preserved seals began to rot, we ate them all up;" and he added, "let us have the one that was last put by; we will have it for a cold dish." It was accordingly brought in and nicely served up, and the host laid the piece that had been rubbed over with the bit of fat uppermost, and set it before his friend, at the same time begging him to partake of it; but just as the visitor was in the act of helping himself to a piece, something from beneath the ledge gave a pull at his leg. This somewhat puzzled him; however, he was going to commence a second time when he got another pull, on which he said, "I must go outside a little," and rose up at the same time and went. Being an *angakok*, the voice of his *tornak* (guardian-spirit) now warned him, saying, "Thy friend regales thee with a base design; turn the piece over when thou goest back and eat of the opposite part; if thou eatest of the part that is now uppermost thou wilt be sure to go mad." Having again seated himself, he turned the meat over; but his host thought it might be a mere accident. When the guest had eaten sufficiently, he felt a pain in his stomach—he had probably touched some of the poisoned flesh; but he soon recovered, and on taking leave, he asked his friend to return the visit soon. When he came home he took a reindeer with velvety horns and treated it in the same manner as his friend had done the seal—rubbing it well with some fat from a dead body; and when his guest came, he instantly regaled him with dried meat and tallow, and never before had the visitor found it so much to his taste. At night the reindeer was set before them with the poisoned side turned up, and putting the knife into it, he said, "There, we have got some cold meat; I have kept it for thee this long while." The friend ate away at it, and several times exclaimed, "This is really delicious!" and the host answered, "Yes, that is because it is so very fat." When the meal was over, the guest felt a pain in his stomach, and, looking hard at every one present, he got up and went outside, but the pains were not relieved. Next day he took his leave, and it was a long time before his friend saw him again; when he went out kayaking he never met him as he had done formerly. At length, when the ice began to cover the waters, a boat was seen to put into the firth from the sea, and was recognised as being the boat of the friend; but finding that he himself was not of the party, he asked, "Where is your master?" "He is ill, and has turned raving mad; he wanted to eat us, and therefore we all took flight." On the very next day the huntsman went out to visit his friend. Nobody was to be seen about the house; but, creeping through the entry and looking over the threshold, he beheld his friend lying on his back, with eyes staring wildly, and his head hanging over the edge of the couch. He went up to him and asked him how he did, but no answer was given. After a short silence he suddenly started up and shouted with all his might, "Because thou hast feasted me basely, I have eaten up all the inmates of my house, and I will now devour thee too"—and he bounded towards him; but the other escaped through the entry, and quickly made for his kayak. He only succeeded in pushing off as his pursuer was in the very act of seizing hold of him. The madman now continued running along the shore and crying, "I feel much better now; do come back. When I have not seen thee for a day or two, I am longing dreadfully for thee." On hearing him speak quite sensibly the friend believed him, and put back again. As soon as he reached the shore, however, the former made a rush at him; but, happily observing this, he pushed off in time. At home he never spoke nor ate from grief for his friend, and his housemates thought him much altered. Towards night he commenced talking to them of his own accord, and told them how he had fared; but the others advised him never to return any more, being sure the madman would eat him too, if he had the chance. Nevertheless, he paddled away the very next morning *as if compelled to do so.* Then it all happened just as on the former day. The madman pursued him right into the house, and fastened the door, so that he was obliged to get out through the window, and he barely escaped to his kayak. The day after, they again tried to detain him; but he was bent upon going. He entered his friend's house and found him worse than before: this time he was lying with his head on the floor and his heels resting on the edge of the bench; his eyes were far protruded and staring wildly, and the bone of his nose as sharp as a knife's edge. On approaching him he started up and pursued his former friend round the room, always crying, "I am starving; I must have thee for food." At last the friend succeeded in jumping out of the window, and reached his kayak; but no sooner had he got clear of the shore than he saw the madman walking on the surface of the water, ready to sieze hold of the prow of his kayak. He now began swinging to and fro in his kayak, and by this means ripples were formed, so that the madman could not steady himself, but was very nearly falling. Thus he once more escaped him. The day after, his housemates again wanted to detain him, but he answered them, "When I have not seen my friend for a whole day, I am ready to die with longing, and cannot desist from going to him." Having arrived at the house of his friend, he found it to be deserted; he searched about everywhere, but did not find him. Outside he observed some footprints winding up hills, and following them, he stopped at a cave in the rock. Here his friend was sitting bent together and much shrunk. As he did not move his friend went up to him, and on trying to lift him up, found him to be quite dead, and his eyelids filled with blood. He now carefully covered and closed up the entrance of the cave, and was henceforth friendless.

## 7.

## KATERPARSUK.

[This is also very commonly known all over Greenland, and the subjoined version is constructed from five manuscripts.]

KATERPARSUK was a poor orphan boy. When he grew up he was anxious to get on in the world, because nobody wanted to take care of him and help him along. At length he resolved, by his own efforts, to try to make himself a kayak ; but, nobody being willing to lend him a knife, he first tried to work with stone tools, and later on with shells. In the same place there happened to live a wicked man, who, instead of pitying the poor boy, took delight in annoying and terrifying him. For this purpose he disguised himself in a bearskin, and stole up behind Katerparsuk, growling like a bear. On turning round and perceiving him, Katerparsuk flung down his work and tools in consternation, and ran away. When the other house-fellows came to the spot and saw his implements of shells and stones, they were quite moved at the sight. Meanwhile the wicked man came forward and said to Katerparsuk, " Instead of pitying thee I scorned thee ; because thou, silly boy, couldst ever think of making a kayak all by thyself : and that was why I frightened thee in a bear-skin." On hearing this his housemates broke out into a fit of laughter at the poor boy's embarrassment ; but he grew mortally vexed, and only thought of revenge and resentment. Subsequently he betook himself to solitary places, and studied angakok science. After a long time he finished his kayak, and exercised himself in rowing and hunting, and shortly afterwards he was even able to hunt seals. Having once, from the top of a hill, seen a walrus dive, he thought, " Oh that I could make him throw off his skin!" He began to sing a magic lay, but without any result. Very much dissatisfied, he went home, but did not rest till he had got up an incantation that would suit his purpose. He tried the effect of it on a hare, and as it proved successful, he more than ever contemplated revenge. One day, when all the hunters were away in their kayaks, he likewise betook himself to his oar, and rowed out to a remote place. There he landed, and having ascended a very high hill, whence he had a view of the sea, he detected a great many walrus diving up and down. He began to sing his magic lay to one of them, which soon approached the beach right below him; he continued singing louder and louder until the animal at last threw off his skin. Katerparsuk at once crept into it, and began to try swimming and diving, and when the kayakers approached, he knew how to harden his skin so that the harpoon could not pierce it. Meanwhile the wicked man had grown old and decrepit, and had given up seal-hunting; he now only went out fishing. Once Katerparsuk put on his walrusskin and emerged from the water close to the place where the old man was fishing. He then heard him exclaim, "Oh that I were young again, what a catch I might have had!" Meantime he returned home, collected all his hunting implements, which he had not been using for a long time, and took them out with him to his fishing-place the next day. "Oh, look! there he is again!" the old man exclaimed, upon which he paddled towards him: but Katerparsuk hardened his skin, and made it tough; and seizing the point of the harpoon, pulled it down into the water along with the huntingbladder, from which he took away the stopper, so that the air escaped, and then he hurried home in his kayak. But the old man was vexed that he had lost his bladderfloat; and at home he said, boasting, "I have again commenced to go out hunting; to-day I pursued a large walrus, but he escaped me, and took my bladder-float along with him." Katerparsuk let him chat on, but in the evening he invited all the men to come and have a feast with him, and the old man was of the party. After the meal he once more began to talk of his chase and of the loss he had sustained. Before their arrival, Katerparsuk had hung up the bladder-float along with the harpoon-line on a peg in the wall; and while the old man was prating, he pointed to them, saying, "Look, there are all thy hunting tools, and thou canst take them away with thee when thou goest home." And the old man looked quite abashed, and left the party in a somewhat confused state. It is said that the resentment of Katerparsuk was somewhat appeased by the fun he had had in playing walrus to the man who had been playing bear to him.

---

## 8.

## A TALE ABOUT TWO GIRLS.

[The text is constructed from two manuscripts, one from Labrador and the other written down in Greenland, anterior to 1828.]

TWO little girls were playing with some small bones on the beach; the one with eagle-bones, the other with whale-bones. Suddenly an eagle came soaring through the air above them, and one of the girls said, "I will have an eagle for my husband;" and the other replied, "Thou mayst rejoice that thou hast already got a husband; I will have a whale for mine." Instantly a whale was seen to spout out at sea. And the eagle took one girl up and flew away with her, and the whale took the other down to the bottom of the sea, having first made her eyes and ears impenetrable, so that the water could not enter. The eagle carried his bride to the top of a steep cliff, and brought her different sorts of little birds for food ; but she gathered all the sinews of the birds' wings, and knotted them together, in order to make a string of them. One day, when the eagle was away, she tried the length of it, and found that it reached down to the level of the sea. Another day she saw a kayaker rowing along the shore ; and when he came just below, she called out to him to send a boat to rescue her. Soon afterwards the boat appeared, and she went sliding down by her string of sinews, and got back to her parents. But the eagle, who missed his mate, soared above the houses beating his wings ; and one of the inhabitants of the place cried out to him, " If thou wantest to show thou hast been married into our family, spread out thy wings ;" but when the eagle did so they shot him through the body. The other girl who had been stolen by the whale was secured to the bottom of the sea by a rope ; and when he was at home, she had nothing to do but to sit picking the lice [1] from off his body. She had two brothers living close by, and both set about building a boat of immense swiftness, in which they intended to deliver their sister ; but when the boat was finished it could not match a bird in speed, and was therefore broken to pieces, and another begun. This boat proved a match for a flying bird, but was nevertheless discarded, and they again built a new one, in which they tried to overtake a gull ; and on finding that this one even outdid the bird, they started from home to fetch back their sister. On becoming aware of their approach she loosened the cord that held her, and twisting it round the stone, she left with the boat. When the whale on his return drew the cord to get hold of her, and discovered that she was gone, he hurried after her. But

---

[1] *Cyamus ceti*, a parasitic crustacean, well known as the "whale louse."

when he came quite close to the boat she threw her outer jacket into the water to him. Having snapped at it he let it go, and again pursued her; and when he had got quite close up with them, she flung her inner jacket at him, which again detained the whale: but he soon reached them for the third time. Then she threw her long jacket, and before he could overtake them again they had already landed; but when the whale reached the shore he was transformed into a piece of whalebone.

---

## 9.

## THE BROTHERS VISIT THEIR SISTER.

[This tale is very popular in Greenland. Traces of it are also found mixed up with other tales from Greenland, and with one from Labrador. Here the text is very nearly a literal translation from a single manuscript, by a native of South Greenland.]

A MAN had three children; the eldest was a daughter. She married a man from a far-away place in the south while her brothers were still little children. In their boyhood they were not aware of their having a sister, because their father purposely never mentioned it to them. At last they had become quite grown up, and began to catch seals, and still they had never heard of their sister, until one day the mother said, "I think ye don't even know that ye have got a sister!" Upon which they immediately began asking about her place of abode; to which the mother replied, " Look there; do you see the high mountains yonder to the south of us? Beyond these is the winter station of your sister, whose hair, strange to say, is quite white on one side. However, ye must not think of going there, for the people she is living among are all cannibals." On hearing this the eldest brother changed his mind, and gave up the idea of going ; but the younger one still longed as much as before to see his sister. The mother tried to dissuade him, but he wanted to go more than ever. The following day the brothers set out on their journey, but the parents warned them, saying, " If ye reach the country yonder in the day-time ye must wait the fall of night, and not go near them until they are all asleep, lest ye should be murdered by them." And when they had gone away the parents gave them up for lost. The travellers reached the high mountains in the south, and began to examine the land below, in order to discover houses. At length the eldest brother said, " When people are found to be living at the foot of the mountains, the ravens will be sure to be soaring in the air above." At last they observed a craggy hill, above which a great number of ravens were flying. The brothers now turned away from the frozen sea and made for the shore, where they at length secured their sledges, and waited the fall of night. But when it had become quite dark, and when they supposed the inhabitants to have gone to bed, they again drew nearer. They were now in sight of many houses, the first of which had three windows ; and having gone close up to it, they cautiously mounted the roof and looked down the vent-hole, and saw a nasty-looking man sitting in front of the lamp beside his wife, who seemed in the act of picking the lice off him, and who appeared to be quite white on one side of her head. The eldest brother now got up and said, " Were we not told that our sister was to be white-haired on one side of her head ? do come and see!" The younger brother now looked down, and perceiving her, exclaimed in great consternation, " Why, that must surely be our sister sitting down there ! Just spit down through the hole, before the lamp, and when they notice that, some one will pro-

bably come out." The moment he spat down, the
woman gave the man a push, and said, "Somebody
must have come from afar to see us; do make haste
and get up!" On which he instantly rose, took up his
bow, and went outside. When they saw him emerge
from the house-passage, carrying the bow ready bent
in his hand, the eldest brother accosted him before he
had set eyes upon them, saying, "We have come here
to visit our sister, and have been told that she is quite
white on one side of her head." The other answered
him in a whisper, "Your sister is within; please go in."
On entering he at once played the part of a brother-in-
law to them, and ordered a meal to be prepared. The
wife put on her boots, and told some of the children to
assist her; and the guests soon understood that the only
housemates of their sister were her children. The beams
for boot-drying were hung all over with boots and skin-
stockings, according to their several sizes, the biggest
outermost. Sometime afterwards a large tub of berries
mingled with blubber was set before them, and their
sister asked them to partake of the meal. The brothers
were almost beginning to feel at ease, and were just
going to help themselves, when suddenly, in the bottom
of the tub, they caught sight of a human hand, cut off
at the wrist, clutching the berries, and very much shrunk.
They merely said, "We don't eat such food as this;"
but she only drew the tub closer to herself, and began
to eat along with the children. When she took hold of
the hand, and had taken a bite of the thumb, the children all cried, "Mother, do let us have some too!" The
eldest brother now got up, and went close beside her,
saying, "Hast thou also turned cannibal?" and giving
her husband a pull, she answered, "This nasty fellow
has made me one." Meanwhile the brother-in-law ordered something separate to be cooked for them on the
lamp, but cautiously added, "Mind ye don't let it burn

too high, lest our neighbours should detect us, and make a row about it." Suspending the pot above the lamp, and at the same time addressing her brothers, his wife now put in, "When our people caught a whale last winter, and it was brought ashore to be cut up and flensed, a man happened to have a fall, and was cut up with it." 'Before the meal was ready the host whispered to his children, "Go out and cut asunder all the lashings of our neighbours' sledges, but beware of making a noise." The children all went out immediately, and when they came back he inquired of them, "Have ye done as I told ye to all of them?" "Yes," they answered, "we have." But still they had forgotten one of them. When the meat was boiled, and they had commenced eating, the host said, "As soon as ye have finished I shall accompany you a little way off; but as soon as ye have left the mainland I'll give a shout, and ye'll just see what will happen." On their departure, after supper, he addressed them, saying, "Ye now know our place of abode; do come back and visit your sister." Upon which he saw them off in their sledges, and away they fled; but as soon as they turned out upon the ice he gave a great shout, and cried out aloud, "The visitors are setting off— the visitors are going to leave!" and when they looked around, the place was black with people, crowding the doorways and windows. Some had just caught hold of their clothes, and others were quite naked, and in this state they all hastened off to their sledges; but when they were about to start, the sledges all broke down. Meanwhile the travellers had taken fright, and urged on their dogs as fast as possible; but turning round they perceived one sledge to be following them, and apparently gaining upon them. The brother-in-law having likewise observed it, hastened to pursue it, and killed the driver, besides a number of the other people, and afterwards filled his sledge with human limbs; and thus freighted, he returned to his house. But the brothers reached home late at night, and reported how their sister had turned a cannibal, and how they had barely escaped death through the aid of their brother-in-law. But they never saw their sister again.

<hr>

## 10.

## KUNUK THE ORPHAN BOY.

[This tale seems to have its origin in historical facts, worked into a tale at a later period. Some parts of it allude to the struggles with the Indians, and the sudden attacks made by them on the Eskimo. Others most probably refer to the wars between the Eskimo tribes themselves, and to their distant migrations, by which they have peopled their wide territories. Several passages of this story are still frequently mixed up in different ways with other tales. The text has been constructed from three copies, in most particulars agreeing with each other.]

SEVERAL men had their permanent winter-quarters near the entrance to a fiord, and with them lived two boys, who were very officious and obliging. In the morning, when the men prepared to go out hunting, the boys helped to turn and rub their gloves, and made them ready for use, and likewise arranged the kayak implements and tools, and fetched the water for their morning drink. When the men had left, the boys exercised themselves in archery, and never entered the house the whole day long, until the men had returned, and they had assisted them in carrying their things from the beach. They did not even think of entering and partaking of their first meal till the last of the men had gone in, and they had once more fetched water. One evening in winter, by moonlight, when they had

gone out to draw water, the youngest said, " I think I
see a lot of faces down in the water ; " and Kunuk, the
elder brother, replied, " Is it not the reflection of the
moon ? " " No, come and look for thyself ; " and Kunuk
looked into the water, and said, " Thou art right, they
are getting at us ; " and presently he observed in the
water (viz., by way of clairvoyance) a host of armed
men advancing towards them. The boys now ran as
fast as possible and told everything to the people at
home, but they only answered, " It must have been the
moon that deceived you. Never mind, but run away and
fetch us some water ; the tub is empty." Off they went,
but saw the same things over again, and went back to
report it ; but still they were not believed. But when
they saw the armed men the third time advancing
quickly towards them, they deliberated what to do with
their little sister ; and when they had determined to go
and hide her, they entered the house and brought her
outside ; and seeing a heap of chips close to the window,
they put her down, and covered her well up with them.
Having done this, they went back and climbed the rafters beneath the roof of the house-passage ; and in helping his brother to get up, Kunuk warned him not to get
tired though he might find it an inconvenient place of
refuge : they were keeping hold of one beam with their
hands, and supported their feet against the next, and
thus lay at full length, with their faces turned downwards. Presently a large man with a spear made his
way through the entrance ; after him another one appeared ; and all told, they counted seven, who came
rushing into the house. But as soon as they got inside
a fearful cry was heard from those who were put to
death by them. While they were still lingering inside
Kunuk's brother was losing strength, and was nearly
giving way, when the aggressors came storming out,
fighting about, right and left, and flinging their spears
everywhere, and likewise into the heap of chips, where

their little sister was lying. When the last of them had disappeared the younger boy fell to the ground, and Kunuk after him. When they came to look for their sister they found her struck right through the body with a lance, and with her entrails protruding; and on entering the house the floor was all covered with blood, every one of the inmates having been killed, besides one of the assailants. Being quite alone in the dreary house they would not stay, but left the place that very night, carrying their wounded sister by turns, and taking care that the entrails did not come out of their proper place. They wandered on for a long while in this manner, and at length they arrived at a firth, which was quite frozen over. There they went down on the ice, but on turning round a steep promontory their little sister died, and they buried her in a cave among the rocks. From the

beginning of their flight they exercised themselves in boxing and in lifting large stones to strengthen their limbs; and they grew on, and had become strong and vigorous men ere they again met with other people. After a great lapse of time they one day noticed a man standing on the ice beside a huge piece of wood, which he had made use of in hunting the small seals. When they approached and told him what had befallen them, he said he would like to adopt them as his sons, and they followed him to a house where he and his wife lived all by themselves. Their foster-parents encouraged them never to forget their enemies, but always to be exercising themselves in order to strengthen their limbs. One night the brothers came home laden with ptarmigan and foxes, which they had caught without any weapons at all, only by throwing large stones at them, which made the old people rejoice very much, commending their dexterity and perseverance. To increase their strength still farther, they lifted very large stones with their hands only. They also practised boxing and wrestling; and no matter how hard the one might be pressing on the other, they made a point of never falling, but rolling together along the ground. At last, with constant practice, they had grown so dexterous that they could even kill a bear without any weapon. At first they gave him a blow, and when he turned upon them they took no more notice of him than if he had been a hare, but merely took hold of him by the legs and smashed him to pieces. When these results had been gained, they began to think of seeking out other people. Where? That was a matter of indifference. They now took a northerly direction, and wandered on a long way without falling in with any human being. At length they came to a great inlet of the sea, where a number of kayakers were out seal-hunting, but only one of them seemed to be provided with weapons. This one was their chief, or the "strong man" among them. He always wanted to harpoon the animals himself which had been hunted by the others—these had only to chase and frighten them; and if anybody dared to wound them, he was sure to be punished by the chief in person; but as soon as the "strong man" had pierced them with his arrow, the others all helped to kill them. Kunuk and his brother were too modest to go down at once, and awaited the approach of evening. Meanwhile they witnessed the cutting up of a walrus, and saw it being divided—each person getting a huge piece for himself, excepting an old man, who lived in the poorest tent, who got nothing but the entrails, which his two daughters helped him to carry home from the beach. The brothers agreed that they would go to the old man when it had grown dark, because they had taken pity on him on account of his patience. Having arrived at the tent, Kunuk had to enter by himself, his brother being too bashful to follow him. The old man now inquired of him, "Art thou alone?" "No, my little brother is standing outside; he is ashamed to enter." On hearing this, the old man cried, "Come in, thou who art standing outside;" and when he entered, he was astonished to see his strong limbs, he being even bigger than his brother. When the meal was over the old man said he would like to have them for his sons-in-law, and that they might go and take his daughters for their wives. Kunuk chose the youngest of them, and his brother got the eldest; and thus they got married. It is said that while going down to the place, they first went to have a look at the boats, and examined them closely; and that on seeing the weapons of the "strong man," they had taken his javelin (or arrow to be flung only by hand) away, with the intention of hiding it, so that the others might get something to look for. They brought it away to a spring, and a little way off they stuck it down into the earth, but pulled it out again, trying another place, where the turf was dry and hard. There Kunuk fixed it so deep in the ground that only so much of it as could be seized with two fingers was to be seen. While they were lying down inside the tent, they heard some one come running along, and partly lift the curtain, but instantly drop it and go off again. It was an old gossip, and mother to the "strong man," who had

been doing this; and a moment later a multitude of
people gathered round the entrance of the tent, to get a
peep at the strangers. In the morning they heard the
chief crying out, " This is a fine day for a walrus-hunt;"
upon which he was silent a while, and then said, " My
javelin has been taken away," which was repeated again
and again by many others. When Kunuk emerged
from the tent he saw several of the men coming out
rubbing their eyes, and saying, " I must surely have
slept too long!" However, it was only out of reverence
for the " strong man " that they spoke thus. While they
were shouting, they heard the old gossip, who had been
away to fetch water, exclaim, " Look, yonder is the
javelin!" and at the same time she pointed to the rock
leading to the spring. All of them now rushed to the
spot, in order to pull it out of the earth, but nobody succeeded in doing it. The brothers were now called, and
were asked to draw it out. They had all been pulling
and biting it with their teeth to get it loose, so that the
end had been quite wasted. But Kunuk just took it
between his two fingers, and disengaged it as if it were
a very small matter. On their way down to the shore
their father-in-law addressed them, and said, " Down
there, underneath the great boat, are the two kayaks of
my dead son. They are perfectly fitted up, and furnished
with weapons, and are quite easy to get at." These
things he now wanted to make over to his sons-in-law,
and he told them that the " strong man " had murdered
his son because he envied him his still greater strength;
for this reason he was now the enemy of his daughters.
Hitherto, however, they had not been able to get their revenge. After a short interval the cry was heard, " Let
the strangers come on for a boxing and fighting match
on the great plain up yonder;" upon which all the men
made thither to behold the spectacle. The brothers followed them; and arriving at the place, they saw a pole
set up on end, and beside it the leader standing with a

whip made of walrus-skin, with a knot on the end.  There
was also a stuffed white hare, and whenever anybody set
foot on it, he quickly lashed them with the whip.   Kunuk was the first who advanced towards the hare, and
the chief tried to hit him, but did  not succeed in reach-

ing him.    Soon after, Kunuk courageously put his foot
on the hare ; but the very moment the " strong man "
lifted up his whip Kunuk stooped down and *hardened*
his limbs (by charm), and when the other smote him
the whip gave a loud crack.   The " strong man " now
believed that he had killed Kunuk, who nevertheless
came away unhurt.   When the crack of the thong was
heard, the " strong man " ordered the younger brother
to step forward.   He, however, cared less than Kunuk : and after the first attempt the chief proposed that
he should take the whip for a change ; and giving it to
him, he went himself and put his foot on the hare.
Kunuk's brother now cried, " Look out and harden
thy body ! " but at the same time smote him, so that he

fell down dead on the spot. All his inferiors now rejoiced greatly, and called out to the brothers, "Henceforth ye shall be our leaders!" but they rejoined, "In
future ye shall have no masters, but hunt at liberty and
at your own will." The brothers now practised all manner of feats belonging to kayaking and seal-hunting, and
procured themselves *bladder - arrows*[1] — the bladders
being made out of one entire blown-up seal-skin. One
day they joined some other kayakers, and went in
pursuit of a very large she-walrus. Kunuk lanced it
four times at a greater distance than usual, and his
arrow went right through the animal, which, pant-
ing for breath, after a minute or two was quite dead.
When the others came on to give it the finishing stroke,
they found that the arrow had penetrated to the very
vent-holes of the bladder; and they all rejoiced at his
great dexterity, and praised it highly. Ordinary seals
even grew quite stiff when his spear merely grazed them.
He once heard a report of a very giant, who lived southward, and was named Ungilagtake.[2] He had a huge
sword, and nobody was ever known to escape him; even
the most valiant of men were vanquished and put to
death by him. On hearing this, the brothers immediately supposed him to have been among the strong
armed men who attacked their housemates at home,
when they themselves were still little children; and they
at once determined to go and find him out, knowing
that they were now more capable of revenging themselves than they had been at that time. They left the
place in two boats, one of which belonged to the youngest; in this the mother of the "strong man" who had
been killed accompanied him. The other boat was Kunuk's, and many kayaks went along with them to make
war against Ungilagtake. A pretty strong breeze from

[1] Small harpoons with a bladder attached to the shaft, but without any
line, and principally used for small animals.

[2] Pron. Unghilagtakee.

the north had sprung up, and the boats hoisted their sails, and the kayak-men amused themselves with throwing their harpoons alongside the boats. It so happened that Kunuk, in flinging the harpoon, hit the prow of the boat, so that it rebounded into the water with a great splash. On seeing this, the old hag chuckled, and went on mocking and teasing the wife of Kunuk till she could not help crying; and Kunuk asked his brother, who was in command of the boat, "Why is my wife crying?" "Oh, that's on account of the arrow," he answered; "she is so mortified because the old woman laughed at thee." Kunuk now purposely dropped astern a little, and holding his harpoon ready, suddenly pushed forward, and flung it across the boat, so that it hit the hood of the old woman's fur coat, while she sat rowing in the fore-end of the boat, even tearing a piece out of it; and this trick he repeated once more. After a while, Kunuk's brother turned his looks towards land, and recognised the burial-place of their little sister. This made him very sad, and he asked for some one to relieve him at the helm, he wanting to go and sit down forward, where, bent down, he went on sobbing, and vainly striving to keep back his tears, while the water from the sea came into the boat, which kept swinging and tossing from his convulsions. He took ill from that very day, and died before they reached their destination, so that Kunuk came alone to Ungilagtake. It was in the depth of winter, and they were met by many people on the ice. A somewhat biggish man invited them to come and put up at his house. This man likewise happened to be an enemy of Ungilagtake; and as soon as the guests had entered, he told them that before the meal he would show them how Ungilagtake used to behave to strangers. He took an entire seal-skin, stuffed with sand, and to the centre of which a strap was attached. Into this he put his third finger, and carried it round the room, after which he ordered his guest to do the same. Kunuk

took hold of the strap with his little finger, lifted the
thing with unbent arm, and put it down without being
fatigued. The host then went on, " Now sit down opposite to me, and I will throw a lance at thee, which, however, won't hurt thee ;" upon which he brought out a
lance and a drum, and began singing, while Kunuk
heard the others saying, " Bend thee down, stranger ! "
Kunuk at once complied, so that nothing but his chin
was visible ; and when his host threw the lance at him,
he lost his aim, merely observing, " This is the way of
Ungilagtake, who always hits the mark, and never fails.
Yet I don't know how thou wilt fare with him ; he will
hardly be able to molest thee. But then he has a companion, called Tajangiarsuk, with a double back, being
as fat in front as behind, who is immensely strong, and
gives him a hand if there happen to be any one he cannot master." Whilst they were sitting down at the meal
a cry was heard without, " Ungilagtake invites the stranger to his house ! " When Kunuk and his wife were
preparing to go, the host said, " Now make a bold entrance, or he will be sure to kill thee at once." The
visitors now went up to a large house with three windows, which was occupied with Ungilagtake's numerous
wives—all of whom he had stolen. Kunuk was ordered
to sit down on the side bench, but his wife was brought
to a seat on the main ledge, and their former host placed
himself opposite her husband. Many other spectators
now entered ; but whenever a new visitor made his appearance, Kunuk asked his first host if that were Tajangiarsuk, until at last he too arrived. Refreshments, consisting of various dishes, were now served before them ;
and when they had finished eating, Ungilagtake ordered
Kunuk to seat himself opposite to him, and presently
drew out a huge spear from beneath the bench, and
striking upon the drum, which had likewise been produced, the whole joined in a song for Kunuk, at the
same time crying out, " Bend thee down, stranger that

has come among us ; the great Ungilagtake, who never missed his aim, is going to thrust his spear at thee." He bent down as before, so that only his chin appeared ; but whilst Ungilagtake was taking aim at him, he nimbly gave a jump, and caught hold of one of the roofbeams, while the spear went far below him; and when it was flung at him the second time, he quickly jumped down, and the spear came flying above him, amid great cheers from the spectators. When Ungilagtake was about to take aim the third time, Kunuk seized the spear, saying that he, too, would like to have a try at killing with it. They now exchanged places. Kunuk, beating the drum, now struck up a song for Ungilaktake ; but the very moment the latter was preparing to bend his back, Kunuk had already taken aim at him, and the spear hit him in the throat, so that he fell dead on the spot. Everybody now rushed out of the house, and Kunuk was following, but soon found himself seized from behind by some one, who proved to be Tajangiarsuk. A wrestling-match soon ensued on a plain of ice, covered with many projecting stones, which he had chosen on purpose, in order to finish off his adversaries by dashing them against the stones. Kunuk felt a little irresolute when he noticed that he had found his equal. However, he took hold of him, and tried to lift him up before he got tired out. He flung him down on the ground, so that the blood gushed out of his mouth. Another champion soon made his appearance, who was of a still stronger and larger make ; and he soon got Kunuk down, and had already put his knee on the heart of Kunuk, when the latter suddenly took hold of him from beneath, grasped his shoulders, and pressed the lungs out of him. The applause of the spectators was again heard, while some of them were crying, " Now they are bringing the last of the lot, him with the lame legs ; " and soon after three boats were seen to carry this champion thither, for he was not like ordinary men, but of an immense size, so that he was obliged to lie across all three boats to get along. Having reached the landing-place, he crept up to the combat-field on his elbows. When Kunuk tried to throw him, his legs never moved an inch ; but when he proceeded to lift him up by taking hold of him round the waist, and began to whirl him round, he gradually succeeded in lifting also his feet ; and when they at last turned right outwards, to let him fall in such a way that his skull was crushed. The people rejoiced, and cried, "Thanks to thee ! now we shall have no masters !" and those who had been robbed of their wives got them back again.

## 11.

## THE FAITHLESS WIFE.

[This and the next tale, with a third one about "the dog's offspring," which has been omitted in this translation, are taken from five manuscripts, one of which was written down in Labrador, the others in different parts of Greenland. In these some parts of the stories were intermixed in various ways, but still they seem originally to have represented the three separate stories, of which two are here given.]

A MAN who was living alone with his wife noticed that she often left the place without his knowing where she went. On his return from his day-work, he seldom found her at home. This made him suspicious ; and one morning he feigned to be going far away, but when he went out in his kayak he only paddled to the nearest point, and went on shore again and hid himself behind some rocks. After a little his wife emerged from the tent in her best attire. He now stole up behind her, and followed her till she reached a lake ; there he observed her throw off something into the water, upon which a masculine being appeared, and she undressing, went out to him in the water. At this sight the husband got into a great rage, and set about gathering all kinds of vermin ; and one day when he was quite alone with his wife he stuffed them into her, and in this manner killed her. From that time he was all alone, but did not wish to go out in his kayak minding his usual business. One day, on his returning to his lonely tent, he was very much surprised to find his supper cooked, and the smoking meat served up. The next day the same thing happened again ; the meat smoking hot was served up on his dish, and his boots were dried and ready to put on :[1] and all this was repeated every day. One day he only paddled a little way off the coast, and then went on shore to hide in a place, whence he could keep a look-out on his tent ; and he soon observed a little woman, with her hair dressed up in a very large tuft, come down the hill and enter his tent. He now quickly made for his kayak, paddled home, and went creeping up to his house. Having softly lifted the door-curtain, he noticed a strong unpleasant smell, and saw the little woman busily trimming his lamp. She was really a fox transformed into the shape of a woman, and this accounted for the strong smell. Nevertheless, he took her for his wife. One day he met his cousin out at sea, and told him about his new wife, praising her loveliness, and next asked him to come and see her, " But," added he, " if thou shouldst happen to notice a rank smell about her, be sure not to make any remarks about it." The cousin followed him at once, and having landed together they both entered the tent. But when the visitor observed how nice and pleasant the wife of his cousin was,

---

[1] The Eskimo boots, or *kamik*, are neatly made of dressed seal-skin. After they are put off they must be dried, and then rubbed with a broad-pointed blunt stick until they are soft and fit to be used again. Rubbing and drying boots and dog-skin socks form a most important part of an Eskimo wife's household duties.

he grew quite jealous; and in order to make mischief exclaimed, "Whence comes this nasty smell?" Instantly the little woman rose to her feet: she had now got a tail, wherewith she extinguished the lamp, and like a fox cried, "Ka, ka, ka!"[1] and ran out of the tent. The husband followed her quickly; but when he again caught sight of her she was transformed into a fox, running up hill as fast as possible. He pursued her, and at last she vanished into a cave. It is told that while he stood outside calling for her, she first sent him a beetle, and then a spider, and at last a caterpillar. He then grew quite enraged, heaped some fuel together at the entrance, and burned her alive; and once more he was quite alone, and at last killed himself in a fit of madness.

---

## 12.

## THE MAN WHO MATED HIMSELF WITH A SEA-FOWL.

AN old bachelor used to amuse himself by playing with skulls of seals, and feigning them to be his children. When he went out kayaking he put them down on the beach, and having placed himself in his kayak, he would say to them, "Now mind ye be good children, and go straight up to the house!" and on still finding them in the same place on his return, he would cry out, "Ye seem to be all deaf and dumb; did not I

---

[1] Or, as the sound is sometimes attempted to be expressed in the books of Arctic voyagers, "Huk, huk, huk!"

tell ye to keep off from the water before I set off?"
Then taking hold of one of the heads, he threw it into
the sea, "Look, there's your little brother fallen into the
water!" Another time, feeling himself very sad and
lonely, he went running far away into the country, and
happened to fall in with a great many women bathing
in a lake. At this sight an idea seized him, and noiselessly he stole away to the place where they had put
their clothes, securing those belonging to the one he
thought the prettiest, and then stepped boldly forward.
When the women saw him they hastened back to their
clothes, and having put them on, they immediately
changed into birds and flew away. Only she who had
been robbed of her clothes remained behind; and the
bachelor went straight up to her, asking her, "Would
she like to be his wife?" and in return she said, "Yes,
thou mayst take me if thou likest, only give me my
clothes." She then got them, but he kept hold of her,
lest she, too, should fly. When she had dressed herself
he took her home and married her. The next morning
he did not venture to go out in his kayak, for fear she
might take flight; and thus it happened that he gave
up kayaking altogether, until one day she declared,
"Now thou mayst leave me without fear, for I do really
love thee, and thou mayst depend upon me;" and then
he again began to go out seal-hunting. At length she
begat a son, and when he grew up, another son was born;
but afterwards they got no more children. When the
children grew on, the mother sometimes took them out
walking; and on the way she would admonish them to
gather bird wings and feathers, saying, "Children, ye
are akin to birds." On a certain day she fastened a
pair of these wings upon one of the boys, who was at
once changed into a sea-fowl, and flew away. She did
the same thing to his brother; and last of all she herself
put on wings and followed them in the shape of a sea-
fowl. When the old husband came home he found nei-

ther wife nor children, at which he grew very sad. However, he did not cease to go out in his kayak, although he no more chased seals. One day he put in close to a sand-hill, and leaving his kayak on the beach, he crossed the hill, and went a good way into the country. Looking round, he saw a man with his back turned towards him, working away at a piece of timber with his axe. On approaching him, he observed that the lower parts of his body visibly trembled. The man now asked him, " From what side art thou drawing nigh ? " and the old man answered, " I am coming against thee ; " to which the other remarked, " If thou hadst come from behind, I should have killed thee on the spot." The old man now addressed him, saying, " Thou shalt have my new kayak if thou wilt inform me whether thou hast seen three persons ? " but the other one answered, " I don't care for thy new kayak, and I have not seen the three persons thou speakest of." The old man again said to him, " I see thou art working in wood, and I will give thee my new axe ; only let me know whether thou hast not seen three persons?" " Well, my axe *is* rather worn. Go and sit down on the tail of a salmon in yonder river ; but when thou hearest the voices of children, mind thou don't open thine eyes ! " The old man obeyed, and sat down on the tail of a salmon, shutting his eyes the while. On hearing a rushing sound he opened his eyes a little, and noticing that he was carried along by a rapid current, he shut them again, and all was silent. He again heard the noise of children crying, " Alas, our father is nigh ! " and the mother answering them, " Lo, we left your father without any means of conveying him hither." The children, however, repeated, " Our father is coming." The father now got on shore, and went to a house with fine windows to it ; he observed that the inmates were all women. Close to the back wall his wife was sitting, and opposite her a man with a pug-nose, constantly repeating, " Wilt thou not marry me ? " But

the woman answered, " No, I have already got another
husband." All the rest now left the house, and only
those two remained. At last, when the fellow with the
pug-nose had left also, the old man made an attempt to
take his wife back ; but she quickly followed the other
out, and while he pursued her she was transformed into
a gull, as were also the rest of the women. The pug-
nosed man was changed into a wild-duck ; and when
the discarded husband turned round, he saw that the
house had been transformed into a gulls-hill.[1]

---

## 13.

## THE BARREN WIFE.

[This very popular tale has been collated from three copies agreeing in all
essential particulars.]

A MAN had a wife who begat him no children. The
husband, who was envious of all the people who
had children, one day told her to make herself trim and
nice, and walk on to a certain spot where an old man,
who had given up seal-hunting, had his fishing-place.
This old man, however, was a great magician. The next
day, while he sat fishing in his kayak, a little way off
the shore, she appeared on the beach dressed in her best.
But as the old man, afraid of her husband, would not
approach her, she soon returned. The husband himself
now went to the old man, and promised him half of his

---

[1] Or birds-mound—viz., a heap of turf and moss accumulated on the top
of small islands which have been long the resting-place of sea-fowls,
and especially gulls, whose ordure has accumulated to a great extent in
such localities.

"catch" if he could think of some means whereby to get children. When the wife appeared on the beach the next day, the old man instantly made for the shore, and went up to her. From this day forwards the husband always put by half of the seals he caught for the old man : and when he noticed that his wife was *enceinte*, he asked the old man to take up his abode in their house ; upon which he rejoined, "Thy wife will bear thee a son. To-morrow when thou goest out kayaking thou must row to the birds-cliff and get hold of a bird,[1] which he shall use for an amulet." On the following day, when the husband had brought the bird, the old man went on, "Farther, thou must fetch a hollow stone, of a black colour, on which the sun has never shone;" and when he had also brought this, the old man said, "Finally, thou must go to thy grandmother's grave and bring home her collar-bone." When all these things had been gathered, the wife brought forth a son, who was named Kujavarsuk by the old man, and the stone was put close to his feet, but the bird was stuck up above the window. The old man now told the father to provide a kayak for the boy as soon as he should be able to make use of it, and have it ready fitted up with utensils and all other requisites for the hunt. When the boy grew up, the father made the kayak; and even before the skins with which it had been covered had time to dry, it was put in the water, and the boy being placed in it, they shoved it off the beach. The old man told what would happen to him, saying, "The very first time he goes out, one of the 'quiet' seals will rise to the surface, and he shall not return home till he has captured ten of them ; and in future he will always get ten seals when-ever he goes out kayaking. The old man and the father now followed him closely, but as soon as they left him at a little distance a seal popped its head above the water, and he paddled on and harpooned it, at which

[1] An "okaitsok"—*Phalacrocorax Carbo.*

the old man was quite transported; and from this time
the boy began to hunt. When he was grown up he took
two wives; and he became of great use to his house-
fellows and neighbours. In times of need he was their
only provider. One winter the sea was frozen over very
early, and ere long there was only one opening in the
ice left, right in front of their dwelling-place; out of this
he every day got his ten seals. Later on the cleft became so narrow that his kayak touched the edge of the
ice with both ends, and at last it altogether closed up.
The whole sea was now covered with ice; great perplex-
ity came over the people, and they deliberated whether
it would not be necessary to call in an angakok. One person mentioned that in the summer-time he had seen the
widow Igdlutsialik's daughter practising the angakok art
in a lake. Kujavarsuk at once sent off a messenger to
let her know that he would give her a large seal-skin in
return if she would make the ice break up. However,
she declined to do so. They next tried to get her to return
by offering her different things, such as clothes and
lamps; but still she refused. Then some one brought her
a handful of beads, which happened to take her fancy;
and she said to her mother, " Bring my summer dress."
When she had put it on, she walked down to the water-
side and disappeared among the loose ice-blocks scattered all along the sea-shore. Shortly afterwards the
spectators heard a splash, and she was seen no more.
She now remained in the depths of the ocean for three
days, and at the bottom of the sea she had a struggle
with the old woman (viz., the arnarkuagssâĸ of the
Eskimo mythology), to make her let loose the animals
of the sea, which she purposely detained, and kept swimming about underneath her lamp; and when at length
she had managed to conciliate her, she again returned
to the earth. On the evening of the third day she reappeared among the ice-blocks on the beach, and let
the people know that she wanted every other seal that

was caught, for herself, of those with the most beautiful skin, as well as of the common *fiord seals*. As yet, however, the sea was all covered with ice. But on the following morning, at dawn, the ice broke up, and an opening appeared near the houses ; and after a while it had become so wide that the men could put down their kayaks. Each of them soon caught two seals, but Kujavarsuk as usual got ten, which made the others very jealous. It now happened one day that his wives had only put by a piece of the back instead of the briskets for his mother's brother, who was expected to come home later in the evening. He was offended at this want of consideration on their part, and resolved to make (by help of sorcery) a *tupilak* for Kujavarsuk. To this end he gathered bones of all sorts of animals, out of which he fashioned it in such manner that it could take the shape of different animals, of birds as well as of seals; and having stirred them into life, he let it loose, and ordered it to persecute Kujavarsuk. First it dived down into the sea, and again appeared to him in the shape of a seal ; but he was then already on his way home, and when it approached him he was in the very act of drawing his kayak on the shore. The same thing happened on the second and the third day. The *tupilak* now determined to pursue him to his house, and then frighten him to death. It transformed itself into a *toogdlik*,[1] and commenced shrieking outside the house. Kujavarsuk went out; but as he could not be brought to look at it, the charm would not work. It then resolved to go underground, and pop up into the room. However, it succeeded no better this time, but rose at the back of the house ; and just as it was about to climb up the roof, it met his own amulet-bird, which at once set about picking and scratching its face. It now, however, turned desperate, and thought, " Why did this miserable fool

[1] The largest sea-fowl in Greenland, *Colymbus glacialis*, or Great Northern Diver.

of a man ever make me ! " and in the height of its wrath
it turned against its maker. Diving down into the
water near his fishing-place, it emerged right beneath
his kayak, and fairly upsetting it, devoured him on the
spot. It now fled far away from the habitations of man,
out on the roaring ocean. Kujavarsuk afterwards remained unmolested, and died at a very old age.

[There are other tales of Kujavarsuk among the Greenlanders. The
following may be taken as a sample of the whole.]

When Kujavarsuk had grown a man he travelled to
a place in the north, where he had had a namesake who
died from starvation. The people of those parts followed the pursuit of whale-fishery, and here Kujavarsuk
made friends with a youth. Those two were always
trying to outdo each other, but Kujavarsuk was more
than a match for him. In the beginning of winter they
were to try who could detect the first whale. Kujavarsuk had never seen any animal of this kind before.
He had by this time taken up his abode with an
old man, who said to him, " When a whale is near at
hand, it cannot be mistaken ; its breathing is at once
roaring and hissing." And Kujavarsuk was always on
the alert to catch sight of them. One fine morning,
when it was quite calm, the old man said, " If the
whales are going to be early this year, they'll turn up on
a day like this." Kujavarsuk remained out in his kayak
all day, listening for the signal, but could not perceive
any such sound at all. In the evening he returned after
a fair hunt, and tried to go to sleep, but was not able.
About midnight he rose, and stepping out he heard a
sound of heavy breathing from the sea coming closer to
him, and stopping at the mouth of the bay ; and on
entering he said, " I wonder what sound it was I heard
just now." The old man walked out, and returned, say-

ing, "Why, that's just the whale blowing; he did not miss his day." Kujavarsuk now went to rest, and slept soundly. But early in the morning his young friend was heard calling without, "Kujavarsuk, the whale is blowing! thou art too late!" But the old man made answer, "Thou art mistaken, he knew it yesterday, and has just gone to sleep." Soon after, the friend said, "Now let us see which of us is the best hand at making bladders for our whale-catching." And next day they went out together to procure seals for this purpose. Close to land Kujavarsuk got two spotted ones, but his friend got none at all. As the weather continued fine, and more whales appeared, the boats were sent out on the watch. At first Kujavarsuk concluded he was not to be of the party because he had no women to row his boat, but on seeing all the hunters set off along with their housemates, women and all, he, too, felt a strong desire to go; and getting hold of some children, he manned his boat with them, and left shore. The other boats, meantime, had stood farther out to sea, and the people shouted to him, "If thou art on the look-out for the whale thou must come out to us; he'll never rise where thou art now." But he did not mind them, and stayed where he was, his mother having said, "I conceived thee on the sea-shore, and for this reason thou shalt watch thy chance near it." In a little while a whale appeared close by; he at once pursued and harpooned it, and the beast could not even draw his bladder under the water. Again the others cried, "If thou wilt not lose it thou must pursue it more seawards." But he only replied, "All the animals of the sea that I am going to pursue will seek towards shore, close to my dwelling-place." And thus he was left alone to kill it all by himself. Whether he got any more than this one is not known; but perhaps he even got his ten of them. When spring came on he returned to his former home, where he still found the old fisherman alive, and to him he presented all the whalebone; the longest and best splits having been all reserved for him.

---

## 14.

## THE TWO BROTHERS.

[This tale is compiled from four manuscripts which differ somewhat.]

TWO brothers lived in the mouth of a fiord—the elder one on the sunny side, the other on the shady side of the inlet. One night the servant of the younger brother happening to go behind the house suddenly perceived something bright glittering out on the sea, and at the same time detected a boat that seemed to grow in size as it approached; on looking sharply she was horrified at recognising it to be an *umiariak* (or supernatural boat manned with fabulous beings). She wanted to run, but was not able to stir; she tried to call out, but found that she could not utter a sound, and so she must needs keep quiet. The next thing she saw was a number of people landing, all carrying glittering swords, and walking straight up to the tent, and sticking their spears through it from all sides. Loud cries were heard from within, and the foreigners rushed down to their boat. She saw the water foaming, and a multitude of seals moving out seawards. She was not able to rise till they were quite out of sight; then she got up and went to the tent, where she found all the inmates killed, and the earth covered with blood. Although it was still dark, she could not possibly wait, but set off at once, and wandered ever so far round the whole bay to reach the opposite shore, where the other brother lived, and having reached his tent she told him what had taken place, and that all her housemates had been put to death. But somehow he got suspicious, and believed that she herself had killed them. Seeing this, she merely said, "First go and look for thyself, and afterward thou mayst kill me if thou likest." He now went across to his brother's station, and when he had seen the tent pierced from all sides he was reassured with regard to the servant, and only thought of finding out the enemies. He bespoke an angakok to come and see him, that he might point them out to him. At night, when the angakok had arrived, the lamps were extinguished, and he spoke, "Look there; far away in the interior of the land, I espy them." When he could no longer descry them he again had the lamps lighted. On the following day the surviving brother paddled up to the fiord head, left his kayak on the beach, and walked, only armed with his spear, to the interior. After a long ramble he at length discovered a house, and stealing to the window he peeped through it, and beheld a man with only one eye sitting down, and busily carving some implement out of wood. On turning round, the man caught sight of the stranger, and at once invited him to come in. Having entered the house, he went and sat down beside the man with one eye, who, however, motioned him off a little, saying, "Don't sit quite so close to me; I might happen to cut thee." When the guest had complied, and moved farther away, he went on, saying, "Let refreshment be brought in for the stranger." A loud peal of laughter was then heard, and from beneath the ledge emerged a lot of *narrayoot* (plural of nârrâjôk, big-bellied), these being the only womankind of his household. They went out, returning soon afterwards with great quantities of meat, chiefly reindeer flesh and tallow. The host now said to him, "To-morrow I will go with thee and help thee to find out thy

enemies, but now thou must lie down to rest here; thou
hast nothing to fear." On the following day the one-
eyed man prepared to follow him, taking with him a
large bunch of arrows, fitted up in a skin cover. Having advanced somewhat into the country, he walked so
quickly that his companion could hardly keep up with
him. At length he stopped, and putting his arrows on
the ground, he said, "Turn thy face towards the interior
and give a shout." Without knowing the reason why,
he turned his face towards the interior part of the
country, and cried out aloud, upon which three large
bears instantly appeared. The one-eyed man aimed his
bow at them and killed them all. Again he said, "Turn
round and call as before!" This done, a multitude of
people appeared, armed with bows and arrows. He was
dreadfully frightened; but his companion, seeing this,
said, "Go and hide behind me; but mind, as soon as
thou puttest forth thy head they'll shoot thee." Having
thus sheltered himself behind his protector, though all
the time trembling with fear, he soon observed the
arrows to be flying about him right and left; but after
a while they decreased in number, and finally abated
altogether. The enemies having discharged all their
arrows had taken flight. The one-eyed man then took
up his bow, and the still revengeful brother his spear,
and both set off in pursuit of them, overtaking and killing the whole of them. On the way home the inlander
noticed his companion's weapon, questioned him concerning it, as he had never seen the like before, and told
him he would like very much to purchase it; and because of his handsome behaviour he had his wish. On
their return they went together to his storehouse, and
he was repaid with the renowned *sea-hare skin* (viz.,
white reindeer skins with black streaks), and one of the
little women was called to take them down. She put
the bundle on her stomach, and ran so fast with it that
the visitor could not keep pace with her. On his reach-

ing home, he found them put on the roof of his house, and from that time his mind was at rest.

NOTE.—This rather mystical tale is in Greenland related in different ways. It seems to have originated from some historical tradition mixed up with the common belief that when seals are chased and killed in too great numbers, the surviving ones will often avenge themselves in the shape of *umiarissat* (plural of **umiariaᴋ**)—that is, armed people in a boat fashioned out of a solid piece of ice. In one of the versions the inlanders here mentioned are called *erkileks*, in another " the men who twinkle *length-wise*," which closely reminds one of the Indians called Loucheux or Squint-eyes, who up to the present day are one of the tribes most hostile to the Eskimo, and described as being able to make themselves proof against the arrows of their enemies by means of a certain movement of their eyes.

---

## 15.

## GIVIOK.

[This tale is chiefly taken from a single manuscript, but nevertheless it is well known all over Greenland. Some slight traces will be found in it of the Indian Hiawatha tale.]

GIVIOK (pron. Ghiviok),[1] it is told, lost his wife, and was about to leave his child and the place where she was buried, in despair. He only waited till the boy had gone to sleep, and then he let himself down from the ledge to the floor; but when the child began crying, he again lay down beside him. Once he was all ready, stooping down to get out of the entrance, but went back unable to leave his son. One day the little boy passionately entered the room, saying, " My mother is walking outside with a stranger." Giviok answered,

[1] The letter G, used, as in this instance, to begin a word, is in the Greenlandish language abnormal. It has been adopted from the original manuscripts, but the name ought perhaps to have been called Kiviok.

" Thy mother is not here; she is lying under the big stones yonder."[1] But the little boy persisted, saying, " Look for thyself, then ;" and when Giviok did look out of the window, he actually saw his wife in the arms of another man. At this he got into a great rage, went out, killed them, and put them on top of each other into the stone grave. Father and son now went to rest: but when the boy slept the father carried out his intention of taking flight; and passing through the doorway, this time resisted the cries of the boy, got into his kayak, and hastened away. He paddled on and on across the wild sea; he came to the whirlpool, and was nearly drawn into it. Somehow, however, he escaped. Then he got among the villainous *sea-lice*. First he tried to keep them back by striking at them with his kayak-stick; but that was soon devoured. Then he threw out his sealskin gloves; and seeing that they lasted a little longer, he bethought himself of covering his paddle-blades with a pair of old gloves, lest the beasts should attack his paddle before he could slip away from them; and then he managed to get past them. Continuing his voyage, he saw a long black line, and on approaching it he noticed it to be sea-weed, which he found to be so compact that he got out; and lying down to rest, he went to sleep on it. When he awoke, he pushed himself and his kayak on with his hands, and in this manner got across the sea-weed. He continued paddling until he came in sight of two icebergs, with a narrow passage between them; and he observed that the passage alternately opened and closed again. He tried to pass the icebergs by paddling round outside them, but they always kept ahead of him; and at length he ventured to go right between them. With great speed and alacrity he pushed on, and had just passed when the bergs closed together, and the stern-point of his kayak got

[1] The Eskimo in Greenland and the greater part of their territories have always been buried under heaps of stones.

bruised between them. At last he caught a glimpse of something dark, and soon after he reached a great stretch of land looming ahead of him. Giviok now thought, "If this country be inhabited, I will be sure to find a bare rock;"[1] and such a one he soon found. He shortly afterwards detected a house by the smoking chimney, and he soon concluded that they were busy cooking inside. He went straight on towards it, upset the funnel, and hid himself close by. Instantly a female came rushing out, saying, "I wonder if any one upset it?" upon which she again put it to rights; and meantime, perceiving Giviok, quickly re-entered the house, but as quickly returned, saying to him, "Thou art invited to step inside." On entering, he saw a hideous old hag lying beneath a coverlet, who ordered her daughter to go and fetch some berries; and, running out, she soon returned with a great quantity of them, profusely mixed up with fat. Giviok, while he was eating them, remarked, "They are really delicious;" and Usorsak (this was the name of the old hag) rejoined, "No wonder; the fat is of quite a young fellow;" but Giviok answered, "Fie! anything of that kind I cannot eat;" and stooping down, he noticed a lot of human heads all in a row beneath the ledge; and when the hag uncovered herself a little, and turned her back towards him, he saw something glittering close behind her. When they were all ready to go to rest, Giviok said, "I shall just go outside for an instant." Accordingly he went, and soon found a flat stone to cover his breast with; and re-entering, he lay down on the ledge beneath the window. No sooner did he seem to be sleeping, than he heard the daughter saying, "Now he is sound asleep;" and instantly the old hag came jumping down from her place on the main ledge; but on his feigning not to be quite asleep, she cautiously returned. When he again had become quiet, and lying on his back

[1] A place used for drying provisions, and therefore without moss.

was exposing his breast, the daughter again said, "He
surely sleeps now;" and again the mother let herself
down, even quicker than the first time, and jumping up
where he was lying, she sat down with all her weight
upon his chest, crying out, "Oh dear!" but instantly
tumbled down. "What a pity!" cried the daughter;
"Usorsak has broken her tail; she provided so nicely
for all of us" (viz., killing men by help of her tail).
Giviok now got up from his couch, let fall the stone,
and escaped through the door, the daughter shouting
after him, "Thou rascal! wouldn't I like to have had a
taste of thy fine cheeks!" but he was already in his
kayak, where he was nearly upset. Rising again, he
broke out, "Shouldn't I like to harpoon her!" and so
saying, he killed her on the spot. He now continued
his journey; and after a while again reached a bare
rock. At a little distance from it he landed; and, as
before, went up to a house where he likewise upset the
chimney-funnel, and afterwards hid himself. A woman
again emerged from the doorway; and when she re-
entered, he heard them wondering at the chimney
having been upset, as there had not been any wind.
When she again made her appearance, Giviok came
forth, and was asked to come inside. Crossing the
threshold, he observed that the walls were covered all
over with hunting - bladders. Here, also, the inmates
consisted of a mother and a daughter. The mother
now spoke—"It will soon be low-water; it is a bad job
for us that we have no one to haul in our draught when
we have harpooned and fixed the bladders to the fishes."
Giviok answered—"I have my kayak close by, and have
just come from the bad women yonder, both of whom I
have killed." "Then thanks to thee!" they exclaimed.
"We, too, have had men in our house, but these monsters
put all of them to death; but now thou hadst better stay
here with us." Giviok at once consenting, they went
on saying, "To-morrow we shall have low-water, and

when thou hearest a roaring noise, thou must hasten back; then the high tide sets in, and thou must be back on shore." They then went to sleep. Giviok was sound asleep when he was awakened by the roaring waters, and saw the daughter glide through the house-passage. He hastened down to the shore; but when he arrived, the women had already caught a number of halibut, which were lying high and dry on the beach. He was only in time to finish off a few when the sound of the rising waters was again heard, and the great waves came rolling over him, so that he had a narrow escape to the coast. The harpooned fish, on account of the bladders, kept floating on the surface, but drove across to the opposite shore. Giviok, however, fetched them back in his kayak, for which the women were very thankful to him; and he remained with them for some time. After a while, the memory of his son haunted him, and he said to himself, "My poor little son! what a pitiful thing it was to hear him cry when I went away! Some day I must go and see him." So he left the place, and travelled on and on, encountering all the dangers he had met with on his departure from home, but once more happily getting past them. At last he reached the opposite country, and he heard people singing. He followed the song, and fell in with a great many boats tugging a whale along, on which stood a vigorous man. He did not recognise him; but this was his son, and he had been catching the whale. The father left him a weeping child, and now beheld him a great hunter, standing on a whale's back.

## 16.

## TIGGAK.

[This is an abstract from three somewhat varying copies received from
Greenland.   In one of the Labrador legends traces of the same tale
appear.]

TIGGAK was a famous angakok and sorcerer.   He
married a girl who had a number of brothers, and
after this he grew neglectful of his duties, and gave up
hunting.   When the brothers-in-law left home in the
morning, they could not persuade him to follow them;
sometimes he even slept till the first of the kayakers
returned, and then did nothing but keep his wife company, and dawdle the time away till bedtime came
round again.   This offended the other men, and they
let him understand that they were vexed with him.
One evening, when one of the brothers had ordered
some boiled briskets, he said to Tiggak when they
were served up, " Do eat some meat — that is easy
work."   Tiggak took a considerable quantity, and did
not pay any attention to the brother-in-law's remarks,
but ate away without giving any answer.   In the midst
of winter, they were one evening awakened by the noise
of the wind.   A gale from the north set in.   The brothers
left off hunting, and lived solely upon their stored-up
provisions; but at last these were brought to an end.
One day, when they could not even go out in the kayak,
Tiggak was missing.   Towards evening they looked
about for him, and there was a terrible snow-drift.
Late at night they heard a call, and they saw him approaching, and dragging two seals along with him.
From that time he rose in their estimation, and was
now highly thought of among them.   He now had the
briskets served up, and addressed the brothers, saying,

" Now come and fall to; the meat is boiled and served up, and eating it is easy work." They all ate, but nobody spoke. Next day the same scene was repeated; and all the winter he continued providing for the others : but in the summer he left off, and let his brothers-in-law undertake this task themselves. Subsequently Tiggak adopted a boy as his son. Once more it was winter, and the sea was covered with ice as far as the eye could see. Tiggak was the only one to roam about upon the ice, looking out for the haze and seeking open holes in the ice, indicating the places to which the sea animals resort in order to breathe. Far off, beyond the outermost islets, he went away for seals. One day the sky was cloudless and the wind down. He had resolved to go out on the ice with the brothers, and he turned to his adopted son saying, " To-day thou mayst come with us and try thy hand at seal-catching." On gaining the remotest islets, Tiggak made an opening in the ice to examine the state of the waters beneath. When he had done he said, " I believe it will come to pass ; the sea-weed seems to be drifting landwards : just look." The brothers then saw that the current, setting towards land, was stronger than usual, and Tiggak said, " We shall have a gale presently; let us make all haste for the shore." And though they could hardly credit his words, the weather being so calm, they left their seals behind and followed him quickly. Then the snow was seen foaming on the mountain-peaks; and when they had only reached the first row of islets, the storm burst strong and fierce, and broke up the ice. Tiggak took hold of his son's hand, running as fast as possible, and leapt across the clefts in the ice. At last they came to a very broad one near the land, and all of them jumped over to the opposite side ; the son only did not dare to try the leap, but kept running to and fro along the edge of the cleft. At last Tiggak took pity on him and returned to him, the others also following him ; but now they all drifted away seawards, and now and then the waves washed over the ice-floe they were standing on, and they grew silent with fear. At last one of them remarked, "It is said that Tiggak is learned in magic art, and we are drifting out to the wild sea." Tiggak said, "I only know a short song treating of the ocean foam;" and he at once began singing. Having finished, they saw an iceberg close in front of them, and in a short time they came up to it, and soon caught sight of an easy ascent. The iceberg, however, kept constantly driving up and down, so that they had to watch their chance to get over. When they were just on a level with the point where they intended to cross, Tiggak took the lead and jumped over, and managed to get a sure footing on it; and after him the others followed. They were all, however, drifting further out to sea, when one of them again remarked, "We will be sure to perish from thirst unless Tiggak knows some charm that will work." He answered, "I only know this one little song to get water." Having finished the incantation, a little spring bubbled forth from the centre of the iceberg. The brothers instantly wanted to drink; but he told them to wait, saying that otherwise it was sure to dry up at once. But when he had tasted it himself, he permitted them to drink; and now it could not change. After having drifted about for a long time, they came in sight of an extensive country; and Tiggak said to his companions, "If any of you is fortunate enough to leap ashore, he must not look towards the sea so long as any of us are behind, otherwise our place of refuge will break up and be annihilated." When they did jump ashore, one by one, none of them looked round; but when the last had safely landed, Tiggak turned round and exclaimed, "Behold our place of refuge!" and lo! nothing remained of it but a heap of foam. They now determined to go and find out the people of the country; and having crossed an isthmus, they came in sight of many houses, and were shortly afterwards invited into

one of them. They relieved themselves of their outer
garments, and hanging them up on the boat-pillars,[1]
went inside. During the meal, a squint-eyed youth
with a shaggy head of hair appeared in the doorway,
and called out, " The strangers from the east are hereby
invited to pay a visit." And shortly afterwards he
returned to repeat the same message. The host now
remarked, " Since he presses you so ardently, you will
be obliged to go." And so they entered another house,
where a great many people were assembled. On the
main ledge a disagreeable giant-like man was sitting,
and by his side a similar old woman, gnawing away at
a big shoulder-bone. The huge man pulled forth a seal-
skin, spread it on the ground, and, in a deep-sounding
voice, exclaimed, " Now come on for a wrestling-match!"
The brothers commenced whispering to Tiggak that he
should take the first turn; but he said, " Not so; you
go down first, then I'll follow." The other guests were
all ordered away, and the old hag fastened the door
with the shoulder-blade. One of the brothers now
hooked his arm into that of the giant. Unable to vanquish him, however, he was soon obliged to give in to
the strong man, who, catching hold of his lower parts,
fell over him, and, with a deep groan, he was crushed to
death. The giant next called out for a rope, and this
being immediately let down through the ceiling, he fastened it round the dead man's body, and had him hoisted
up to the roof of the house, where a sound of knives
was presently heard, and whence one cried out, " Here
is his eye; let it be kept for our master." Tiggak meanwhile thought, " In this manner I shall soon lose all my
brothers-in-law;" and therefore he whispered to him
who was going to stand forward, " Just let me take a
turn with him!" They now hooked their arms together, and the giant, taking a pull in good earnest, nearly
succeeded in hauling Tiggak's arm across to him. For-

·[1] Poles for supporting the boat during the winter.

tunately, however, he stopped him.   Then pausing a minute, he feigned to have been overcome by his adversary,
but suddenly threw him down, and leapt upon him.
The brothers now came to his aid, and assisted in putting him to death in the same way as he had treated
their brother.   Imitating the voice of the other, Tiggak
now called out, "A rope, a rope!" which instantly appeared, and was made fast round the neck of the giant;
and again he cried, "Haul away!"   Once more the
sound of knives was heard; but after a while all was
silent, and at last one cried out, "Are we not flensing
our own master?  We'll make them perish down below!"
And presently they commenced pouring water down
upon them.   They tried to leave the house, but found
no means of escape.   Suddenly, however, Tiggak remembered that his amulet was sowed up in the lining
of his outer jacket, which he had left on the boat-pillars
on their arrival, and he called out, "Bring me my coat
that lies outside; I want it for a shroud!"   Contrary
to his anticipations, it was instantly thrown down, and
catching hold of it, he loosened something from within
the fur-lining, and there was his amulet all right.   He
put it into his mouth, and, after saying "Revenge us!"
he again took it out.   Already they heard voices outside crying, "He is falling!—and he too!—and there
is another one!" and so on; and after a while the amulet returned, covered with blood.   Having well wiped
and cleaned it, the owner again threw it out and cried,
"All of them!"   When the amulet next time returned
no sound was heard outside.   They now pushed forward, and from a corner of the ledge they found their
way out.   Not seeing any person alive, they went back
to the house where they had been first received, and
again set to work at their meal.   But the silly-looking
youth again appeared in the entry, and said, "I'll tell
you what—Apiak is now doing her very worst: she is
cooking the brains, hands, and feet of her son."   Tiggak,

however, could not understand him. The youth returned
and told the same thing over again; but still Tiggak
did not understand him, and let him go. One of the
brothers—the same who had made the remark that
Tiggak was learned in magic art—now said, " It will
be the brains, hands, and feet of the one thou didst kill
up yonder, and his mother probably intends to regale
thee with a dish made of them. When thou hast been
asked to go, thou wilt perceive an oblong dish right in
front of the entrance, filled with brains nicely served up.
On entering the room thou must quickly take hold of it,
and standing erect with thy face turned towards her,
and with thine eyes shut, thou shalt eat it all up—if thou
eatest it with open eyes, thou wilt go mad and die ; and
after having tasted it, thou must turn the dish upside
down, and put it back in its place. That done, open
thine eyes again, and sit down beside the lamp. She
will then turn her gaze upon thee, and thou wilt still
remain unchanged ; and when she takes the dish and
turns it round, the contents of it will be all restored, and
thou shalt say to her, ' Now, please, eat something thyself, as I have done.' While she is eating, with her looks
turned upon thee, just see what becomes of her ! "
When the brother-in-law had thus spoken, the squint-
ing youth again appeared, saying, " The foreigner is invited to follow me ! " Tiggak walked up to the house
of the old hag, and acted exactly as he had been told ;
and having eaten, the wicked old woman turned raving
mad and died. Tiggak now returned to his brothers-in-
law, saying, " I have killed the old hag, but they will
go on in this manner if we stay here; so we had better
leave the place altogether and make for our home again."
They again crossed the isthmus, and saw a snow-covered
hill sloping down to the water's side. There they stopped, and Tiggak asked the eldest brother, " What kind
of amulet didst thou take when thou hadst to make thy
choice ? " He answered, " A small piece of bear-skin."

Tiggak said, " That is first-rate." He then asked the
second one ; and he had the same amulet, and so had all
of them : but when he questioned the youngest of them,
he answered, " I am not quite sure ; but I believe it's
a piece of bear-skin ; " whereat Tiggak said, " That's
all right ; you will all do very well." When, however,
he asked the son he had adopted, he only answered,
" I don't know indeed." But Tiggak then said, " We
shall leave thee behind if thou wilt not tell." " But I
don't know it." " If thou goest on that way, we shall
certainly leave thee alone ; so pray tell us ! " He then
said, " When I was able to judge for myself, I got
a *snow-bunting*[1] for my amulet ; " at which Tiggak
became silent, and shook his head. After a while
he remarked, " And yet it may do ; thou must perch
down on us ; " and Tiggak let himself slide down-
hill, right down into the sea, where he disappeared, and
again reappeared in the shape of a bear. He shook the
water from his ears, and turned to the others, saying,
" Now follow me all of you ; " and they were all transformed into bears. When the son's turn came, he had
not the courage. However, when the others had long
besought him to follow them, he went gliding slowly
down ; and when he reached the margin of the water,
he grew a snow-bunting, and as such was able to fly.
Meanwhile all the others were swimming homewards ;
and when the little snow-bunting got tired, he took a rest
between their ears. At length they landed a little to
the north of their old homestead ; and when they first
climbed up the shore, Tiggak shook himself well, and
his bear-skin glided off. The rest all did the same.
When the son's turn had come, he shook off the snow-
bunting's skin ; and thus all of them marched home,
except the one who had been killed.

[1] *Emberiza nivalis.*

## 17.

## MALAISE—THE MAN WHO TRAVELLED
## TO AKILINEK.

[This story has been collated from two separate copies, one of which was written down from the verbal narration of an East Greenlander. Akilinek signifies a fabulous country beyond the seas.]

WE are told that Malaise (pron. Malysee) was a jolly, fearless fellow, who lived in prosperity with his two sisters, both younger than himself, and that he had his winter - quarters at the mouth of a fiord. When he went out kayaking, his sisters followed him on foot, going along the beach; and returning as soon as they saw him put back, they reached home at the same time. One day when the sea was all covered with ice the sisters went away to the outermost islets, to gather some roots. Suddenly an eastern gale overtook them; the ice broke up, and they were taken far out to sea in very bad weather. After a while the sky became clear, and they came in sight of some high land. They drifted on towards it and landed safely, but almost starving with hunger. On looking round they saw that the ice-floe on which they had floated had turned into foam. Each of them had part of a gull for an amulet. They now wandered across the country, and arrived at a little bay into which a river emptied itself, and the eldest said, "There will be salmon yonder, I warrant, or there would not be so many gulls about. Let us go and have a look at the place." Coming down to the riverside they found it abounding in salmon; and having instantly caught one, they made a fire by rubbing pieces of wood together, and put the fish on a slab to fry it: but though they only ate half of the tail-piece, both were quite satisfied. It was now getting low tide, and they saw the beach turning quite dry, and all along the coast there were numbers of spotted seals (*Phoca vitulina*), and various other kinds besides, of which they killed as many as they required with big stones. Having taken up their abode in this place, they one day observed two kayakers, who were out hunting for spotted seals. On seeing the girls they were heard to exclaim, " Well, he who gets ashore first shall marry the prettiest of the two ; " upon which they both took to their paddles, and he who first reached the shore touched the elder sister, the other one taking the younger ; and quite forgetting their hunt, they hastened home to fetch a boat. Before long they returned with a good crew, got the girls into the boat, and brought them to their house, where they lived as happy as could be for some time. After a while each of them had a daughter ; but subsequently the eldest one noticed that her sister had quite lost her spirits. One day, when the two happened to be all by themselves, she asked her why she was always sobbing and crying ; and the sister answered that her husband had told her that he would kill her if she next time bore him a daughter. The eldest sister advised her to feign that she was quite content, and went on saying, " We'll pack up our clothes, and as soon as the ice forms, we'll return to our old home ; but don't let them suspect anything." They now made themselves new clothes, and put them by in their bags, which had been concealed beneath the boat outside about the same time that the ice covered the sea. The seal-hunting ceased ; and the men having nothing else to do, went out visiting at a large house close by, where they amused themselves with dancing. The elder sister now proposed that they should try to make their escape at a time when the men had gone away to their dancing ; and they only waited a convenient opportunity. One night when there was to be a dance, and all the other women had gone to look on, so that nobody was to be seen

outside, the sisters first walked up and down outside
the house, lulling their children to sleep.   That they
might not be suspected, they had only put on their
short breeches.   The little girls who used to nurse the
children came running out after them, so that they
could not get off immediately; but soon afterwards
they heard singing within the house, and as it seemed
to be a funny song, the girls went in to listen.   Upon
this the sisters hastened away to the boat, and having
got on their breeches and put the babies into their
*amowts*,[1] they started.   At first they kept on shore,
but subsequently went out on the ice, and there they
wandered all the night long.   At daybreak they went
to hide behind some blocks of ice, and before long they
heard the sound of sledges, and perceived that their
traces had been followed.   Where their footprints were
lost, they heard their pursuers halt and call out to them,
"Your poor little children are crying for you;" but
they did not leave their place of retreat until evening.
They then set forth and continued their journey; but
on the way they suffered their babies to freeze to death,
and having put them down on the snow, left them there.
Some time afterwards they reached land and recognised
the place where they had formerly had their winter-
station.   They proceeded a little further, and behold!
there was their own little house, just as they had left it.
Malaise was very much astonished to see his sisters
entering, and immediately questioned them about Akilinek and the hunting in those parts, but he could not
make them tell anything.   After the return of his sisters,
Malaise displayed great energy in fishing and hunting.
When the days were beginning to lengthen, he one
morning came back to the house, having put on his
kayak-jacket, and stepping inside he said, "This is a
fine day to go out kayaking;" upon which the sisters

---

[1] Cor. sp. **amaut**, hood on the back of a woman's jacket to carry the
child in.

turned to him, saying, "Though almost nothing is to be got in this poor country, it cannot be denied that Malaise strives hard enough to provide for us; but, to be sure, in Akilinek there *is* something for a hunter." Hearing this, he put his jacket aside and said, "Well, then, let me hear something about it;" and from that day they began telling him all he wished; and even in fine weather Malaise did not stir out. Once when they had been telling him of the many seals they had found on the dry beach, he could not forbear saying, "I really must try Akilinek—in spring when the saddleback-seals[1] appear. I will give my women's boat a threefold covering. Then his wife began crying, being of a very timid disposition; but Malaise only laughed at her. As soon as the seals appeared, he caught as many of them as they wanted for his purpose. The boat got three coverings; and he only waited a favourable opportunity for starting. One day he rose very early, went outside, and ascended a hill to ascertain the state of the weather. On finding that not a breath of wind was stirring, he returned, and on entering the house, observed, "The day is fine and it is quite calm now; let us be off for Akilinek." His wife again cried; but Malaise laughed down her fears, and made preparations for their departure. When the boat was ready, his wife, still sobbing and crying, was put into it; then they pushed off from shore, and heading westward, at once put out to sea. The sisters had to row all by themselves, and their sister-in-law continued crying in the bottom of the boat. When at last she left off a little, Malaise, further to tease her, rose from his place, and looking aft, observed, "I think we are going to have a gale, it is getting quite black out there!" after which she again commenced crying in good earnest, to his very great diversion. At last they entirely lost sight of their own country; but

---

[1] *Phoca Greenlandica*, the âtâᴋ of the Greenlanders, the most common of the large seals. The skin is used for boat-covers.

Malaise thought they were very slow in getting on, and he cut the outer covering away because it had grown too wet. Before they had sighted any land, he likewise cut off the second cover, and then they again went on a good while; but all on a sudden Malaise sprang to his feet, saying, "I see the loom of the land yonder!" On hearing this his wife also got up and stuck to the oars bravely. They soon came close to this land, and the sisters recognised the bay in which they had first landed, and at the same time observed their former husbands, who were now coming on to attack them. Before their departure, however, Malaise had been out to the grave of some relative in search of a pair of reindeer-skin stockings, which he had brought away with him. He now took a drinking-vessel, which he filled with water, and having poured some dust mingled with the hairs of the stockings into it, he put the tub down on an adjacent rock, where their adversaries were obliged to pass by. When the eldest came up to it, he took a drink of water, but was at once transformed into a reindeer, which was shot by Malaise, and rolled into the sea. The other one had no better luck; and in this manner Malaise killed all their companions excepting one, to whom he said, " I will spare thee that thou mayst live on, a miserable specimen of thy countrymen." Some time afterwards he again gave his boat three separate coverings, filled it with narwhal-horns, *matak* (the edible hide of the whale), salmon, and many other valuables, and reached his former home, where he stayed content until his death.

## 18.

## NAVARANAK OR JAVRAGANAK.

[This apparently historical tradition has been given in two separate narratives, the original copies not agreeing sufficiently to admit of their being combined into one, although they have evidently sprung from the same source. The variants of this tale exemplify in a very remarkable manner how the narrators have practised their habit of localising events. The first copy is one from North Greenland, where the inlanders are meant to represent the fabulous inhabitants of the interior of Greenland ; the second is one from Labrador, in which the native Indians of that country are plainly alluded to ; and it is very remarkable that a third record of the same events has been received from South Greenland, in which the inlanders are represented as being identical with the ancient Scandinavian settlers in those parts of the country.]

THE inlanders and the coast-people in the beginning were friends. A servant-maid called Navaranak used to be sent out by the inlanders to the coast-people in order to fetch back *matak* (edible whale-skin), and in exchange brought them reindeer-tallow ; but after a time she grew weary of this work, and resolved to free herself by making them enemies. For this purpose she told the inlanders that the coast-people were going to attack them, and to the coasters she asserted that the inlanders were making ready to invade them. At length she provoked the inlanders to such a degree that they resolved upon attacking the coast-people. They chose a time when they were well aware that the men had all gone out hunting ; and, accompanied by Navaranak, fell upon the helpless women and children. In their fright some of the mothers killed their own children, but one woman who was pregnant fled down beneath the ledge ; and when Navaranak was sent back by the inlanders to find her out, she promised her all she possessed not to betray her. Some also escaped by hiding themselves among the rocks, but all the rest were killed. When the men returned, those who were left alive ran down and told them what had happened ; and on coming up from the beach to their houses and beholding all their dead, the men were almost desperate. When the time came for flensing and cutting up the whale, Navaranak did not arrive as usual ; she seemed to have disappeared altogether. When summer had again come round, the men prepared a great many arrows, and set out for the interior to take revenge on the inlanders. On their way they called out, as was their wont, " Navaranak, come on ; we have got matak for thee ! " but no one appeared. Again they went on a good distance, and then repeatedly called out, " Navaranak," &c. And this time she answered the summons, and went up to them. On noticing their arrows, she was about to take flight. Reassuring her, however, they told her she had no need to do that. When she had ventured quite close to them, they asked her where her countrymen were to be found, and she said, " Further away in the interior of the country ! " but now they made her fast to a rope, and dragged her along with them until she perished. At length they arrived at a very large lake, where the tents of the inlanders were pitched all around, and they saw people going out and in. But they waited till all had entered the tents, and then they made their attack. Arrows came flying from both sides ; but those of the inlanders soon grew fewer in number, and the coast-people remained all unwounded. When they had done with the men, they went inside, killing women and children ; and having thus satisfied their revenge, returned to their homes.

[On the island of Okak, in Labrador, this tale is told as follows :—]

At Kivalek, on the island of Okak, there once lived a great many people, among whom was an Indian woman named Javraganak. From her childhood she had been

living with the coast-people, whose servant she was ;
but nevertheless she had always remained a stranger
among them. One day when she was hungry, and
longed for one of her Indian dishes, she said, "At
Pangma my countrymen have plenty of tongues;" upon
which an old man sneeringly replied, " I daresay thou
hast many brothers and relatives away there; thou hadst
better make them come over here,"—and at night she
wandered away to give them warning. In those times
hares were very abundant, and sometimes you might
even hear them run about on the house-tops. One night
when Javraganak had come with a great number of
her countrymen, those within heard a murmuring sound
outside, and the old man said, "Well, if that is not the
hares again ! They are very lively, it seems." Besides
him there was not a man at home ; they were all out
hunting. And so it happened that all the inhabitants
were put to death by Javraganak's Indian countrymen.
Many of them sought refuge in a cave, where some were
suffocated and others murdered. On their return the
men found their wives and children all killed ; but
shortly afterwards they set out to kill the murderers.
Among these men was an angakok, who made a road
for them right through a mountain, and the countrymen
of Javraganak were all destroyed. She, however, was
not to be found, having gone to hide herself ; but the
men had great trust in their angakok. At last a man
happened to call out, " How I wish that Javraganak
would serve me again !" upon which she immediately
appeared, looking very comfortable. But they soon all
fell upon her, wound a cord around her body, and
dragged her along the ground till she died. And in
this way she was paid back for what she had done to
them.

## 19.

## AVARUNGUAK OR AGDLERUT.

AT a well-peopled place the trick of pinching was a favourite amusement with the inhabitants. One night a girl, who was an only sister with a number of brothers, came running in, crying, "I wonder who it can possibly be who is always running after me and paying court to me?" They told her that when he again made his appearance, she had better bring him into the house. When at length she brought him in, it was a man totally unknown to all of them. Avarunguak —such was his name—had grown up in solitary places, and when he came among people he married this girl, and after a while learned to manage a kayak, and grew an excellent hunter. Once they had some visitors from the south, and an old woman of the party accosted Avarunguak thus, saying, " If Avarunguak were to hear of the nice hunt, and the many auks[1] we have down in the south, I am sure he would be wanting to go there!" So saying, she went away; but having heard her, Avarunguak could not sleep, so great was his desire to go at once. Already the next morning he ordered his housemates to make ready for the voyage; he wanted to be off for the south, he said. They loaded the boat and got under way. On the way out they asked the people they encountered whether the place was still far off, and all made answer that it was not very nigh yet. At length they put on shore, to rest from the toil of rowing, at a place where the people said that to-morrow they might possibly gain their destination. " When ye leave here, and have doubled the cape, ye will come in sight of a very large tent—this ye must shun ; but soon afterwards ye will perceive a little

---

[1] *Alca arra*—Greenlandish, **agpa.**

white point, and having also passed this, ye will fall in with a great many people. To those ye shall go up." On leaving, they soon observed the little white promontory right enough. Avarunguak steered his boat towards the large tent, unheeding the advice of his companions. On landing, a huge man came out from the tent towards them, and receiving them very civilly, went on saying, " It is really a matter of difficulty to get any one to keep company with here ; pray stay and live with me ; " and accordingly they prepared for wintering there.

Every morning Avarunguak awoke at an early hour, but somehow his housemate was always out and off before him. One day in autumn he happened to meet him on their look-out hill ; and when the huge man observed him, he said, " It will soon be the time when the auks will come screaming across the country ; then thou must be sure to get up in good time." But rise as early as he might, Avarunguak was never able to be beforehand with his companion, but always found he had gone out first. One day, when he again overtook him on the hill, he said, " There, the auks are coming across the sea. Make haste to thy tent; but mind, shut the curtain closely, so that only one bird can get in at a time ; and do not begin to catch any of them until the tent is quite full." When Avarunguak had entered and drawn the curtain close, he heard a tapping and rustling, and the birds began to flutter in. He could not, however, take time, but began catching them too soon, upon which the birds instantly left; and at the same time he heard the man scolding, and saying, " Didst thou not mind my telling thee that thou wert not to catch them till the tent was quite full, lest I should be in want of food ? " Still, Avarunguak had got a great many birds, quite sufficient to live upon for a good length of time. Some time after, his house-fellow said, " Now it is near the time for the walrus, but I do not pursue them ; the red walrus is a very ferocious beast, and at that time I do not venture out at all." When these animals appeared, Avarunguak grew very excited about going, taking a great interest in all kinds of hunting that were new to him. When he lanced his first walrus, his big companion came down to the beach, took half of the walrus, and dragging it along with only one hand, passed by Avarunguak's tent, and carried it off to his own. Avarunguak wondered, and said to himself, " I doubt if I shall have a taste of my first walrus ;" and entering, he saw the big man busy eating it all by himself, his wife and daughter only looking on ; but he did not dare to make any objections. Next time he got a walrus the big man's wife came, and at once carried off his prize, and, after her, their three daughters did the same by turns. Not until they had all got their walrus did they desist ; and then, at last, he could think of providing for the ensuing winter. In the beginning his huge friend proposed that they should come and live all together in his house ; and when Avarunguak consented, the big man added, " We are five individuals ourselves, and consequently have five windows. Now I suppose that thou wilt add as many as ye count persons." To this Avarunguak answered, " Why, we have never built any more than two or three windows for a company of travellers, with only one boat, whatever their number may be."[1]  " Then just do as thou mayst like, and put in two or three windows, but only do come and live with us." In the beginning of winter Avarunguak always caught plenty ; but the big man having no kayak of his own, never went out. As time wore on, the sea froze up, and all hunting ceased. The master of the house then spoke, " Here we are all badly off ; but I know that behind our country there is good hunting enough, and thither we intend to go to-

[1] A house with three windows is considered a very large one ; those with five must have been very rare.

morrow." Avarunguak had a great mind to accompany them; but the other asked him, "How swift mayst thou be?" "Why, I think I can run a race with any of the quadrupeds." But still the man was very unwilling to take him with him, and only consented at last after much beseeching. The next day they departed, all of them carrying cords of sealskin round their necks. They crossed the neighbouring mountains, and in the distance beheld a bare land, and then the big man spoke: "Dost thou see yonder lofty mountains far away? Behind, there is a sea where the *white whale* in abundance are found; but when we get so far, thou must only aim at the small ones, because thou wilt not be expert enough to carry home one of the larger ones." As they wandered along, the daughters had to take hold of Avarunguak by his arms to help him along, because he was not quite able to keep up with them. When they reached the appointed place, each of them watched at a cleft in the ice. No sooner did Avarunguak see a huge white whale rise to the surface than he at once aimed at and killed it. Then the other party came on, each of them bringing up two fish; but when the master saw that Avarunguak had disobeyed his orders, he gave him a scolding; and when they prepared to return, they wanted to tie his fish to their own, and make him sit down on the top of it, and thus be dragged home. But he answered, "Since I commenced hunting I have never let my game be carried home by any one but myself, nor shall I do so now. I have caught the fish myself, and will take care to bring it home." They let him have his own way, but in a moment they disappeared from his sight, as if they had been blown away. It was evening, and again beginning to dawn, before he could even see his home, and he met the others coming back to fish anew. It was not till the fourth day he got home; and on the way he had been obliged to eat all the matak (skin) of his dolphin. Meanwhile his

relatives had been very anxious about him, thinking
that perhaps his companion had killed him. About this
time, Avarunguak's people had a dog that happened to
whelp.  When the first whelp appeared, the huge man
whispered something to his wife, on which she brought
it him, and he took hold of it and examined all its joints.
The wife then put it back in its place, and subsequently
brought each new-born whelp to him to be examined in
the same way ; but when they had handled the seventh,
which was also the last, they were heard saying, " This
one is perfect ; there is not a limb wanting." From that
time they seemed despondent ; and Avarunguak, who
began to fear their intentions, one day said to them,
" If you would like to have a dog, you are welcome to
take the one you like best."  This seemed to please
them highly, and they chose the last born, and becàme
so fond of it that they let it stop on the ledge and sleep
at night beside them.  From this time Avarunguak
himself became a great favourite with his other house-
fellows.  While the winter lasted, the big man once
spoke as follows, " We intend soon to go and visit our
enemies."  Avarunguak was very desirous to join the
party, but his house-master answered him, " No, friend ;
thou wouldst too soon be worn out : for, in the first place,
thou canst not eat blubber and flesh enough ; and
secondly, because of thy clumsiness and want of speed."
He answered, " As to the blubber and flesh, methinks
I do well enough as regards both of them."  Whereat
the big one rejoined, " Well, then, try to lick out the oil
of all the lamps here, beginning with the outermost."
Avarunguak succeeded ; and only a few days after, the
leader told him " that now he might accompany them
to their enemies," adding, " when we have entered, and
begin licking the oil, thou must be sure to help us.
Next they will present each of us with one large white
fish, and thou must thrust thy knife right into it, turn
it round, and put the piece thou has cut out into thy

mouth, and suddenly exclaim, 'I must go outside, but I will be back in a moment, and go on eating; I enjoy it very much.' But when outside take to thy heels, and run for home as fast as possible, and before thou hast been off long, we shall empty the lamps, and soon overtake thee." Some time after, they carried out their intention of visiting their enemies in their place of abode. They at once set about licking the oil of the lamps, beginning with the first, Avarunguak joining them to the best of his ability. When the hosts saw a stranger among their visitors, they regarded him keenly, so that the huge man interposed : " That is a new housemate of ours; he is living with us at present, and assists us every way,"—and they went on praising and flattering him very much, and making a great deal of his dexterity and strength, adding that he was more than a match for them every way. This was anything but the truth; but they dared not do otherwise, for fear of their enemies. The host now said, " Bring in the meal for the visitors," and the women instantly went out, and returned, bringing in large white fish. The guests soon fell to; but Avarunguak forgot he had been advised to leave off in good time, and never remembered till he was quite satisfied. He then observed his companions making signs to him, and quickly pronouncing the words he had been told, took himself off, and commenced running as fast as possible. On coming near their own house he turned round, and looking back, he saw that the creatures he had been visiting were transformed into bears, pursuing him closely; but his own housemates soon overtook him, and the daughters again took him by the arms to speed him on. When they had almost reached the house, the enemies seemed at their very heels, and Avarunguak was deserted by his protectors, who gave him a blow, so that he fell, and the bears instantly gathered round him. But he chanced to have a salmon for his amulet, and this did him good service in making him too slippery to be caught hold of, and thus he escaped. When spring came round, Avarunguak took a fancy to remove to another place ; and on departing, his huge companion said to him, " I hope thou wilt soon return and stay with us; but wherever thou goest, mind to tell the people never to kill a bear when one appears." Thus they departed ; but on turning round, they now saw that their housemates too had been transformed into bears: they had been wintering among bears in human shape. Later on they heard that some people in the south had killed a bear, and still later Avarunguak and his wife died.

---

## 20.

## THE GIRL WHO MARRIED AN ATLIARUSEK.[1]

AN aged couple had a daughter who had a great many suitors ; but the old people were very selfish, and wanted to keep her at home. Meanwhile a man came who was very anxious to get the daughter. At last he fought them, and had nearly killed them; but the old man escaped, and got into his boat. The other men of the place despised and scorned him ; but they got the boat loaded, and left. The others shouted to him contemptuously, " It won't be easy for thee to get a husband for thy daughter ! The poor old thing, who is quite unable to hunt—he to dare reject any one ! Only let him come to be in want of necessaries, and

---

[1] The *atliaruseks*, probably identical with the *ingnersuaks*, were a sort of elves or gnomes, supposed to have their abodes within rocks along the sea-shore.

then look out if there be any one to help him!" But
he set off without deigning to answer them, and landed
at one of the outermost islets. There they built their
house, and put up for the winter. One morning the old
man awoke, saying, "I wonder what I have just been
seeing? Methinks I saw a man gliding through the
doorway." He questioned his daughter; but she keeping silence, he got suspicious. When he awoke the next
morning, he saw a real man slip out of the doorway;
and on being closely questioned, the daughter confessed
that she was married to an *atliarusek*. On hearing this,
the father was very happy; but she went on saying,
"For fear thou wouldst not like him, he keeps out of
sight; but if thou dost not mind, he will come and live
with us." The father said it was all right, and he might
come and take up his quarters with them at once. The
next morning the old man, on awakening, turned his eyes
towards the entrance, but saw nothing remarkable there;
but on turning round to his daughter's resting-place, he
saw a stout man sitting there beneath her lamp. The
father was very well pleased, and leaned back on his
couch; but listening again, and peeping out, the man
was not to be seen. Towards evening the daughter
several times left the room. At last she stayed away
rather long, but after some time returned with a hunting-line, which she hung up on a nail to dry, saying that
he had returned and brought home the produce of his
hunt, but that he must take some part of it to his
relatives. When her parents went outside, they saw
many seals on the beach, and they rejoiced very much
at their sudden prosperity. The following morning the
old man peeped over the screen of the ledge, and there
beheld the stranger reposing beside his daughter. The
old man again lay down, believing him to be asleep.
In a little while, however, he heard something stirring,
at which he arose; but the son-in-law had already taken
himself off. He again spoke to his daughter, saying,

"Why do you not make him come and stay with us? We like him very well indeed." In the evening, when he again returned with his catch, he went inside and made himself at home; and the parents were very civil to him. In the spring he wanted to go further inland along the fiord-side, as was generally his custom, but told them that he was obliged to join his parents, he being their only son, and as such he ought not to let his sisters be without protection. He then went away to his own home; and when they again met, he told them that now they were ready for starting. On hearing this, his father-in-law likewise put his boat into the water; and when it was ready loaded, and they were going to set off, another boat appeared, coming straight out of the beach. Both went along together, and made the land at the same time in the evening. Next morning they again started; and when they approached an inhabited place, the head-man of the atliaruseks told them always to keep close in their wake; and all of a sudden they saw his boat sink beneath the surface, and totally disappear. At this sight the old man got rather frightened; but on arriving at the spot, their boat dived down in the same manner, without any damage to the crew. Presently they caught sight of their companions' boat right ahead of them, and they continued their course beneath the waves of the sea. Having safely passed the inhabited places, they once more rose to the surface, and continued their voyage without further peril; and when they had arrived at their place of destination, went reindeer-hunting, and got their boats fully laden. When the old people had again taken up their winter-quarters, the son-in-law provided amply for them, and they prospered and were well off. About this time intelligence reached them that the men who had once scorned and abused them were living in great want, and the old man determined to help them. He loaded his kayak with matak, and brought it to them.   On his arrival, they asked him whence he had got it—whether it was not taken from the carcass of a whale that had been driven on shore accidentally. However, he left them without deigning them an answer to this question ; and talking over this matter on his return home, the son-in-law exclaimed, " I should really like to have a look at these people ;" whereat the old man went back to fetch off all the men who had formerly been his daughter's suitors, and returned with a large train of kayaks following him.   They landed, and were very hospitably received, and regaled with reindeer-meat and seal-flesh ; and when they had satisfied their appetite, the old man accosted them thus : " I wonder if ye can still remember what ye were telling me a long time ago when ye had nearly killed me, wanting by main force my daughter for your wife ?   Your words were these : 'Thou wilt surely never get a clever husband for thy daughter.'   But you see I have, for all that. Likewise ye said that ye would deny me your assistance if ever I came in want : now help yourself, if ye please, and eat as much as ever ye like."

---

## 21.

### THE LOST DAUGHTER.

AN old woman lived with her three children, two sons and a daughter.   The sons were good hunters, and loved their sister exceedingly.   As time passed on, the mother observed a change in her daughter's manners ; and one day it happened that she went out by herself, and stayed away for good. The brothers sought her far and wide ; but at last they gave it up, and again took to kayaking and hunting, and now lived alone with their mother. But one day, when she was all by herself in the house, and had lain down to rest on the ledge beneath the skin coverlet, she remarked a thing like a shadow gliding across the doorway, and on turning that way beheld her long-lost daughter ; and perceiving the *amowt* (hood) she wore, she asked her to come and sit beside her, and admired her beautiful clothes, the amowt particularly, which was made of soft and thin reindeer-skin. When a low cry was heard from within it, the mother asked her to take out the little one she was carrying to let her see it. But the daughter answered her, " What I carry on my back is no human being. Thou hadst better hide thyself beneath thy skin coverlet." The mother accordingly did so ; but peeping through a small opening, she was dreadfully alarmed at seeing her daughter produce a large reptile, which she allowed to bite her lips so as to make them bleed ; and having caressed it in a motherly way, she let it suck at her breast. Then having replaced it in her amowt, she asked her mother to look up again, upon which the latter asked her, " Where is thy dwelling-place, child?" " My house lies far from here, in a very large valley ; but my husband is not of human race : so none of you must ever think of coming to see me," she added, and left. In the evening, when the sons returned, the mother told them what had happened, saying, " I have seen your sister, but in a very low and contemptible state. Only think ! she carried a vile reptile in her amowt, and was also married to such a one !" The brothers got into a great rage on hearing this, and at once prepared their bows and arrows to attack the vermin. Starting together, they took the direction which their mother had pointed out to them, and soon found the great house in the valley. After a careful inspection of all the mountains, they ventured to peep through the window, and there saw their sister comfortably seated in a snug and well-furnished room. They entered at once, killed her offspring, and having torn it to pieces, threw it outside. They did not leave their sorrowing sister during the day-time, but towards evening they saw her dreadful husband approaching the place from some remote part of the country: its size was like the wall of a house; and in its mouth it carried a large reindeer. When it came nearer, the brothers went out to hide themselves at the back of the house, whence they saw the reptile drop the reindeer on the ground, and afterwards enter the house. They again ventured a peep through the window, and saw the creature twining itself closely round the body of their sister, so that only the tuft of her hair was visible. They tightened the strings of their bows, keeping them ready bent, and then made a little noise, in order to alarm the beast. The instant it emerged from the house, it was aimed at from both sides by the brothers; and when all their arrows had been spent, they finished it off and killed it with their spears. Having accomplished this, they made for their home, bringing their sister along with them, as well as all her things, and some dried reindeer. And now the sister was once more with her parents; and they warned her to leave off her former bad habits. After a little, however, her manner towards them again suddenly changed; and they perceived that she was always carrying something about in her hand. This appeared to be a small worm or reptile, with black streaks round its body. Every day it grew in size, so that before long both sides appeared out of her hand; and now she disappeared a second time. The brothers again went in search of her, this time taking their mother along with them; but she soon died on her way; and one brother had his leg broken: and henceforth they gave up all hope of ever finding their sister.

## 22.

## ANGUTISUGSUK.

THERE were three brothers, the eldest of whom was called Angutisugsuk. They had never lived apart; and all of them were clever hunters, especially Angutisugsuk. One winter the weather was dreadfully severe, and all the neighbours were in great want. Only the three brothers had enough to spare, and the others claimed their assistance. It so happened that two old men came to them with that intention; and during their visit the wife of Angutisugsuk remonstrated, saying that they were having rather too many visitors about the place, at which the old men quickly took offence; and in spring - time, when Angutisugsuk's family left their winter - quarters, and were away on some long excursion, they visited the place in their kayaks, entered the empty house, and practised all manner of sorcery and witchcraft upon the wall adjoining the ledge occupied by Angutisugsuk's wife, in order to produce discord among the family when they came back from their travels. In autumn they all returned to the old house as usual. One day Angutisugsuk did not go out kayaking, but stayed at home to make a wooden plate and spoon. At that time he had got two wives, both of whom were very clever at needle-work; and he offered to give her who would mend his fur jacket for him the wooden plate and spoon. The first wife made answer, before the second could put in a word, " I want to have them—I will mend the jacket;" and she worked very quickly on it. The second wife, however, who happened to be the best beloved, on her part became envious, and got into a passion. Perceiving this, the husband struck her, because of her having borne him no children. At

this his youngest son began crying; and seeing it, the
child's uncle fell upon the father, who was still ill-treating his second wife. In this fight Angutisugsuk thrust
his brother against the door-sill with such force that his
thigh-bone was bruised; and he would have followed up
his advantage over him but for the younger brother and
some others, who interfered in the quarrel. Thus it came
to pass as the old men had planned when they went
and bewitched the empty house in their absence. After
having lamed his brother, Angutisugsuk next day loaded
his boat and went off in it, taking a small roofless house
for himself which he found a little north of his former
station; and as a substitute for roof-beams he made a
shift with his tent-poles. His proper wife he left behind,
and only took the second one along with him. Seeing
that his brother was now able to stir, he resolved to
kill him, and repeatedly returned to despatch him; but
somehow he always found his younger brother or his
nephew by his side, and never succeeded in accomplishing his end. These two watched the sick man by
turns; and only one at a time went out in his kayak.
Angutisugsuk one day encountered his nephew at sea,
and resolved to pursue him; but as soon as they came
within sight of the house on shore, he left off and turned
back. When the nephew got home, he told them that
Angutisugsuk had been persecuting him; and his father
(viz., the invalid) said, "To-morrow thou must go and
ask our neighbours to assist us in getting Angutisugsuk
out of the way, because he has gone raving mad; but
two or three men will not suffice, for he is immensely
strong himself." The son went the following morning
to several stations, and brought a considerable party of
kayakers along with him; and the invalid accosted
them, saying, "Let us agree to kill Angutisugsuk. Every
day he comes this way intending to take my life; but
as soon as he sees anybody staying with me, he desists
and turns back." All the men prepared to pass the

night there, hiding their kayaks behind the house ; and
early in the morning they saw Angutisugsuk in his
kayak emerging from behind a rocky point close by.
As nobody was to be seen, and he did not even observe
the kayaks of his brother and nephew, he supposed them
to be off, and made for the shore as fast as possible.
An old man among the strangers now drew his hood
closer to his head, and pronounced a magic spell, adding
that, if it were likely to succeed, Angutisugsuk as a sure
sign would turn the back of his hands downwards,
instead of using the palms in ascending the beach.
Watching him very closely, they noticed that he did as
the old man had foretold, and they no longer had any
doubt of their success.   Having got out on the beach,
he only drew his kayak half-way out of the water, and
went straight up to the house as if to enter it at once ;
but bethinking himself of something, turned back to the
large boat to get hold of a flensing-knife, and then proceeded to the entry.   The men were all reclining on the
side-ledge couches except two, who stood posted at the
inner entrance ready to seize him.   When he saw his
brother sitting on the main ledge, he addressed him in

the following words, saying, " Here is a brave man for
thee !   I'll show thee the way to fight !   Didst thou
really believe I did not intend to kill thee ? "   Thus
speaking, he advanced a step or two, but was soon seized

by the two men, and quickly disarmed. He was at once conducted outside, where all the rest fell upon him ; but nobody could manage to overthrow him. At last, when they had got him hamstrung, he fell ; whereat they seized him, and held a council as to which of them should first stab him. At last the invalid brother was carried out, in order that he might finish him off. They put him down close beside the other, and he said, " Go and fetch me my spear from under the boat." When he had got it, he lanced his brother several times in the shoulder, saying, " Now let go your hold ; if he boasts himself a man, he will be sure to rise." He did get up, and went towards his kayak on the beach, but fell down dead before he reached it. Then the surviving brother exclaimed, " Alas ! we have killed him who did well towards us. In the short, dark days, when we were almost starving, he did not mind toiling away for us. I am sorry indeed : now do kill me also !" He asked his brother, his son, and all the other men ; but finding that nobody would do it, he said, " Well, then, go and fetch his second wife, and kill her at any rate ; it was she who began it all." They did so ; and the person who slew her admonished the bystanders, saying, " Now put together all her things, and all her clothes, all her jackets of reindeer-skin, her breeches and boots of seal-skin—get them all together, and carry them along with her ; and mind you close up the burial-place well, and heap plenty of stones on top of it." Later on, when the invalid recovered, he felt great remorse for his act of violence ; but the old magician was quite satisfied that Angutisugsuk should have been killed by his brother.

## 23.

## SITLIARNAT.

[This tale having much resemblance to Nos. 16 and 19, the text is here somewhat abridged.]

THERE were three brothers, the eldest of whom was named Sitliarnat. One day they all went out hunting on the frozen sea, accompanied by a person who was in no way related to them. All of a sudden a south-east storm arose, the ice creaked and gave way beneath their feet, and nothing remained to them but to mount an iceberg. Having got there, they drifted far away out on the great ocean. They were nearly starving with hunger when they at length touched upon an unknown shore and landed there. They now went roaming about the country in search of people, and passed an isthmus on which they observed a little hut with only one window. Sitliarnat then spoke, " Let them make me their first prize ; " and he went on and crossed the threshold in front of his companions. Inside the house they only found an old couple, who seemed to be its sole inhabitants. The four strangers seated themselves on the ledge ; but finding that nobody spoke, the old man began to eye them more closely, and having breathed upon them, asked them, " Whence do you come ? " Sitliarnat answered him, " Some time ago we set off from the land on the other side of the ocean, and went out on the ice to catch seals ; but a gale from the south-east came on, breaking up the ice and drifting us across to your country. So here we are ; three of us are brothers, and the fourth is a companion of ours." Turning to his wife the old man observed, " After travelling so far people are apt to get hungry," upon which they added some words which the people did not understand. The wife fetched some blubber in a pan, put it on to boil, and gave it them served up in a wooden dish; but though they were almost fainting with hunger, they only tasted a very little of it. Soon after, however, a proper meal was set before them, and then the old man said to them, "Our only provider is staying away a long time; we have been expecting him back this last month. He left us to go out hunting, and has not yet returned; we are much afraid he may have encountered some wicked people and have come to grief." While he was thus speaking, the guests began to think, "What sort of people may these be?" Meanwhile the visitors stayed on, and for some time the old man provided food for them. One morning, when they were all sitting together, they heard a voice calling from without, "I want to get in; do let me get in!" whereat the old man rose from his seat and went outside, but soon returned holding his son by the hand, who was looking very pale and haggard. After supper he lay down on the side ledge, and remained thus for several days, until one morning when he rose up very early. He had now recovered his health and strength as well as his appetite, and had regained his former aspect also, and again took up his task as provider of the household; but strange to say, he was never seen to carry any weapons. The visitors meanwhile prolonged their stay for several years; and one evening the old man, addressing the eldest brother, questioned him, "What did they give thee for thy amulet when thou wert born?" Sitliarnat replied, "In my infancy I got a *carrion-gull*, one of those that always seek the carrion farthest out to sea." On hearing this the old man responded, "So thou mayst be sure of returning to thy own country at some time or other." One of the brothers now put in, "All of us have got the same bird for our amulets;" but when the stranger was asked, he told them that his was a raven, a bird that always seeks his prey landward;

on which the old man replied, " I doubt if thou wilt ever
see thy country again, if it is so." The old man used
to rise the earliest of them all, and when the others at
length came out, he was always seen to be on some
mountain-top, marking the state of the air and the
weather. He one day entered with this remark, " When
the wind goes down and the weather gets settled, I
shall take you across." But they wondered, and said,
" How will he manage to carry us yonder, as there is
no ice at present, and neither boats nor kayaks are to
be seen hereabouts, and we don't even know in what
direction our country is situated ? " One morning when
they were still fast asleep, he cried, " It is no time for
sleeping now. Make haste and get up, if ye really
long for your homes; I shall see you along myself :" and
they now rose as quickly as possible, and followed him
down to the steep shore, where they had landed years
ago. Here the old man said, " Now watch me !" Then
taking a run, he leapt into the sea, dived down, and reappeared in the shape of a bear, saying, " If Sitliarnat
really has a gull for his amulet, it will soon appear to
him. Do as I have done, and throw thyself into the
water." Sitliarnat, however, still lingered a little ; but
the bear went on, " If thou dost not follow me into the
ocean, thou wilt never get home." Sitliarnat now ran
on and took the leap ; and as soon as he had plunged
down, he again rose and merely touched the surface
with his feet, gliding along as if he were on solid ice,
instead of being on the waves of the sea. At the same
time the gull also made its appearance, and a large iceberg was seen which he climbed, both his brothers
following him. The old man now turned to the fourth,
saying, " Thou, too, wouldst like to return, I know ; now
try thy wings !" He, too, plunged into the sea, trying
to fly, but went right down instead, and would have
lost breath but for the bear, who put him on shore,
saying, " No, thou wilt never get home, because thou

hast got a raven for thy amulet; thou canst return to my house as before." The bear now spoke to the three, " Shut your eyes and sit close together. If ye open your eyes, ye will never get home. I shall now put my shoulder to the iceberg, and push you away." Presently their place of refuge began to shake beneath them, and they had started on their journey. Thus they moved onwards until they at last felt a quake as if they were touching something hard. Here the bear ordered them to open their eyes, and they beheld a country spreading before them, and recognised it as their own. They had landed just a little south of what had been their former habitation. They asked the bear to enter, that they might recompense him in some way or other ; but he said, " No, I don't care for being paid—I merely intended to do you a good turn ; but when in winter-time ye should happen to see a bear with a bald head, and your companions prepare to hunt him down, then try to make them desist, and put some food before him." After these words he plunged into the sea, and instantly disappeared. The brothers now went up to their former house, and knew it to be inhabited because of some little boys who were seen at play outside. These children had been named after them by their parents, in remembrance of their lost friends. Their wives had all married again ; but their other relatives rejoiced greatly at receiving those whom they had given up for lost a long time ago. Inquiries were also made about their companion, but they answered that they had left him " on the opposite shore." Perceiving that the husbands of their own former wives feared them, they reassured them, saying, " We don't intend any harm towards you. Many thanks to you that ye have provided so well for our relatives." But the wives, nevertheless, were given back to them. During the winter the bear was almost forgotten, till one evening, when they were all at home, some of the men exclaimed, " A bear is making for the shore!" When they were collecting their arms, the brothers interfered, crying, "Just wait a little ; we must first have a look at him." They instantly recognised their own bear, and said to the others, "Without his good aid we should never have reached home again. Don't hunt that bear; make haste and give him a feast." When the bear had got on shore, he went right up to the house, sat down on his haunches before the entrance, his head turned towards it. The people put several entire seals before him, and beckoned him to eat ; and all the men gathered round him. When the meal was ended, the bear lay down to sleep, while the children played round him. After a while he awoke, and having eaten a little more, he arose, and following his own traces back to the beach, leapt into the sea, and was never seen any more. It is said that the descendants of Sitliarnat were very prosperous and multiplied greatly.

---

## 24.

## THE REINDEER-HUNT OF MERKISALIK.

[This story is compiled from two copies, one of which had been noted down in North Greenland before 1828.]

MERKISALIK had only one son to assist him in providing for his family. In the summer-time they always used to hunt along the shores of the same fiord without any other company. Growing old and infirm, Merkisalik at length had to give up hunting and leave the providing to his son. Once when they had again taken up their abode at the fiord, and the son, as was his wont, had gone out hunting, the old people were left by themselves, expecting no visitors. Taking a turn outside the tent, they suddenly observed a boat sailing up the inlet right before the wind, accompanied by several kayakers. Merkisalik was much pleased at this sight, and ordered his wife to put out some dry meat, to let them have a bite on landing. He rejoiced to think that his son should henceforth have companions on his hunting excursions. There were a great number of men among the visitors, some of whom were old and rather talkative and entertaining. When the son returned from the mountains, he was likewise very glad of the company they had got. He treated them with the utmost hospitality, and invited them to partake of the meal as soon as it was boiled and ready. Meanwhile they all conversed very politely, and soon agreed in going out together the next day. They did so, and before long came in sight of a number of animals feeding on the grass down in the valleys. When the drivers were all sent out, the hunters proceeded to make walls of earth, furnished with loopholes. The visitors now proposed that Merkisalik's son should be the last to shoot, and he agreed ; but when the drivers had surrounded the animals, and began to drive them on towards the loopholed walls, the thought struck him, "What if they are too greedy to leave me any chance at all?" Meanwhile the others took aim, and shot all that were to be got. He afterwards assisted them in stripping off the skins ; but on their descending the hills towards the tents, he remained a little behind. When the strangers returned they at once set their women to cook and prepare a meal, to which Merkisalik and his people were invited. During supper one of the men remarked, "There must be any amount of animals in this place, since even Merkisalik's son is capable of getting at them." The Merkisaliks heard this slight in silence ; but afterwards, when they got into their own tent and sat down together, the father said, "It can't be otherwise ; we must just let them have their way, seeing that they are

so many." The following day was spent in the same
manner ; they treated Merkisalik's son as they had done
the day before, only allowing him to take up his position
as far away as possible from the drivers : but on their
way home he again kept back a little. Before long,
however, he rejoined them, and on their return home
the Merkisaliks were again invited to eat of the day's
hunt. The man who the day before had scorned Merkisalik's son, now spoke to him in a similar fashion, at
which he got into a great passion. However, they set
out together the next day, and got to the entrance of a
great valley, which appeared to be almost overcrowded
with reindeer. As before, they ordered him to choose his
hiding-place, and make his loophole behind them all, at
which he murmured to himself, "If this is to go on, I shall
never be able to get anything. I think I will give the
beasts the alarm, that they may all run away." When
the flock approached, driven by the drivers, he feigned
to be busy about something or other. At last he was
warned to be quiet, that the animals might not see him ;
but he only stopped a moment, and then began to move
about again. In the mean time the flock was close by,
when, all of a sudden, the leader stopped short, turned
round, and bounded off as fast as possible. On perceiving this, the others began to follow him, but dropped
short one after another, so that at the other end of the
valley but one of them had kept up with him, and this
one soon tired out ; and when he was about to mount
the slope he was left quite alone. Merkisalik's son
shortly disappeared on the other side of the hills, pursuing the fast-running animals. Slowly the men followed
in his traces : but when they got to the top of the hill,
they beheld numbers of deer with white bellies ready
killed in the valley on the other side ; and on a stone
close by, the huntsman was seated, already quite cool
and refreshed. The others now arrived, their faces all
red with heat and wrath, and nobody spoke. They at

once set to work, stripping the deer; but while the
others finished one, he stripped and cut up two, and
packing his bundle, he said, "Ye may all of you take as
much as ye like." The man who had formerly ridiculed
and mocked him did not altogether like this speech, but
became quite mute, and would not join the rest. On the
way home they separated. Merkisalik's son had now got
into his old ways, and was in front of the rest. Carrying
his burden on his back, and now and then resting himself a little, he got home first of all. When the others
came without anything, the Merkisaliks had already all
their pots and pans on the fire, and, after their wont,
invited the foreigners to join them. During the meal the
host tried to begin a conversation, but without success ;
they all remained mute, and even their old father kept
silent. Having done eating, they retired, excepting the
father, who now began to be a little talkative, and, as if
by chance, remarked, " We want something that would
do for a gimlet ; would ye mind letting me have that
knuckle ? " Merkisalik gave it to him willingly, saying,
" We have got lots of them." On the following morning the Merkisaliks were aroused by a clattering noise,
as of poles, and peeping out, they saw the visitors pulling down their tent and preparing to depart. Thus
they were once more alone ; and their son again went
out hunting all by himself. One day, when he was still
busy bringing down the deer he had stalked to their
station, he told them that he had got a swelling at his
knee. It grew in size, and was getting worse and worse.
The parents were much distressed, and at length he
died, but not till he had made known to them that his
disease was solely caused by the father of their former
visitors, who, in order to hurt him, had bewitched the
knee-joint he had asked of them, which had worked
back upon him and killed him. The poor old people
were inconsolable. It was now autumn ; the little lakes
began to be covered with ice, and it was time to leave

the inland country for the sea-coast : so one fine morning
they made preparations to go. They first wept at the
tomb of their son, and, still wailing and complaining,
they went down the firth with a light easterly breeze.
Having arrived at their winter-quarters, Merkisalik's
mind was filled with hatred, and he was always contem-
plating revenge. In order to carry it out, he resolved
to make a *tupilak* to destroy his enemies. To this end
he every day collected bones of all sorts of animals, and
put them into the brook close by to whiten, and then
mixed them up with hairs taken from boat-skins ; and
when he had got as many as he required, he made them
alive, and put them into the brook which flowed on to the
sea. While he was watching the tupilak, he saw it was
taking the shape of an *agpaliarsuk*,[1] that dived down
and turned round to its owner ; but he said, " Thou art
not the thing I want thee to be yet." Instantly it
dived down and reappeared in the shape of a *dovekie*.[2]
Again he said, "That won't do neither." It underwent many changes and took the shape of all sorts
of birds ; but he rejected them all. Then it was transformed into all manner of seals and dolphins ; but they
did not suit him either. At last, after another dive beneath the surface of the water, its breath was heard like
a mighty roar, and he beheld a small whale, and then
he said, " This will do ; thou shalt avenge us." The animal now seemed to inquire, " Where am I to go ? " and
he replied, " To the hunting place of *the many brothers.*"
At these words it took one long breath, then dived
down into the sea ; and the man returned home and
bided his time, waiting to hear how the family would
fare who lived a little to the north of them. One evening a kayaker appeared rounding the northern point,
and in him he soon recognised a poor relative and very
old man, who for some time had had his quarters at the

[1] The smallest auk, *Mergulus alle.*
[2] Another common sea-fowl, *Uria grylle.*

same place as their former visitors.   On their way from
the beach up to the house, he related what follows :
" Some days ago an accident occurred up at our place ;
one of the many brothers has not returned home.   The
day before his departure he told us that he had harpooned a little whale, adding that he would now go out
in search of it ; but he has never yet returned."   The
maker of the tupilak feigned compassion, saying, " He
must, of course, have managed awkwardly somehow ; "
but inwardly he rejoiced at this intelligence.   When
the visitor departed, he asked him soon to return, but
he did not do so for a good long while.   When at
length he did come, he again reported : " Yesterday the
same accident happened to another of the brothers."
When the visitor was about to depart, Merkisalik encouraged him soon to return, saying, " We are always
glad to see thee ; now come back as soon as thou canst."
After another long interval he once came back, and told
them that the last of the brothers had now disappeared,
adding that the poor parents were very much grieved
because of their bereavement.   On hearing this, Merkisalik's wrath was somewhat appeased.

## 25.

### N A M A K.

[Of this story there is only one manuscript, written down in North
Greenland before 1828.]

THE parents of Namak were both killed by their
house-fellows ; and while he was as yet but a
weak and helpless child, a man happened to take pity on
him and adopted him for his son.   But this same foster-

father was fond of worrying the boy, and inventing
stories to frighten and excite him. Sometimes, when the
child was asleep, he would cry out, " Namak, thy enemies have come to kill thee, too." At first he was
much alarmed, but by degrees he got used to it. But
sometimes his foster-father would say, " Ah, how forget-
ful that Namak is! Here are his parents newly murdered,
and he forgetting all about it." At this, Namak would
get into a great rage. When he was still a child, his
father one day made him a present of a sling, saying,
" I don't mean to give thee a kayak, because I believe
that thy enemies will kill thee for all that; but take
this sling and practise with it." Namak instantly began
to do so, and soon got very clever in using it. In the
spring he would betake himself to solitary places, practising his sling, always pondering over the things his
foster-father had said to stir up vengeance within him.
At home he spoke little, but inwardly rejoiced at his
growing strength. Sometimes he brought in hares, and
sometimes ptarmigan; he got them entirely by means
of his sling. In the summer he never slept at night, but
always in the day-time. Sometimes, when he had gone
to sleep, his father would bring home a seal, and he was
then awakened to assist in carrying it up to the house;
but he would then hide his strength, and make-believe
it was very hard work for him. One day, however, he
said that his sling was too weak, and his father went to
cut him a stronger one out of a very thick piece of seal-
skin; and after that time he left off gibing the boy,
because he began to fear him. During the winter it was
reported that the enemies of Namak intended to remove
farther to the north in spring. He got quite enraged at
the thought that they would be going away before he
could be revenged; and from that day his manner
changed altogether. When spring came round, and
they left their winter-house for the tents, he one day
said, " I wish I could get myself a new sling." On

hearing this the father went out in his kayak, and had the good‐luck to catch a thong‐seal.[1] This he brought in while Namak was still asleep. When the women were busy flensing it, and preparing the skin for boat-covers, the husband said, "It just occurs to me that Namak is wanting a sling." He then roused him, saying, " Namak, thy enemies are making ready to depart." He awoke and ran out, and stood staring at the neighbours. On his way down to the beach, his foster-father said to him, "Just cut out a line for thy sling, wherever thou choosest." Keeping an eye upon his neighbours, he took the knife from his father, lifted up the seal by one of the forepaws with only one hand, and turning it over without any difficulty, cut himself a sling to his liking, all in one piece. On seeing this his foster-father got quite frightened. Some time after this, their neighbours were really going to depart. Namak slept, and his father roused him with these words, " Namak, this time thou mayst believe me ; thy enemies are in the very act of departing : " but Namak did not think fit to stir ; he had been cheated too often. The father again cried to him, " Now they are taking their tents away,"—and as he himself could hear the clatter-ing of the bars and poles, he rose and put on jacket and boots, but without getting into the sleeves of his jacket, and catching hold of his sling from under the ledge, he hid it inside. Further down on the beach were some large stone-heaps ; there he lay in ambush. Now that he had determined to revenge himself, he no more concealed his strength. While some were yet bringing down their luggage, the first boat put out, rowing briskly, and when right athwart of him, Namak put a big stone in his sling, and threw it into the boat, where it made a large hole, so that it instantly began to sink. " Alas ! alas !" they cried. The other boat hurried on to rescue them, but underwent the same fate. The third one tried to save

[1] *Phoca barbata.*

itself by turning in time, but at that instant he flung the
stone at it, hitting the prow and cleaving right through ;
and thus he destroyed three boats, crews and all, and
his mind now got rest.   One boat was saved from destruction, as it had gone out to sea at once, instead of
keeping along the shore.   His enemies increased in
number after they had established themselves some-

where in the north ; and seeing that they had reason to
fear him, they trained themselves to be as vigorous as he.
Namak married, and though he had never had a kayak
himself, he taught his son to practise kayak-paddling.
He grew up and came to be an excellent kayaker, and
subsequently owned a boat as well as a tent.   Now and
then reports reached them from their enemies that they
were numerous, and also strong.   At last he persuaded
his son to go and look them up ; and in spring they
went away northward in their boat, asking the people

they met with, "Where are Namak's enemies?" "Farther north" was the constant answer. At last they learned that their station was close at hand; and from that time they did not as usual land in the evening to take rest, but rowed on incessantly. On their arrival they asked the people who came down to the beach to meet them, "Where are Namak's enemies?" To this, however, they made no reply, but entered their houses, and the travellers had to make their way on shore by themselves; neither were they afterwards invited to visit them. However, they took up their winter-quarters at that very place, and settled down for the time. In the beginning of their stay, Namak advised his son to watch them closely, but afterwards they got less suspicious. That same winter, one morning, it blew a gale from the south-west, and the kayakers remained at home, and on that day it was announced, "They all want to see Namak." He was ready in a moment; the son likewise went: and thus they were going to visit their enemies for the first time. There was only set forth meat for two. The son did not taste much of it, but the father continued eating till the dish was nearly emptied. The visitors did not speak; but at length one of the other party proposed different sports, saying, "Ye ought to try strength at the *pulling-thong* first;" and then he took out the string fitted with walrus-teeth from beneath the ledge, and threw it upon the skin which was spread on the floor for the champions. But Namak said, "This is but child's-play for people who really want to try a match;" and so saying, he took hold of and tore the thong asunder with one hand, and then flung them down on the floor. Another offered to try strength with him, by hooking their arms together, and trying to pull each other over. Namak did not hesitate, but at once sat down on the skin. They now tried one after another, but nobody was able to move his arm in the least. Seeing that they were not able to match him, they all departed. The son went home, but Namak never stirred, but stayed on. At last, however, he prepared to put on his outer coat, and did it very slowly and deliberately, always expecting an attack. They were never invited afterwards. In spring they again wanted to go to the south, and at parting he let his

house-fellows first go into the boat, while he kept back, still expecting an attack from his enemies; but seeing that they did not come, he finally left the place.

NOTE.—The native writer has added the following very characteristic remark : " It is generally supposed that if his foster-father had not continually excited him, he would scarcely have grown to be so immensely strong. People say that among our ancestors, before they became Christians, there was no lack of strong men, because their bad consciences induced them to cultivate their strength. Nowadays, since people have turned Christians, and have no bad consciences, there are no strong men among them."

## 26.

## THE LONELY BROTHERS.

[This tale is here somewhat abridged, and derived only from one manuscript, in which the journey across the country is represented as having
been achieved from the west to the east coast of Greenland, an idea
which can *only have originated by transplanting* the same story from
another Eskimo country, where such a journey might be more practicable than across the frozen, impassable interior of Greenland.]

TWO brothers had taken up their abode at a fiord;
there they lived alone, and having no female assistance, they were obliged to cook and make their garments themselves. One day when they were out kayaking, they passed a little rocky point, and turning their
eyes landwards, they observed a woman standing on
the beach. The eldest brother now said he would go
and fetch her, and with this view he went ashore; but
when he approached her she fled, at first slowly, till, when
he commenced to run, she hurried on so that he gave
her up and returned to his kayak. The younger brother
now ascended the beach, and as he approached she stood
quiet, making no resistance, but let him take her down.
They fastened the kayaks together with strings, and
when she was seated behind the men, she said to the
eldest brother, " I observed thy intention to be bad, so
I fled; but thy brother there has a better disposition."
They now paddled homewards, all the time keeping a
sharp look-out upon her. But it happened that they left
off watching her for a moment; and instantly they heard
a clattering noise, and there she was gone. They searched
all around, thinking she might have fallen into the water,
but there were no traces of her to be seen anywhere, and
after a while they gave her up, saying, " No matter, perhaps she was not a real woman " (*i. e.*, she had fled from

mankind, and was a кivigtoк, endowed with supernatural swiftness). They again untied their kayaks and made for home ; but lo ! there she was, standing outside the tent mending their boots. They ran up to her in case she wanted to run away ; but she said to them, " Pray let go your hold of me, I don't want to leave you." For the first few days they were quite unwilling to leave her alone, lest she should take flight in their absence. Afterwards they started, but did not leave her neighbourhood ; and they did not venture to go away from her for any length of time, until she had said, " I like to stop with you, and ye may go as far as ye like." As they could now employ all their time in hunting, having a woman at home to cook and sew for them, they got more prosperous than before. She bore a male child in due time ; but from that period her manners were altered, and she grew restrained and silent. The eldest brother proposed to the younger one that he should question her as to the cause. At night when they lay down to rest he did so, and she answered him, " It is because of our baby boy ; I would like him so much to go and see his mother's brothers. I cannot forget those dear ones, and that is the reason why I have grown so silent." The brothers agreed that they could not deny her the pleasure of paying a visit to her parents, and said that they would themselves accompany her. Delighted at the prospect of going, she prepared for the journey, and packed up a bundle of boots, as well as several new pairs of soles and other necessaries ; and being ready for their departure, they started to cross the country. The wife with the child in the amowt (hood) constantly went ahead of them, and the others could scarcely keep up with her. For several days they wandered on in the same manner, but at last the woman exclaimed, " If my brothers be still alive, and are to be found in the old place, we shall certainly come in sight of their sea to-morrow ; I recognise all the mountain-hills of my old home." They still wandered on the whole of the next day, and towards evening they sighted an open water. At this they all began crying for joy, and were obliged to stop a little. The wife now said, " If we descend at once we shall not find my brothers ; at this time of the day they always used to be out kayaking. Let us therefore stay here till to-morrow, and be down with them before they start." Accordingly they lay down to sleep for the night, and in the morning they descended the hillside together. A great many tents soon appeared in the valley below, and pointing to one among them remarkable for its greater size, she cried, " That is the tent belonging to my relatives, but I would fain go down by myself; meanwhile you must keep behind,"—and so she went. The sun rose bright and warm, and a moment after, an old woman came forth from a tent holding a child by her one arm and in her other carrying a large seal-skin for sole-leather, which she was going to stretch on the ground to dry. All of a sudden the little one turned round, exclaiming, " Why, is not that my aunt coming there ? " " No, don't speak such foolish things. Thou knowest very well thy aunt fled away never to return any more, because of these quarrels and fights for her sake." At this rebuke the boy was silenced, but in a little while again went on, " Indeed, indeed, it is my aunt, and there she is coming ! " The old woman, however, was still bending over the piece of skin, and busy in fastening it down. She only rejoined, " What stupid nonsense ! thy aunt has gone away from us for ever. I only wish I could manage those pegs " (viz., for fastening the skins) ; but as the boy would not give over chattering about his aunt she got into a passion with him, and tore out the holes made in the skin for the pegs. Then for the first time she looked up and cried out, " That is she, sure enough. Why did not I believe the little one ? " she continued, and went on caressing the boy. In the meantime the brothers had also in some way or other

been informed of what had happened, and each of them
cried out, "Oh, my dear sister! ye have not cared so
much for her as I have; ye have not missed her so
much neither; ye have not longed so much for her as I
have done." And each of them wanted to be the first
to greet her, and to take hold of her. They all ran towards her, but out of reverence for the eldest they allowed
him to be the first to give her welcome. They now began questioning her about her fellow-travellers; and she
told them that the men were waiting on the mountain-
side above, and they ran to bring them down, and the
entrance to the tent was soon blocked up with inquisitive neighbours, all eager to see the travellers who had
crossed the whole breadth of the country. The brothers
stayed at home all day, and for joy at the meeting could
do nought but sit down together and regard each other
lovingly. In the evening the eldest proposed that some
kind of amusements should be got up, and they agreed
to try strength with one another at " hook and crook;"
upon which one of them drew forth a skin for the purpose, saying, "When strangers meet, one always likes
to see which is the better man;" and acting upon his
word, he at once undressed and seated himself on the
skin. Seeing that none of the visitors moved, one of his
own brothers sat down opposite to him, and they hooked
each other's arms, and the eldest of the two beat his
brother's back vigorously in order to encourage him to
pull hard. However, neither he nor any of all the brothers were able to stretch out his arm; but when they
had all done, he still retained his place sitting down on
the skin. The eldest of the visitors now whispered to
his brother, "I shall first take my chance, then thou
take thine;" and he likewise undressed and sat down,
stretching out his right arm and hooking it inside his
adversary's. The visitor, perceiving his strength, thought,
" I will try to conquer him before he is tired out, so that
it may not seem to be too easy a job for me;" and he

gathered all his strength, and slowly pulled on the arm of his adversary till it touched his own breast, and the other now tried to draw him back, but his features grew quite convulsed, and the skin came off his arms in the attempt. They changed places and tried the game over with their left arms, but with the same result; and at last the host rose, with these words, " I now see that we have acquired some very strong friends;" and taking his seat on the main ledge, as the principal person of the house, he continued, saying, " We, too, have got a man of great strength among us, and ye will scarcely escape him; I almost fear you won't come off alive." The next morning a call was heard outside the tent, " The visitors are requested to come and fight!" At this summons they quickly dressed and went outside. There they saw a number of people ascending the heights; and following in their wake, they reached a plain, where a still greater crowd formed a circle about a fellow with a frame like a giant: and the elder bro- ther whispered to the younger one, " It won't do for thee to go first—thou dost look so very dejected; I had better go myself." So saying, he suddenly rushed at the champion, and thus took the huge man by surprise. This was at sunrise, and at sunset they were still fight- ing; and the visitor thought, " I must try to throw him over before I get too tired." Taking hold of him, he slowly lifted him off his feet, and held him swinging in the air. He had noticed a pole stuck up among some rocks. However, he did not choose to knock him down against that, but hurled him right out among the spec- tators, where he fell down, the blood gushing forth from his mouth. A loud roar was now heard among the people—some rejoiced, others wept; and in descending to the valley below, they all gathered around the eldest visitor, merely to have the satisfaction of having touched him, and some addressed him, saying, " Thou shalt have my windlass in reward for that job." This, however, he did not understand at the time. The whole crowd now vanished with one cry, " Ye shall be our masters henceforth ; " and for a while they remained at their new station, kayaked, and were always together. When the frost set in, and the sea began to be covered with ice, the men chose a day for putting their hunting and fishing implements to rights ; but the brothers did not join their work, because their manner of hunting was quite new to them. The next day they all started, and towards evening the eldest of the men came dragging along two large *saddleback* seals, others *blueside* ones,[1] while others had caught thong-seals. On the following day the visitors accompanied them to see their ways of hunting. They had left the shore far behind them before they fell in with the frost-smoke and reached the first apertures in the ice, at the edge of which walrus-teeth had been stuck down. These were what they had been calling their windlasses.[2] The eldest of the men now said, " Do not try to harpoon the big ones, but aim at the little firth-seals, and leave the others to me." They both obeyed his orders, and as soon as they had each harpooned a small seal, they wound up their harpoon-strings round one of the large walrus-teeth, and made it fast there. When all the seals had been slaughtered they prepared to return, letting the elder take the lead. But he had not gone far when, turning round, he remarked, " Now ye may go on just as ye like ; " and so saying, he went off as if carried by the wind. The others followed in due order, but came home late. When they had all entered, the eldest of the men took out the dish with the boiled meat from beneath the ledge, and said, " I am afraid it is not particularly good ; it will have lost its flavour, having been ready this long time." They went

[1] The *Phoca Greenlandica* in a full-grown and in a half-grown state.

[2] This manner of catching seals, noticed by travellers among the nations of Smith Sound, seems to have been known to the narrator of this story only as a very remarkable tradition.

out the same way next morning. That day the visitors each caught a large seal, and the chief of the men said, " They will not get home with these by to-morrow morning." But on their way home the elder brother said, " This won't do ; we won't get any credit unless we try to be the first,"—and off they went, in order to forestall the others. The master of the house came in later, and was greatly astonished on seeing their outer clothes hanging outside the hut, but supposed that some other visitors might have arrived. On entering the house, however, the brothers put the supper before him at once, saying, " We fear the meat has got tough, and has lost its flavour ; it is ever so long since we boiled it." At first he remained silent, but soon became more talkative, and said he was glad that he had got such able and clever helpmates. When spring came on, the brothers began to long for their own home, and they asked their former companion whether she preferred to stay or go with them. She answered, " I will rather return with you." Her parents making no objections, they went away together, and were never more seen or heard of by any of their kinsmen after the day of their departure.

---

## 27.

## SIKUTLUK.

SIKUTLUK and his cousin were living together, and loved each other dearly. At that settlement the cousin was the only one who possessed a dog. One day Sikutluk observed his cousin sitting before his tent doing some work, the dog beside him. When he came close up to him the cousin suddenly said, " Pray, shoot

my dog." "No, I won't, because we are friends." But
the cousin still persuaded him, saying, "Pray do it,
nevertheless." He brought his bow accordingly; but not
yet satisfied, he again inquired, "But wilt thou not really
get vexed when it is too late?" "No, indeed, I shall
not;" and the other killed the dog. The cousin, however, took offence for all that, and challenged his friend,
saying, "He had a mind to kill him at once." But
Sikutluk shot him right through the breast, and he fell
down dead. Immediately after this, Sikutluk went and
covered his cousin's boat and tent all over with heavy
stones, and left the place along with his wife; but the
murder he had committed had made him thirst for blood,
and he went on intending to kill whatever he met with.
At first he was content with killing ptarmigan and reindeer. They both brought with them as many arrows as
they were able to carry. After a while they fell in with
an *amarok*.[1] They first discovered the young ones,
but towards evening the mother arrived with a young
buck in her mouth. From their retreat they noticed
her dropping the burden on finding that her young
ones were killed; and then sniffing the air, she followed the scent of human beings, and with a fearful
howl came running on towards them at full speed. The
woman screamed, "I fear she will devour us!" but he
made no other reply than, "Ah, my cousin, my beloved
cousin, I murdered thee!" and he crept forth from his
ambush, aimed at the beast, and killed it on the spot.
They hid themselves again, and soon afterwards saw the
male return, also carrying a buck between his teeth.
After the same words, "Alas, my cousin, my beloved
cousin!" he shot this one also. They still wandered
on and on, and killed everything living they met with
on their way. One day the woman caught sight of
a *kilivfak*,[2] which stood scratching the earth with its

---

[1] Fabulous animal originating in traditions of the wolf.
[2] Another fabulous animal.

feet. When the husband had also seen it, he first
went to look out for a hole in the earth close by, where
he ordered his wife to go and hide, and remain quiet
till he should let himself down to her. He now stole
down to encounter the animal. Whenever it turned to
look round he bent down to the ground; but when it
stood scratching the earth, he crept on towards it. At
last he had got quite close, and ventured a shot at it,
and then hurried back and let himself fall down to his
wife. After him came the wild beast tumbling down
into the cave, where it entirely filled up the opening;
but after much toil they got out again. They continued
roaming further away; and in crossing the glaciers he
carried his wife across the crevasses. At length he again
reached the sea, and at the same time observed a kayaker close by. This man said he would take them to
his own place if he would wait a little while he brought
a boat for them; but the crew of the boat were all men.
They took up with these people; but soon found out
that they had come among *erkileks*.[1] One day Sikutluk
told his wife that he would return and look for some of
their kinsmen, and named a certain time by which they
expected to be back; but in vain they waited for him.
When the appointed time had elapsed, they promised an
angakok a great reward if he could tell what had befallen the traveller. After some meditation he replied,
" I observed he killed a pair of amaroks with their
brood." The wife acknowledged it. " And a female
kilivfak besides?" " Indeed he did so." " Then be
assured the male beast devoured him." But the wife
of Sikutluk lived on with the foreigners until the time
of her death.

[1] Fabulous inlanders.

## 28.

## THE GIRL WHO FLED TO THE INLANDERS.

[The details of this legend are somewhat defective, owing to the imperfect state of the manuscripts from which it was compiled. The tradition itself is widely spread over Greenland, but does not appear to be known any more perfectly by the relators themselves, and is perhaps gradually passing into oblivion. It is probably one of the oldest, and certainly one of the most remarkable, as pointing out the relations between the Eskimo and the Indians, and gives us several hints with regard to the customs of the latter, such as their dancing and their modes of disguising themselves.]

THERE was once a young maiden who happened to break her elder sister's needle, which was made of reindeer-horn and was very precious. The sister got dreadfully angry with her, although she lived in great prosperity, being well married. So angry was she, that she told her sister she might as well take herself off, and henceforth keep away from the coast-people. The girl at once obeyed, and wandered about the country for many a day. One night when she was sitting down on a stone crying, she heard a voice beside her saying, "Why dost thou cry thus?" and turning round, she saw a very tall man, whom she recognised to be an inlander (viz., fabulous people), standing beside her. Again he repeated, "For what art thou crying?" "Because I broke my sister's needle, and she sent me away." "And I was sent away in the same manner because I spoiled my brother's precious snare." Then he asked her to follow him, and they went away together to his house, where he made her a present of deer-skins, some for outer garments and some for inner clothes, and he took her for his wife. This inlander used to go and catch eider-ducks in a certain lake, by wading out in

the water and taking the birds by stealth.   One day he
proposed that she should accompany him on a visit to
his relatives, and told her that when they came in sight
of the house he would call out, "*Kung, kung-kuyo!* and
they will know me at once," he said.   They went; and
as soon as from one of the hill-tops they could make
out the house of his relatives in the valley, he made the
sign, and they heard the children of the place calling
out, "Somebody is saying, 'Kung, kung;'" and they
saw his mother appearing in the doorway repeating the
same words.   They now descended, and entered the
house.   He had a sister who was an idiot (considered as
a clairvoyant), and very talkative.   He told her not to
mention that a coast-woman had come among them,
and he went to hide his wife in some remote corner of
the broad ledge; but when his brothers came in they at
once remarked, "There is a smell of coast-people about
the place!" and when the fool went outside, she could
not forbear saying to his neighbours, "Ye haven't got a
sister-in-law like mine, with beads and necklace—a real
nice one—one of the coast-women!"   After this the
inquisitive people thronged about the window to get a
peep at the stranger.   Some crept up on the roof and
made themselves a peep-hole there, and in no time the
house was quite full.   Subsequently there was some talk
of a boat that was shortly expected, and one morning it
was announced to be coming.  She knew them to be inuarutligaks.[1]  On coming up from the beach, they stopped
outside the house and commenced singing to one another,
and then brought forth gifts of skins, and stayed with
them a whole month, enjoying each other's company
very much, feasting a great deal, and singing songs continually.   At one of their banquets an inlander stood
forth, and, by way of entertaining the assembly, he sang
and danced.   During the dance he transformed himself
into a reindeer; but at this trick the children of the inu-

---

[1] Fabulous dwarf inlanders or mountain-elves.

arutligaks got dreadfully frightened, so that he again quickly changed himself into a man. Another, in his turn to divert the company, took upon himself the shape of a hare ; but the inlanders' children cried out aloud, and he hastened to re-change himself as fast as possible. One inlander, when he danced, pulled the skin from off his whole body till it only adhered to a small portion between his eyes ; but when the urchins cried, he soon put it all right again. At last one of the inuarutligaks came forth to dance, and he danced in such a way that the whole house soon leaned over, and all the inmates rolled down to one side with such force that one woman and a child were crushed to death. The entertainment now ended, and the next day the inuarutligaks departed, after having first invited their late hosts to visit them. In a month's time they made preparations to start, and they had a boat made of stone for the purpose. They agreed that the coast-woman might as well be of the party, but told her not to open her eyes during the voyage, saying that the boat would not move on if she did so. She complied ; but as soon as the crew could make out the sound of children's voices, they permitted her to open them again, and she perceived a very little house, and wondered how they should all get room in it. While, however, she was looking at it, it seemed to grow bigger—the inuarutligaks knew how to enlarge their houses by means of rubbing them. They now went inside, bringing their bundles of skin, one for each person, with them, and then commenced their feasting and merry-making. One of the inuarutligaks stepped forward, and after having performed a dance, flung himself down on the ground transformed into an *orsughiak-stone* (viz., a sort of white, glistering felspar). The inlanders tried to lift it, but being quite unable, he soon rose up in his proper shape. One of the inlanders now advanced, fell to the ground, and was transformed into a common stone ; but the inuarutligaks managed to lift

it, and flung it against the door, where it flew to pieces.
In this manner the inlanders lost one of their people,
and they left on the following day. In the summer-
time preparations were made for reindeer-hunting, and
the coast-woman was to accompany them. She had
two girls for her enemies because she married so early,
and they were always molesting her, and trying to
make her ridiculous. They said that she was not so
smart and lightfooted on the march as the inlanders;
and one of them added, "To-day I even pursued and
overtook a young deer!" On hearing this, the old woman of the house produced a pair of boots, which she
filled with all kinds of vermin, and ordering her to put
them on, she tightened them round her legs, the husband
encouraging her, saying, "She must needs bear it in order
to get agile and smart." But presently she fell into a
swoon, and the skin dropped off her feet and legs. When
she was restored to her senses, she perceived new flesh
and new skin to be growing on them, and she had now
become swift and nimble as the inlanders themselves.
On their return from the reindeer-hunt she said she
longed for her relatives, and was desirous to go and see
them; and the next summer her husband accompanied
her thither. Approaching the coast-side, they saw a
kayaker, whom they hailed, and asked to bring a boat
to take them the remainder of the way. On getting into
it the inlander was dreadfully afraid, and fell down flat
on his face at the bottom of the boat, where he remained
till he landed close to their home. They stayed that
winter at her parents, and once her father said, "I wish
I could have got another son-in-law instead of this one
—one who knew how to trap eider-ducks." The inlander had a habit of stopping in the house all day, but
at these words he only asked a trap of him; and one
day he returned all covered with ducks. The other men
of the place in the winter-time often used to ridicule
him, and always wanted to persuade him to accompany

them out on the ice for the *mowpok*-hunt (cor. sp. **mau-poᴋ**, seal-hunt, by watching the breathing-holes). In the summer he resolved to visit his countrymen, and on parting said to his wife, " If I find our son in health, I will return with more companions." He now set off, and did not return till next spring, and then reported that their son had died. He told his wife that it was now his intention to return to his own people ; and when he left they never saw any more of him.

## 29.

## THE ORPHANS.

AT a well-peopled settlement there lived an old couple, with an only son and a younger daughter ; but the parents died before they were grown up. They, however, soon got foster-parents, but these did not love them—they were always scolded, and left to seek their food on the beach at low-water. One spring, when the people were going to start on their summer travels, they put the children into an empty house, with a small portion of food, closed the entrance with large stones, and then left them. When the poor orphans were wellnigh starving, they rummaged about the empty room to find something to allay their hunger, and fell to eating all the old leavings they could get hold of. When these were finished, the sister found an instrument for boring. As they could not reach the ceiling, they heaped up stones to stand upon, and in this way managed to make a hole in the roof to creep through. The brother first helped his sister to escape, and then got out himself. Outside they could see tents standing in rows on the islets, they being themselves on the mainland ; by

the smoke they observed, they knew them to be cooking
all the day, and they could see the kayakers pursuing
the seals.  Being hungry, they went to the place where
the seals used to be stripped and cut up in the winter,
hoping to find some old bits to eat, and they were fortunate enough to find the head of a small thong-seal.
When they had eaten a part of it, the sister stripped off
the skin, prepared it, and said to the brother, "I am
going to make a disguise for thee; dost not thou remember the magic song our mother taught us?"  "Indeed I do; and I even remember one for raising a storm.
Make haste and get ready the skin."  She rubbed it
hard, at the same time singing over it, and all the while
it grew larger and larger.  He tried it on, but found that
it only touched his knees.  She rubbed still more, and
at last he could wrap himself quite up in it.  The sister
fastened it on him, saying, "There, thou lookest just like
a young thong-seal; now try the water,"—and he went
to the beach.  He leapt down, while she remained singing the magic lay, and saying, "Now dive down!"
When he reappeared on the surface she said, "Thou
art looking like a little dovekie (see p. 201); I will
sing again:" and when he again appeared, she said,
"Well, now, thou art quite like a thong-seal; come!"
When he rose the next morning and came outside, it was
fine weather and quite calm; and seeing that no kayaker
from the islets had left land, he took a fancy to play the
seal.  He put on his disguise and leapt into the sea.
No sooner was he observed from the tents than they
called out, "There is a young seal; let us be off and
chase it!"  There was plenty of joking, and a great
bustle, and the men got their kayaks down into the sea
in a great hurry.  In the meantime he dived, but as he
could not keep his breath all the time, he rose to the
surface behind one of the kayakers, and took breath
without being observed.  In the hurry of the moment,
some of the men had forgotten to put on their kayak-

jackets, though they were rather far out at sea.   These
the disguised boy had picked out to wreak his vengeance
on.   He sang the lay for raising the wind, and all of a
sudden a gale began to blow.   The hunters hastened
to put back and reach home; but those who were not
in proper trim had their kayaks filled with water, and
perished.   When the brother came on shore, he said to
his sister, " I believe we may safely venture to let them
see we are still alive.   Now they have lost some of their
people, we may probably be of some use to them, and
may be they will fetch us off;" and they proceeded to
make signs to attract attention.   As soon as they were
observed by the people on the opposite islands, these
said to one another, " Let us get them over ; we are in
want of people."   A boat was soon despatched; and after
a while the orphans recovered.   Later on in the summer
they were taken into a boat's crew as rowers, and went
up a firth for a deer-hunting station ; but their master
was not kind to them, and when he had got his first
buck, he gave the boy the knee-pan, and said, " Until
thou hast swallowed that, thou shalt have nothing else
to eat."   He was almost choked with it, but at last
managed to make it go down, and then had his meal ;
but he never forgot the knee-pan.   When the deer-
hunting was at an end in the autumn, some people were
leaving for the north, and the orphans were among their
party, and thus left their former masters.   They were
not yet quite grown up ; but they went on practising
all manner of hard exercise, in order to increase their
strength.   In this they both succeeded ; and the brother
turned out to be an excellent seal-hunter besides.   Some
years afterwards, they travelled back to the south, and
again came across the man who had made him swallow
the knee-pan, but he had now grown quite old.   Game
was scarce in the middle of winter, but the young
man still went out and tried his luck.   One day he
brought home a large thong-seal, and ordered the sister

to boil down the blubber into train-oil. This done, he invited all their neighbours; and when the meal was served up, he addressed the old man, saying, "I would like to know whether it be easier to swallow a knee-pan or to drink boiling-hot oil? Just thou try, or otherwise thou wilt have no supper." The old man hesitated, but drank it off at last; but his throat got scalded, and he died in the act of drinking. The young man was thus appeased, and left the place on the first thaw.

NOTE.—There is a story of some other orphans, that they were left help-less and destitute at the winter-quarters when all the rest of the people went deer-hunting; but when they were at the point of starving, they heard a noise on the roof of the doorway, and on looking out to see what it was, they found a ptarmigan. The next day came a small seal, and when that was finished, a large saddleback seal. Of other orphans it is told that the eldest, a boy, died of starvatiom; but that the girl, left alone, one day happened to see some kayakers hallo-hunting (viz., by driving the seals). When they had finished, one of them brought her a little seal; and when they again put out to sea, she observed them all turning into gulls and fly-ing away. When she had returned, and lay all alone in the house, a queer little woman brought her a fire that could never be extinguished. Of an-other orphan the legend is, that he taught himself to walk on the surface of the ocean.

-----

## 30.

## THE GIRL WHO WENT AWAY IN SEARCH OF HER BROTHER.

[From two rather defective copies.]

ALEKATOKAK went away with her brother Asu-vina, to set up fox-traps. Having arrived at the place they had fixed upon, she told her brother that she wanted a flat stone to make a door for the trap, and asked him to bring her one. He went to get it; but as he was rather long in returning, she went off to seek him : but in vain ; he had completely disappeared ; and she was obliged to return by herself. On her coming home, her father said, " I suppose thou hast hurt him— perhaps even killed him : I shall be sure to punish thee." He had often threatened to make away with her, having never liked her, but put her down as an idle wench, unable to make herself useful in any way. Her mother pitied her, and advised her to flee the society of men ; and accordingly she made up a little bag with some clothes, and went far into the country. She kept wandering about, and could even overtake the rein- deer. Having once passed a cleft in the mountains, she saw a little house down in a valley, with an opening in the centre of the roof. She approached the house, and peeping down observed a giant-like fellow, who returned the look, and addressed her, saying, " What dost thou want here, thou miserable daughter of the coast - people ? Dost thou think that I will let thee off like that ? " He then rushed out to seize her ; but meanwhile she had found a hiding-place ; and when he had returned to his house, she again hastened on her way farther into the country ; and at last she came to another house, which had three windows. She noticed that cooking was going on inside, as well as other business, without any people being visible. Though not aware of it, she had been coming all the way to the place of *shadows*. A voice was heard saying, " Thou little one from the coast-side, come in, come in ! " and when she had entered, a dish with boiled meat was set before her ; and her hunger being stilled, the invisible shadows among whom she now found herself invited her to stay and sleep there. After farther wanderings, she at length reached the sea ; and around a little creek she observed a great many tents pitched up near the strand. She waited till evening before venturing to go down ; and sitting on a slope, she heard the children of

the place call out, " A kayaker is coming ! he is towing
a seal ! " Presently a kayaker appeared from behind a
point. She heard them repeat, " Asuvina has got a
seal ! " and she felt sure that she had found her lost
brother. The people of the place had a chief, whose
tent was larger than all the rest ; and beyond this was
a plain, where they used to practise ball-playing. She
recognised her brother accompanying the men thither,
and saw that he was ordered to lift up a large round
stone ; but not being able to do so, the others threw him
down. In the evening she descended the hill, and
went straight on to his house. He wondered very much
at her coming, and told her that he had lost his way in
seeking the slab for her fox-trap, but that he was now
married, and that his wife had a sister. He went on to
tell her that they had an idiot at the place, who—viz.,
by clairvoyance—would probably soon be aware of her
arrival; and that she had better hide herself a while
behind the skin-hangings of the wall. Next morning
the fool entered, saying, " In the night I dreamt that a
woman from the coast-side, and sister to Asuvina, came
among us ; " but Asuvina answered, " I have got no
sister," upon which the other went away ; but Asuvina
stayed at home the whole day long, enjoying his sister's
company. In the evening she went with them to the
ball-play on the plain, disguised in the clothes of her
sister-in-law. When the chief had lifted the round
stone, he made a false hit, and let it fall down upon
his own feet, and fairly crushed them. Alekatokak now
told them quickly to fetch a little dog ; but on hearing
that they had not got one in the whole place, she hurried
away and soon overtook and brought back a young deer.
She cut an opening into it, and let the chief put the sore
feet down among the entrails, and in this way cured
him. She got married there, and had a son. At his
birth they brought her an oblong dish with certain
entrails of a fox, and ordered her to swallow them,

shutting her eyes the while. This was the custom with them, when they desired the new-born child to be clever and dexterous. After this remedy she was at once restored to her usual health, and her boy grew to be a very swift runner; and they remained in the place and had numerous descendants.

## 31.

## THE DOG.

[This tale is taken from a single manuscript.]

AN old married couple had two sons and a little daughter. The sons were renowned for strength, and for being able hunters. They used to return with their seals towing in a long line behind them. But one day they did not return. While the parents were still expecting them, a man brought the sad news that he had seen them both hanging on an inaccessible rock. They were hung up by the feet, head downwards, and nobody could get at them to save them. This deed had been done by the inlanders. While the old parents were in deep affliction for their loss, they heard that some of their neighbours had a dog with a great many whelps. The mother sent the daughter away to fetch one, which she adopted, and had it always on the ledge beside her, nursing it with her own milk. In the winter, she noticed that the dog (being endowed with magic power) sometimes went on scratching his face, and at the same time always commencing to speak, and asking, " What do I look like now?" Towards the end of the winter they were in great want, having lost their protectors. The dog then said he was going for a walk into the country. One night he roused his foster-mother, and having given himself a scratching, inquired, "Am I still good-looking? I shall be off to-morrow." The reason for thus scratching itself was *to frighten people to death* (viz., by charm). He came upon the inlanders while they were busy conjuring spirits. The angakok soon foretold his coming, and cried, "Fire! fire!" but the dog scratched his face, and rushed into the passage, hiding itself there. When the people came out, bringing lights with them, the dog frightened them to death on the spot. Next he set off in search of their storehouse, and carried some victuals back to his foster-parents, and showed them the place where they could find the rest. But from that time upwards the woman began to fear him; and in the spring, when the boat was loaded and ready for starting, she asked the dog to go back to the house and bring her something she had forgotten. As soon as it had disappeared to obey her orders, they pushed off from land, and set out on their journey. But the dog went on following along the shore until they gained the last point, from which it could follow them no longer. There it remained whining and howling. It is supposed that this is the origin of the present custom with the dogs to follow the departing boat along the coast, and go on howling at them from the last point of land.

---

## 32.

## THE WIDOW'S VENGEANCE.

[From one of the older manuscripts.]

THERE was a widow with a son named Kujanguak; beyond her house was another one, inhabited by a number of brothers, all clever at their profession, and well off. Whenever they had brought home any seals, the widow, according to the custom, would send her son to get a *tamorasak* (viz., little bit of blubber); but the men generally replied, "Thou lazy beggar, thou never assisted us in providing anything; so thou wilt not get anything neither." On his returning with this answer, his mother only said, "Never mind—just let them talk." One day they caught a *mamartok* (viz., a delicious kind of seal—one that has shed hair). The mother now took a stronger fancy than ever for a little morsel, and sent her son for it; but he was treated as usual: the men took a bit of whatever they could lay hand on, and flung it at him. When he came back and gave their message to his mother, she was in a great rage; and taking one of her boots, seated herself in a corner of the ledge to practise some charm. On the following morning, when her son looked into the pot, there was an eider-duck in it. The mother merely remarked, "Just take it." Part of it she boiled, and the rest was put by for future use. In the evening she repeated her charms and spells, and a small seal was found in the water-tub. The third day, the son, to his great surprise, saw standing on the floor a completely furnished kayak; the mother took him down to the beach, and made him practise paddling, as well as upsetting and again righting, till he had got quite expert at these things. The following day she let him go out again, and pointing to an iceberg, told him to round it in his kayak. He pushed off at her bidding, and when he was out of sight, she returned to the house. The neighbours likewise set off, and saw Kujanguak attacking a bear, which at last took refuge on an iceberg. The eldest of the brothers tried to climb it, but was not able. After him Kujanguak made the attempt; and having first asked the other to take care of his kayak, he clutched hold of the ice, and scrambled up. At the very top he encountered the bear, and immediately fell upon it; and taking hold of it by the neck,

flung it down into the sea, stone-dead.  The youngest of
the brothers, Sanak, cried out, " I have got a bear!" but
Kujanguak quietly descended, got into his kayak, fastened his towing-line to the bear, and paddled home,
followed by the other kayakers, who had given him their
assistance.  The mother now went down to the beach,
accompanied by the sister of the brothers.  While they
were busy dragging the bear up to the house, the mother
mockingly observed, turning to her, " Who knows how
nourishing that flesh may be!" adding, " Now haul it
up the rest of the way thyself; I am going to fetch
water."  Having finished this task, however, she returned to the bear, and now divided it into two equal
parts, of which she gave her companion one, saying,
" The skin thou mayst keep for a ledge-cover."  She
then boiled the flesh, and invited the whole party tó
partake of it.  The other woman she asked to sit down
on the main ledge; and when she had served the meal
up she remarked, " It is a pity one cannot make sure
whether there is any nourishment about this game of
Kujanguak's."  The woman visitor said, " I have been
longing ever so much for bear's meat lately."  They all
ate well; and on taking leave the female visitor thanked
her saying, that she had altogether found it a delicious
and hearty feed.  The following day Kujanguak again
set off to the iceberg, and got a large seal.  When he
was returning towing it homewards, he chanced to encounter the brothers.  Happily his mother had advised
him beforehand, " If ever they venture to persecute thee,
take some water out of the sea with thy left hand, and
moisten thy lips with it."  Kujanguak tried this as soon
as they all came rushing in upon him.  The eldest brother began the attack by catching hold of the kayak
point, doing his utmost to upset it; but no sooner had
Kujanguak tasted the water with his lips than the other
let it go.  Sanak now said, "Look at the foaming breakers
there! let us try which of us can first get beyond them;"

and all of them pushed on as fast as possible.  Kujanguak, who had a seal on his line, was first obliged to
tighten it ; but this done, he pushed on like a shot, and
soon came up with the eldest brother, ahead of the
others ; and while they rowed outside of the breakers,
Kujanguak went right across them, carried along by the
surf.  When the waves retreated, he jumped out upon
the rocks ; and when the breakers came rolling on again,
he hastened back into the kayak.  On the way home the
brothers secretly consulted to surround him ; however,
he made his escape from them.  Meanwhile his mother
suddenly missed a certain lock of hair, and knowing this
to be a bad omen for her son, was very anxious about him,
until it shortly afterwards proved to be in its proper
place on her forehead.  Reassured with regard to her
son, she now mounted the hills to look out for his return.
On landing he was received on the beach by her along
with the other woman, who asked him how her brothers
had fared.  He answered her, " I wonder thou carest to
bother thyself about those stupid fellows ! "  When the
flesh of the seal had been prepared, and the men were
supping upon the briskets, the mother of the many sons
grew envious and resentful because she was not invited
to share the good fare.  On hearing this the widow cut
a piece of the loin, and having pronounced a spell upon
it, carried it to her by way of a present.  When they
sat down to eat it, Sanak was almost suffocated, and
presently his old mother likewise cried for water.  Having got a drink, she recovered ; Sanak, however, expired.  When the widow re-entered the room, the eldest
brother accused her of the deed, saying, " You only fed
them to work their destruction—it is none but thou who
hast killed them ! " and, at the same time, he rose and
rushed against the house-pillars, in order to shake it
down and make it fall over her : but the widow replaced
them quickly.  Again he rose from his seat, and turning towards the widow herself, he quickly snatched off

the two points of her jacket—the one in front as well as the one behind. Little heeding this affront, she now ran out, and told her son that two of their adversaries had now been despatched. In the enjoyment of the happy event, they both bolted across the boat in great glee; however, the mother happened to break her back. When Kujanguak had got her indoors, she took some filth from beneath the place where her dead mother used to put all kinds of dirty refuse, and threw it out at the house of their enemies. This brought sickness upon them, from which all of them died excepting the sister, who turned *kivigtok* (*i.e.*, one who has fled from mankind).

---

## 33.

## A LAMENTABLE STORY.

[From one of the older manuscripts.]

AN old man had taken up his position on the ice watching the breathing-holes of the seals, in order to spear them as they appeared. Meanwhile some little girls were playing on shore in a cleft between some rocks, as usual, carrying their little baby sisters and brothers in the *amowts* (hoods) at their backs. Just as the old man was in the act of spearing a seal, the children happened to give a shout, and the terrified seal at once dived to the bottom. On this the old man got into a great passion, and cried out aloud, "Shut up, mountain-cleft!" and accordingly it closed upon all the playing children, who were not able to escape, but were now buried in a cavern, wide at the bottom, and narrow towards the top.

The babies soon began to cry for thirst, and the girls put their fingers into their mouths to suck at, trying to hush them by telling them, "When mother has finished soling the boots, she will come and suckle thee." At length the mothers came to the spot, and poured water down in the cleft. The water trickled along the walls, and they licked it up, and the mothers could very well see the children, but as it was impossible to get at them, all of them were starved.

## 34.

### UVIKIAK.

[From one of the oldest manuscripts.]

UVIKIAK was travelling to the north, accompanied by one son and two daughters. Whenever he came to a favourable shore, the son kayaked ahead of them, and when the others came up to the spot they had fixed to land upon, he was already standing in waiting. They generally remained on land for the night, and travelled further the next day; in the evening the son roamed ahead, as usual, to await them ashore, but when they landed and looked for him he was not to be seen. They pushed off again, and having doubled a point of land and got into a bay, they saw his lifeless body, standing erect, pierced with sharp weapons beneath his arms, and his eyes covered with some of his entrails. At this sight his father groaned with despair, and left the place to get hold of the murderers. Some way off he observed some tents, and he went and asked, " Have ye seen no travellers pass by this way ? " " To be sure we have: yesterday a boat passed by; they were singing some kind of mock song about a young lad whose eyes had been covered with his entrails, and at which they laughed and scorned him." At this re-

port the father was still more provoked; and always lamenting the lost one, they continued their journey of discovery, making inquiries at several other places, where they always got the same information, that a boat had newly passed by. Uvikiak still travelled on, with his wife and his two daughters, never now coming on shore in the night. At last they again reached some tents, and on making the usual inquiries, got the answer that a boat had lately passed by, the crew of which were singing very sadly about a young man they had killed; and the wrath of the old Uvikiak somewhat subsided at their mild words. They continued their journey for several days without being able to sleep in the night for excitement ; but at length they set foot on the spot where lived the murderers. They put in and landed somewhat at the back of their dwelling-place; and having got the boat on shore, placed it keel upwards, and gathered crowberry plants and grass to cover it up with. Uvikiak's wife betook herself under the boat, while he himself went away with his daughters across the isthmus. They soon heard a noise, and listening on one of the nearest hills, just above the spot where they used to have dancing and other games,—they heard distinctly that one of them was singing about Uvikiak's son. The song being finished, two young men came walking up-hill, flushed with heat and quite undressed. The new-comers at once inquired something about the singers. " It is our master," they answered; "he was just singing about a young man whom we happened to meet with down in the south, and killed—it was mighty amusing !" In a great rage, Uvikiak instantly seized the one of them, and the daughters the other. They soon got the better of both ; and having killed them, put them in exactly the same position as that in which they had seen Uvikiak's son; after which they hid themselves at a little distance. They had not to wait long before they heard a cry of vengeance; but their hiding-place was not discovered ; and they escaped without any harm, and then returned to their home in the south.

## 35.

## THE SUN AND THE MOON.

[This tale, one of the few already mentioned by other authors on Greenland, has been translated from one of the oldest manuscripts.]

A N old married couple remained at home while their children travelled about all the summer. One day the wife was left alone as usual while the husband was out kayaking. On hearing something moving about close by, she hastened to hide beneath her coverlet, and after a little while, when she ventured to peep above it, she saw a little *snow-bunting* (*Plectrophanes nivalis*) hopping about on the floor and chirping, "Another one will soon enter, who is going to tell thee something." In a little while she was alarmed by a still greater noise; and looking up again, she beheld a *kusagtak* (another little bird—the wheat-ear—*Saxicola œnanthe*), likewise hopping on the floor and singing, "Somebody shall soon enter and tell thee something." It left the room, and was soon followed by a raven; but soon after it had gone she heard a sound like the steps of people, and this time she saw a very beautiful woman, who entered. On asking whence she came, the stranger told, "In bygone days we often used to assemble in my home to divert ourselves at different plays and games, and in the evening, when it was all ended, the young girls generally remained out, and the young men used to pursue and court us; but we could never manage to recognise them in the dark. One night I was curious to know the one who had chosen me, and so I went and daubed my hands with soot before I joined the others. When our play had come to an end, I drew my hands along his back, and left him, and was the first who entered the house. The young people came in, one after another undressed, but for some time I observed no marks. Last of all my brother entered, and I saw at once that the back of his white jacket was all besmeared with soot. I took a knife, and sharpened it, and proceeded to cut off my two breasts, and gave him them, saying, ' Since my body seems to please thee, pray take these and eat them.' He now began to speak indecently to me, and courted me more than ever, and while we raced about the room he caught hold of some bad moss and lit it, but I took some that was good, and also lit mine. He ran out, and I ran after him; but suddenly I felt that we were lifted up, and soared high up in the air. When we got more aloft my brother's light was extinguished, but mine remained burning, and I had become a sun. Now I am on my way higher up the skies, that I may give warmth to the orphans (viz., going to make summer)." Finally she said, "Now close thy eyes." The woman turned her eyes downwards; but perceiving that she was about to leave the house, she gave her one look, and observed that at her back she was a mere skeleton. Soon after she had left the house the old husband returned.

NOTE.—Among the rare cases which we have of any Eskimo tradition from the west about Behring Straits, the above legend is reported as known at Point Barrow, and was communicated to John Simpson, surgeon on board the Plover. In this the sister says to the brother, " *Ta-man'g-ma mam-mang-mang-an'g-ma nigh'-e-ro*," which corresponds to the Greenlandish **tamarma mamarmat âma neriuk**, " *My whole person being delicious, eat this also*"—almost the same words as in one of the copies from Greenland.

## 36.

## N I V N I T A K.

[The high esteem in which personal dexterity and strength, combined with
courage and hardihood, have been held by the natives, is pointed
out to us in this curious story, which especially aims at bringing these
qualities to bear against the influence of old age.]

NIVNITAK went away and settled far off to the
north, at a certain place favourably situated for
all kinds of hunting.  He had many grandchildren, who
all grew up to be skilled hunters while he was still in
the prime of life ; but none of them ever came to be a
match for him.  At last they also married in their turn
and begat children before Nivnitak had got one grey hair.
It once happened that the winter set in very severely, with
hard weather every day.  When the sea was getting all
covered with ice, the young people gradually left off
hunting.  Nivnitak, however, was constantly on the
move hunting, alternately on land and on the frozen
sea.  Later on the young men did not even rise from
their couches, but remained at rest on the ledge.  One
evening Nivnitak said, " To-morrow I won't go out
hunting, but I intend to climb the highest mountains to
have a survey of the sea ; " and he departed early on the
following day, and returned late in the evening, saying,
" I climbed the highest, and saw the frost-smoke at different places far out at sea.  No doubt there will be animals to be got there ; to-morrow I shall try."  When
the midnight stars shone brightest he left the house.
He gained the outermost islets at dawn of day, and
when he had quite lost sight of them on his seaward way
the sun rose above the horizon, and then for the first
time he observed the haze hanging above the open
water, which he had plainly seen from the hills the day

before. Meanwhile his house-fellows were anxiously
expecting him ; when all of a sudden a noise was heard,
and soon after he entered the house, pushing a seal on
before him, and saying, " If we are in want of game, I have
found a hole where plenty of seals, large as well as small,
are to be had." But at this speech his children and grandchildren only murmured and sulked a little, and then
asked for a morsel of blubber. The next morning he was
again off at an early hour, and did not return till late
at night, when the same noise was heard; and, covered
with sweat, he again entered the room with a very large
seal. This day the young men had risen, and were sitting on the ledge with their boots on. The following
night, when he again brought in a large seal, he found
them mending their hunting tools ; and on the ensuing
morning some of the ablest among them at length accompanied him ; but because of their slowness he ordered
them not to attack the larger seals. When they had got
at the aperture, Nivnitak roamed about by himself a
little, and detected the marks of a sledge leading right
out to sea. Having examined them closely, he returned
to his younger companions, and soon lanced a couple of
seals. Dragging them along by the tug-line, he now
made for home ; but on the way he fancied that his
grandchildren, each of them having but one seal, were
too slow for him, and prepared to leave them, saying,
" Ye know your way, of course, and can go on by yourselves." Upon which he proceeded on alone, and reached
home much earlier than they. When they were all sitting together in the evening, he observed, " If the weather stands, it is quite a treat to go out hunting ; now ye
may stop at home if ye like : I will take care that we do
not suffer from want of food." On the morrow he left as
usual, but in the evening they expected him back in
vain. Nivnitak remembered the track of the sledge he
had discovered the preceding day ; and having found it,
he followed it across the sea. The mountains of his

own country were lost to his sight, but others appeared ahead of him, and he landed on a foreign coast at the opposite side of the ocean. Here he passed through a valley, and again beheld a sheet of frozen water; and close by he observed a little house, with some poles stuck in the ground beside it. A woman emerged from it, and perceiving a stranger approaching the house by such an unwonted road, she stood hesitating an instant, but then asked him to come inside. On entering the house he saw two young girls sitting close to the wall, and he secretly determined that they should be his future wives. He felt very hungry, and hoped that he should be offered something to eat, but in this he was disappointed. After a while one of the women left the room, but presently returned, saying, "Yonder he is coming!" on which Nivnitak looked out at the window, and saw a man running along the ice at a great rate, tugging two seals after him. Near the beach he disappeared among the loose blocks of ice scattered about there; however, he soon reappeared, bounding along towards the house; but seeing the outer garments of a stranger hung up on the poles he stopped. Nivnitak seated himself, and shortly afterwards the other man entered, seemingly pleased, and smiling at the visitor. Having relieved himself of his clothes, he took a bear-skin from beneath the ledge, and spreading it mid-way on the floor, exclaimed, "When two men meet for the first time they always try to outdo each other; let us have a try." Nivnitak did not hesitate a moment, but having undressed himself sat down on the skin opposite to him, hooked his hand into his adversary's arms, and pulled away with all might, and almost succeeded in mastering him. They then stopped, and the host seated himself on the main bench [ledge] and inquired if the visitor had got anything to eat. He answered "No." "Why, then, make haste and treat him to your best;" on which the women set forth several dishes. Nivnitak now fell eagerly to, and when the host was going to begin the dish was already empty. He now looked at the two girls, who were flensing the seal down on the floor, one cleaning the entrails, and the other blowing them up. In this way they soon finished the task ; and before the seal-flesh was boiled, the entrails had been dried, and the girls were busy making a jacket of them for their father. The host now got more talkative, and said, " I am in want of a companion on my hunting excursions ; we have plenty of good hunting hereabout. Away on the ice is a place where the thong-seals have their breathing-holes." When they were about to retire for the night he added, " If thou wantest a wife, thou art welcome to take one of my daughters." And thus Nivnitak became his son-in-law. Next day the father put on the jacket of seal-entrails from yesterday's hunt ; and they wandered a great distance on the ice together till they reached the apertures made by the seals. The father-in-law then said to Nivnitak, " As thou hast not got my alacrity thou hadst better not catch more than one at a time ; it is as much as I can manage to drag along two of them." Meanwhile he soon caught a couple of them. Nivnitak thought, I should like to do the same. When he had caught the first, and the father-in-law had turned a little aside, he hastened to pull up another, and thus he had two. They now prepared to return, hauling their seals along with them, the host continually observing the sun, and guiding himself by it. After a while he said, " I suppose thou knowest thy way by this time ; I think I will leave thee to follow in my wake." When the father entered the main room he said, " We cannot expect him before late, but still ye must keep a look-out for him." The daughters kept waiting and waiting for him, but he did not come home till late in the night. The father-in-law never spoke to him, but the daughters were delighted to see him, and at once cut up the animals ; but when they were preparing to make the dress, the entrails had shrunk, and got too small; and this was the reason why the father made such haste in returning, that the entrails might not get cold on the way, lest they should shrink and be unfit for use. He was now displeased at having got a son-in-law, who was not as clever as he wished him to be. They went out together all the same next day, with a similar result, and on the way home the father again told him, that as he could not keep up with him, he would go on beforehand. This time, however, Nivnitak was saying to himself, " To-day I should just like to run a race with him." However, he soon lost sight of him, and lost his way besides; but at the same time felt that his burden was getting lighter. He continued running still faster, and turning round he saw that his two seals were swinging round in the air after him. He passed by his host in a great circuit, and was home in good time long before him. His wife instantly prepared the meal; and seeing the blown-up entrails clean and shining, Nivnitak did not doubt that they would make him a nice jacket. He let the meat be kept ready dressed for his father-in-law, and the women had the jacket finished even before his arrival. He put it on at once, and was standing outside mending his tools when the host made his appearance. At first sight he thought that some visitor had arrived during his absence, and not till he had passed the iceberg did he recognise Nivnitak; but on finding it to be him he was very well pleased, and again spoke familiarly to him, saying, " That's right, we will always succeed in the end;" but Nivnitak did not quite understand this speech. Having seated themselves at the meal prepared, he said, " Why, it has been getting quite cold and dry;" and he did not quite like it so; nevertheless he was as gay and talkative as could be. They now went on having the same good luck, and Nivnitak totally forgot his home and his grandchildren, and would not leave his young wives. One day his father-in-law accosted him,

saying, "The moon is now in the crescent, and our
neighbours will be coming to pay us a visit and practice
ball-playing; to-morrow I shall stay at home and make
tools for the games, and we must all be smart and trim
in new dresses." Next day Nivnitak likewise stayed at
home, and his father-in-law brought in six large shoulder-blades of walrus. While preparing them he said,
"When the play has begun, and the ball has been
thrown, we must follow its course, and always be ready
to strike it; if any one throws it wrong we shan't win ;
so thou must mind what thou art about. With this
spoon-like instrument we hit the ball; I shall throw
it to my wife, and she to her daughter, and they will
send it on to thee ; take care that thou dost not make
any mistake, or miss catching it, lest we should be
mocked and scorned." They also remained at home
the next day, and kept looking out at the windows as
well as at the entrance of the house for the expected
guests. At last a great many people appeared passing
round the southern point, and Nivnitak along with his
new relations quickly put on his new clothes and ran
out to meet them on the ice, shouting to them, " Here
we are with our new relative Nivnitak ! Let the play
begin at once ! " The strangers answered with a loud
yell. The ball, consisting of a large seal-skin stuffed
with sand and clay, and fashioned like a real seal, was
now brought out ; and the master of the house determined that Nivnitak, being the most dexterous, should
stand next to the adversaries. He then began the play
by throwing the ball to his wife ; and she running along
beneath it, thrust it to her younger daughter, she in her
turn to her elder sister, and she to her husband. But
when Nivnitak was about to strike it, he thought to himself, " I only wish I may do well." That instant the
ball hit him with its whole force and knocked him down,
so that he was unable to rise. On this the enemies
shouted and yelled in great triumph, and took up the

ball, carrying it towards their dwelling-place. Their opponents, however, pursued them, but without any result; and on turning round the host saw a multitude of people, and not observing Nivnitak among them, he suspected some evil. Hurrying on to his assistance he found him almost dying. Some were filling his clothes with snow, and others were actually trampling on him. He drew him from out the heap; but the enemies left him with great glee and loud halloos. Nivnitak's clothes had been quite spoiled with the snow and the mud, and in this state they got home—the father-in-law sullen and cross. Soon afterwards he said, "It will soon be time for us to pay our neighbours a return visit; get everything ready;" and on departing, Nivnitak looked very nice in his new suit; but the father-in-law once more admonished him, saying, "We must do our utmost to vanquish them, and if thou doest wrong this time, we will have nothing more to do with thee." Nivnitak, however, did not deign to answer him. Having approached the abode of the neighbours, a tumultuous roar was raised to welcome them, as was the custom, and the ball was soon brought down on the ice. They posted themselves in the same way as last time, and began the play according to the former rules. When it was Nivnitak's turn to strike, he gave the ball such a blow that it turned round in the air, and then flew straight forward. It was now the father-in-law's turn to run for it; but Nivnitak had already reached it, and hit it a second time. The adversaries now advanced to give it a stroke; Nivnitak, however, always forestalled them in getting up with it, and sending it higher and higher aloft. Nobody could cope with him, and thus he went on, pursuing the ball until he at length reached home. Their rivals had at last to give in, and retired to their house very much dejected, and Nivnitak's host cried out to them, "To-day ye lost the game, better luck next time!" On the way home he kept

constantly repeating, "That's right, we will always succeed in the end." It was only now that Nivnitak understood what the other had meant by saying so before.
Some time after, Nivnitak began to think of his old relatives whom he had left in poverty and want; and one
day returning from his hunt he said to his wives, "Make
me a suit of tight clothes, jacket, breeches, and boots."
They at once set to work, and when the clothes were
ready he tried them on. They fitted him as if they had
been glued on to his body; and where they were a little
too wide he at once had them altered. He then made
the suit into a bundle, and went to hide it beneath the
boat; and from this time secretly planned to return to
his own country. One night, when the others were
sound asleep, he tried to leap down on the floor; but
on touching the edge of the bench, one of his wives
awoke, and he again went back, and quietly lay down
beside them. For several nights afterwards he repeated
his attempts, but was always obliged to turn in again.

One night he succeeded in getting down without anybody awaking. In order, however, to make quite sure
that they were all fast asleep, he again stepped up on
the ledge. On finding that the noise had awakened no-

body, he jumped down on the floor above the entrance of the room, and gliding out noiselessly, he went and dressed himself in his tight clothes, which had been hidden beneath the boat. Having also put on his outer coat, which was hanging on the poles outside the house, he took hold of his spear, and climbed the low roof of the house, and sallied forth in the opposite direction he wanted to take, making circular tracks in the snow as he went along. After a while he jumped and crossed the little promontory, and got down on the ice, which stretched away as far as his own country. There he again made large round tracks, always leaping from one side to the other, so that his family should not be able to be guided by his footmarks. Proceeding on his way, he at length reached a coast with a steep ascent and high slope, covered with heath. Having once more formed plenty of round circles on the ice, he jumped ashore and climbed an edge of the rock, where he stuffed his outer coat well with moss, and again leaped down. On the ice he built a snow-hut, and placed the stuffed coat inside it, spear in hand, with the back turned outwards, that it might resemble a living man. After this he again went back, and climbed the steep rock, awaiting the arrival of the pursuers. At sunrise several people who had come out in search of him were to be seen on the ice, sometimes single, sometimes making joint efforts to find the track. At last, halting at the snow-house, they approached it cautiously; but no sooner had the foremost detected the figure in the doorway than he thrust his spear straight at it, and Nivnitak heard them call out, "Well, well, we ought to have kept a better watch upon him while he was with us, showing well enough that he was not a real man; but anyhow we have done with him now;" and then they returned, satisfied that they had killed him. When they had quite disappeared, Nivnitak again leapt down the rocks.

The sun was then high in the heavens; but before it had quite set, he reached the shore of his own country, and found his grandchildren, who had totally given him up, prospering and doing well. In the spring-time, when the ice had vanished, he got a fancy to go and see his native place; but having arrived there, he determined

to spend the rest of his days in this place, and did not travel any more. He lived to see his grandchildren's grandchildren, but at length the flesh of his body became all shrivelled and shrunk; and finally, at a very old age, he died.

## 37.

## THE BROTHER WHO WENT TO AKILINEK IN SEARCH OF HIS SISTER.

[In regard to this story, which is very widely known in Greenland, we refer to the introductory sections, where it is pointed out as one of those most probably resting upon a historical basis, representing the invention of dog-sledging, or the teaming and training of some wild animal, from which the present Eskimo dog has descended. Akilinek is now by the Greenlanders considered a fabulous country beyond the sea ; but it may be supposed to have been a real country opposite to the original homesteads of their ancestors.]

AN old man had a son and two daughters.  His son being a first-rate hunter and provider, the father at length gave up kayaking himself.  His son could overtake and outrun every animal on shore; and at sea he was an excellent hand at harpooning.  His eldest sister used to follow him along the shore, where she amused herself by catching partridges in little traps, and generally got a good many.  At a time when the sea was frozen over, they one day went away to the outermost islets.  There the brother saw a fox and set off to pursue it.  After a short absence among the islets, he returned with the fox ; but meanwhile the sister was gone.  He looked for her everywhere, and called out, but she did not come.  At length he detected the trace of a sledge, but as it was growing dark, he had to go home without his sister.  On his return, he grew silent and reserved, but after a while said to his father, "Oh how much I should like to have a sledge !"  The father rather favoured this idea, and at once set about making him one.  The next morning the son set out on foot, but returned at nightfall without having killed anything, and went to sleep without saying a word.  In the morning he asked his father to provide him with some cords, saying that he wanted to fetch home an animal to pull his sledge for him ; and then he went off and stayed away. Towards evening a strange noise was heard, and the little sister went outside to see what it was, but instantly returned in great alarm, exclaiming, " Oh, what dreadful monster is this my dear brother has brought home with him ? " When he entered, the father asked him, " What beast is it thou hast got ? " " Why, it is only a little bear I have caught to drag my sledge ; I hope thou wilt make a harness for it; I want him to be trained shortly." The father complied, and the son left off hunting for a while in order to train the bear; but when he had finished this, he took him along with him on his excursions. Another time he again returned late in the evening quite exhausted, and turned in without speaking a word. The following morning he asked his father for more cords ; but this time they must be still stronger. Having received what he wanted, he went away. In the evening a strange noise was again heard, on which the little sister went outside, but returned quite horrified, saying that it was still more frightful than the last time. When he had entered, and the father questioned him, he answered, " Oh, it's nothing but a little *amarok* (wolf or fabulous animal) I have caught to match the bear." These two, however, could not agree ; and he had often to use his whip to part them when they were going to fight. After training, however, they pulled very well together ; but now he wanted a third one, and having set out for it in the morning, he did not return till late at night, when his parents had long been quite miserable on account of his long absence ; and he went to sleep as before without speaking to any one. The next morning he applied to his father for strings and lashings, but this time none but the very strongest would serve him ; having got them, he went off as usual. In the evening there was a terrible noise outside, for now he had got the bear, the amarok, and an *agshik* (a fabulous monster) fighting each other. At length he had them all tamed and trained; and he once more turned to his father, saying, "All I wish for is a sledge." His father was quite willing, and made him one of very hard wood, with many knots in it. When the sea was frozen over, he went out to try his team, following the coast southwards, and returned towards evening on the same day. When his father questioned him as to how far he had been, he answered: "If thou wert to leave with a boat early in spring, thou wouldst not have reached the place I got at to-day before autumn. In going home we made great speed, but the bear got tired, and I was obliged to take him into the sledge beside me; but the agshik is incapable of tiring, and will be of great use to me." The next day he travelled on in the same manner to the north, returning home at night; and having made some similar remarks, he added, "The agshik, I find, is soon provoked, and goes off in a fury; he will be rather dangerous for strangers to encounter." The ice now covering the sea all over, and not having broken up, although it had been very stormy, he supposed he might trust himself out on it; and the weather again became settled and beautiful. He then spoke to his parents thus: "Don't ye remember the day I wandered out on the ice with my sister and lost her there? Since that day I have sought her far and near all over our country: where can she have gone to? Not even the bones of her corpse did I find; but on the day I lost her, in looking for her, I noticed the marks of a sledge on the ice, leading right to sea. Any other trace of her I have never seen; and therefore I should now like to go across to Akilinek, as I shall certainly not be at rest until I have found her." The parents tried to persuade him to stay, saying, "It does not matter for thy sister, who has been lost to us for such a great length of time; don't go away in search of her as far away as that, but bear in mind thou art now our only provider. Out yonder is a cleft in the ice so wide that thou mayst never cross it." The son then rejoined, " To be sure my animals cannot swim ; the bear only in some degree is capable of that : but if I don't succeed, I shall, of course, return." The parents repeated their warnings, but he got all the more bent upon going, come what might, so that he should only find his sister. When he arrived at the exact spot where he had formerly seen the trace of a sledge, he turned right seawards, and after a while lost sight of the land. The bear now got tired as before, and being only a hindrance, he took it on the sledge. Driving continually straight on, he again came in sight of land, and observed the tracks of many sledges ; and on approaching the shore, he saw them in all directions. He now looked all around him to find out which way he had better turn. In the meantime he had made fast his animals to an iceberg near the strand, and went to shore himself to see if any people were to be found there. He had not walked long before he saw a number of houses, which made him stop and consider ; but after a while he advanced, and having found an entrance, he walked up to a large house and went inside. Having entered and given the inmates a look, he at once recognised his sister sitting down with a baby on her lap. When he had seated himself on the side bench, she also recognised him, and they began to speak to each other, and she said, "On the same day thou left me to pursue thy fox, a man in a sledge happened to pass by ; and in no time I was taken up and carried away to this place, and that is the reason why thou seest me here. I am married, but at present my husband is out as usual. However, I expect him home very soon, and when he comes thou must look at him well." The brother now rejoined, " Since that day I have done nothing but try to find thee out ; all over the country I have travelled in search of thee ; how lucky it is that I

find thee at last ! " Whilst they sat waiting, some one
called out, " There he is coming ! " and looking out at
the window the brother-in-law saw his sister's husband
driving on towards the house with a number of young
reindeer pulling his sledge. Though he sped on at a
good rate, the other thought his own animals still
swifter, and considering himself to be quite a match for
the new-comer, he again seated himself without any
further remark. When the husband entered, he kept
his eyes constantly fixed on the visitor sitting beside his
wife ; and without a word to any one, leaned back on
the ledge after having taken his place upon it, so that
nothing but his heels resting on the edge of it were
visible. The relatives being thus interrupted, left off
speaking for a time ; however, she told her brother that
it was for fear of her husband, who used to speak very
little, she added, being of a shy disposition. On hearing
this he came a little closer to them, and they began to
converse together. The guest spoke of his happiness in
seeing his sister so well off, and said, that seeing she had
such a good provider, he would not trouble himself any
more about her in future ; and further, he proposed that
they should come and visit him and his parents on the
opposite shore. But his brother-in-law did not fancy
this much : he gave as a pretext that the cold would be
too severe for the children. Both now wanted to persuade him to stay, but he said he must needs go and
look after his animals, without mention of what kind
they were. His relatives gave him some of the children's clothes for a gift to the parents : he put them on
his shoulders, went to his sledge, and departed. When
he had got so far that he had lost sight of the land, the
bear again got tired, and was taken in beside him. On
his return, his parents rejoiced greatly at seeing the
clothes of their daughter's little children, and on hearing
that their long-missed daughter was coming to visit
them. One day during fine weather, when they were

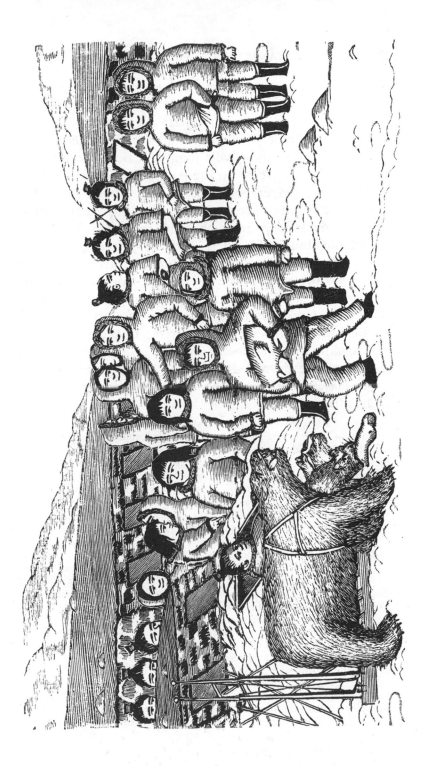

anxiously expecting them, sledges were seen coming across the ice, which made them all very happy, and the little sister, who was of a merry temper, was hardly able to contain her joy. When her sister's sledge had come still closer, she gave a jump and bounded over the boat, which was put up on the boat-pillars. But all of a sudden the sledgers were seen to put about—probably they took fright at seeing her brother's animals and at the girl indulging in such wild pranks. They now called out loudly for them, and the parents were very much distressed and wept together. This sight made the son take pity on the old people, and to punish the fugitives he let loose the agshik, being the most furious of the lot, to pursue them. In a moment the sledgers as well as the agshik disappeared ; but on his return the agshik was all bloody around the muzzle. In all likelihood he devoured them all. The brother did not go in search of them, as he did not expect any of them to be alive.

NOTE.—The tale here given is nearly literally translated from one manuscript; besides which three copies have been received, and one verbal narration has been written down by the author himself. The latter, comprising the most frequent variations of the tale, substitutes a cousin in the place of the brother. When he had turned mute and sorrowful on account of his having lost a dear companion, his father spoke to him saying, "At the neighbouring hamlet to the north of us, there are several old people, and old people generally are rich in stories; go to them for the purpose of cheering thy mind." One morning the son at length took a fancy to go and visit these old folks ; and on his arrival there, one old man told him how in the days of his youth, when he had been roaming about in quest of sport and excitement, he had once on the brink of a rock happened to discover a *kukissook* (fabulous animal with great fangs) with its young ones. While he was gazing at these awful beasts, a little sparrow happened to pass by, flying over their heads. At the same moment the old animal, which had till then been couchant, bounded into the air, snatching the body of the sparrow so that the wings fell to the ground separately, at the sight of which the man had been struck with terror, and fled the spot for ever. The visitor on hearing this asked exact information about the locality of the place, and having returned to his father, made ready for an excursion, upon which he captured a kukissook. The remaining part of the story agrees with the version given. But when the cousin with her husband and child comes to visit their relatives, instead of being frightened and turning back, they decided to stay with them ; but the brother-in-law from Akilinek did not dare to step outside the house for fear of the sledge animals, and being too tall for the ledge, he was obliged to lie on the floor. At length he grew tired and ventured outside, whereupon the cousin of his wife set the kukissook upon him, causing him to be torn to pieces. He then also went on to kill the child, saying it was of no real human descent, and might grow like its father. The two cousins then adopted their former mode of life, roaming about their home together, where their bones are now resting. The illustration accompanying the text refers to one of the written variations of the story.

---

## 38.

## USSUNGUSSAK OR SAVNIMERSOK.

[This tale, taken from two of the older manuscripts, is given here on account of its apparent mythological reference ; otherwise it will be found to be somewhat fragmentary and obscure.]

A NUMBER of people once lived together in a large house. Among them was a man named Ussungussak, who generally came home empty-handed, when all the others returned with what they had caught, for which his wife used to scold him. One night she had gone on rating him worse than usual, and in the morning he had disappeared. He kayaked along shore, and having rounded a point he saw a man standing on the beach. At first he was frightened ; but then he thought a little, and finally concluded, "Why should I be afraid at the very moment I have resolved to go and lead a solitary life all by myself?" When the man on shore called him, he alternately approached and again turned back ; but when he had come pretty close to the beach, the other threw out a trap, by which he drew him in, and ordered him to follow to the inland. They now wandered along together and came to the gulf of the earth. There, poor Ussungussak began to whine and howl; but the inlander put a cord round his neck, straining it so hard that he was nearly choked; when he again untied him, however, they had safely passed the fearful precipice. Having next crossed a beautiful meadow, they gained the house of the inlander, who had a wife but no children. In the morning Ussungussak was ordered to remain at home, while the master of the house went away himself, and returned very noisily in the evening with what he had taken. In this way several days went by; but at length Ussungussak got desirous to see his own home, and the inlander accompanied him on the way. This time they did not see the precipice; but arriving at the coast they saw a great many killed seals on the beach, being those which the inlander, standing on shore, had caught in his trap. When Ussungussak was about to take leave, the inlander said, " Henceforth thou canst take some of these seals, but mind, thou art not to be too greedy: thou mayst take one at a time to begin with; afterwards thou mayst take two." Ussungussak then returned to his homestead and housemates, who were having good hunting at the time. The next day he again disappeared, but in the evening returned with two seals. The following day he brought home three; the others asked him whereabouts he had got them. He answered, " Out at the most seaward place;" and they demanded of him whether they might not accompany him thither. But when he had carried away the very last of the lot, he one night returned without anything at all, and was again scolded by his wife. The day after he left as before, and kayaking along shore he at length turned a point, and again beheld the inlander. This time he willingly approached him when he was called, and went along with him; but when they had gained the precipice, he did not get over this time, but was fairly strangled. When Ussungussak's relations and housemates had been expecting him in vain for five days, one of the kayakers went out in search of him. He encountered the inlander, and asked him whether he had not seen a man. " To be sure I have, and I killed him myself!" At this the other thrust his harpoon at him, and he ran on with the hunting-bladder dragging behind him, and thus disappeared. The coastman now took his spear and bladder-arrow, following him swiftly,

and found him drawing out the point; but he now lanced another spear at him, while the inlander kept running on so fast that the bladder flew up high in the air. Finally, he flung his arrow at him, and this at last did for him, and he expired; upon which the pursuer cut him up, and put his knee on the nape of his neck.

## 39.

## THE CHILD-MONSTER.

AMONGST a number of people who lived in the same house, one woman was in the act of child-birth, when all of a sudden the midwife attending her cried out in great dismay, " Ah, it is a monster, with great big teeth ; it is tearing my arm! " As she spoke, all the inmates fled away to the boat, which was turned keel upwards, and to the top of a great rock ; only two boys with their sister could find no room there, and they therefore hurried out to the pro-vision - house. Meantime the monster appeared, drag-ging along his own mother, her hair all loose and flying about her, and it soon turned upon those on the boat. Not being able itself to climb, it ate away the pillars beneath, so that, when they gave way, all the people came tumbling down, and were devoured. It next came to the rock, and those who had taken refuge on it pushed and knocked against each other for horror, till all but one lost their footing, and came down heads over heels. The monster now ordered the rock to upset, and the very last of them was made away with. When these were all killed, the beast turned against the provision-house, but stopping, entered the main house instead ; this process was repeated several times, and it always remained inside a little longer each time. During the last interval the children fled out of sight, and went far into the country, until they came in sight of a house. They went in and told their story and the cause of their flight, and stayed there for the night. Most of the inmates had gone to sleep ; the sister, however, did not dare to do so, and kept awake. At midnight she heard some one saying, " They have probably themselves put their housemates to death, though they tell us a different story. The safest thing will be to have them killed in the morning." At this speech she got greatly alarmed, and when the others had gone off to sleep, she roused her brothers, and once more they fled on and reached another house, where they met the very same fate. But when they made their escape from this place the second night, the sister took one of her brother's boots and thrust it several times against the house-door, at the same time pronouncing a spell, that the people within might all perish. Pursuing their way, they fell in with a man of extraordinary size, carrying one half of a reindeer on his shoulders. The sister said to the youngest brother, " Go and try to make him understand why we have come here;" and she told him how to put his words. When the boy had finished, the big man took them along with him to his own house, the interior of which was nicely furnished and hung with reindeer-skins all along the walls. There they remained, and made a meal upon some dry meat. This done, the girl said to her brothers, " Reindeer-meat is good eating, no doubt; but what would make it eat .still better ? "— " Mixing it up with some nice partridges, to be sure."— " So thou must make haste and go out and get some." Off they went ; a flapping of wings was presently heard, and lots of birds were brought into the house. While they were busy eating them, the sister repeated, " Partridges are very nice, sure enough ; but what would make them eat still better? "—" Mixing them up with some nice hares, to be sure !"—&c. ; and so they went out and caught a great many hares. The sister once more repeated what she had said, mentioning all kinds of game and fowls, and at last she said, " Young *serdlernaks* (fabulous birds) are exceedingly nice, but the large ones,—oh, be quick, be quick !" But the huge man said, " I never hunted that fowl without some misgivings ; when she is hatching her eggs on the lee side of yonder point, and catches the seals, she is rather dangerous." Still, they all ran out to have a look at it ; but seeing it perched on its rock, and sometimes rising to snatch at them, they were afraid, and again retired ; only the younger brother remained, and was torn asunder by it. Then the sister shouted, " It is now time for me to interfere ; " upon which they all ran out together ; she quickly pulled out her boot, struck at the bird with it, and killed it on the spot. She now cut it up, and found its pouch filled with seal-bones, among which she likewise found those of her brother. When these had all been singled out, she carried them with her. While she was yet on the way, she felt them move ; and when they got close to the house she put them down, and the brother quickly revived, seemingly quite unhurt, and they all of them reached home safely.

NOTE.—We find several stories treating of this same subject, generally representing the monster as the revenger of some act of atrocity or misbehaviour and injustice. In one of them the monster at first is an imbecile child, called Tungavik, neglected and ill-treated by its housemates, till all of a sudden, having been mute before, it acquired the faculty of speech, and set to eating its mother's breast, afterwards devouring both its parents and all its housemates, excepting two orphan children, who had shown kindness towards it.

---

## 40.

## THE KIVIGTOK.

[This story, taken from an old manuscript, is only a sample of the many narratives treating about this very popular subject, which will be found more or less intermixed in various other tales of this collection.]

THERE was once a man who had several sons ; of these, the second son turned *kivigtok* (viz., fled the society of mankind). This happened in the wintertime ; but next summer the father, as well as his other

sons, went away from home in order to search for the
fugitive. In this manner summer went by and winter
came round, but still they had not found him. When
summer was again approaching, they made all preparations for another search, this time to other places, along
another firth. Late in autumn they at length chanced
to find out his solitary abode, in an out-of-the-way
place, after having traversed the country in every direction for ever so long. His habitation was a cave or
hollow in a rock, the inside being covered with reindeer-
skin, and the entrance of which had been carefully
closed up. At the time of their arrival the kivigtok
was still out hunting ; but a little later they saw him
advance towards the place from the inland, dragging a
whole deer along with him. The brothers were lying
in ambush for him; and when he came close to them
they seized hold of him. He recognised them at once,
and gave a loud cry like that of a reindeer, and said,
" Do let me off; I shan't flee." The father now asked
him to return with them, adding, " This is the second
summer in which we have given up our hunt in order to
find thee out, and, now we have succeeded, thou really
must come home with us ;" and he answered, " Yes,
that I will." They remained in the cave during the
night, enjoying each other's company. Next day they
had much to do with the things that had to be taken
back with them, the store-room, besides his dwelling-
place, being filled with dry meat and skins. They
tied up bundles to be taken down one by one to the
tent of his relatives, which was pitched at some distance
near the firth by which they were to travel home.
When they were about to set off with the first loads,
they wanted him to follow them ; he excused himself,
however, saying, " When ye go down the last time I
shall follow ; but I must stay and take care of these
things." They went without him ; but on their return
the kivigtok had disappeared, and taken the remainder

of the provisions with him, and the brothers grew exceedingly vexed with themselves, that they had thus
relied on his word, without leaving any one in charge of
him. But all too late. Some time afterwards, when
they had gone out again to look for him, he terrified
them by yelling and howling at them from the summit
of a steep and altogether inaccessible rock. How he
had got there they could not make out, but finding it
impossible to follow him, they were obliged to give him
up for lost.

----

## 41.

### THE WOMAN WHO GOT CONNECTED WITH THE INGNERSUIT[1] OR UNDER-WORLD PEOPLE.

IT once happened that two men went out deer-hunting,
accompanied by a woman. On the way they scolded
her, at which she got vexed, and tied up her boots in
order to remain behind. They waited a while for her,
but at length went along without her, and soon lost
sight of her, as she had purposely hidden herself behind
some large heaps of stones. She heard them seeking
for her close beside her hiding-place, and lamenting
their loss ; but nevertheless she remained quiet until
they were gone. When she was thus left alone she
crept forth and went off in an opposite direction. After
some time she came to a *gull's mound*, and observed a
man coming out from it ; she tried to escape, but he
seized hold of her, and asked her to follow him to his
dwelling-place in the gull's-hill, as he wished to marry

[1] Cor. sp. **ingnerssuit**, plur. of **ingnerssuak**, signifying a sort of elves
or spirits, having their abodes in the rocks along the sea.

her. She followed him reluctantly; but when he opened it to her, she noticed that it was covered with reindeer-skins on the walls, and on the whole looked quite comfortable. She now left off crying, entered the hill, and became his wife, and in due time she bore him a child, whom the father wanted to be named Imitlungnarsunguak. The wife, however, remonstrated, saying, "That she had not got any relatives of that name;" but the husband answered her, "It did not matter; he would take care to make a great huntsman of him,"—and then she let him call the boy as he liked. When he grew on, and his mother had spent a good many winters in this place, she longed for her former home, and wished to return. The husband merely answered her, "I claim his first catch, mind!" and then she left him along with her son, and went back to her old relatives and house-mates, and once more lived with them. When the other children played with her son, she used to tell them not to do him any harm; and for fear of his unknown father they desisted. When he was quite grown up, and saw the men prepare for the hunt, he was very desirous to join them; his mother observing this, went outside and shouted out aloud, "Now get him some tools!" When she came out next morning she found them lying on the ground, close beside the entry. When the son brought home what he had caught for the first time, she again went out and cried with all her might, "Imitlungnarsunguak has caught a seal!" and when she was about to re-enter, the people were all very busy in dragging this seal into the house. When they had reached the farther end of the passage, it could not be lifted across the threshold into the room, but rolled back, and in no time had vanished. The father, of course, had taken it away. His next catch the mother got; but when he went out hunting the third time, he remained away. His mother now mended his clothes and put them to rights, and in the evening went outside as before, shouting something at the pitch of her voice, upon which his garments came flying out of the house, and she hurried after them. When they had got as far as the beach, the coast-ice appeared to be lifted up, and left room for the clothes to slip down beneath,—the mother following them closely. She now came to a house under ground belonging to ingnersuit, and there found her son, tied hands and feet. Loosening him she hurried him into his clothes, and brought him away with her. Her own name was Nagguanguak.

---

## 42.

## ABOUT THE CHILDREN OF TWO COUSINS.

THERE were once two cousins living together at the same winter-station, and at the time, their wives were both childless. In spring they parted from each other, saying, "Well, we will see who first gets a child." One travelled away to the south, and established himself for the coming winter. At this place he lived in prosperity, and his wife bore him a child. When the boy grew up, the father took a fancy to return to his cousin. He, however, had still no children; and for this reason he caught a young deer, and trained it up for his amusement. At length it improved so much that it could understand human speech. About that period the cousin returned, and he first beheld the calf running about outside the house. The cousins once more lived together, and the boy and the calf became playmates. The calf, however, soon grew stronger, and sometimes knocked over the boy, at which he wept. For this reason the boy's father went and shot the calf, though he loved his cousin dearly. The childless man got into a great rage at this, and at once challenged his cousin, and they met, armed with their bows ; the childless man shot his cousin on the spot, but was very much afflicted afterwards, and burst into a flood of tears. The son of the man that had been thus killed removed to a distance, for he could not endure the sight of his father's cousin. When he was full-grown and strong he returned to the place, but he had come too late—the cousin was no more. He heard some rumour of an enormously strong man who used to rob other men of their wives ; he challenged him to a wrestling-match, and overcame and killed him, and returned the women to their own husbands.

---

## 43.

## THE GIRL WHO WAS STOLEN BY AN INLANDER.

[This tale appearing somewhat obscure and fragmentary, has been added here only on account of its probable relation to Nos. 28 and 30. The details in the different manuscripts of these three stories appear to be more or less confounded and intermixed.]

A BROTHER and a sister once lived together, and were very much attached to each other. The sister, who was very desirous of going off for the salmon-fishing, asked her brother to take her up to a salmon river. Not being able to deny her, he put the boat into the sea and went with her to the fishing-place ; but when they had landed and discharged the boat, putting all their things on the beach, she climbed a little way up the rocks, and went across a smooth level to the brook. All at once she saw an *inorusek* (fabulous giant-like inlander) close beside her. Stupefied with terror, she tried to escape; but he caught hold of her and carried her further and further inland. The others plainly heard her shrieks for help, and hurried off to rescue her; but she was already gone, and her cries soon died away among the mountains. In the meantime the inorusek carried her up through the highlands till they stopped at a place with a number of huts. He intended to marry her, but first brought her to the house of a neighbour, where he put her down on the ledge and seated himself in front of her. She cried incessantly, but whenever she tried to run away, he took hold of her like a little child and put her down again. While she was thus sitting, an old woman peeped across the screen of the ledge, asking her, "What wouldst thou like to eat? dost thou like *talu?*" and the unhappy girl thought to herself, "I wonder what *talu* is like!" She soon heard the old woman step down to fetch something, and though still weeping, she peeped through her fingers, and perceived it to be the fat of a deer's heart they were giving her. However, she would not take it, and the old woman again retired. Then she again asked her, "Wouldst thou like some *ernowt?*" and the girl still crying, answered, "What may it be like?" This time she saw the old hag produce some common tallow, saying, "Now do eat that and be quiet;" but she would not take that either. Being very disheartened, she continued to weep; and the old woman now menaced her, and threatened to take away her boots, at which she cried still more. Then she heard a rattling noise, and peeping through her fingers, she saw a strange figure, all bones and joints, creeping along the ledge towards her. This creature warned her, saying, "Leave off crying, lest they should treat thee as they did me. I was once like thee; I was stolen and brought to this place, and because I would not leave off crying, they took away my boots and gave me others filled with reptiles, spiders, and vermin. They fastened them on my legs, and when they were taken off, the flesh was all gone." When the skeleton had done speaking, she cried all the more. The old hag now in an outburst of ill temper and vexation approached; and she saw her holding a pair of boots, in which she observed something crawling about; but the giant took hold of them and flung them away into the corner of the room, and then at length she was able to leave off crying. Her husband, however, kept a close watch upon her, and led her by the hand whenever she wished to go out. One day she said to him, " Don't go on watching me so; I have no intention of leaving thee now; I like thee very much, and thou mayst safely leave me and go out deer-hunting as usual." After that she feigned to go behind the house ; but she started from her hiding-place and ran up and down hill, and continued running towards the coast until she reached the tent of her parents, where she burst right through the door-curtain, not giving herself time to draw it before entering. She hastened to say, " Let us be off at once and remove to some other place ; the inlanders are sure to come and seek me here." They at once left the mainland to settle down on one of the farthest-off islets ; and after that time they never again ventured to pitch their tents on the continent.

## 44.

## THE CHILD THAT WAS STOLEN BY THE INLANDERS.

A MAN, whose name was Tungnerdluk, had his fixed abode by a firth, from which he made his regular excursions into the highlands to hunt the reindeer, and generally he was lucky. In winter he carried on seal-hunting at the mouth of the firth. One summer he was out chasing the deer as usual, and during his absence his wife went away to gather berries among the heather, with their only child. She put the boy down on the sod, and left him a moment; but she had hardly turned away before she heard him crying out. Although she instantly turned back, she did not find him in his place, but only heard his lamentations a long way off from where she was standing. She returned to the tent in great afflic-tion, and told how she had suffered her child to be taken by the inlanders, adding that she feared her husband's anger. In the evening he returned, heavily laden, and they heard him call out, "I have got plenty of reindeer-flesh for thee." On finding that nobody answered, he at once knew that some mischief had befallen them in his absence. He hurried in, and breathlessly asked if his son had died. The wife made no answer; but the others enlightened him, saying, "She let the inlanders take him;" upon which Tungnerdluk asked his trembling wife to put new soles on his boots—he wanted to go and consult his cousin, who was an angakok. This man pointed out the place to which the boy had been taken, and accompanied the father on his way to find him. At a good distance they reached a large house; and the angakok now told him he must go up to it alone, and that he himself would have to return. Tungnerdluk peeped in at the window, and saw two terrible women quarrelling and fighting about his weeping child. He leapt down into the outer passage; but he was obliged to creep on hands and feet to get through the inner one up into the main room. Having at last succeeded, he made his way up to the two hags to snatch his child; but whenever he tried to take it from one woman, she directly handed it to the other, and thus they went on a good while. A huge man at length entered, who said he would assist him, declaring that he had sprung from the coast people. He said, " Thou'dst better run on beforehand: be sure I will soon come after with the child; but mind be quick—my house-fellows will soon be pursuing us." And Tungnerdluk came running at full speed, and entered his tent, saying, " Make ready to depart at once;" and meanwhile the other entered with the child. They folded their tents, and quickly loaded their boat; and at the very moment they pushed from shore they saw their enemies descending the hills. When they had fairly got down to the beach, Tungnerdluk could not resist putting back to fight them, and he soon despatched one of them with his harpoon, and then followed his own people out of the firth. After this his son fell sick, and again he consulted an angakok, who was not, however, able to find out the cause of his complaint. He then called another one, who was besides renowned as a performer of *headlifting* (a peculiar charm for discovering the cause of sickness). He conjured and called up spirits; and lying down on his back, he first let go his breath, then rose up, and again began to breathe, saying, " The child's spirit is still with the inlanders." The father rejoined, " Then lose no time in preparing for an *angakok-flight* to bring it back and restore it to us;" and he flew away to the inlanders, fetching the spirit of the child home with him. On his return to the parents, he heard the voice of the child growing weaker; but by restoring the spirit to it, the baby soon recovered. Tungnerdluk paid the angakok well with different kinds of victuals, adding, "Whenever thou shouldst happen to be in any distress, I will gladly assist thee." Shortly afterwards he had two visitors who had come on purpose to mock him. On their approach, he observed that one carried a lot of whalebones with him. They addressed him, saying, "We have heard of the celebrated Tungnerdluk, who fetched his child back from the inlanders; pray tell us some of thy achievements: we will make thee a present of our whalebones in return." Tungnerdluk answered, "I am not in want of any such thing,"—whereat he took them to his storehouse, where he showed them his large stock of whalebones as well as of walrus-teeth. Seeing this, they respectfully retired, and left the place without so much as entering the house.

NOTE.—A story very similar to this has been received in another manuscript, and through a verbal narration written down by the author. The principal difference consists in the fact of the inlanders being replaced by the *amarsiniook* (a fabulous monster, which lived upon one of the mountain-tops emerging from the inland ice). The old *k'elaumassok* (or angakok of an inferior class), who brought back the child, was again overtaken by the amarsiniook, who put both of them into his hood. The angakok then summoned his *tornaks*, the *slinghitter* and the *falcon*, of which the latter succeeded in vanquishing the monster, and making him drop the old man and the child out of his hood.

---

## 45.

## THE ANGAKOK'S FLIGHT TO AKILINEK.

[The following three tales are here given separately, but nevertheless put under one number, their contents being, on the one hand, interesting with regard to the information implied about the art of *angakut* (plur. of angakok) in general, while, on the other, they are somewhat imperfect and obscure, so as to make it difficult to decide whether we have one or two original stories before us. The first was written down in

North Greenland before 1830 ; the second in the southernmost part of
Greenland, about 1860 ; and the last has been written down by the
author himself from a verbal narration, but is given here only in an
abridged form. Akilinek is the fabulous country beyond the ocean.]

(1.) THERE was once a very clever angakok. When
he was about to practise his art, and his limbs
had been tied and the lamps extinguished, he took flight,
and having found the wind favourable, he flew across the
sea, but did not sight the opposite shore before daybreak,
when he was obliged to return. Several times he tried
to get farther away, but was never able to pass beyond
this mark; and therefore he determined to educate his
son for an angakok, hoping that he might possibly be
brought to excel him. When the boy was grown up, he
went through all the grades and branches of the angakok-
science with him ; but when the father proposed to give
up teaching him, the son turned very moody and low-
spirited. The father now questioned him, saying, " Is
there any part of the science thou thinkest we have
overlooked, and neglected to practise?" and the son
answered, " I think there is ;" whereat the father recalled all the exercises they had gone through, one by
one, but after due meditation asked him, " Didst thou
visit the graves?" The son told him he had not ; and
the father said, " Well, I will take thee thither this evening ;" whereat the son was very glad. At the time appointed, they wandered to the burying-grounds, where
the father opened one of the graves, and undid the pall
of a corpse beneath the waist, and made his son thrust
his hand right into the flesh of the deceased body. This
done, the father left him as if nothing at all were the
matter. When the son was about to follow him, the
father remarked, " As yet thou hast observed nothing
particular at this tomb ; but wait till thou seest the last
rays of the setting sun, and take not thy eyes from its
splendour : but the moment thou dost notice a spark of
light falling down from it, beware, and flee the place at

once." While he was yet standing and gazing at the declining sun, the father suddenly beheld something glistening through the brightness of the sky, at the sight of which he immediately took flight, but the son remained with his hands attached to the corpse, unable to extricate himself. Not until midnight did he return, 'all smiles and joy; and now the father deemed him thoroughly tried and expert in his art. On the night of the following day he resolved to bind him for his first flight. When the lamps had all been extinguished, the son flew out. Having no particular end or aim, however, he only went backwards and forwards, but saw nothing very remarkable: his father questioned him concerning the currents of the air, but he did not happen to have taken note of any. The next day he again prepared for an angakok flight, and this time observed that the wind was favourable. He crossed part of the sea, and soon perceived that he was taking the same course as his father. At last great perpendicular rocks arose in front of him, and he had reached now the limit of his father's journey. He continued his flight towards it; and having with some difficulty succeeded in passing it, he saw an extensive country: crossing it in a southerly direction, he came upon a small house, and alighted close beside it. It was a house with two windows; and peeping within, he saw one man standing at each window, and watching him closely. One of the men went out and beckoned to a woman: on seeing the stranger, he invited him to step inside; and as both were entering, they met the woman in the passage ready to follow, and he now turned to her, saying, "Thou seest I have brought a visitor." Having passed the doorway, the angakok seated himself on the side-ledge to the right, and on the opposite side he saw a squint-eyed person, whose breath was like fire (peculiar to angakut, and also only to be observed by them). At his feet were chips of bone, at which he had been working. Further away he observed a woman, whose body was all over hairy. When the squint-eyed man noticed that he was being looked at, he said, "Why dost thou thus stare at me?" "Oh, I was only looking at the chips at thy feet." The other answered, "In the summer I have not got time to make chips, and that is why I am at it now." Some of them said, "Perhaps our visitor would like to show us some of his art?" and he answered, "Why, I am not unwilling, though it is but the second time I have practised angakok science." They all repaired to the *kagse* (their house of festivities). The squint-eyed person, who was always keeping close at the visitor's heels, asked him what fearful *tornak* (guardian spirit) he had got at his service; and he answered, "If I succeed, a large iceberg will presently appear." They all entered the dark *kagse*, and he also observed the hairy woman, the sight of whom he did not like, suspecting her to be dangerous to his purpose. When the conjuring had begun, and he felt that his tornak was drawing nigh, he said, "I fancy that something is approaching us." They looked out at the window, and whispered to each other, "A monstrous iceberg is close upon the beach." The angakok said, "Let a young man and a maiden step forth and post themselves in the middle of the floor." When they had taken their place, a tremendous noise proceeded from the iceberg bouncing ashore and suddenly calving. Then a married couple was ordered out on the floor, and a loud roar from without followed. Thus they were all called forth, one after the other, and at last it was the turn of the ugly woman to step out. When she was about to advance, she missed her footing on one of the flags, and got beyond the proper stepping-stones, and at the same time the iceberg turned over, and came tumbling over the shore, crushing the house to atoms. Only the angakok visitor and the man with the squint came out unhurt. He now tied his limbs, rose high in the air, and returned, accompanied by a swarm of croaking ravens. He was silent and dejected; and when his father questioned him as to the reason, he answered, "I am heavy with grief because I have practised my art badly: I did wrong in calling forth the hairy woman; and by this fault of mine many happy and vigorous people have perished." Next day the squint-eyed person made his appearance in the house, and observed, "Perhaps I too may be allowed to exhibit my art? I too am an anga-kok." To this the old angakok remarked, "My son there is just telling me that he has killed many brave and strong people by his want of experience." The other answered, "So he did, the bad one." The squint-eyed was now tied hand and foot, and began his flight in the house, which was still lighted up, and as soon as they began singing, he flew out of it. Somehow they suspected that he was likely to be dangerous to them, and accordingly they extinguished the lamps, in order to prevent his re-entering the place; but on look-ing out at the window, they saw him take a direction to-wards his own homestead, and soon after proceeded to light the lamps, concluding that, at any rate, he would not return the same night.

(2.) Of an angakok called Ipisanguak, who was still a novice in his art, this tale is told: On a certain evening, when he was just ready to set out on a flight, he said, "I intend to go away in search of the little house my forefathers have often spoken of, outside of which lies the bloody sword." Having spoken thus, he set off, making a circuit all round the horizon, without having anything particular to relate on his return; but the next time he flew straight across to Akilinek, and alighted right in front of a house, where lay the bloody sword which was to be taken by him. He went up to the entrance, from whence a man emerged whose eyes were all dim, like those of an unborn seal. He re-entered the house without noticing the stranger, and another man now appeared whose eyes were like the blackest berries, and this one asked him to step inside, where the inmates of the house welcomed him, saying, "Thou art just in time to join us at our meal." After a while the angakok observed, "I want another to fill my place at home to-night, otherwise my relatives will not believe that I have been here." The dim-eyed man answered him, "I should very much like to be thy substitute, but I am rather a slow one." They now proceeded to have him tied. Presently he was lifted up within the house, and then soared out into the open air, while Ipisanguak enjoyed a happy night in the company of his pleasant hosts. At dawn of day he broke off, saying, "The night is done; I must be off." Again he crossed the sea; and about midway he saw a glare as of a great fire shining about him, which appeared to be from his substitute, who likewise was on his way home, and thus meeting, both aimed at each other. Ipisanguak again visited Akilinek next evening, and at the same time his substitute exclaimed, "I hear him coming; behold, there he is!" whereupon he also went off, and again they encountered each other on the way, and smiled as they met, and returned in the same way at daybreak. On the following day, when Ipisanguak returned from a trip in his kayak, he said he had met several kayakers from an adjoining place, called Kagsimiut, and likewise reported that he had heard them say of himself, "Ipisanguak has turned angakok, and almost every day exchanges place with an angakok from Akilinek. Let us go and hear him." On the following day a great many kayakers and several boats' crews arrived; and when he suffered himself to be tied, and left for Akilinek, he was soon replaced by his comrade, who entered the house, and entertained the guests all the night long. Some time after this Ipisanguak paid a visit to Kagsimiut; and during his stay one of the seal-hunters said: "Seals are rather scanty with us at present: a clever hunter can hardly get one at a time; thou mightest bring on the seals, I should think, and thus improve the hunting." At the same time Ipisanguak observed a handsome young woman, to whom he at once took a fancy, standing outside the house. In the evening he conjured spirits; and during that interval an immense iceberg appeared, fast approaching the beach. He now let the women advance one by one; but she to whom he had taken a liking would not come. At length one appeared with a fine new ribbon round her topknot, and at that very moment the iceberg began to waver and shake; the angakok immediately sank down beneath the floor, and reached his own house by an underground way, while the iceberg came rolling on, tumbling right across the beach, crushing the house to atoms. On getting home he had all the lamps lighted; but in less than a moment the angakok from Kagsimiut made his appearance to avenge his people. However, they hit him with stones, and drove him back, and his voice had become inaudible. The following day Ipisanguak went to have a look at the destroyed house, but not a trace was left of it. The girl with the new topknot was possessed of an *anghiak* (the ghost of an abortion, or a child born in concealment), and it was all owing to her that Ipisanguak had been the cause of the accident that had happened to her housemates.

(3.) A great angakok at his conjurations always used to talk of his having been to Akilinek, and his auditors fully believed him. Once he forced his little son to attend his conjurations, sitting upon his knee. The boy, who was horribly frightened, said, "Lo! what is it I see? The stars are dropping down in the old grave on yonder hill." The father said, "When the old grave is shining to thee, it will enlighten thy understanding." When the boy had been lying down in his lap for a while, he again burst out, "What is it I now see?—the bones in the old

grave are beginning to join together." The father only
repeating his last words, the son grew obstinate and
wanted to run away; but the father still kept hold of
him. Lastly, the ghost from the grave came out, and
being called upon by the angakok, he entered the house
to fetch the boy, who only perceived a strong smell of
maggots, and then fainted away. On recovering his
senses, he found himself in the grave quite naked, and
when he arose and looked about, his nature was totally
altered—he found himself able at a sight to survey the
whole country away to the farthest north, and nothing
remained concealed from him. All the dwelling-places
of man appeared to be close together, side by side; and
on looking at the sea, he saw his father's tracks, stretching across to Akilinek. When going down to the house,
he observed his clothes flying through the air, and had
only to put forth his hands and feet to make them cover
his body again. But on entering the house he looked
exceedingly pale, because of the great angakok wisdom
he had acquired down in the old grave. After having
become an angakok himself, he once went on a flight to
Akilinek, and entered a house where a number of men
were assembled, one of whom he observed to be dim-
eyed. By help of his angakok sense he discovered this
man also to be an angakok, and remarked some bone-
chips lying at his feet. These chips (probably supernatural ones, and only visible to a clairvoyant) the dim-
eyed man had in vain tried to get rid of; because they
arose from some work he had taken in hand before the
appointed days of mourning for some person deceased
had gone by, thereby provoking the invisible rulers.
While staying here, the angakok visitor was requested
to make a conjuration, in order to procure a plentiful
seal-hunting. He summoned his tornak called a *kivingak* (viz., an iceberg, steep on one side, but sloping down
on the other, all covered with seals). The iceberg quickly
approached with the latter side towards them, and bend-

ing over, was just about to cast off all the seals into the water. But it so happened that among the housemates who had stepped forth on the floor there was a woman with an anghiak, which immediately made the iceberg turn on its steep side; and tumbling over with a tremendous roar, it crushed the house and all the people within, all of whom perished excepting the two angakut, who took care to make their escape at the right moment.

<hr />

## 46.

## THE KAYAKERS IN CAPTIVITY WITH THE MALIGNANT INGNERSUIT.

[The following abridged stories are only variations of the popular theme, which appear to exhibit one of the principal dangers which could be encountered and braved by renowned angakut. As to the Ingnersuit, or gnomes of the sea-shore, in general, we refer to the Introduction.]

(1.) KUVITSINA left the boat and the crew who had been his companions on their summer journey, and whom he had followed down the firth, and in his lonely kayak went along the shore. As he approached a low steep rock, it opened of its own accord, and seeing this, he entered. No sooner had he got inside than he was surrounded by ingnersuit, who tore his kayak from him and smashed it to pieces. They took him away into the house, and put him down on the side-ledge, and their old housewife first sharpened her knife, went up to him, and cut off his nose, and tied him to one of the pillars. In this plight he at length bethought himself of his tornaks. The first he called, however, were not at all noticed by the ingnersuit, and had no effect upon them. It then occurred to him to call forth two tornaks he had amongst the benevolent ingnersuit. Their approach was instantly heard; and one of them was named Nepingasuak, the other Napatarak. The latter of the two, however, was the first to hasten to the spot, crying loudly, "What have ye been doing to Kuvitsina?" He was in a terrible passion, and at once severed the strings, and, further, gave Kuvitsina an amulet, saying, "Make haste, and be off!" and he had thus escaped even before Nepingasuak arrived. On coming down to his ruined kayak, Nepingasuak merely breathed upon it, which soon made it all right; and thus he again returned to his own world, while Napatarak warned the ingnersuit, saying, "Ye should never lay hand on the people who live on the face of the earth: ye ought much more to hold them in awe, because they can vanquish the beings we hold in fear, such as whales, which they catch by means of the bladder." Kuvitsina had another name, which was Akamak. On his way home he met Nepingasuak, and at the same time observed a strange noise overhead: this was his nose, which came whirling along in the air, and adjusted itself in its proper place—only it became a little awry; and thus Kuvitsina reached his home.

(2.) Katauk, a very skilful hunter, used to catch seals by fastening the harpoon-line to his kayak without any hunting-bladder. Once, however, he happened to be capsized and drawn out of his kayak. Being on the point of drowning, he gave himself up for lost, when all of a sudden he was surprised at the sound of kayakers approaching from the shore. He saw that they were the ingnersuit, and of the malignant sort; but still he thought it better to be captured by them than drown. He was carried off to their place, put down on the window-bench, and encouraged to talk. But seeing that he remained quite mute, they first cut off his nose, and then tied him up beneath the roof-beams. Being in the greatest distress, he called his tornaks, three of whom instantly appeared and relieved him, after a hard struggle. On going outside he found his *erkungassok* (the wise man among the tornaks) prostrate and killed; but quickly made him revive again by breathing on him. When he had pushed off in his kayak he heard a voice calling behind him, and a whistling besides; turning his face round, he beheld his nose, which came flying through the air, sent by his erkungassok; it soon fitted itself into its due place. In the evening, when he had gained his home, he felt a pain around his waist and loins, and looking at them, he perceived one of the thongs with which he had been tied still attached. He cut it up in small bits, which he gave to young people for amulets, for the purpose of making them good kayakers.

(3.) Ulajok, while looking for seals outside the islands, came to a rock, which was being washed by a heavy swell. At the same time he observed a bright kayak making great haste towards him; but getting sight of Ulajok, the white kayak turned back and made for the rock again. Ulajok, suspecting that he might be an ingnersuak, wanted to turn his kayak homeward, but tried it in vain. The prow of his kayak always kept turning round, pointing anew at the rock, and insensibly he was drawn behind the white kayak. When close to the rock he saw it being lifted high up; and within houses and people presented themselves. Ulajok was pulled to the shore, where the people put by his kayak and paddle, conducting him into a large house. (The rest of the story is much like the preceding two.)

## 47.

## THE ORPHAN BOY ILIARSORKIK.

IN a house which was occupied by a great number of people lived a married couple with only one son; the parents, however, both died while he was quite a baby. Another family adopted him; but on finding that he gave them more trouble than they had expected, they soon grew tired of him, and he became nothing but a bore to them. Others took him up, but in a little time neglected him; and thus it befell that all the families in a house came to take charge of him by turns. His last foster-parents had him for rather a long time; but on a certain day when the man happened to return home without any catch, and was cross and moody, he addressed his wife, saying, " This boy is a mere good-for-nothing; cast him out on the dunghill at once." Meantime a widow, whose son had just commenced to try his hand at seal-hunting, took him in. She brought him up, and he did well, and was well provided for from that time. One autumn the weather turned bad with heavy gales; and snowdrifts coming on earlier than usual, there had hardly been a chance of any catch for the inhabitants. Before the days had begun to lengthen the sea was quite frozen over, and the bad weather still continuing, the many hunters and providers about the place entirely ceased to go out. All their provisions had been spent, and the lamps were not lighted in the evening. The only lamp still burning was that of the widow, and the only person that made any attempt at hunting was her adopted son Iliarsorkik. One of his housemates, a man who did not possess any kayak, used to take him by the hand every morning, and give him a run uphill; and by continuing this exercise he soon got to be very swift and agile. Meanwhile the inmates of the crowded house all remained in bed for hunger and cold; but every evening the widow went to her little store and took out a handful of *angmagsat* (dried fish, *capelins*, the chief winter provision), and bestowed a small share upon each of them; her own son got four, her adopted son three, and the others half a one: all had a little morsel of blubber besides. One morning at low tide Iliarsorkik saw some small spots off the rocky shore free of ice, and coming nearer he saw a great number of little sandpipers there. He at length caught one, which he brought to the house. His foster-mother was just getting anxious about him when she heard him slide down the outer passage; and soon after entering the room, holding up his bird, he exclaimed, " Look here, what I have got!" The men who lay on the ledge cried out, " Oh, he has actually got a sandpiper!" and they reproached each other for having driven him out, saying that he might now have been able to provide for them. The mother cut the little bird through at all its joints, and gave every one their share, but still some one went on crying for more. The next day Iliarsorkik brought two, and every succeeding day one more; and the widow always divided them, and gave their house-fellows something, each in turn. One day he again met the man who used to give him a turn up the hills, who pointed out to him a spot where the partridges were sitting in the snow with their black beaks peeping forth, and he went on directing him how to get at them. He returned bringing one home the first day; but every following day the number increased, and the widow went on distributing what he had caught; but the men were constantly repeating, " What a pity we ever cast him off from us!" One day when he was away among the mountains in search of partridges with his friend, he observed a mist hanging above the waters, at one time growing thicker, and shortly after dissolving; and this

his companions hailed as a good sign, informing him
that it was a sure token of holes in the ice, kept open
by the sea animals that gathered there to breathe.
They now climbed a still higher mountain to take a
more correct survey, and make sure of the place. In
the evening Iliarsorkik said to his brother, " To-morrow
I don't intend to hunt on shore ; I shall just take a
walk on the ice, and give a look round to find out the
breathing - holes." His foster - brother answered him :
" Yonder beneath the boat thou wilt find my hunting-
tools: I shall soon put thee right, and make them smaller
for thee ; but mind they are put deep down in the
snow." Iliarsorkik dug away for them, and having
found them brought them to his brother, who fitted
them for him. Early in the morning he was off ; after
a while he fell in with the frost-haze. He followed the
direction of it, and soon arrived at the brim of the aperture, where he saw the seals diving up and down, and
playing about in large crowds in the open water. Finding it difficult to get a sure footing on the slippery edge,
he lost no time, but at once took aim and fixed his harpoon into one of the smaller seals. Having hauled it
up upon the ice, he fastened it to his towing-line, and
made the best of his way home. When the starving
creatures heard him dragging a seal along through the
house-passage a great clamour and strife ensued. The
widow first cut very thin slices of blubber and skin together, and handed it to them. Some of them, however,
were not able to bide their time, but came creeping along
on the floor, stretching out their lean hands ; but the
widow merely said, " Each of you will get a piece in his
or her turn." She likewise took a piece of flesh of the
size of a hand and boiled it, after having lit some lamps ;
but even this meal did not satisfy them ; several of them
cried out for more food, while others protested they had
got no food at all. In the night some of them even
came creeping across the floor to steal the raw flesh,

but they were so faint that they were not able to get back and climb the ledge for their couches. Iliarsorkik brought a larger seal on the following day, and the widow was now able to light all the lamps, to warm up the house; but she was still very careful in sharing out the meals, and continued to give them very small rations. From this day forth Iliarsorkik every day brought home seals. One time when he had got two very big ones, and had already got half-way home with them, he was suddenly caught in an easterly gale, with a snow-storm blowing right in his face, so that he was not able to see anything at all. He continued to walk straight against the wind, but as it happened to haul round to the south he, of course, took a wrong direction, and lost his way. Towards evening, however, he concluded that he must have gained the coast-side, by the loose blocks of ice scattered about on all sides. Leaving his seals on the beach, he stepped up on shore, and came across a house. On entering it he saw that only the foremost lamps were burning, and behind this a widow and a young man were sitting, the latter with his chin buried deep in the fur collar of his jacket; but behind, in the more remote corner of the house, the lamps were all extinguished. Iliarsorkik said, "I have not absolutely come here on a visit, but I was not aware that the wind had changed, and thus lost my way in the snow-drift." The widow replied, "Then thou hadst better stay here till to-morrow; and when the weather alters for the better thou mayst return to thy home." Iliarsorkik said, "If ye have any fancy at all, ye are very welcome to one of my seals." No sooner had he uttered these words than a faint sound of wailing was heard from the dark corners of the room. These people were likewise starving, and he had just come in time to save them. The weather being fine on the following day he reached his home, and when he had told his mother how he had solaced the hungry and starving, she answered him,

" Always act in that way, and the number of thy captured animals will always increase." Another time
when he was just making ready what he had caught to
carry it home, he suddenly heard a tremendous roar,
and at the same time the ice seemed to quake beneath
his feet. He looked round, and seeing nothing but icebergs right and left, he thought it might have been one
of them calving (bursting and moving). When the
roaring sound was again heard, and had come much
nearer, he again turned round, and saw that what he had
taken for an iceberg was a great bear, all covered with
ice, and standing erect before him. When he saw the
beast preparing to attack him he ran on towards an iceberg at some distance, and kept on running about, always pursued by the bear. Each time he rounded it
he managed to hit a blow in the same spot on the iceberg, and in this manner he had soon made a cave, into
which he hastened to creep, while the animal still hurried, and followed the scent of his footmarks. Whenever
the bear passed him he thrust at it with his *tok* (tool for
making holes in the ice) ; each time he thus hit it some of
the ice-cover dropped down from its back, and at length
some bleeding was visible ; snorting and roaring, it
circled round the iceberg, but at length stopped short
and fell down motionless. Iliarsorkik descended, and
found it to be dead. He cut out a piece of the flesh,
and made the best of his way home ; having arrived
safely, he gave notice at the dwelling - places in the
neighbourhood, that whoever chose might go and fetch
away some of the bear's flesh ; he himself went along to
the spot with his house-fellows, who had in the meantime fully recovered, to flense and cut it up, on the following day. Having gone on for some time he saw a
black spot on the ice, which soon appeared to be the
body of a dead man : further on they came across another one ; and so on all the way. These were the
corpses of people who had been on the point of starva-

tion, and had expired in making their attempt to reach
the bear ; a few of them had succeeded in reaching it
and getting a bite of the flesh, but afterwards dropped
on their way home, worn out with hunger and fatigue.

## 48.

## THE BROTHERS WHO WERE LOST ON THEIR JOURNEY UP THE FIORD.

SEVERAL men were living together in the mouth
of a fiord.  Each of them used to go out kayaking
by himself ; but it so happened that all those who went
up the fiord entirely disappeared one after another. Two
brothers, both strong and able men, were still left, and
of these, the eldest first went out in search of the lost
ones.  He kept close along shore ; but having arrived
at a certain spot, he could not master the strong tide,
but was carried along by it to a place where two old
people were standing, who (by magic) drew him to their
shore.  When he got upon land he saw numbers of
people, who were all sons of the old couple ; they seized
his kayak, smashed it asunder, and put the pieces of it
on the top of the turned-up boat.  He was then asked
to enter the house, and a dish of berries was put before
him ; but perceiving part of a human hand sticking up
among them, he left it untouched.  The people he had
thus encountered were the murderers of his lost friends.
At nightfall they entered to attack him also ; and with
this view they as usual took out a sealskin and spread
it on the floor, for a trying-match at hook and crook.
Seeing, however, that nobody was able to conquer him
in this way, they dared not downright kill him.  His

kayak being destroyed, he was deprived of all means of returning. His brother in vain awaited his arrival, and therefore at length resolved to follow him. He took the very same course, and had the same fate, being likewise drawn towards the shore by the two old people. But before the young men could seize hold of his kayak, his own brother, who all the while had feigned to know nought of him, caught it up and placed it in safety on the top of the boat. At night he said to the men of the place that they might as well go to sleep, and that he would take charge of the stranger; but at midnight he suffered him to escape; and not till he believed he had gained a safe distance did he awake the people of the house and make known to them what had happened. The boat was quickly got down and put out in pursuit of him. The brother, who was given charge of the steering-oar, feigned to be pulling exceedingly hard, and in so doing, purposely broke every oar he got in hand in order to delay the pursuit. Meanwhile the fugitive escaped them, and on reaching home went off in search of helpmates to the north as well as to the south. In the ensuing winter they started in great numbers to take revenge on the fiord people. When the latter had been apprised of their approach, the elder brother, who was still staying with them, said he would rescue them, and they had better go and hide themselves in a cave close by; but no sooner had the assailants arrived, than the brother hastened to point out their hiding-place, and they commenced the attack, pouring their arrows into the cave, killing all but one, for whom there was not an arrow left. Presently, however, a bird came flying out of the cave; but one of them quickly got an arrow from an orphan boy, who had just been practising bow-shooting, and hit the bird with it; and when they came to look more closely at it, the bird turned out to have been one of the men. They cut him to pieces, and at once took out his entrails.

Part of them were sunk in the depths of the ocean, and the rest brought to a place on which the sun never shone.

NOTE.—This tale is taken from two copies. Besides these there are two much resembling it. In the first, all the men having disappeared, only an old bachelor is left with the women, who persuade him to go in search of the lost men. On returning after having revenged them, the women, for sheer joy, suffocated him by their caresses. In the other, the inhabitants of two different islands were living in friendly relations to each other until an ill-natured sorcerer at one of those places took it into his head to kill the visitors successively arriving from the other island. His mode of attacking people was to fly at them like a bird from the top of a mountain, striking off their heads at one blow. At length, however, he was killed by the arrow of a boy who had been trained for the purpose.

## 49.

## THE SOLITARY KAYAKER.

THERE was once a kayaker who had only one certain hunting-place to which he always resorted, and whither he was never accompanied by any one else. He was well skilled in his craft, and generally brought home a great quantity of seals. Not far off, to the north of his habitation, lived a number of other people in a large house with three windows. One day he had started as usual for his solitary hunting-ground ; but for the first time found it preoccupied by another hunter. On coming closer to him, he recognised in him one of his northern neighbours. This man spoke to him and was so talkative that the other found it rather difficult to mind his work. At home he reported, "To-day I at length had a fellow joining me at my hunting-place ; he turned out to be one of our neighbours : but to-morrow I intend to be off earlier and try to forestall him." Accordingly he started sooner than was his wont, but on reaching the place, he found that the other man had already arrived, and was even more loquacious than on the first day. It was almost day-break before they had begun their work. When they had both caught their seals they returned. But the first kayaker on coming home, remarked, "It seems almost impossible to be beforehand with this man ; however, I will try it once more." He started early the following morning, while it was still pitch-dark ; but the other one was on the spot. He rowed close up to him, hoping to find him in his usual polite mood, but to-day he did not speak at all ; not until daybreak did he utter a single word, and then went away. The next day it was the same thing over again, he never spoke till sunrise ; then he remarked, " To-day she remained in bed altogether ; the day before yesterday she fell sick, and all the while she is growing worse and worse." It is to be understood that he was speaking of his wife, and this was the reason why he had thus changed. He now added, " If thou dost not meet me here to-morrow, thou mayst judge that she is still worse, and then pray look in upon us to-morrow and see how we are doing." Then the other made some further inquiry, and went home with his catch, relating his adventure to his family. He did not meet his new comrade the next day, and therefore called on him the day after. Entering the house, he found all the men within ; not one of them was out kayaking that day. He entered the room and there remarked a man sitting far back upon the ledge and staring straight before him, and he soon recognised him to be his former companion. His wife had died and he had already buried her. Observing the general silence, he rose and moved alongside the widower, saying—" I have come to give thee some solace ; thou wilt be sure to stand in need of some one to talk to thee at such an unhappy time : and if thou wouldst like it, I will be-

think me of something to tell thee." But at this the
widower uttered some unintelligible words, at the same
time looking very fierce and angry. Suddenly he advanced and took hold of the visitor by the throat and
threw him down into the doorway. Taking it all for
a jest, he quickly got up and re-entered the room ; but
he was again seized and thrust right against the door-
posts and broke his spine, which immediately caused
his death. The murderer again with downcast eyes
seated himself on the ledge. Meanwhile a youth, the
son of a widow, coolly proceeded to whet his knife ; and
when he had got it well sharpened, he sprang up behind
the widower and made a long cut on each side of his
back ; the blood rushed out, and in a few minutes he
fell down dead. At this sight they all got infuriated
and took to their knives, and a terrible slaughter ensued ; the widow and her son, with an adopted daughter,
were the only ones that remained unhurt ; and having
made their escape through the window, they went to
take up their abode in the storehouse. But subsequently the winter became very severe, and the frost
fearfully keen, so that the widow's son at last had to
give up hunting, and remain indoors. They had almost
finished their stock of provisions, only a few angmagsat
(small dried fish) and a small bag with blubber were
still left ; and accordingly they could not afford to eat
their fill every day. Not till supper-time did the widow
venture to share out their portions. The son then
got two and a half fish, while she herself and her
stepdaughter had one and a half. Owing to this sen-
sible management, they kept alive, though badly
enough, and did not altogether starve with hunger, because they always got a morsel of blubber besides.
For three succeeding days they went on like this, but
on the fourth, the young man disappeared. However,
he had only gone out to take a look round from some
of the neighbouring heights. In the evening he put his

weapons and tools to rights, and on the very next day
he returned home, dragging an immense white whale
with him.   The women were transported with joy, and
at once began to flense and cut it up ; but presently the
daughter complained of her feet being so dreadfully
cold.   This was because the blood of the fish had got
into her boots and filled them.   Her mother, however,
pretended not to heed her, and told her to go on helping
her.   A little afterwards the girl said that she saw all
the mountains double, and then she was ordered to go
inside ; but the moment she bent down to descend
through the entrance, she broke in twain, and was dead
on the spot.   In the evening the son wrought a spell
upon the body of the deceased, and not till then was her
mother aware of his being an angakok.   They extinguished the lamps and he called forth the spirits, and
restored her to life and health.   They all remained
living together at this place, and he afterwards married
his adopted sister.   At length they died there without
removing to any other place, and without any accidents
ever happening to them.

---

## 50.

## KASIAGSAK, THE GREAT LIAR.

KASIAGSAK, who was living with a great many
skilful seal-hunters, always returned in the evening without a catch of his own.   When he was out, his
wife, named Kitlagsuak, was always restless and fidgety,
running out and in looking out for him, in the hope that
he might be bringing home something ; but he generally
returned empty-handed.   One day, being out in his

kayak, he observed a black spot on a piece of ice, and
it soon turned to be a little seal. His first intention was
to harpoon it, but he changed his mind, and broke out,
saying, " Poor little thing ! it is almost a pity. Perhaps
it has already been wounded by somebody else ; perhaps it will slide down in the water when I approach it,
and then I need only take hold of it with my hands."
So saying he gave a shout, at which the seal was not
slow to get down. Presently it appeared close before
the point of his kayak ; but he called out still louder
than before, and the seal went on diving up and down
quite close to him. At length he made up his mind to
chase and harpoon it ; but somehow it always rose at
a greater distance, and was soon entirely lost to him.
Kasiagsak now put back, merely observing, " Ye silly
thing ! ye are not easy to get at ; but just wait till next
time."

Another day he went seaward in bright, fine weather.
Looking towards land he got sight of the other kayakers, and observed that one of them had just harpooned
a seal, and that the others were all hurrying on to his
assistance. As to himself, he never stirred, but remained
quite unconcerned in his former place. He also noticed
that the one who had caught the seal tugged it to the
shore, and made it fast to a rock on the beach, intending to return in pursuit of others. He instantly put
further out to sea ; but when he had got quite out of
sight he returned to the beach by a roundabout way,
and made straight for the other man's seal, and carried
it off. The towing-line was all around ornamented with
walrus-teeth, and he was greatly delighted at the prospect of getting home with this prize. Meanwhile his
wife had been wandering about in expectation of him,
and looking out for the returning kayakers. She at
length cried out, " There is a kayak !"—at which more
people came running out ; and shading her eyes with
her hand, she continued, " It looks like Kasiagsak, and

he moves his arms like one tugging something along
with him.   Well, I suppose it will now be my turn to
give you a share, and ye shall all get a nice piece of
blubber."   As soon as he landed she hastened to ask
him, "Where didst thou get that beautiful tugging-
line?"   He answered, "This morning at setting out I
thought it might come in handy, as I was bent on having a catch, and so I brought it out with me; I have
kept it in store this long time."   "Hast thou, indeed?"
she rejoined, and then began the flensing and carving
business.   She put the head, the back, and the skin
aside; all the rest, as well as the blubber, she intended
to make a grand feast upon.   The other kayakers successively returned, and she took care to inform each of
them separately that a seal was already brought home;
and when some of the women came back from a ramble
on the beach, she repeated the whole thing over to them.
But while they were sitting down to supper in the evening, a boy entered, saying, "I have been sent to ask
for the towing-line; as to the seal, that is no matter."
Turning to Kasiagsak, his wife now put in, "Didst thou
tell me an untruth?"   He only answered, "To be sure
I did;" whereto his wife remarked, "What a shame it
is that Kasiagsak behaves thus!" but he only made a
wry face, saying, "Bah!" which made her quite frightened; and when they lay down to rest he went on
pinching her and whistling until they both fell asleep.

Another day, rowing about in his kayak, he happened
to observe a black spot away on a flake of ice.   On
nearing it he made it out to be only a stone.   He
glanced round towards the other kayakers, and then
suddenly feigned to be rowing hard up to a seal, at the
same time lifting the harpoon ready to lance it; but
presently went to hide himself behind a projecting point
of the ice, from which he managed to climb it and roll
the stone into the sea with a splash, making it all froth
and foam.   Meanwhile he got into his kayak again,

making a great roar in order to call the others to his assistance. When they came up to him they observed that he had no bladder, and he said, "A walrus has just gone down with my bladder; do help me to catch sight of him; meantime I will turn back and tell that I have lanced a walrus." He hurried landwards, and his wife, who happened to be on the look-out, again shouted, "A kayaker!" He called out that he had made a lucky hit. "I almost do believe it is Kasiagsak; do ye hear him in there?" Meantime he had approached the shore, and said, "In chasing a walrus I lost my bladder; I only came home to tell you this." His wife now came running into the house, but being in such a hurry she broke the handle of her knife. However, she did not mind this, but merely said, "Now I can get a handle of walrus-tooth for my knife, and a new hook for my kettle." In the evening Kasiagsak had chosen a seat on the hindermost part of the ledge, so that only his heels were to be seen. The other kayakers stayed out rather long; but the last of them on entering brought a harpoon-line and a bladder along with him, and turning to Kasiagsak observed, "I think it is thine; it must have been tied round some stone and have slipped off; here it is." His wife exclaimed, "Hast thou been telling us new lies?" at which he only answered her, "Why, yes; I wanted to play you a trick, you see."

Another day, when he was kayaking along the coast, he remarked some loose pieces of ice away on a sandy beach at some distance; he rowed up to them and went ashore. Two women, gathering berries, watched his doings all along. They saw him fill his kayak with bits of broken ice; and this done, he waded down into the water till it reached his very neck, and then turned back and got upon the beach, where he set to hammering his kayak all over with stones; and having finally stuffed his coat with ice, he turned towards home. At some distance he commenced shrieking aloud and crying, "Ah me! a big iceberg went calving (bursting and capsizing) right across my kayak, and came down on the top of me;" and his wife repeated his ejaculations, adding, "I must go and see about some dry clothes for him." At last they got him up on shore, and large bits of ice came tumbling out of his clothes, while he went on lamenting and groaning as if with pain, saying, "I had a very narrow escape." His wife repeated the tale of his misfortunes to every kayaker on his return home; but at last it so happened that the two women who had seen him likewise returned, and they at once exclaimed, "Is not that he whom we saw down below the sand-cliffs, stuffing his clothes with ice." On this, the wife cried out, "Dear me! has Kasiagsak again been lying to us?" Subsequently Kasiagsak went to pay a visit to his father-in-law. On entering the house he exclaimed, "Why, what's the matter with you that your lamps are not burning, and ye are boiling dog's flesh?" "Alas!" answered the master, pointing to his little son, "he was hungry, poor fellow! and having nothing else to eat we killed the dog." Kasiagsak boastingly answered him, "Yesterday we had a hard job at home. One of the women and I had our hands full with the great heaps of seals and walruses that have been caught. I have got both my storehouses choke-full with them; my arms are quite sore with the work." The father-in-law now rejoined, "Who would ever have thought that the poor little orphan boy Kasiagsak should turn out such a rich man!" and so saying, he began crying with emotion; and Kasiagsak feigned crying likewise. On parting from them the following day, he proposed that his little brother-in-law should accompany him in order to bring back some victuals, adding, "I will see thee home again;" and his father said, "Well, dostn't thou hear what thy brother-in-law is saying? thou hadst better go." On reaching home, Kasiagsak took hold of a string and brought it into the

house, where he busied himself in making a trap, and
taking some scraps of frizzled blubber from his wife's
lamp, he thrust them out as baits for the ravens.  Suddenly he gave a pull at the string, crying out, " Two !—
alas! one made its escape;" and then he ran out and
brought back a raven, which his wife skinned and boiled.
But his brother-in-law had to look to the other people
for some food ; and at his departure the next day, he
likewise received all his presents from them, and not
from Kasiagsak.

Another day he set off in his kayak to visit some
people at a neighbouring station.  Having entered one
of the houses, he soon noticed that some of the inmates
were mourning the loss of some one deceased.  He
questioned the others, and on hearing that they had
lost a little daughter named Nepisanguak, he hastened
in a loud voice to state, " We have just got a little
daughter at home, whom we have called Nepisanguak;"
on which the mourning parents and relations exclaimed,
" Thanks be to thee that ye have called her by that
name;" and then they wept, and Kasiagsak also made
believe to be weeping; but he peeped through his
fingers all the while.  Later in the day they treated
him richly with plenty of good things to eat.  Kasiagsak went on saying, " Our little daughter cannot speak
plainly as yet ; she only cries ' *apangaja !* ' " but the
others said, " She surely means ' *sapangaja* ' " (**sapangat,**
beads) ; " we will give thee some for her ;" and at his
departure he was loaded with gifts—such as beads, a
plate, and some seal-paws.  Just as he was going to
start, one of the men cried out to him, " I would fain
buy a kayak, and I can pay it back with a good pot ;
make it known to the people in thy place."  But Kasiagsak said, " Give it to me ; I have got a new kayak,
but it is a little too narrow for my size."  At length he
started along with his presents, and the pot stuck upon
the front part of his kayak.  At home he said, " Such a

dreadful accident! a boat must surely have been lost;
all these things I bring you here, I have found tossed
about on the ice;" and his wife hastened into the house
to give her cracked old pot a smash, and threw away the
shoulder-blades that till now had served her instead of
plates, and ornamented her coat with beads, and proudly
walked to and fro to make the pearls rattle. The next
day a great many kayakers were announced. Kasiagsak instantly kept as far back on the ledge as possible.
As soon as the kayakers put in to shore, they called out,
"Tell Kasiagsak to come down and fetch off some
victuals we have brought for their little daughter;" but
all the reply was, "Why, they have got no daughter at
all." Another of the men now put in, "Go and ask
Kasiagsak for the new kayak I bought of him;" but
the answer was, "He certainly has no new kayak." At
this information they quickly got up to the house, which
they entered, taking their several gifts back, and last of
all cutting the flaps ornamented with beads away from
the wife's jacket. When the strangers were gone she
said as before, "Kasiagsak has indeed been telling a lie
again." His last invention was this: he one day found
a small bit of whale-skin floating on the top of the
water, and bringing it home he said, "I have found the
carcass of a whale; follow me and I will show you it:"
and the boat was got out, and they started. After a
good while they asked him, "Whereabout is it?" but
he merely answered them, "Away yonder;" and then
a little bit further, "we shall soon get at it." But when
they had gone a long way from home without seeing
anything like a floating whale, they got tired of Kasiagsak, and put a stop to all his fibs by killing him then
and there.

## 51.

## THE REVIVED WHO CAME TO THE
## UNDER-WORLD PEOPLE.

A HUSBAND and a wife, with an only son, were living together with an old married couple, who had got no children at all. On a certain day, while together on the fishing-place, the former lost their son, and left the place before the five subsequent mourning days were over, leaving the old childless people behind. Not knowing any way to get food without assistance, the man said to his wife, "Let us go up to the tomb." Having arrived there, he went on, "Thou being a woman, must open the grave;" but she told him that he, being the man, ought to do so. However, she proceeded to take away the top-stone, after which the man set himself to open the grave. When they had got the corpse taken out, and had done chanting over it, it began to move, and after a while it rose up, and began running straight against the man. The woman now said to her husband, "Stand steady;" but the very same moment he was overturned, and in the next she was herself thrown over; and lastly the youth also fell down. The old man first rose, and going up to him said, "Now, dear, come along and stay with us;" and the revived youth went home with them, got a kayak, and became their provider. Once his real father came back to see what had become of the old people, who he almost expected had starved for want of food. Coming round the point, and seeing blood upon the stones on the beach, he thought, "They must have been to the grave and taken away the corpse;" but coming closer, he observed marks of seal-flensing besides, and therefore inquired, "Whoever might have caught these for you?" They made answer, "Thy own son, whom we have restored to life again;" but he at once prepared to kill them, because he doubted the truth of this assertion, and believed they were mocking him. The old man now said, "Just wait a little; and if he then does not come, it is time enough to kill us!" Before he had finished speaking, the son appeared from behind the point. They both cried out, "Don't touch him at once!" but the father could not forbear so doing, and consequently he again fell down dead on the spot. The old people again sang some magic lay over him, and by this means restored him to life. Once more he moved, rose up, and ran right up to his father, whom he threw down, and likewise his foster-mother, but then stopped. His father would fain have taken him home to his true mother, but the son answered him, "No, no! ye left me before the five mourning days were over, and therefore I will remain with those who have revived me;" and the father started off by himself. One day the youth returned in his kayak, but in a strangely silent mood, whereat his father said, "Why doesn't thou speak, dear?" to which the son answered that he had gone and taken an *ingnersuak-woman* for a wife. The old people were sorry that he should have to leave them, and asked him if they might not accompany him; and one day, on meeting an ingnersuak, he inquired of him whether he could bring them with him. He answered that they might come, but at the same time told him to warn them not to look back when they approached the rock which enclosed the abode of the *ingnersuit*, lest the entrance should remain shut for them. He told them this, and impressed on them all the way to keep their eyes fixed on the point of his kayak. They then instantly loaded the boat, and made ready to depart. When they had reached the cliff, and were rowing up to it, it forthwith opened; and inside was seen a beautiful country, with many houses, and a beach covered with pebbles, and large heaps of flesh and matak (edible skin). Perceiving this, the old people for joy forgot the warning and turned round, and instantly all disappeared: the prow of the boat knocked right against the steep rock, and was smashed in, so that they all were thrown down by the shock. The son said, "Now we must remain apart for ever; but build your house on yonder cliff: they will no doubt provide you with food." They built their house on the cliff, and every day they got their meals without trouble from the ingnersuit.

---

## 52.

## THE OLD BACHELOR.

THERE was once a queer old bachelor who had a singular dislike to singing: whenever he heard people sing, he would take himself off immediately. One day, being out at his hunting-place off the coast, he heard people singing, and it proved to proceed from the crew of a boat which was going up the firth right against the wind, and without being rowed. This song pleased him; and he went up to the boat, which he several times noticed to be lifted up into the air, soon to sink down again on the surface of the water, and constantly advancing, although the crew seemed resting on their oars all the while. He now asked leave to be one of the party; and the steersman said he might follow them if he chose, but that he must keep close to them; upon which they tied his kayak to the boat, and then continued singing, ᴋangátarsa, ᴋangátarsartigut! (let us be taken aloft!) imaᴋaja, ah, ha, ha. They were instantly lifted up and taken away across the country.

Being now on the top of a very high mountain, they took a little rest there, but soon after travelled on through the air until they alighted close beside a house. They discharged the boat; and the old bachelor also got out of his kayak on land, and he entered a house to pay them a visit. He came to like them, remained with them, and learned their magic song. But at length he bethought himself of his relatives, who were sure to be missing him, and be concerned about his fate, and he resolved to return. His hosts proceeded to fill his kayak with victuals, after which he got in: and singing the magic lay, he flew away in the same direction he had formerly come from; but when he reached the high mountain, he got a strong fancy to repose for a while on the summit of it, which happened to be a very steep peak. After a while he wanted to be off again, but found that he had suddenly forgotten the lay, and then he sat down all at a loss on the steep mountain-side. At last he lost his balance, and was about to fall down. He tried to catch hold of the proper words, and sang, "'immakaja!'—no; not quite that; 'kanajaja!'—no, that's not it neither;" and now he began crying and tumbling down the precipice. When he was quite close to the stone-heaps at the foot of the mountain, he remembered the song, and was again carried through the air, and thus saved from destruction. At last he saw his dwelling-place, where his house-fellows had quite given him up for lost. They were just assembled outside, when all at once they heard a song from above, and looking upwards, perceived a kayaker overhead rushing through the air, and before long they recognised their own old bachelor. He directed his course staight towards the entrance, never stopping until he sat right down on the ledge, his kayak's point crushing against the wall of the room; and this was his first and last journey through the air.

## 53.

## SALIK THE KIVIGTOK.

SALIK went off to the north; and during his journey
the frost set in, and cut off his passage home, and
he established himself for the winter at a very solitary
place. The following spring he drew still farther north.
After some hours travelling, he remembered that they
had left their axe fixed in one of the cross-beams of
their deserted house. He at once returned and entered
the dark house through the open window. Just as he was
going to take hold of the axe, he heard something moving
about beside the ledge, down on the floor, and on looking
more closely, he caught sight of a man. The stranger
began to whistle aloud; but soon after he spoke thus:
" Though I am always aware of what is going to happen,
thou hast for once chanced to take me by surprise. This
is the way in which I manage : being very quick, it is my
wont to go about from one place to another, picking up
odd scraps and leavings after people move away to other
parts." Having delivered himself of this speech, he
added, " I think it is the custom when meeting a man
for the first time to ask him his name." The former
rejoined, " My name is Salik;" and the stranger said,
" Why, so is mine; and since thou hast, to a certain
degree, outdone me, who have never before been taken
aback, I shall relate the history of my life to thee : In
former times, when we were still children, we used to
leave the house every morning with our father; and
while he was away we used to spend the day joyfully,
practising bow-shooting and making ourselves expert at
flinging stones, and never thought of entering the house
till he returned. Then he would say to our mother,
' Have not they had anything to eat as yet?' Upon

which she used to put a large plate with meat before us. This was always our first meal each day, and we swallowed it greedily. But we were ten children, and therefore the plate had to be filled thrice before we were quite satisfied. One evening, when our father had come back and gone into the house, we also went inside as usual, but on entering found the manners of our parents altered. Though it was after twilight, the lamps were not lighted, but lay tumbled down on the floor, bottom up. At this sight we seated ourselves silently on the main-ledge. After a while my father turned round and said to our mother, 'These will probably be hungry: I am not going to do like my mother's brothers, who fled from mankind because he had been scolded by his wife.' Our mother at first remained silent, but then bestirred herself, and in her turn replied, 'If he had any sense at all, he would not speak in that way.' She now put the usual dish before us. Our father partook of the meal with us; and then they began to talk to each other as if nothing had passed: my brothers and sisters were also soon quite at their ease, but I was not able to forget my mother's harsh words, though they had not been addressed to me. I could only take one little morsel; and when the dish was filled the second time, I had not yet swallowed that. Winter passed by, and I still wondered over my mother's speech. In spring father took us all away to the firth for *angmagsat*-fishing; and all were happy, and helped mother in drawing the fishes up on the beach. She used to say, 'Now we had better stop: we might be getting too many, and have a difficulty in carrying them away before the tide sets in;' and then we helped her in spreading them out to dry. When father brought his catch in the evening, we likewise assisted her in cutting the flesh into strips for drying. About that time the mountain-brooks burst through their ice-coverings, and father taught us to build a dyke at the outlet of the brooks, in order to stop and catch the salmon. At full tide he used to catch them in his kayak, and we from land by throwing stones at them; and when the tide was out we could easily take the fish that were stopped behind the dykes with our spears. We had all work enough in helping to carry them up to our mother and assisting her in cutting them up for drying. My brothers enjoyed that busy time; but I had not yet learned to forget those words of my mother's, and my spirits grew more and more depressed. One day a great many salmon had been caught behind the dam we had made for them; but as father had left, and we had to lance them and bring them up to mother, I asked my brothers to do my part of the business. How-

ever, they all agreed that I was to do it myself; but on seeing my youngest brother drawing his fish on a cord, I turned to him saying, 'I think I see a partridge yonder: pray take my lot of salmons along with thee while I pursue the bird.' He willingly obeyed me, and I darted off;

and running straight on for the interior, I never stopped my flight till nightfall. I lay down to sleep as best I might. All the summer-time I roamed about snaring partridges, and in the autumn I set to build myself a suitable house for the winter: the birds, however, were now getting scarcer. One morning there was a terrible snow-fall, on account of which I stayed at home. Now and then I looked out of the window, and once saw something brown moving about in the snow. As the storm was going down, and the sky clearing a little, I recognised a large male reindeer seeking for food beneath the snow. I was dreadfully hungry at the time; and, although it was very unwise, I could not suppress a loud cry on seeing it. The knife I have got here"— showing a stump of a knife hardly a finger's-length— "was then considerably longer: I took hold of it, and crept up to the animal very cautiously, not to frighten it. When the snow fell thicker I took to running; but when it cleared off a little, I lay down flat on the ground to hide. Once I entirely lost sight of it concealed in a cloud of snow, when all of a sudden I rushed at it, thrusting my knife several times into its flanks. It ran on, nevertheless, but I followed up its bloody tracks, and soon managed to get it killed. I brought it quickly to my house, and found it to be a fat buck; and thus I was provided sufficiently for the winter. Next summer I travelled to a place abounding in those animals, and I soon became well skilled in hunting them. But I was constantly getting very low-spirited: I did not much care for that sort of thing, but went in search of more daring excitement. However, I only happened to meet with some poor old *kivigtut* (plural of ᴋɪᴠɪɢᴛoᴋ). I had got to be very nimble-footed, and could run a race with any animal that ever was. Once I ascended the highlands, and got to the verge of the large glacier; and from thence I climbed my way on to an ice-bound land. My boots having got poor and soaked through, I proceeded to take out the skin-stockings in order to have them dried in the sun. Meantime, surveying the immense plain stretching out before me, at some distance I perceived a tiny black spot; moving on, I took it to be a raven, but presently it grew to be more like a fox, and this set me wondering in what manner a fox could possibly have got on to the glacier. When I again examined it, it had become the size of a reindeer; then it appeared like an *amarok*, or something like that. As I had all the time been in search of something appalling enough to rouse my dejected spirits, I resolved to front and attack the animal: on its approach, however, I found myself turning somewhat irresolute. As I stood mending my boots, I saw the beast bending down, and the ice flying about it on every side. Inwardly I wished it would keep to windward that it might not get the scent of me. I hastened to get on my boots, and fastened all my clothes about me to keep out the wind. Meantime the beast stood sniffing the ground; but all at once it bounded right towards me, and seeing this, I took to my heels, trying to gain the ice, where it was less smooth and slippery. The animal followed close at my heels, and I was thinking that all my diversion would likely end in being devoured by a monster. I now reached some large clefts in the ice, but soon noticed that, when I was obliged to leap, the monster merely took a long stride over, and I therefore looked out for a very wide crevice, thinking it would be quite as well for me to fall down the precipice as to be swallowed up by the beast. I barely managed to cross it: and no sooner had I gained the other side than I heard a fearful yell, and turning round, beheld the monster hanging perched on the edge of the icy rocks, unable to get up again. I sprang towards it; but before I had time to kill it, it was tumbling down the precipice—and thus I lost my prize. At the beginning of every winter I filled two storehouses with victuals, remembering the terrible want of the first winter. One evening, seated at my work in the house, I suddenly heard somebody passing through the entry, and two little women presently appeared before me: both were light-haired, and had a cleft in their upper lips. They each carried a bag with berries; and when they had sat down, no room was left in my little house. I treated them civilly, however, because they were my very first visitors. Both now poured out their berries, and begged me to eat with them; and I in my turn brought in grease and meat: but of this they would take nothing. I partook of the meal with them, and was much amused at their lively talking all the evening through. One of them jestingly said, 'When people don't keep an eye upon their stores, the wicked little foxes will come and carry them off; and then, when they happen to take them by surprise, they will run away, the tails turned right out;' and they went on laughing till they were quite out of breath. I joined their merry laughter, and felt very happy indeed. At length, however, they left me, taking their bags with them; and I now perceived for the first time that my guests had been hares disguised in the shape of women. Another evening, when I again sat working, two other little women entered the house; but these had a darker complexion and larger tufts of hair: they were still more amiable than the former ones, and likewise poured out their berries before me, and I brought forth tallow and dried meat as before. They ate of this with great pleasure; and having done, they said, 'These silly little hares, whenever they happen to meet folks, they sit down staring at them—they look so very funny with their cloven lips; and when they take to run, and people only say *itek*, they sit down on the spot.' In such wise we chattered away, and spent the evening very pleasantly together. Now I have got practised in running, and skip about from place to place whenever I know that people have newly left. Accordingly I came here. Thou alone hast taken me

by surprise; otherwise I seem to hear everything. When
the partridges sit down yonder behind the high moun-
tain-ridges, I shall be sure to hear them as if they were
quite close by: but thy steps I have not heard." From
the upper part of his boot the first Salik produced a
knife, and handed it to the narrator with these words,
" I have got nothing else wherewith to pay thee back
the pleasure thou hast given me." When both were
leaving, the story-teller said, " I feel a little indisposed
immediately after the meal, but just follow me with a
look;" and off he ran. Beyond the house was a high
sloping hill: this he went up as swiftly as a flying raven
that soars smoothly along, barely touching the earth,
and thus he went quickly out of sight. But Salik often
repeated the interesting tale of his namesake.

## 54.

## STORIES ABOUT THE ANCIENT KAVDLUNAIT.

[The four following tales are given in one section on account of their more
local character, being known only to the west Greenlanders, especially
the southernmost of them, and representing the only trace of intelligence left concerning the ancient Scandinavian settlers which the
author has been able to discover by inquiries made in the country.]

### (1.) UNGORTOK, THE CHIEF OF KAKORTOK.

IT once happened that a kayaker from Arpatsivik
came rowing up the firth, trying his new bird-
javelin as he went along. On approaching Kakortok,
where the first *Kavdlunait*[1] had taken up their

---

[1] Plur. of **kavdlunâk**, a foreigner, a European, a Dane.

abode, he saw one of them gathering shells on the beach, and presently he called out to him, "Let us see whether thou canst hit me with thy lance." The kayaker would not comply, although the other continued asking him. At last, however, the master of the place, named Ungortok, made his appearance, and said, "Since he seems so very anxious about it, take good aim at him;" and soon the kayaker sent out his spear in good earnest, and killed him on the spot. Ungortok, however, did not reproach him, but only said, "It certainly is no fault of thine, since thou hast only done as thou wast bidden." When winter came, it was a general belief that the Kavdlunait would come and avenge the death of their countryman; but summer came round again; and even two summers passed quickly by. At the beginning of the third winter, the same kayaker again rowed up to Kakortok, provided with the usual hunting tools, bladder and all. This time he again happened to see a Kavdlunak gathering shells, and somehow he took a fancy to kill him too. He rowed up towards him on that side where the sun was shining full upon the water, and launching his spear at him, killed him at once, upon which he returned home unobserved, and told how he had done away with one of the Kavdlunait. They reproached him with not having let their chief know of this; and the murderer answered them, "The first time I only killed him because I was asked over and over again to do so." Some time after this occurrence, a girl was sent out to draw water in the evening; but while she was filling the pail, she noticed the reflection of something red down in the water. At first she thought it to be the reflection of her own face; but turning round, she was horrified at seeing a great crowd of Kavdlunait. She was so confounded that she left the pail behind, and hurried into the house to tell what had happened. At the same time the enemies posted themselves in front of the door

and the windows. One of the inmates instantly ran
out, but was soon killed with an axe, and cast aside.
They were all despatched in this way : only two brothers
remained unhurt. They happily escaped out on the ice.
The Kavdlunait, however, soon caught sight of them,
saying, " Those are the last of the lot; let us be after
them ; " and at once began the pursuit. The leader now
said, " I am the quickest of you ; let me start after
them ; " and he followed them out on the ice, where the
speed of the brothers had been greatly retarded owing
to the younger one having got new soles to his boots,
which made them slippery, and caused him often to lose
his footing. At length they reached the opposite shore,
and Kaisape (pron. Kysapee), the elder, succeeded in
climbing the icy beach ; but the younger fell, and was
quickly overtaken. Ungortok cut off his left arm, and

held it up before his brother, saying, " Kaisape! as long
as thou livest thou won't surely forget thy poor brother."
Kaisape, who was not armed, could render him no assistance, but quickly took to his heels. He crossed the
country for Kangermiutsiak, where his father-in-law was
living. Here he remained all winter, and was presented
with a kayak. In summer he kayaked southward to
learn some magic lay that had power to charm his
enemies. He again wintered at Kangermiutsiak ; but
when the summer came round he went away to the
north, in order to find himself a companion. At every

place he came to, he first inquired if there happened to
be a couple of brothers, and then he went on to examine
the inside fur of their boots to see whether they had
any lice in them ; and he travelled far and wide before
he found two brothers, of whom the younger one was
altogether without lice.   This one he persuaded to
assist him, and made him return with him to Kangermiutsiak.   He was now very intent on catching seals ;
and of all he caught he had the hairs removed from the
skins, which were then used for white skins.   This done,
he went out in search of a large piece of driftwood, and
at last found one to suit his purpose.   He now proceeded to excavate it with his knife until it was all
hollow like a tube, and made a cover to fit tightly at
one end ; and both sides he furnished with little holes,
for which he also made stoppers of wood.   Being thus
far ready, he first put all the white skins inside the
hollow space, shut it up at the end with the cover, and
likewise closed the little side holes.   He then put it
down into the water, upon which all the kayakers joined
in towing it down the inlet to Pingiviarnek, where they
landed it ; and having got out the skins, attached strings
to them, then hoisted and spread them like sails, so
that the boat came to have the appearance of a somewhat dirty iceberg, the skins being not all alike white.
The people now got in : it was pushed off from land,
and Kaisape gave the order, " Let the skins be spread ! "
This was accordingly done ; and the people on shore
were astonished to see how very like it was to an iceberg floating slowly along.   Kaisape, who wanted to
take a survey of the whole from shore, said to the crew,
" Now ye can take the boat out yourselves, while I step
ashore to have a look at it."   When he beheld the work
of his hands, he was well pleased with it, and ordered
the boat to load again.   The skins were all spread out
to dry in the sun ; and when this had been done, he
remarked that he had not yet forgotten his brother.

They were now ready to go to Kakortok and have their revenge, but for some time they were obliged to station themselves at Arpatsivik, waiting a favourable wind to carry them up the inlet. When the fair wind had set in, the firth gradually filled with broken bits of ice of different form and size. Now was the time for Kaisape to spread all sail and get in. Several boats followed in his wake, but the crews landed a little north of Kakortok to gather fagots of juniper; while Kaisape and his helpmates, well hidden in the hollow wood, and keeping a constant look-out through the peep-holes, drifted straight on towards the house. They saw the Kavdlunait go to and fro, now and then taking a look down the inlet. Once they distinctly heard it announced, "The *Kaladlit* (plur. of kalâlek, a Greenlander) are coming:" upon which they all came running out of the house; but when the master had reassured them, saying, "It is nothing but ice," they again retired; and Kaisape said, "Now, quick! they won't be coming out for a while, I think." They got out on shore; and, well loaded with juniper fagots, they all surrounded the house. Kaisape filled up the doorway with fuel, and then stuck fire to it, so that all the people inside were burned; and those who tried to make their escape through the passage were also consumed. But Kaisape cared little for the people in general; his thoughts all centred in Ungortok; and he now heard one of his helpmates exclaiming, "Kaisape! the man whom thou seekest is up there." The chief had by this time left the burning house through a window, and was flying with his little son in his arms. Kaisape went off in pursuit of him, and approached him rapidly. On reaching the lake, the father threw his child into the water that it might rather die unwounded. Kaisape, however, not being able to overtake his antagonist, was forced to return to his crew. Ungortok ran on till he reached Igaliko, and there established himself with another chief

named Olave. On finding that Kaisape would not leave him at peace there, he removed to the head of the firth Agdluitsok, where he settled at Sioralik, while Kaisape established himself at the outlet of the same firth. The following summer he again left in pursuit of Ungortok, who, however, succeeded in getting to the coast opposite the island of Aluk. Kaisape traced him right along to the north side of the same island, where he took up his abode; and he now consulted the East-landers with regard to some means of killing Ungortok. At last one stood forth, saying, " I will get thee a bit of wood from a barren woman's boot-shelf, out of which thou must shape thine arrow." Having pronounced some spell upon it, he handed it over to Kaisape, who acknowledged the gift saying, " If it comes true that this shall help me, I will be bound to give thee my aid in hunting and fishing." He now went on making as many arrows as could be contained in a quiver fashioned out of a sealskin; and last of all, he added the precious charmed one, and then with his helpmates left for the great lake in front of Ungortok's house, where Kaisape stuck all the arrows in the ground at a certain distance from each other; and finally also the charmed one. He let his companion remain below by the lake, and cautiously mounted some high hills by himself, from whence he could see Ungortok striding to and fro outside his house. He heard him talk to himself, and mention the name of Kaisape. However, he resolved to await the coming of night to carry out his purpose. In the dusk he stole away to the house, and looked in at the window, holding his bow ready bent. Ungortok was passing up and down as swiftly as a shadow, on account of which it was impossible for him to take a sure aim. He therefore levelled his bow at Ungortok's wife, who lay sleeping with a baby at her breast. Ungortok, hearing a noise, gave a look at his wife, and perceived the arrow sticking fast in her throat. Mean-

time Kaisape had quickly run back to the margin of the
lake to fetch another arrow, while Ungortok sped after
him with uplifted arm holding the axe that had formerly
killed his brother in readiness for himself. Kaisape
launched his second arrow at him, but Ungortok escaped
it by falling down and making himself so thin that
nothing but his chin remained visible ; and before long

Kaisape had spent all his arrows, without having hit his
mark. Ungortok broke them in twain, and threw them
into the lake. But at last Kaisape caught hold of the
charmed arrow, and this went straight through the

protruding chin down into the throat.  As Ungortok
did not, however, expire immediately, Kaisape took
flight, but was shortly followed by the wounded Ungortok.  Kaisape had been running on for a good long
while, when all of a sudden he felt his throat getting
dry, and fell down totally exhausted.  Remembering
Ungortok, however, he soon rose again, and running
back to see what had become of him, found his dead
body lying close by.  He now cut off his right arm, and
holding it up before the dead man, repeated his own
words, "Behold this arm, which thou wilt surely never
forget!"  He also killed the orphan child; and taking
the old Eastlander with him, he travelled back to Kangermiutsiak, where he sustained the old man, whose
bones, according to report, were laid to rest in that
same place.


### (2.) THE FIRST MEETING OF THE KALADLIT WITH THE ANCIENT KAVDLUNAIT IN GREENLAND.

In former times, when the coast was less peopled
than now, a boat's crew landed at Nook (Godthaab).
They found no people, and traversed the fiord to Kangersunek.  Half-way up to the east of Kornok, near
Kangiusak, they came upon a large house; but on
getting closer to it, they did not know what to make
of the people, seeing that they were not Kaladlit.  In
this manner they had quite unexpectedly come across
the first Kavdlunak settlers.  These likewise for the
first time saw the natives of the country, and treated
them kindly and civilly; but the Greenlanders nevertheless feared them, and made for their boats.  On
getting farther up the fiord, they found many Kavdlunait
stationed.  However, they did not put in anywhere, but
hastened away as fast as possible.  When the boat and
its crew returned from their summer trip in the fiord,

they told their countrymen all around of their encounter with the foreigners, and many of them now travelled up to see them. Many boats having thus reached Kanger-sunek, they now began to have intercourse with the Kavdlunait, seeing that they were well disposed towards them. Later on in the summer, many more Kaladlit arrived, and the foreigners began to learn their language. At Kapisilik a Kavdlunak and a Kalalek, it is said, became such fast friends that they would not be separated, but were constantly together. They tried to excel each other at different games and feats of dexterity; and their countrymen on both sides were greatly diverted as lookers-on; but being both first-rate archers, their arrows always fell side by side. One day the Kavdlunak said, " Come, let us climb yon lofty hill; but first we will stretch a skin for a target to aim at on that little islet yonder; then we will try which of us can hit the mark. He who fails shall be thrown down the precipice, and the other remain the conqueror." The Kalalek answered, " No, I will not agree to that, because we are friends, and none of us shall perish." But the Kavdlunak persisted so long that his own countrymen at last said, "Well, let him be thrown down as it is at his own will;" and the Kalalek at last gave in, and they climbed the mountain together, accompanied by a crowd of spectators. The Kavdlunak was the first to shoot, but altogether failed; then the Kalalek came in for his turn, and pierced the skin in the centre. According to his own desire, the Kavdlunak was hurled down the precipice, and his countrymen only thought it served him right for having thus recklessly pledged his life. From that day until the present this mountain has been called Pisigsarfik (the shooting-place).

NOTE.—The two preceding stories are compiled from six different manuscripts, in which the contents of both are partly mixed up, and the same events have been localised for each of the two tracts of coastland in which ruins of the old settlements are still to be seen—viz., the district of Julianehaab, now most generally supposed to have been the old Easter-bygd, and the district of Godthaab, identified with the ancient Westerbygd. The second story, however, is only told by the Godthaab narrators, who appear to have linked the first one to it, having previously altered and adapted it for their homestead fiords of Kapisilik, Pisigsarfik, and Amer-alik, and inserted the tale of Navaranak (see No. 18) to explain the beginning of the warfare. The name Kakortok signifies Julianehaab itself, as also some very remarkable Scandinavian ruins about eight miles distant from it. Arpatsivik is an island between these places, upon which some very ancient sod-covered Eskimo ruins are still to be seen, and are pointed out as Kaisape's house.

(3.) THE ANCIENT KAVDLUNAIT'S RUIN NEAR ARSUT.

A kayaker one day went to the bay of Iminguit to catch thong-seals. Arriving there he observed a tent belonging to some Kavdlunait. He heard them jesting and prating inside, and was strongly minded to go and look in upon them. Accordingly he left his kayak, went up to the place, and began to strike on the sides of the tent. This made them apprehensive, and they now became quiet, which only encouraged him to continue all the more, until he succeeded in silencing them altogether. Then he took a peep in at them, and behold! they were all dead with fear. At Ikat, the Kavdlunait living there were also taken by surprise by the Kaladlit, and four fathers fled with their children out upon the ice, which, however, being too thin, broke through with them, so that all were drowned; and it is said that only a few years ago they might be seen at the bottom of the sea. It is a common tradition at Arsut, that whenever they become visible it is a sure foreboding that one of the people will die.

## (4.) ENCOUNTER OF KALADLIT WITH THE ANCIENT KAVDLUNAIT ON THE ICE.

[A tale received from North Greenland.]

It is said that the Kaladlit of the south country at times were attacked in the autumn season, when the lakes were frozen over, and the sea-shore was all bordered with ice. It once happened that a man had been out hunting, and came home with two white whales. In the evening a couple of girls came running into the house crying, " The enemy is coming upon us ! " At which the man got into a passion, and tore the fishing-line which he was busily winding up. But when he was about to go out, the Kavdlunait were already making an onset upon the house. The housewife, who had been newly delivered of a child, was by means of sorcery got through a window, and several escaped the same way ; but all those who attempted to get through the entrance were miserably killed. The master of the house, who had escaped along with his wife, returned to bring his mother out, but finding her badly wounded had to leave her to her fate. Some had in this manner escaped, and hastened away to hide themselves among the stone-heaps, from whence they heard the enemy's wild shouts of triumph. And the man had to witness his mother being dragged across the frozen lake by a rope fastened to her tuft of hair. Though greatly enraged, he tried to keep quiet in his hiding-place, but ordered the two girls down on the ice, saying, " Now ye go on to the edge of the water, and when they overtake you plunge yourselves into the sea." Sobbing and crying, they did as they were bid. No sooner had they been observed by the Kavdlunait than they were seen to run out after them ; but the ice was too slippery for them, and they lost their footing. Some fell on their backs, others sideways, and some went tottering about. The angry Kalalek now asked his people how many of the enemy had gone out on the ice, and whether any of them were still on shore. About this, however, they did not agree; but at last one of them said, " That all of them had now got down." Immediately the furious Kalalek rushed out on the ice, spear in hand, and another one in store. The first of the Kavdlunait he met with was instantly speared; the others fell on approaching him, and were likewise killed. When the point of his spear had got too sticky with blood, he would only take time to blow it away; and before the girls had reached the open sea, he had despatched the whole of them. However, he turned back again, and pierced them through their bellies, in order to complete his vengeance, and then returned to the house, where he found the inmates all killed.

## 55.

## PISAGSAK AND THE KIVIGTOK.

[This tale, having only been received from one narrator, appears too doubtful to be included among those that treat on the ancient Kavdlunait.]

PISAGSAK one day went out kayaking in order to try his new bird-javelin, and in the excitement of the sport was carried far away from his homestead. At length he arrived at the foot of a steep mountain-wall, from the top of which a long ladder was suspended; and having reached the top with great trouble, he surveyed a little plain spreading below him on the other side, covered with cotton-grass, the down of which was car-

ried along by the wind. On the further side the plain
was bordered by another mountain-wall. He climbed
this likewise, and far below, on the other side, he now
beheld a little house. He stole along to it and peeped
in at the window, but only saw one old kivigtok sitting at his work. When he was about to withdraw as
noiselessly as he had come, the old man accosted him,
saying, " Of course I have seen thee, so please to come
inside." Pisagsak now entered ; and the old man, all
shaky and shivering, in a peevish voice continued, " I
would like thee for my companion ; thou hadst better
stop with me ;" and so saying he went out, and soon after
returned with some dried meat and tallow. Pisagsak now
satisfied his hunger ; his host then went out, and took
some boiled reindeer out of a large pot, which pleased
him even more. At night Pisagsak could hardly sleep
for fear of his aged housemate. When he awoke in the
morning the old man had gone off, but on looking round
he perceived a great number of boots dangling on the
cross-bar beneath the roof. He took them, overhauled
them, and put them up to dry, and then proceeded to
do the cooking. In the evening he heard a noise, and
soon saw the old man coming along with two large
bucks. He now said to him, " Here is some work for thee
to put thy hand to ; come away and skin them at once."
Pisagsak remained with him, and took charge of the
household work ; he learned to snare partridges and
shoot reindeer, and after some time grew very dexterous as a sportsman. One evening the old kivigtok went
on, saying, " To-morrow is the day when the women of
the Kavdlunait use to come here to fetch water. I daresay there will be some young girls among them : we will
go and have a look at them." The following morning
they started, and arrived at a place from whence they
could see a great many houses, beyond which a spring
was visible ; and they went to hide themselves behind
some large stones. About sunrise the first girl came,

filled her pail, and retired. Others followed, some of whom were handsome, others were old and slow. A young and very beautiful woman now approached, and had just put down her pail, and commenced pouring in water, when Pisagsak noticed that the old man was getting very excited, and trembled all over. The next moment, however, he sprang on the young girl and carried her away, having first stuffed her mouth to keep her from calling out; and Pisagsak of course followed them. Having reached their house, they took away her boots to prevent her from running away, and only went out to hunt by turns, in order to keep watch on her. However, the girl at length got reconciled to her fate, and gave up all idea of flight; and they could now venture to leave the house together. On their return they always found the work of the house ready done, and their clothes and boots mended. Another day Pisagsak again accompanied the old man to the spring to look at the girls. This time the old man ordered Pisagsak to catch a nice one; but he lingered and waited till an old woman, wrinkled all over, made her appearance; then he rushed on and took hold of her, and brought her home; and when the old woman had passed one day with them, she came to like them, and did not care to go back. Now they had two women in the house, and they did exceedingly well. One day the kivigtok said to Pisagsak, "To-morrow the Kavdlunait will be making an assault on us from the sea-side; let us go and look out for them." The next morning they went away to the top of the high cliff, where the ladder was made fast, and they saw several boats approaching the coast. The old man now spoke: "Now they begin to land; but when they have all got on shore and try to climb the ladder, I will loosen it on the top, and then thou wilt see a sight." Pisagsak now stood in great expectation; and presently they had all got on the ladder; but not until the first of them appeared wielding his lance above the summit of the steep mountain-side did the kivigtok loosen the cords from the stone. A tremendous cry now followed, and the Kavdlunait were all swallowed up by the sea. Not one escaped. After this catastrophe the others for some time lived on in their usual way, but the old woman at length took ill, and died from sheer old age; and after that Pisagsak began to long for his own home. When he told his master, he did not object, but remarked, "Tell the Kavdlunait yonder that they had better not attack me; if they do, I shall certainly destroy them." Pisagsak now returned to his relatives, who had totally given him up, and he likewise brought them the message of the kivigtok, and never afterwards left home.

---

## 56.

## THE ANGAKOK TUGTUTSIAK.

[This tale, only received in one copy, has been adopted for the present collection on account of its referring to the process of being *angakok poolik*, frequently mentioned by the older authors in connection with the Greenlanders.]

TUGTUTSIAK and his sister were a couple of orphans, and lived in a great house. It once happened that all the grown-up people went away berry-gathering, leaving all children at home. Tugtutsiak, who happened to be the eldest of them, said, "Let us try to conjure up spirits;" and some of them proceeded to make up the necessary preparations, while he himself undressed, and covered the door with his jacket, and closed the opening at the sleeves with a string. He now commenced the invocation, while the other children got mortally frightened, and were about to take flight. But the slabs of the floor were lifted high in the air, and rushed after them. Tugtutsiak would have followed them, but felt himself sticking fast to the floor, and could not get loose until he had made the children come back, and ordered them to uncover the door, and open the window, on which it again became light in the room, and he was enabled to get up. He told his companions not to mention it to the old ones when they returned; but as soon as the boat landed in the evening some of the younger children forgot their promise, and said: "We have had great fun to-day; Tugtutsiak played at angakok, and when we got frightened and took to our heels, the slabs rose up from their place on the floor and followed after us." The elder people were astonished, but agreed to let him try it over again in the evening. At this proposal Tugtutsiak got frightened, and took to crying; but afterwards, when the hunting became bad, they wanted him to conjure up the sea-animals, and he was made to sit down and call forth a bear and a walrus, which were soon roaring outside the house. The bear went ashore and took hold of Tugtutsiak, and flung him along to the walrus, which again hurled him out to the bear. In this manner Tugtutsiak alternately was thrust from the walrus to the bear, and from the bear to the walrus, until he lost sight of his native country, and at length a new land rose in front of him; but this country was lower than the one he had left. Close to the shore the bear for the last time seized hold of him, and threw him upon the beach. Having got there, his senses revived, and close beside him he observed a house, and on the roof, above the passage leading to it, was a terrible dog, which, showing his white teeth, howled and snarled at him when he drew nigh. Nevertheless he approached, and for the first time observed that a bridge as narrow as a knife's edge led into the inner room,

which appeared totally dark. Still he proceeded, and
made his way to the main room, where the female owner
of the house lay on the ledge, suffering great pain. Her
hair was all loose and dishevelled, and her face turned
to the wall. On seeing Tugtutsiak, she started to her
feet, crying out aloud, " What hast thou come for ? thou
canst not take away what makes me suffer." But from
the narrow passage he rushed right upon her, took hold
of her by the hair, and flung her against the door-post.
Having, however, got his hands entangled in her long
hair, he was himself dragged along with her, and could
not extricate himself. He tried to throw her off, but
his hands could not be got loose ; and she surrendered
herself to him, saying, " Now I see thou mayst be capable of removing my sufferings." On closer examination Tugtutsiak found her eyes, nostrils, and mouth
stuffed with dirt and filth. He cleaned it away, and
threw it outside, after which the hideous woman grew
somewhat composed, and after a while resumed, " Now
do my hair." He put it up in the usual tuft, upon which
she took down some eagles' wings from a nail in the wall,
and stirred up the smoking lamp, so as to make it burn
brightly. For the first time he could now see that the
walls were hung with skins like those used for boat-
covers ; and though the lamp was now burning quite
clearly, he could not distinguish any objects in the more
remote parts of the room, which were in total darkness. A moment after he heard the horrible woman
saying, " My guest ought not to go alone ; let some one
accompany him out : " and presently a little man with
a very short nose emerged from out of the wall, and
after him a host of similar creatures, who all passed out
of the doorway ; when the last had vanished, they were
all heard to cry out, " Kah, kah—sa, sa !" just like the
shrieks of auks. Other varieties followed soon—some
with flat noses, and others with crooked ones ; but when
they were getting too numerous she cried " Stop !"

When the last were about to pass Tugtutsiak, he scratched some of them in the forehead, because he noticed that they were transfigured as soon as they passed the doorway, and he put a mark upon some of the most beautiful specimens, that he might know them again if he happened to catch them. Afterwards several other curious creatures appeared, some of them with large heads and great beards, and as soon as they were getting too numerous she again cried "Stop!" When these had all passed by, he observed that the lamp burned still brighter, and the way through the passage was now quite smooth, and sufficiently wide, and the dog wagged his tail quite amicably at him. Simultaneously with all these strange doings, his house-fellows at home observed that his belongings were shaking. On his way home he was again alternately thrown along by the bear and the walrus; but the last time by the bear, and he gained his homestead, where his relatives sat singing for him on his return. Being apprised of his arrival through the noise caused by his entrance, a great man among them gave orders, "Light the lamp for him;" and they could now see that no single spot of his body had remained unwounded. This arose from the teeth of the bear and the walrus, and they could not hear him breathe. The lamps were again extinguished, and the singing commenced; some time after he began to revive a little, but at daybreak they saw that his wounds were not yet healed, and so they continued the singing. There happened to be among them one ostentatious fellow, who on the following morning went out to have a look at the ice. On his return he exclaimed, "I guess it will be a meagre hunt he will procure us;" but Tugtutsiak only muttered, "Wait a bit —let my wounds first heal, and then we will see;" and when they began healing, a gale from the south-east had suddenly set in. A man who had gone out to reconnoitre quickly returned, reporting that the ice was

rapidly receding from the shore, and instantly afterwards auks and dovekies were seen in numbers. The inhabitants soon hastened out with their fowling-spears,
and they had their kayaks filled before evening. The
boaster, however, only got one bird. When they began
to catch seals, they gave to the angakok the first one
they caught, of all varieties; and he examined all he
got closely, hoping to find out those he had marked, but
all in vain. Some time after, however, the report came
that far away at Illulissat there had been caught a thong-
seal and a spotted seal both with a mark right between
the eyes.

## 57.

## THE WITCHCRAFT OF KULANGE.

IT was Kulange's (pron. Koolanghee's) business to
bring up and down the fishing implements, tools,
and arms of the kayakers. Having no kayak of his
own, he only roamed about the country. He had
but one friend; and on a certain day he saw his friend
engaged in opening a new grave and cutting a piece
out of the dead body. He had taken a morsel of flesh
and the bladder. He approached silently, and after
having watched his proceeding, he asked him what he
was about. The friend turned round, explaining to him,
" I want it to work some witchcraft." But having thus
been taken by surprise, he got ashamed and wished to
make it over to Kulange, saying that he might use it
advantageously any time he wanted to injure some great
hunter. He informed him that he ought to dry the
morsel of dead man's flesh, and put it beneath the point

of the hunter's harpoon, and that in this manner he might in less than a moment turn a clever hunter into a very poor one. The bladder he was likewise to dry, and if ever he happened to get an enemy, he was to blow it up, and, while the other was asleep, press the air out upon him. At length Kulange accepted the gift, and after making the grave up anew, they both departed. Meanwhile Kulange put by the things, intending to try them on the first occasion. About the beginning of winter one of his house-fellows had a particularly good hunt, and consequently got quite rich. Kulange at once determined whether he could put an end to his great good luck; with this view he put a bit of the flesh beneath the point of his harpoon, while the owner was sleeping, after which he sneaked silently away to his couch. On the return of the kayakers the following evening, it happened that only he on whose harpoon the bit of flesh had been concealed, was unsuccessful; and this continued from day to day until one day Kulange again took it away and cleaned the point well where it had been deposited. No sooner had this been done, than the kayaker returned tugging a large seal after him like all the rest, and he had the same good luck ever afterwards. Kulange now thought that he had sufficiently tested the magic power of the flesh, and he only awaited an opportunity to make somebody angry with him in order to try the effect of the bladder. It so happened that his daughter-in-law got offended with him, and in her wrath called him "the nasty Kulange." The next day it blew a gale from the south, and he went out to fill the bladder with air. When she was asleep in the evening, he went up beside her and let the air out upon her. At dawn she awoke with a swelling in her side, and later in the day she was swollen all over. Her husband instantly rowed away to fetch an angakok from a neighbouring place. He came back with him, and after having practised his incantations for some time in the darkened room, he knew enough to tell that the misdeed had been done by Kulange, who immediately confessed his guilt, saying, " I certainly did it, and here are the implements given me by my friend." Having heard the whole state of the case, the bewitching objects were sunk deep in the sea ; but the wicked friend was put to death.

----

## 58.

## THE OLD MEN'S REVENGE.

TWO men were living together, each of them having a son. When the young men were beginning to provide for them, the old ones resolved to abandon hunting altogether, and gave themselves up to their ease and comfort. One of them, who most valued a life of idleness and ease, soon got rid of all his tools and implements, while the other one had still a few left. Their sons used both to start in the morning as well as to return together at night; and they were accustomed to brave the fiercest gales, so that the parents were never alarmed on their account. Nevertheless, one day when they had left with fair weather in the morning, they happened not to return as usual in the evening. The reason was that they had fallen in with a man of more than common strength, well known in those parts as a formidable man-slayer, and he had killed them both. Under these circumstances, the old men had again to take to their kayaks ; but as one of them had no hunting-tools, he made a bird-javelin, the point of which he fashioned out of a sharp-edged piece of bone, for want of iron ; and for the point of his lance, having

nothing better, he used the rib of a seal. Their preparations made, they said to one another, " We may as well
run the risk and be off; we are not of much account
anyhow." Early the next morning they set off in their
kayaks, and soon lost sight of the outermost islands;
turning more to the north, they took care to keep right
in the glittering sunshine, that they might not so easily
be perceived. After a little while they detected an
almost giant-like kayaker hunting to the north of them.
They quickly paddled up to him, all the time keeping in
the sun. While he was stooping down, resting on his
paddle, they had recourse to charms, and hoped by this
means to get the better of him. When they had got
still closer, the one that had no weapons said to his companion, " When thou thinkest him to be within thy aim,
lose no time in thrusting thy harpoon at him : if he sees
us beforehand he will be sure to catch us both." At
these words the other rushed forward and lifted his harpoon. His companion thought he was going to throw
it, but while he was in the act of so doing, he took
fright and whispered, " Where ? where ? when ? " At
length, however, he did fling the harpoon ; but in the
meantime the murderer had heard the noise, and as
he was turning round to look for the cause, the other
missed him, only hitting the kayak. On this his companion exclaimed, " Did not I tell thee to be quick lest
he should forestall thee and make us both his prey ?
Now look well after thy bladder." The other merely
replied, " Now is thy turn ; lance thy javelin into him."
It cleft the air with a whizzing sound, and though it
first went beyond him, it quickly rebounded and struck
the manslayer on the crown of his head with a crack.
He was seen to stagger and fall over on one side ; and
now the first kayaker launched his spear at him, and
another splash was heard. When they had thus killed
him between them, they examined his body and found
that the javelin with the bone point had killed him

without even penetrating as far as the barbs. They now thought, " If we leave him here his relatives will know nothing of him; let us rather bring him to the coast." Tying him to their kayaks, they tugged him to the shore, where they soon discovered his house near the beach, and saw a person emerge from it, who, shading her eyes with her hands, took a survey of the sea, and then re-entered. This person was the daughter of the strong man, who, not expecting any other kayak, was only on the look-out for her father. She soon came out again, and seemed greatly astonished that the strange kayakers had already gained the coast. They now called out to her, " This is only what thou mightst expect. He killed our sons, and we have paid him back in the same manner." She remained quite motionless for some time; but at last she said in a low voice, " You are in the right; it is only what he deserved : " but she briskly added, " Ye ought to come up and visit our house." She could not help wondering that those two wretches had been able to conquer her powerful father. When she went on urging them to come up, and herself came further down the beach to welcome them, one whispered to the other, " Since the father was so fearfully strong, the daughter, no doubt, is not less so, so don't go." Though they had already started, she followed them running along the water-side, still beseeching them to come. But the old men were only the more afraid of her ; and though they had made a great distance from the shore, they could still see how she undressed herself, first taking off her jacket, then her boots, and at last her breeches, and seated herself thus naked on the water-edge. One of the old men seeing this, thought it good fun, and wanted to go back to her ; but his companion rebuked him saying, " What is it thou art about ? She will be sure to take thy life if thou goest." He gave up his intention, and having put further out to sea, they once more looked round and

saw the woman jump up and run up to the house without ever minding her clothes. The second kayaker
now remarked, "Being so strong, she will very likely
pursue us in her boat;" and he was not mistaken. Immediately they saw her creeping down beneath the
boat, intending to carry it down on her back; and they
could still hear her gnashing her teeth, calling out,
"Would I could kill them both like this!" at the same
time crushing a piece of wood to atoms between her
fingers. They at length lost sight of her. At home
they related how they had despatched the well-known
murderer; and their mind was somewhat relieved by
having had their revenge.

---

## 59.

### ATERFIO.

TWO widows, having each a son, had chosen their
winter quarters at no great distance from one
another. Both of them happened to have several neighbours; but though these principally consisted of rich
and prosperous people, they did not think of assisting
the poor orphans. Having lost their supporters, the
widows suffered much from want, and they therefore
admonished their young sons to be wise and kind to
the other children, lest they should be deprived of the
scanty help they now enjoyed. At last, however, the
relatives furnished the orphans with kayaks. He who
lived furthest south was named Aterfio, and the other
one living to the north was called Sukallassok. They
grew up to be much renowned for their strength and
vigour. They always chose their hunting-places far off

the coast ; and even in hard weather and heavy gales
went out, and never came home empty-handed.  On
their return they always used to give the orphans a
plentiful repast, and had special stores of provisions set
apart for orphan children against hard times.  One day
Aterfio had gone out hunting beyond the skerries and
islands ; the wind was northerly and the sky clear.  He
had already got two seals, and, expecting to catch some
more, he still rowed on, till all of a sudden he heard a
noise, and turning round, beheld Sukalassok with raised
arm aiming his harpoon at him.  Not being able to
make any resistance, he was obliged to await his fate ;
keeping his eyes on him, he capsized his kayak towards
him so as make the harpoon only touch the side of it.
As soon as he again had risen, the thought flashed
through him to revenge himself on Sukalassok ; but he
gave up the idea and turned towards home.  On his
arrival he did not mention the matter at all ; but sometime later, in a gale from the north, the same thing happened over again.  He forebore to take revenge ; but
this time told those at home that Sukalassok had twice
attempted to kill him.  But his mother bade him not to
take revenge.  " Never mind," she went on ; " let him
go on as he likes, only thou shun his companionship."
Soon after, however, Aterfio being busy in his hunting-
grounds, suddenly heard a whizzing sound close by,
and presently afterwards was grazed by an arrow, which
fell into the water alongside of him.  His wrath was
now up, and he could not resist paying him back.  In
less than no time he levelled his harpoon at Sukalassok
and killed him right off.  At home he reported his
deed, and said he would flee to the south, thinking it
probable that the relatives of Sukalassok might take
part with the slain and pursue him.  But his mother
told him he need not fear his new enemies, and he remained at the old place as before.  Soon after he married and got a son, whom he called Akeralik.  One day

an old man came to visit them, who reported that the
relatives of Sukalossok were ill-minded towards Aterfio ;
to which he rejoined, " They are quite welcome to anything ; and thou mayst tell them that I myself, my little
son, and the rest of the household, are ready to receive
them whenever they like." But from that day they
grew suspicious, and not long afterwards a great many
strange boats appeared off the coast. At the sight
Aterfio went in, relieved himself of his jacket, went
straight down to the beach, and seated himself on a flat
stone with his back turned to the sea. Rowing on, the
kayakers deliberated among themselves who should be
the first to wound him. Some of them quickly gained
upon the rest, and on coming quite close to him, the
foremost took up his harpoon to strike him ; although
it hit the mark, it did him no harm, but the harpoon
broke in three pieces. The next kayakers likewise un-
launched their harpoons at him, but had them broken in
the same manner without wounding him in the least.
They now held a council, and agreed in landing to try
a match with him on shore. Aterfio willingly attended.
The strangers stayed the night over ; and early the next
morning four stout and powerful men made their way
through the entrance ; but Aterfio said, " My house is
too small, let us fight in the open air." Having reached
the meadow above, one of the strong men instantly
rushed in upon Aterfio to try a wrestling-match with
him ; but Aterfio only turned to him and thrust him
down as easily as if he had been a fox, upon which he
soon died. The foreigners now made a general assault
on him, but he shook them off like children, and on the
way home he killed the whole of them. After this
Aterfio trained his son to all kinds of daring feats on
land as well as at sea ; and thus Akeralik grew to be a
man, and was still stronger and even more fearless than
his father. His hunting-ground was far out at sea, and he
hunted seals and white whales alike, and could keep his

breath under water as well as any seal.   One day when
they were a long way off the coast, a small-topped cloud
rose on the horizon.   Aterfio asked his son, "Dost thou
see the cloud yonder ?   When the mists come up from
that side it will not be child's-play ; let us put back with
all speed."   They put their seals on the top of their
kayaks and made them fast with the harpoon-lines, and
headed for the shore.   Each of them had captured two
seals.   Scarcely had they put about, before a heavy gale
came rushing down upon them, turning the sea into one
mass of foam, and completely hiding the land.   A roaring noise was now heard, and Aterfio said, " Take care
we don't smash together ; keep further away from me."
At the same time he saw a great sea topped with foam
close upon them, and turning side on, bolted across
them ; but notwithstanding, they kept their breath and
rowed away under water until they soon afterwards
both emerged on the surface.   At last his son got a tear
in his thick outer jacket ; then he spoke to his father,
" Now mind thine own self, I must needs speed on ; "
and he skimmed the surface like a falcon pursuing his
prey, and was lost to sight in less than a moment.   Both
safely reached home.   About this time the Southlanders
happened to hear the fame of the mighty Aterfio and
of his son Akeralik, who with his kayak matched a
falcon in speed.   Among this people of the south there
was a strong man named Tajarnek, who greatly longed
to have an encounter with Aterfio.   One day Aterfio and
all his family remained at home.   The air was clear
and the weather fine.   They saw a great many boats
and kayaks apparently passing by their place ; but
Aterfio came down to the water's edge, and hailed
them, shouting, "Where are ye for ?   It is late in the
evening ; ye had better put in and take shelter with us
for the night."   One of the men replied, " We have
heard of the mighty Aterfio, and have come to offer him
a match."   Aterfio replied, " He whom ye see is nothing

extraordinary, but his son is a man of great strength ; "
so saying, he pointed to him as he stood at his side, to
let them know of whom he was speaking. The kayakers
stopped short in great amazement, never thinking him
to be the person in question. But Aterfio went on,
" But here is a first-rate landing-place, and ye can pass
the night here." Accordingly they landed ; and after
a needful rest, they all resorted to a level spot above
the houses. Tajarnek first seized Aterfio, but was soon
thrown over — without being hurt, however. Several
times they closed with him, but Aterfio was as staunch
as a rock. Akeralik now thought it time for him to
interfere ; every man he touched was soon thrown down.
At first they turned them over without injuring them
further ; but at length they slew Tajarnek and all the
rest. All the Southlanders, women and children included,
were thus put to death. From this time upwards
Aterfio roamed all along the coast-side, and father and
son were equally renowned ; and they both ended their
days without ever having been wounded.

## 60.

## INUGTUJUSOK.

SEVERAL brothers lived in a large house with five
windows. About the time when the youngest of
them had grown to manhood, a widow with one beautiful daughter happened to live at a place not far off.
The brothers were very kindly disposed towards the
widow, and when the youngest had made the daughter
his sweetheart they grew still more intimate, and the

brothers never failed to bring her part of their hunt. Every night the bridegroom used to cross the country to see his bride, but unhappily there lived in that neighbourhood a wicked angakok, a man-slayer, named Inugtujusok. He had made himself a hiding-place by digging out a cave in the snow like those formerly used for fox-trapping. Close by the way on which the young man used to pass on going to his girl, Inugtujusok slyly made his cave, and went to hide himself there in order to waylay or murder him. One evening the young woman accompanied her lover home; when all of a sudden they caught sight of Inugtujusok emerging from the cave. On seeing him armed with a lance, they both took flight, and he pursued them closely, crying out to the girl, " Help me to tire him out ; if thou canst not I will kill you both." The girl pitied her lover, but being obliged to help the dreadful angakok she pretended to be pursuing him, and before long he was overtaken and killed. She returned home, and mentioned naught about the matter to her mother. The following morning, however, the brothers all came up to her house, calling out, " Where is our brother ? " No reply was made. Again they cried, " Where is our brother ? " but again no answer came. At last they tore a hole in the window, and constantly repeating their question, went on to break down the roof. Nor until the mother said, " They have begun to unroof our house, do give them an answer," did she exclaim, " Yesterday, on his return from our house, I accompanied him on the way, and saw him killed by Inugtujusok ; " and then she burst into tears. The brothers likewise returned in tears, and filled with hatred towards Inugtujusok. Well knowing that he was a great angakok, they durst not attack him at once, but gradually prepared themselves to defy him. At this time they heard that Inugtujusok intended to leave for the north for fear of his enemies. Inugtujusok travelled all the summer, and did not

settle down till late in the autumn, in the far north.
There he got a son, whom he brought up with great care,
saying, " That since they had many enemies he ought
not to grow up a good-for-nothing." When he was full-
grown he was so clever and dexterous that he could
catch the very *tikagugdlik* (beaked whale, *Balænoptera
rostrata*) with nothing but the ordinary kayak tools.
When he had attained to his perfection, and could not
be conquered by mere human beings, they remained no
longer where they were, but travelled back to the south.
The brothers had not meanwhile left their abode ;
but hearing that their enemy was drawing nigh they
went on to meet him half-way. One had furnished himself with a girdle of whalebone three fingers wide ; he
had first made it out of the skin of a thong-seal, and
tried to burst it open by pressing back his breath, but this
was not nearly strong enough ; and then he proceeded to
make the one of whalebone, as much tougher. This man
was thought the hardiest and strongest of all the brothers.
While they had gone to lie in wait for him on the islands
outside the country, Inugtujusok and his son happened
to set off in their boat, but on seeing their enemies they
would not go back there, but went to the place where
the brothers had formerly lived. Having passed the
night, they loaded their boat in order to proceed on
their journey. In the meantime the brothers had also
loaded their boat, ready to pursue them as fast as possible. Discovering their intention, Inugtujusok did not
proceed, but returned to his former quarters ; and the
brothers said, " Let us rather remain where we are, that
we may not frighten them away." Winter had now set
in, and a little daughter belonging to one of the brothers was taken very ill. They now advised " Let us call
in the angakok Inugtujusok that he may come and try
his art upon her ; and when he has done we will of
course put him to death." An old bachelor who lived
in the house with them was now sent off on this errand ;

and when he had brought his message to Inugtujusok, the angakok answered, " Well, let it be so." His son was away at the time ; but he was beginning to think that in the course of time their feelings had probably softened, and their thoughts of revenge been given up. He was himself beginning to grow old, and he accompanied the bachelor back. On entering, the brothers cried, " Poor thing, thou art getting rather aged ! " " I am so," he answered ; and this was all he spoke. They treated him to a good meal, and in the evening the invocation commenced ; and soon they agreed that the little girl improved at once, The brothers thanked him, saying, " Thou mayst sleep without fear, and go back to-morrow." When he awoke and found himself all alone he suspected evil, and started up. On raising his head in stepping over the door-sill of the outer entrance, he encountered a man standing close by, who accosted him, saying, " It is very fine weather, but it is only daybreak, and rather dark yet." On hearing these words he trembled. After speaking, the man, though not he with the strong girdle, struck him on the head, and almost stunned him, upon which the others rushed in upon him, beating him so that his head was bruised, and the brain gushed forth. The next morning the son of Inugtujusok came on, ready for them. He was taking such strokes with his oars that the prow of his kayak rose right out of the water, and he exclaimed, " I suppose ye have done for him ! " They made answer from land, " If thou venturest to approach this place we shall send thee straight after him." At these words he rushed on in a great passion ; but they stood ready to receive and shake him off. Finding it quite impossible to get on shore he at length gave it up, and wheeled round, crying, " To-morrow ye shall be my spoil ! " The old bachelor, however, warned him, saying, " Thou hadst better give it up, and leave thy father alone. He was only paid back according to his deserts, being himself a

man-slayer." And the son of Inugtujusok responded,
"Let it be as thou proposest; perhaps I shall only
get new foes if I carry out my thoughts of vengeance.
People seeming to have no relatives, when they get
enemies generally have some relations (viz., avengers)
turning up." And report says that in this manner they
were reconciled.

## 61.

## THE SONS WHO AVENGED THEIR MOTHER.

A GREAT many brothers were living in a house together, with but one female; that one being their
old mother. Beside the house they occupied was another inhabited by an old couple, whose children consisted of girls only; and they never left their parents.
When the brothers removed to the other side of the
fiord in search of provender the old people followed
them, and took up their abode a little further down the
coast. Here the mother of the many men died, and
being bereft of their housewife, the youngest brother
had to do the general work. On alternate days the
elder ones went out kayaking, and repaired to their
mother's grave to mourn her death. At last they
moved back to their usual winter station, and the old
people likewise resorted to their hut. From this place
also the brothers continued alternately to go out hunting one day, and visit their mother's grave the next,
whereas the youngest always stopped at home to flense
the seals and attend to the other house-work. One day,
on reaching the grave, they noticed that the top-stones

had been disturbed, and were out of their proper place ; the day after they again went to the tomb, and, after hiding their kayaks, concealed themselves behind some heaps of great rocks. When dawn had changed into broad daylight they saw a kayaker putting off from their own shore, and when he came nearer, they recognised him as their own old neighbour. They first supposed him to be going to a small uninhabited house down on the coast ; but this he passed by, and went right up to the grave, where he at once began to rummage about. The brothers now said, " There is plain proof ; he is the criminal ; let us kill him to-morrow." They soon saw the old man descending to his kayak, and pulling back across the fiord to his own home, and followed him. The next morning they sought him in his tent : he had not yet arisen. The eldest brother went first, and after him followed the others. The leader now accosted the old man, saying, " It is not without reason we have thus come to thee, but because the tomb of our mother has recently been disturbed." " But who could possibly have done it ? " the old man exclaimed ; " I am but a poor decayed fellow, and am hardly able to get up to the little house on the shore." The eldest brother answered him : " Notwithstanding, I know thou art the trespasser, inasmuch as we all saw thee pilfering about the grave yesterday ; " and so saying, he rushed upon him, and hauling him outside the tent killed him on the spot. This done he returned to the hut, and going right up to the eldest girl, said to her, " Thy father shall recompense me through his daughter ; " upon which he brought her home and took her for his wife. The next day the younger brothers were to watch her during the absence of the elder ones, lest she should make her escape. She remained there for a long while, but continued to be very obstinate, and could not be made to lie down on the ledge, but remained sitting up till dawn of day. At last she determined to kill her husband.

He always used to put his knife in front of the lamp on coming in for the night. One evening when all were fast asleep, and her husband lay beside her, she took hold of the knife, having first tied on her boots well. The thought struck her, however, "If the others awake at his cry, they will no doubt turn upon me at once; but let them take my life too, as they have already taken that of my poor father." Putting aside her fears, she stabbed him in the bosom, and in a moment he silently expired. Without drawing the knife back, she hurried away to her mother's house, saying, "Pack up thy things speedily and let us be off; I have killed the eldest brother." That same night the boat was loaded, and they started. She who had slain her husband questioned the man at the steer-oar, "What way are we going?" He answered, "I shall follow the coast up north." But she thought that the pursuers would most probably likewise take that direction; when he turned to the south, she feared that they would do the same, when they had sought them in vain to the north; and she advised him to steer right to sea. No sooner had they turned their prow off the land than the foremost of the women-rowers broke her oar. She asked for that of her neighbour, but broke that too; and thus went on to break them all, one after another, and at last wanted the steersman to give up his too. He then asked her, "What wouldst thou have me steer with?" She said, "With thy kayak-paddle, of course." They now rowed on with the only oar left, he steering with his paddle. The mother, who had her place in the bottom of the boat, said to her son, the steersman, that they would soon be in sight of land ahead of them, and told him to steer straight towards the sun, and follow the coast southwards. As she had said, a great looming land soon broke upon their sight; and observing a house on the shore, they landed there. It so happened that only one man was standing outside; with this exception all there happened to be women. They were invited to come in, and they accordingly entered.

In the meantime the brothers of the murdered man, who were left behind in their former place, awoke and found him stabbed, and steeped in blood beside them. They hastened along to the house of their neighbours, and finding it empty, at once made ready to pursue them. First they scanned the coast to the north, and asked intelligence of everybody they met with ; but not gaining the information they sought, they put about ; and having again passed by their own place, they now rowed south. There they had no better luck ; and having roamed about for a long time, they only returned home in time to get settled for the winter. Next summer they also put out to sea, intending to cross the sea for Akilinek, but having reached the land on the other side, they made to the north instead of to the south ; and having put many inquiries to different people they happened to meet with on the coast, they gave up the chase, and settled down there.

Meantime the second of the sisters that had escaped had got married to the only man of their place ; and their brother, on his side, had chosen a wife among the sisters of his brothers-in-law. On getting a son, he called his name after that of his poor deceased father. The grandmother ordered them, " Bring me my bag !" and having got it she produced the *whetstone of the inuarutligaks* (mountain-elves) from the bottom of it ; and rubbing the new-born baby with it, she went on repeating : " Child ! be as *hard* as this stone" (viz., invulnerable, by charm) ; and each time the child got a new suit of clothes she would give him a rub with the stone, repeating the words, " Be hard," &c. In course of time, when the son had got more children, he one day chanced to ask whether there were no more people in that country. One of the women answered him, " Ah, yes, to the north of us are plenty of people, but having never been

there we don't know them." After this he tried to persuade his brother-in-law to follow him thither. At first,
however, he would not consent to go to these strange
people; but when the other went on entreating, he at last
agreed, and they started with only one boat. After a
rather long journey, they at last passed by a foreland,
under shelter of which they saw a great many tents
pitched round a little bay. The fugitive, next morning, ascended a hill; but seeing a kayaker shove off from
land he hastened down, and likewise got into his kayak
in order to make his acquaintance. On getting up with
him, he thought he knew his features, thinking them to
be those of the next younger brother he had been living with in his former home. On their way to the
hunting-place, he went on to question him thus: "Art
thou a native of this country?" "Yes, I was born
here." "Art thou also grown up here?" "No, I am
neither born nor grown up here, but in the country opposite. When our eldest brother was killed by his wife
we left our land in search of her, hoping to find her out,
and finally landed here." The fugitive said, "Art thou
married?" "Yes, I am." "Are all thy brothers married?" "Yes, excepting the youngest." "Hast thou
got any children?" "Yes, two—both boys." "Have
thy brothers got children?" "Yes, and all of them
boys." On his return from the hunt, after having been
seated a little while in the tent, the inmates heard a
noise of many people outside, and presently all those
brothers came rushing in. He who was now the eldest
sat down opposite to his former sister-in-law, and at
once exclaimed, "These people are easily recognised."
To this the fugitive answered, "Maybe we are easily
recognised, but so ye are too, although ye pretend to be
foreigners." The eldest brother said, "Can we possibly
let them remain alive, now that we have at length fallen
in with them?" Their old adversary, the woman who
had committed the murder, was busy making sewing-

thread. Her brother said, "They say that womankind
are not fit to revenge themselves on men;" and taking up
a large knife, he gave it to the other, saying, "Look
here ; that poor boy is named after my father, whom ye
killed, appease your thirst of vengeance by killing him
first." The bad man at once thrust his knife at the
boy, who was standing erect in the centre of the tent;
but the knife glided off him, and a sound was heard as
if it had struck against something hard. On finding
that they were not able to pierce him through, he examined the knife and found it broken ; on which he returned it to the owner, and they all left the tent. Shortly
after, the former fugitive went outside and saw to his
amazement the people preparing to leave the place. He
then determined to do the same ; and both parties
started at the same time. The brothers crossed the sea
to go to their own country ; but the fugitives remained
for good at their new place of abode, where they lived,
they and their successors, and where their bones are
said to rest.

---

## 62.

## ERNERSIAK THE FOSTER-SON.

LITTLE Ernersiak lived with an aged stepmother
at a place where a number of men, who were all
brothers, housed together, and at that same place there
was also an immensely strong man. In the autumn the
youngest brother fell sick, and getting worse and worse
at length died. They all agreed in suspecting Ernersiak's
mother of having caused his death, and they only waited
a time when they should find her alone in the house to

charge her with the deed. One morning Ernersiak furnished himself with some strings, and went away to set up fox-traps, and the brothers, profiting by his absence, entered and struck the old woman dead. But the strong man took pity on Ernersiak; and when he saw him returning he went out to meet him, and said, "Don't thou go into the tent; thou won't see her any more; the brothers killed her this morning as soon as thou wert gone;" and the strong man adopted him, and, for want of a better, gave him a bit of his dear mother's backbone for an amulet. The strong man brought him up, and trained him according to the rules of strength: early in the morning he lifted him off his couch by the hairs only, and the boy did not awake till he was put down on his feet. His new parents gave him a suit of clothes, but these did not last long, because he had always to exercise himself throwing and carrying stones. One evening, when they were late up, his new father took a skin, and spreading it on the floor he began to teach him how to draw hook and crook. But he admonished him not to join the other children at ball-playing, and for this reason Ernersiak was always seen standing with one arm out of his sleeve (a token of modesty), and regarding them from a safe distance. One day, however, while he was thus looking on, he got a severe stroke on the top of his head, at which he fell to the ground in a swoon; when he came to himself, nobody was near. Another time he was again struck down in the same manner, but on rising he plainly saw some one sneaking away. Hurrying after him, he found him hiding behind a rock; and making right up to him, he took hold of him by the collar of his jacket, and, hurling him several times round in the air, flung him to the ground with such force that the blood gushed out of his mouth and nose. "Ernersiak has been up to mischief," was now all the cry; and a large skin was produced to carry the wounded boy away upon, while

Ernersiak seated himself on a little mound in front of the house. Soon after the kayakers were seen to return, and they were welcomed with the same cry—"Ernersiak has been up to mischief." When his foster-father heard this, he speedily loosened his towing-line, and running up to Ernersiak said that they intended to kill him. The brothers by this time had also got on shore, and hearing what had happened, one among them ran to fetch his spear, the others all following him. The father of the wounded boy flung his lance with all his strength at Ernersiak, who remained sitting, his back turned towards them; and though Ernersiak remained unhurt, the lance was broken in pieces. The others now tried their lances, but with no better luck. In this manner, we are told, his foster-mother's amulet wrought its first wonder. They now gathered round him and caught hold of him; but though they were so many that he could hardly be seen in the crowd, they were not able to throw him over. All of a sudden, he turned round upon them, seized them one by one by their fur collars, and hurled them all bleeding to the ground. His foster-father now advised him to stop, lest he should get too many enemies, upon which he followed him into the house, where he seated himself, but could not be made to eat or speak. In the evening his foster-father fetched him some liver, hoping he would relish that, and on entering with it, remarked, "The very last boat is now leaving us, and we shall have no neighbours henceforth." On hearing this, he leaned forward and chuckled grimly, well knowing that he had been the cause of their hasty departure; he enjoyed the idea vastly, and from that moment he began to find his appetite. His father, who now deemed it only fair that he should have his own kayak, set to building him one, and subsequently began to teach him how to manage it, and before long the pupil proved himself very apt at paddling as well as hunting in kayak.

When his father awoke in the morning, his son had already fetched his kayak-jacket, and when the father went away for his own jacket, the son was already seated in his kayak, waiting for his father, and invariably returned home with some capture. One day he had been waiting in his kayak for his father to come down and start with him ; but thinking him too long about it he paddled away alone, following the coast southwards, and there, behind a cape, he suddenly fell in with another kayaker. This man, however, did not recognise Ernersiak, because he left him before he had got his kayak. He asked him to go with him and visit his people ; and presently they came upon a place covered with tents, in front of which a number of people were engaged in building boats, kayaks, &c. On catching sight of Ernersiak and his companion, they shouted, " Look there ! Ernersiak has turned a kayaker." At this moment Ernersiak's companion paddled on in advance of him, intending to make the shore before him ; but Ernersiak followed him close, and almost before " He is going to kill thee " had escaped the bystanders, Ernersiak lifted his harpoon and killed him from behind, then paddling up to him, drew it out and turned his back upon them. Having passed the cape he put ashore and climbed the top, there to await his pursuers ; but when night set in, and no one had as yet appeared, he again set off for home. On reaching it he sulked, and would not eat. His father guessed he had been guilty of some murder, and then went on warning him against making too many enemies for himself. After this he was again persuaded to take some food. The following day the father kayaked the same way past the cape, and came in sight of the tents, with the people at work outside them. He paddled quite close to the beach and cried out, "If ye remain in this neighbourhood I and my son Ernersiak won't fail to despatch the whole of you ; but I have heard of plenty good hunting away to the north, and I will encourage

him to go thither." After this speech he returned, and
did not fail to tell his son the exciting report, and found
him very anxious to try that place. In the spring they
left their old quarters, and travelled northwards the
whole summer-time. Just as the frost was beginning to
harden the earth a little, they got to a place with many
tents, and being hailed from land to put in there, they
went ashore accordingly. They were very civilly received, and were not allowed to trouble themselves
about their luggage ; the inhabitants of the place un-
loaded and carried it all up for them. It happened that
Ernersiak being somewhat fatigued with kayaking, had
seated himself in the boat for a rest ; and on finding his
tools and weapons so heavy that they had to carry them
on their shoulders, the people remarked, that he was not
likely ever to have more use for them. The foster-
father overhearing their talk, in the evening repeated it
to Ernersiak, who, tickled at the idea, burst out laughing. This was his first mirth since the murder. In this
place they passed the winter. One morning, on coming
outside, Ernersiak was astonished not to see any one
about the houses as usual ; but on glancing round he
observed them standing on a hilltop looking out upon
the sea. When he had joined them, they enlightened
him as to the reason, saying, " We are watching the red
walrus." Ernersiak, on seeing the ocean all a foam,
hastened down to his kayak, and set off towards them.
He soon detected a large walrus, comparatively quiet.
When he came close to it, the animal lifted its head
above the surface, and holding back its breath quietly
regarded him ; but when it had come quite close, it
tossed back its head, blew a great puff of air at him, and
rushed towards him, while he kept steadily moving in
upon it. About the distance of an arrow-shot, he aimed
his weapon at it, and when the animal bent down and
curved its back, he lanced and thrust, instantly de-
spatching it. Having towed it ashore, he went back

to catch one more before he landed for good himself. Towards spring they again prepared to go south, but their hosts invited them to come back and pass the winter with them. They thanked them very kindly, but being once more in the south, they stopped, and never afterwards visited the north.

---

## 63.

## THE OLD SOUTHLANDER.

IN days of yore there was an old man who lived down south with his only son, a very dexterous and able sportsman, in the country near Agdluitsok (South Greenland). When this son was able to supply their wants, the father left everything to his care, and for his part lived only to eat and sleep. One day the son did not return as usual in the evening. It was the season for the large *hooded seals* (bladder-nose *Cystophora cristata*), and the father thought he was lost. In sight of his abode was a plain with many tents, the inhabitants of which consisted partly of a number of brothers, among whom there was one of great fame. There also was a cousin of the old man living there ; and whilst the latter was bewailing and mourning the loss of his son, this cousin came to see him, and informed him that his son had been put to death, and that the middlemost among the brothers was the transgressor. The old man was greatly enraged at this intelligence. That same spring he secured a large piece of driftwood, which he cut up and wrought out of it various heavy tools, such as a harpoon and a lance. He also provided himself with a new bladder. From that time he resumed all his former habits—going out kayaking, always hoping to find an opportunity to avenge his son. One morning early, he went off to one of the hunting-grounds farthest out at sea. After a while he came back inside the reefs, and on approaching the shore encountered a kayaker towing a seal and making for the land. This was the murderer of his son. Keeping right in the sunlight, he looked carefully about to see if they were alone; and having first made sure of his man, who did not detect him, being blinded by the sun, he suddenly rushed in upon him, and, lifting his weapon, gave him the death-stroke. He towed him towards land; but on seeing an iceberg driven up on the rocks by the tide, he made him fast to this; and leaving him there, pursued his way landwards to let his brothers know what had happened. They were all at home, and his cousin was among them. They were sitting in the open air outside their tents, when they suddenly beheld him paddling in with unwonted speed. He stopped short, and called aloud to those on shore, " Since your brother wanted to get rid of his life, I have done away with it." He then turned quickly away, and made for his own abode. They all stood gazing wonderingly at him while he was making such way through the rushing waters, all foaming about him. Then the brothers began to cry, and prepared to fetch home their dead. They found him awfully massacred. But the old man again ceased kayaking and hunting from the time he had killed the murderer. Whilst he still had his tent pitched alongside of his winter-house, his cousin one day came to tell him that the brothers had been calling several relatives together with a view to attacking him in company. When he heard this, he employed himself in making a great supply of arrows, but otherwise remained quietly at his place, not leaving home at all. One day he espied the long-expected kayakers crossing the bay to attack him in his loneliness. He went to fetch his bow; and, dividing his arrows into three portions, he brought each portion down to a different little point on the beach. Having thus prepared for them, he stood awaiting his enemies with no other arms than his bow. One of the men was just making ready to jump ashore when the old man, perceiving it in time, came running on to the nearest point, and pulling out one of his arrows, aimed at him, whereat the other retreated. Another now tried to land on the second cape, but the old man as quickly reached it, and had his bow ready bent for him. At the third point they fared no better; and becoming awed by his great expertness, they soon retreated. Subsequently he was again informed of an intended attack, and that they were coming in still greater number; but he said, "They may come whenever they please; this time I am not even going to use any weapons; I only intend to show my face." His tent, they say, lay just above the water-mark. The tide happened to be full; and there he sat within singing a magic song to have his face enlarged; and as he sang, it grew in size, but he went on until it fairly resembled the full moon. He then went out into the front part of the tent, hiding himself among the skin-curtains. At this time one of the men had just got out of his kayak, and prepared to enter; but turning round, he started at seeing the terrible face which the old man poked out towards him through the entrance. "A face! a face!" was all he could utter in his terror; and almost capsizing his kayak, he put about, and quickly rowed away. Another was now ready to enter, but met the same face; and merely by showing his face, he succeeded in keeping them all off, and was attacked no more. When they were all gone, he sang a counteracting lay to get his face to its proper shape again. Next spring, he heard that his enemies, in company with some others, were chasing spotted seals. He now made himself a couple of very large bladder-arrows;

and one fine day kayaked away to have a look at them. Before long he heard them shouting; and catching sight of them, he rowed right in amidst them. The foremost of them had just flung his arrow at a seal, but on thus suddenly beholding the old man with his tremendous arrow, both he and his companions were startled; and whilst they all sat staring at him, the wounded seal dived up in front of the old man's kayak. He darted on to pierce it with his two big arrows; and tearing out the first one, he threw it contemptuously to the owner. With one hand he lifted the seal upon the kayak behind him, and left his enemies in utter amazement. They never afterwards ventured to attack one who, notwithstanding his great age, had such strength and vigour left. The old man at length died in peace without being killed or even wounded.

---

## 64.

## NAUJARSUAK AND KUKAJAK.

[A tale from South Greenland.]

NAUJARSUAK and Kukajak were friends, and both skilled hunters. They lived apart; but being very fond of each other, they were often together. In spring, when the first seals had made their appearance, they used to bring full-loaded boats with dried meat to their storehouses. Once Kukajak happened to have put by a greater store than his friend, and this made Naujarsuak jealous. Kukajak used to go away deer-hunting in the spring, and did the same that summer; and on his way home in the autumn, he was as usual to pass by his store-places on the coast, and take out some dried seal-meat for a welcome feast at home. He was longing greatly for some dried seal-flesh himself. But on arriving at his stores, he found that the foxes had been there beforehand, and had left nothing for him. On a close examination, he found out that some one had been making little holes in the stone coverings, just large enough for a fox to pass through. He got extremely vexed ; and at home he learned that Naujarsuak had made the holes during his absence. At this intelligence he became still more angry ; but nevertheless he could not help longing for his friend ; and he started on a visit to him the day after. Naujarsuak, in his turn, was longing as much to see Kukajak ; and as soon as the other had arrived, he hastened to draw his kayak on land, and take him to his house. During the meal, Kukajak carelessly observed, " I also had a small portion of dried meat put by, but the foxes have carried it all off, which has never happened to me before." Naujarsuak remarked, "Thou hast been wrong in coming so late to look after thy stores." At this speech Kukajak got inwardly enraged. Having passed the night beneath his friend's roof, he, as usual, invited him to accompany him home to have some dried reindeer-flesh. While they were thus talking, they saw from land some kayakers stopping outside, lying in wait for seals, when, all of a sudden, Kukajak came upon his friend from behind, and sent his harpoon right through him. The little son of Naujarsuak was standing on the beach, and saw his father being killed, while Kukajak called out, " I paid him back, because he spoiled my stores," and then turned his back upon them, and rowed home. The old father of Naujarsuak now took away the corpse of his son, and had it buried ; and when the usual days of mourning had gone by, he accosted the little one thus—" Now thou hast seen thy father killed, it will not do for thee to grow up in idleness." He then resolved

to leave his place, where he was continually reminded
of his lost son. They travelled on to Amerdlok (the
present Holsteinsborg), where they established themselves for the winter. Here the boy grew up under the
constant care and unceasing admonitions of his grandfather ; and he was never seen to smile. While they
were still at Amerdlok, he grew to manhood, assisted
at the whale-fishing, and turned out an able and expert
kayaker. Under these circumstances, the old man
advised him to go southwards and revenge himself on
Kukajak, if he were still alive ; and during this last
winter he carefully secured the whalebones whenever a
whale was caught, knowing them to be a rare article,
much in request in the south. When the first thaw set
in, they started ; and at every place they passed by,
they inquired, " Have ye heard nothing of Kukajak ? "
but invariably the answer was, " No ; we don't know
him." Far away south, however, they met some people
who told them—" Kukajak ! ah, yes ; he is all right !
but getting rather old now, and has taken to frog-
fishing." At length they reached their former home,
and settled there for good. All their relatives immediately came to see them after their long absence ; and
on leaving they presented them with some of the longest
and best whalebones. They had many unexpected
visitors, some of whom only came in the hope of
getting their share of whalebones, which were well
known to be desired for gifts. As time wore on, they
had to change their tent for a winter hut ; but as yet
Naujarsuak's son had had no opportunity of avenging
the murder of his father. He one day requested his
grandfather to make him a very big harpoon, with a
strong line to match. The grandfather got it ready for
him the very next day ; and, regarding it with great
satisfaction, the son smiled, and thanked him, and concealed it carefully beneath the ledge. Some time after,
Kukajak took a great fancy to go and ask the son of

his betrayed friend for a piece of whalebone for his
fishing-line, but on further consideration gave up the
idea, fearing that he might bring down vengeance upon
himself if he carried it out.   However, the people there-
about were always telling him of the gifts they had
received, saying, " If thou goest, thou wilt be sure to
get some too : it was only the other day the old man
said that he longed much to see thee."   On hearing this,
he could resist no longer, and started the very next day.
He got a friendly welcome, and was beginning to think
" they had forgotten all about the murder."   A plentiful
repast was soon served up before him ; and the talk went
merrily round all the evening ; but somehow, whenever
there was a short silence, he always thought, " there,
now, it all returns to them."   At daybreak the following morning, when Naujarsuak's son went outside the
house, the thought struck him it was just on such a day
that his father was killed.   The air was soft, and light
clouds appeared and passed by overhead.   At this his
former wrath awoke with full force ; but on entering the
house, he looked quite guileless.   At Kukajak's departure, he also was presented with whalebones.   Still he
apprehended some evil, and kept glancing back to be
sure that he was not pursued ; and thus he succeeded
in getting a considerable way off.   Now, however, was
the time for Naujarsuak's son to make use of his new
weapon.   He took the bone-point which his grandfather
had made, brought it down, and fixed it with a loud
jerk.   Kukajak heard the sound, and recognised the
meaning (viz., charm) of it ; and seeing his enemy in
full pursuit, he hastened on as quickly as he could, but
found his strength fast failing.   Perceiving this, his
enemy pursued him more slowly ; and Kukajak began
thinking that he might reach home unharmed.   At that
moment, however, his adversary again darted on, and,
just outside his own house, took aim, and sent his lance
with a great crash into Kukajak's body.   The son of

Naujarsuak now turned to the bystanders, saying, " I saw him treat my father in the same way ; and I have only paid him back ; if ye care for his corpse, ye may take it." Having finished this speech, he left for home ; and from that day his father was not always in his thought, though he never quite forgot him.

## 65.

## THE TWO FRIENDS RESCUED BY THE BENEVOLENT INGNERSUIT.

ONE widow lived all alone with her son at a winter station ; and a little more to the south another widow, also with an only son, had her residence. The young men were fast friends, and used to go out kayaking and perform their several tasks in company. But one morning the one who was to the north seeing the clear bright sky and a light breeze from the east, resolved on going to the hunting-place by himself, without waiting his friend's arrival. After he had been on the hunting-ground for some time, he suddenly heard a noise from the sunny side of the bay, and, turning round, he saw his friend with gloomy looks and hand uplifted, about to throw his harpoon at him. Having no other choice, he kept his look steadily fixed on him ; and the moment the harpoon came flying towards him, he upset himself, kayak and all, so that the weapon touched the edge of the kayak, and fell splashing into the water beside him, after which he again rose by means of his paddle. The other now proceeded to coil up his harpoon-line ; and without further reference to the matter, the friends as usual remained together, catching their seals, and speaking pleasantly to each other on the way home. Still he kept an eye upon his companion, but did not find anything to rouse his suspicion. Another time he again left home without waiting the arrival of his friend, and the same thing happened. After a third similar attempt, however, he resolved to revenge himself. He did so in the following way: As soon as he rose above water after having capsized his kayak as before, he aimed his harpoon at his friend, who, however, averted the danger by likewise upsetting himself; but before he was able to get his kayak righted, the other was by his side and kept him from rising by running the point of his own kayak right across the one that lay bottom upwards. After having killed his friend in this manner, he rowed towards land; but before he reached the first islets, he noticed the water coming fast into his kayak. He pulled as quickly as possible, but all in vain, and was only kept above water by means of the bladder. He then happily remembered that he was himself an angakok, and that he had several tornaks (guardian spirits) among the ingnersuit (under-world people). No sooner had he called them than he saw three kayakers coming straight towards him. Two of the strangers put their paddles, one from each side, into the sinking kayak to hold it up; and, at the same time, the third mended the kayak as well as possible, by filling the leak with blubber, and hastened to give the drowning man his dry breeches to put on. He was now again placed in his kayak, to which they made fast their seals, all strung together in a long row; and they told him to tug them along, that he might get warm. He rowed in front, and they closely followed him with the greatest speed. They came to a high island, with only one house; there they landed, and at once entered. When they had seated themselves, he saw the master of the house, a man so very old that his wrinkled skin was hanging, and almost hiding his eyes; but the old man pushed it aside a little, and then looked at the new-comers. Presently some one called out that two kay-akers were approaching, tugging seals along with them. Those whose business it was to bring them up to the house soon returned with hauling-thongs, ornamented with fittings of bright walrus-bone ; and then followed the seal-hunters themselves. On entering the house, they accosted their brothers, and reproached them, say-ing, " Why were ye not quicker in giving him your assistance before he got to be so cold ? " but they answered, " He did not call for our aid till then." They now ordered the women to bring some dry meat. After the meal, the old man moved aside the wrinkled skin from off his eyes, gave a look out of the window, and said, " Go and call our other relatives ;" upon which the youngest immediately went away, and after some time came back covered with sweat. The stranger on seeing him reflected, " Where can he have been, since no house seems to be near ? " and soon after five other brothers, much like his hosts, and also accompanied by an old man, entered the house. There was also another man, who turned out to be his former friend and com-panion, whom he had killed in his kayak. He sat down right opposite, and hardly dared to look up. When they had had their meal, the eldest brother brought out a skin, spread it on the floor, and first tried a wrestling-match with his own brothers, and afterwards with the visitors ; but no one was able to hold his own against him. The master of the house now challenged the other old man, who, however, had to give in to him. Having thus been vanquished and put to shame, the strangers prepared to leave their hosts ; these reproved them sharply for their former behaviour, and told them henceforth to give up quarrelling, and be friends again. When the rest had all withdrawn, the stranger who had been saved remained five days longer ; but on the sixth he left. On passing his usual hunting-place, he encountered his friend, who had been restored to life in the same manner as himself, and they spoke to each other. It so happened that they were both angakut, and that each of them had his tornaks among the ingnersuit. From this time they were quite reconciled.

<hr />

## 66.

## THE STRONG MAN ON THE ISLAND OF K'ERKA.

A LITTLE north of Pamiut (Frederikshaab) there is an island called K'erka. In olden times there lived on this islet a man who had no equal in kayaking. His paddle was so thick that he had to cut it narrower where it was to be grasped. He was alone in this place. Once in the winter time, when he was far out on the open sea, he was suddenly caught in a furious gale from the north. He tried hard to make the land, but the coast had altogether vanished in the tempest. At length, however, he knew by the great breakers that he must be right off Tulugartalik (close to the large glacier); and having passed those isles, land soon appeared ahead, and he observed a light from a window on shore. Landing his kayak, he went up towards the house, and stopped short on hearing some one singing within. After listening for a while, he found that he had unawares landed on Ukevik, the homestead of his adversary, who happened to be practising a nith-song (satirical song), with which to abuse him when they met in the spring. He took great care to impress the exact words on his memory, and then went silently down to his kayak, leaving the place in the dark; and having again crossed the heavy surf about Tulugartalik, he reached his own home. The following spring, his adversary came from Ukevik to have a singing match with him; but as he had well remembered, and knew all the taunts and spiteful things beforehand, he soon gained an easy victory over him. The lonely resident of K'erka also had some enemies among the southern people. During the summer, when he was one day out at sea kayaking in fine calm weather, he noticed some kayakers coming from the south, and from their numbers guessed they were his enemies coming to attack him. On this surmise he fled towards the shore, with the rest in full pursuit after him; but reaching a large iceberg, he happened to observe a great cave on the opposite side of it, and quickly glided in, kayak and all. The prow turned outwards; and, holding his lance ready lifted, he lay in wait for his enemies. When the first man came up in front of the cave, he speared him, at once drawing his lance back; the second of them met the same fate; and all the others fared alike, excepting two, whom he left alive that they might inform their countrymen of what had happened. All those Southlanders had intended to kill their foe, but happened to be killed themselves instead.

## 67.

### NIAKUNGUAK.

A NUMBER of brothers always used to have their fixed winter quarters at a certain place, while several of the older ones were married. Niakunguak, one of the younger brothers, had as yet no wife. His dis-

position differed greatly from the others, who were all
wild and boisterous. He would never join in any of
their noisy pastimes and wanton tricks, although they
tried to persuade him to do so. At last he got so weary
of their company, that he would stay with them no
longer. One morning he did not join them in their
day's excursion, but as soon as they were well off,
betook himself to his kayak, put out from land, and
coasted away south. He travelled on for many days
without seeing a human being; and he had fairly given
up the hope of falling in with any, when suddenly he
was hailed from shore, and at the same time discovered
a little bay with many tents pitched round it, and
people shouting to him to land. When he reached the
beach, he was received by a crowd of men, who welcomed him very civilly, although he did not know any
one of them. An old man now invited him to come to
his tent. There were only his two daughters inside, but
before long it was crowded with visitors, who were all
very friendly and pleasant. The visitors having left,
the old man said, " In case thou wouldst like one of my
daughters, thou mayst choose for thyself." He took
the youngest for his wife, and henceforth became the
support and provider of the old man. The people there
got very fond of him, and liked him for his great
modesty; and he, too, felt very happy amongst them.
When they assembled for social intercourse, boasting
was not heard, nor boisterous manners displayed. When
the days lengthened, and seals got scarce, Niakunguak
chose his hunting-place at a good distance out. His
wife in the meantime had borne him a son; and during
his childhood a boat's crew of Southlanders arrived and
took up their winter abode among them. It soon appeared that one of the strangers was presumptuous and
full of conceit, though Niakunguak in his modesty felt
loath to contradict him. One morning after the winter
solstice, when the cold was very severe, Niakunguak

was the only man of the place who thought of starting. The bragging stranger, on seeing this, offered to go with him; and both put out to sea in quest of seals. Meantime the wind increased; but Niakunguak, nothing daunted, lanced his seal, hoping that his companion would come and help him to kill the animal. However, he showed no such intention, but had already turned homewards, frightened at the fury of the gale. Niakunguak made his seal fast to the tug-line, but did not return till he had got another. Meantime his companion had gained the shore, where Niakunguak's little son was standing on the beach gazing out upon the heaving sea, on the look-out for his father. The boy at once inquired about his father, having seen them go out together; but the other one answered, "Thou mayst as well go home; thy silly father will never return; there is no kayaking in such weather." The boy entered the house, and there kept tranquil and silent—he was already of an age to understand the ways of mourning —but the other men still kept outside the house on the look-out for Niakunguak's kayak. The opening of the bay was a very narrow one, and consequently a mass of foaming surf. Towards evening they espied two little black spots upon the white foam; these were his seals with the spears still sticking in them, and tossed along by the breakers setting in upon the shore. A third black spot on the surf appeared to be himself, carried quickly on across the heavy seas. Having got on shore and reached his house, his son told him what the other man had said—that no kayak could live in such a sea; and the father replied, "In such a sea and such weather one might go out even in a very poor kayak." When the briskets were boiled, the men were invited to partake of the meal; and when the dish was ready served, and the guests all assembled, Niakunguak during a pause remarked, "When I had harpooned my second seal, I looked about in vain for a kayaker to assist me in

securing it." Later on the guests grew talkative, and
all passed the evening pleasantly, excepting his companion of the morning, who never spoke a word. When
the days grew still longer, and there were no seals to be
had, the men entertained themselves with ball-playing.
Once there was a general calling for Niakunguak to
come and join the ball - players. Though not disposed to do so, he at once obeyed their summons, but
only went to look on at some distance. While occupied
in watching the ball-players, and standing modestly
with one arm drawn out of the sleeve of his jacket, the
other kayaker owing him a grudge now approached, and
threw him down. While Niakunguak was rising and
shaking the snow from his garments, the men gathered
round him, saying, "Is Niakunguak going to stand
this?" On hearing this, his antagonist seized hold of
Niakunguak, who, seeking no strife, only tried to keep
his footing ; but finding that the other would not let go
his grasp, he was forced to defend himself, and a struggle
ensued, ending in favour of Niakunguak, who soon got
the better of his adversary, and hurled him to the ground
with such force that his bowels burst, and the blood
gushed from his mouth. His brothers instantly left off
playing, and brought him into the house, where he soon
expired. Niakunguak had now, much against his will,
made himself enemies ; and he told his young son that
he ought to mind this, and train himself to endure hard-
ships that he might attain strength and vigour. He
should no longer practise lifting and flinging stones,
but should try to pull up shrubs and bushes by the root.
Afterwards he taught him everything belonging to
kayaking. Before long he came to be his father's equal
every way, and even in the roughest weather chased the
seal far out seawards. Once another party of Southlanders arrived, and among them were two sons of the
man whom Niakunguak had formerly killed. They
also had been reared to manly exercise in order to pro-

mote their strength. The strangers were polite and friendly enough, and chose to settle with them for the winter. The equinoctial gales proved very strong that autumn, with much bad weather; and often no kayaking was possible. On such a day Niakunguak with his son and other housemates was invited to the foreigners. They were well received, and afterwards regaled with many dainties; and there was no want of lively talking at the meal. At last there was silence; and during this, one of the two brothers stood forth, and, taking a bit of dried liver (this being exceedingly hard), raised his voice, saying, "I have been told that I have an enemy in Niakunguak." At the same time he tried to crush the piece of liver he held in his hand; but failing to do so, he again put it by. Silence still prevailed, when Niakunguak's son advanced, and, taking up the same bit, crushed it to atoms with his fingers, so that it fell like dust upon the floor. All were utterly amazed, and not a word was spoken. Niakunguak and his relations still felt some suspicion of their enemies; but these departed peaceably as soon as spring came on; and henceforth the Niakunguaks remained undisturbed until their death.

---

## 68.

## AUGPILAGTOK.

AUGPILAGTOK, who was living in the southern part of the country, chanced to hear that Kangek (pron. Kanghek—at the firth of Godthaab) was an excellent place for seal-hunting. He accordingly started for it; but the autumn set in, and the ground was hard

with frost before he arrived; so on coming across an
old deserted house at Ikarisat, not far from Kangek, he
decided to stop there, and set about preparing an abode
for the winter. At first he had fair hunting; so much
was he able to store up, that it might have been thought
the seals came to his house of their own accord. Heavy
northern gales were blowing, and the fall of snow was
so great that he was forced to take his store of seals into
the house, and live entirely upon them. At last, however, they were finished. The weather was getting
calmer, but the sea was still covered with ice. In these
circumstances he made himself a small harpoon for
hunting on the ice, but first went out to reconnoitre, and
find out the breathing-holes of the seals. The first day
he roamed all around the bay Ameralik without finding one opening in the ice. The next he tried Kapisilik, but also in vain. The third day, having had the
same bad luck at Kangersunek, and having nothing to
eat, he set to whetting his knife in the evening. He
had a dog with drooping ears, and his knife was intended for this poor animal. He killed it, and cut a
piece from the loin, which he ate raw, skin and all, only
scraping off the hairs; and when the rest had been
boiled he again ate with a hearty appetite. The following day he remained in the house. On the next he
climbed the highest mountains to survey the neighbourhood, and discovered an opening in the ice, not far
from his dwelling-place, but it was then too late to start.
The following morning he set off, carrying his kayak on
his head as far as the water's edge. Having rowed for
some time along the margin of the ice, he unexpectedly
detected a number of huts; and the beach was also red
with blood from sea-animals which had been killed.
He pulled away; and on arriving had a friendly welcome from the inmates, who asked him to their huts.
This place was that Kangek which, for want of better
knowledge of the locality, he had not been able to reach

before the winter overtook him.  In ascending the beach
he saw the frozen entrails of some auks thrown out upon
the dunghill, and not till he had swallowed some of
these could they get him to go inside, where he soon got
a proper meal, and had his kayak filled with stores for
his departure.  A short time after this he removed with
all his household to Kangek.  Every day he alternately
went out seal-hunting and spearing birds; and during
this period his little son was provided with a kayak of
his own.  When auk-hunting his father told him, "When
thou goest out for auks and I am not with thee, thou
needest not look so much for my kayak, but be watch-
ful of the others; there are those among them whom it
would be no joke to disturb while they are busy at their
hunt."  One day, however, when they had gone out together after birds, Augpilagtok had got to a little distance from his son.  Suddenly he heard angry voices,
and turning round saw the small kayak surrounded by
the other men.  Augpilagtok, who at once suspected
something wrong, quickly produced his amulet from
out the edging of his jacket, and hiding it inside his
mouth rowed on as fast as possible.  Having reached
them he tossed up the amulet, saying, " Whomsoever !"
at which one was instantly overturned, then a second,
then a third, and so on, till all were drowned excepting himself and his son, who returned home together.  Not feeling secure in this place any longer,
they removed farther north to Antangmik in the spring.
During their stay there the father recommended the
son to exert himself to grow a match for his enemies,
from whom they might expect an assault some day or
other.  The son soon became a first-rate kayaker, and
chased the sea-animals at the remotest places.  On his
excursions he was often accompanied by the middlemost of several brothers living at the same settlement.
One day when he thought himself quite alone, he was
surprised to hear a sound like that of an approaching

kayak, and turning round he saw with some amazement his usual companion deliberately aiming at him with his harpoon. He narrowly escaped by overturning his kayak ; and when he rose again the other said it was only in fun, although it had been an attempt on his life in good earnest. At home he told his father of this occurrence, but he advised him to take no notice of it, lest he should stir up more foes for himself. The next day the same thing happened, and he barely escaped. The third time he resolved to revenge himself, and killed his antagonist. After the deed he returned home, having first put the seal on his kayak, but turned tail foremost. By this sign his father at once knew what had happened; but the brothers of the deceased, who were standing outside the house-door, thought he had placed it the wrong way to ease the kayak while rowing against the wind. Augpilagtok's son on landing said, " I have put it thus because *it was the next one after a man;* he thrice attempted my life, and was in the act of killing me; if ye are longing for him ye may go and look for him." At this news they all began to cry, and entered the house, to observe the usual mourning ceremonies. After this the youth became cautious, and never started except when the weather was too bad for the others to venture out. Once in the spring he was invited with his father to visit the brothers. Augpilagtok said to his son, "We may as well make a bold entrance, and I will go first, and take a good leap across the doorway, right to the entrance of the room." They thus entered, and saw all the brothers stretched out at full length on the ledge, only their feet visible on its outer edge (a sign of wrath). They were treated to some frozen liver in an oblong dish; but when they had got only half through with it, the frozen roof fell in and covered the dish with turf-dust. The eldest brother now said, " When the roof falls down like this, it only can be by sorcery. The Southlanders are rather deep, and know a thing or two ; we had better leave them alone." Augpilagtok now said to his son, "Slip off thy clothes ; " and taking a knife cut up his belly. But when the entrails began to fall out, he merely drew his hand across the cut, and instantly it healed. Some time after they once more repaired to the south.

---

## 69.

## THE ANGAKOK ATAITSIAK PRACTISING HIS ART WITH THE BENEVOLENT INGNERSUIT.

ATAITSIAK was a very celebrated angakok, who had his hunting-place close to his abode, and he used to frequent it all by himself. If he ever wanted company he used to invoke some of his tornaks belonging to the ingnersuit, and they always came at his call. One day he had just harpooned a seal, and was about to slacken the line, when suddenly the seal gave a pull which capsized his kayak, throwing him headlong out of it ; and he could barely keep his head above the water by taking hold of the line. It was not till he began to grow stiff with cold that he thought of calling his tornaks. No sooner had he done so than they appeared, coming from the shore in their kayaks. The foremost called out to the others, "Quick, or he may be drawn down ; make haste !" When the first was taking hold of his kayak he perceived that he was already lifted up, and when the others came up he saw that the kayak was emptied of the sea-water, whilst others supported his weak limbs. They then replaced him in his kayak, giving him dry warm clothes. Being well propped up, he noticed that his seal and kayak

were being towed along by the others, and that they
carried him out seawards. They soon saw a great new
land, and the oldest said, " Take care that the blood of
the seal does not drop to earth ; for in that case he will
never see his home again." When they were near enough
to hear what was said ashore, they heard people cry that
a dolphin was probably caught ; to which they answered,
that they were only bringing their old angakok. Having got him inside, all the lamps were lighted. They
first laid him naked down on the floor, and covered him
well up ; and after a while he again recovered his lost
senses, and began to walk. In the evening they served
all kind of victuals before him. During the meal he
noticed a poor young man, who was very ill, lying down
on the ledge. The oldest among them said, " A most dis-
tressing case with the lad yonder ; he is failing fast.
When he chased the reindeer in the autumn we feasted
and were well off ; he was equally clever at stalking
deer and chasing white whales ; and even in the worst
season was always lucky ; will you examine his case to-
night ? there must be something particular the matter
with him, preventing his recovery." He said he would
fain do it ; but as he was going to set about it, he noticed
the sick man's aunt (viz., her soul or ghost, she being a
witch) going close up to him in order to touch him. On
seeing this he said, " It would be an easy matter, and
he would look to it the day after." When he began his
conjurations the following night he saw the woman approaching still nearer to the sick youth, and then said,
·" In the practice of my art I must speak the truth ; it is
the woman there that does him the mischief." They
cried with one voice, " Take her, do take her away."
But Ataitsiak replied, " I must first question her." The
base woman now explained, " Whenever he returned
from the hunt, he used to supply me abundantly with
sundry good things ; but the last time he was out,
though he brought home deer as well as dolphins, and

I was in the highest expectation, he never gave me a bit. From that day I determined to blast and wither him, and but for thee I would have touched him now." Ataitsiak turned to the others, saying, " If you really want the young man to recover I must slay her; but mind you hold the harpoon-strings fast." He was about to hit her, but as long as she looked at him he could not conquer her. As soon, however, as she turned to the wall, he thrust at her, and a loud cracking noise ensued; but she, having watched him sharply, as soon as he moved, let herself down beneath the floor, and the harpoon only caught the sole of her foot. She went dragging the line down with her, so that the men with all their strength could hardly stop her. One after another they let go their hold. At last there was only one man at the line when Ataitsiak was happily in time to help him; and catching hold of a bit of bone, made fast to the line, he entirely stopped it. After a while he said, " Now go and see how his aunt is." She lived in a little house close by. They returned and reported that she lay on her couch with a bleeding foot. On the ensuing morning Ataitsiak went back to his home loaded with gifts. His family had not as yet given him up, being assured he would return before the three days were over. One day, at a later period, when he happened to be out in his hunting-ground, a great many kayakers were seen approaching, and first among them was the sick young man whom he had restored to health, bringing many gifts for Ataitsiak, and at the same time reporting that his aunt, the base old hag, had died.

## 70.

## THE STRONG MAN ON UMANAK.

ON the isle of Umanak in the Isortok firth (South
    Greenland) lived a very strong man, besides a
great many other people. He gained great fame from
his extraordinary strength, and was likewise considered
a first-rate hunter and skilled angakok. He was in
fact a principal provider for the whole place, and their
angakok into the bargain. He used to take his little
son on his knee when conjuring, in order to teach him
his art. The people themselves had no lack of good
hunting off the coast in the autumn season ; but after
the winter solstice the angakok used to roam about on
the open sea all by himself, and when he had caught a
couple of big seals, he used to put them upon his kayak,
one in front and the other behind (viz., instead of towing them), making them fast with his harpoon - line.
Before the sun had gone round to the west he was sure
to have reached home with his two seals ; and then lost
no time in ordering the women to cook the briskets.
When the meal was served, the men sat down to it, and
generally the angakok started the conversation by saying, " I was again caught in a heavy snowstorm from the
north." This seemed very strange, for on shore the weather had been fine, and far away seawards only a small
mist-band had been noticed. Being a man of such rare
qualities, he naturally wished his son to come up to his
own standard, and carefully trained him with this view.
When full grown the son also would go far out to sea
in all weathers, and bring big seals home with him.
From that time the father grew quite easy about him,
and occasionally remained at home himself, though perfectly hale and hearty. Once in the long days the son

had started by himself, and at night the father in vain expected his return. The next morning at daybreak he set out in search of him. When so far from land that the southern islands looked quite dim and shadowy, he heard a voice calling out "*Eek !*" On hearing this strange voice, which he soon knew did not belong to any of his countrymen, he hastened on southwards, steering towards the sun ; and in a little while he suddenly stopped short, again hearing a voice shouting "Where ?" Soon after he came in sight of an immense kayak, and on nearing it found it to be a *kayariak* (fabulous kayaker). The huge kayaker had a paddle with only one blade, which he plied vigorously by shifting it alternately from one side of the kayak to the other. Approaching him from behind, he discovered one of his son's arms lashed on to the after-part of the kayariak. At this sight he got into such a rage that he instantly darted his harpoon and killed the kayaker. Having drawn out the harpoon, whose point was the length of half an arm, he kayaked still further along, until he heard the former cry repeated. He answered it, and continuing his way soon fell in with another kayaker, who carried the second arm of his son, aft on his kayak. Having killed him also, he stood out to sea, till the high mountains of his own country were almost lost to sight. He again heard a deep rough voice, belonging to a similar kayaker, who was the father of the two he had already killed. The weather being calm, with a swell from the south-west, he put in his oar, and having secured it by means of the kayak-line, drifted along, steering only with his hands. Approaching the great kayaker thus, he discovered his son's body behind him on his kayak. He did not throw his lance, but rowed right in upon him, and kept alongside of him by hooking his oar into the stranger's kayak-straps. This somewhat startled the former, and he was heard to exclaim, "Where are those whom I am seeking?" and then the angakok understood of whom he was speaking.

Turning landwards, they soon fell in with one kayak, floating bottom up. The angakok now inquired, " Canst thou revive him there ? " To this the kayariak rejoined, " Why, yes, I could ; " and lifting the wounded man up he merely touched him, and brought him to life again. Then they reached the next, and the father did the same to him. Being now four in number, the angakok went on, " Perhaps ye would not mind making him alive too whom ye have got there on your kayak. The other replied, " It might be done if a fitting place can be found to manage it properly." On reaching a piece of floating ice they landed upon it, and when the kayariak had joined the severed limbs together, and had revived him that had been slain, the father said, " What is to be done next ? he has got no kayak ; can't we have the loan of one of those ? " " Well, take it, but be sure ye bring it back immediately, and when ye land do not let any one look into it." The angakok now returned with his son, who found his kayak such a size that he went down into it to the pit of his arms. On reaching land he cried out that no one must look down into the big kayak. But one unbeliever among their placemates did so, in consequence of which the son of the angakok who had made use of it grew lame in his legs. The unbeliever also was found close by, having been frightened to death at something he had seen inside the big kayak. Meantime the angakok brought the kayak back to the big man, who stood waiting for him on the ice. The sons now both descended into their kayaks, but the father remained a while, and first took a general view of the whole horizon, and then producing a small pipe he had hidden in his own boat, he blew it successively towards the four quarters of the horizon, and then repaired to his boat. When the angakok left them the weather was fine and calm, but he was hardly off before clouds arose, the sky became overcast, and all of a sudden a heavy gale was blowing. The wind rushing on from different quarters almost prevented his making the land. However, he went ahead undauntedly, having a first-rate kayak covered with skins, joined together lengthways. When the storm abated, and the stars again shone out, a high land became visible, which he recognised to be Akilinek, on the shore opposite his own. He was again caught in a tempest; but this having also subsided, he landed at the southernmost point of our country (Cape Farewell), and finally reached his own home, where his family had long believed him dead.

----

## 71.

## KIGUTIKAK WHO WAS CARRIED OFF BY THE WHALERS.

[This curious story appears to be founded upon a real event, one of the numerous acts of violence committed by the first European visitors to Greenland. If we wish to appreciate properly these reminiscences of the original account given by Kigutikak on his return home, we must take into consideration first the manner in which he probably was treated by his European keepers, merely as an object of curiosity and jokes; next, the difficulty he had in explaining his strange experiences and adventures to his countrymen, who had seen nothing but Greenland; and lastly, the continued endeavours at localising and adaptation by which succeeding narrators have altered it, until it became capable of being understood by every assembly in Greenland, merely as an object of entertainment, without needing any further explanation. From this point of view the tale will be found interesting and instructive with regard to the notions of the natives, and the development of traditions in general.]

IN former times when European ships used to come to the Ameralik shore, the whalers and natives met for trading. Once a whaler warned Kigutikak and his brother: "Ye had better beware of approaching my countrymen yonder; they intend some evil." One day

Kigutikak had got some gifts from the sailors; his brother on seeing this envied his good luck; and gathering some of his goods for barter, went off to the malevolent whalers. Kigutikak also collected some trifles and followed his brother; but when the brother approached the ship, a well-manned boat came off to meet him. They seized him and hoisted him on deck, kayak and all. Kigutikak having shared the same fate, the ship weighed anchor and stood out to sea. When fairly clear of land, the wind rose and the sea ran high; once a great wave came sweeping the deck, and the sailors all rushed below for safety. Kigutikak alone remained on deck, and as the sea washed over, he took firm hold of the gunwale. Except a small space where Kigutikak had planted himself, the sea carried away every part of the gunwale with a loud crash; and when the sailors appeared on deck they could not but see that he had been in great danger. Afterwards, when the storm had passed, and they had made a good distance off the land, which was now out of sight, it blew another gale. This time the sailors persuaded him to go below with them before they shipped another sea. Approaching their own country they shortened sail, although the wind was fair, lest it should be known whom they had brought with them. Only at midnight they stood in for the land and anchored. People on shore were heard to call out, "The trading ships are coming." At this news all the houses were quickly illuminated, and afterwards the seamen were invited to come on shore, but the captain would not leave the ship before next morning. The following day he went on shore, taking the *Kalaleks* (Greenlanders) with him. People having got news of their presence, gathered like gnats in great swarms to catch sight of them. In the boat the captain gave orders to them saying, "When I am going among people on shore, ye must not be staring about you, but keep your eyes fixed on my heels;

if ye don't mind my words, and take your eyes off my
heels, ye are sure to be lost in the throng ; " and they
answered him, " Well, we will follow thee closely." On
landing there was not a spot to plant their feet, such
was the crowd. At last a soldier appeared and undertook to clear a passage for them by dividing the masses,
and following in his wake they managed to get through.
Arriving at the captain's house the brother of Kigutikak
was missing ; in looking round he had lost his way, but
had fortunately been picked up by some other great
man, with whom he remained. When Kigutikak
entered with the captain, they found his wife moody
and sulking—fancy the idea ! she had a fit of jealousy.
However, when the captain produced a doll from his
pocket, and put it on the table before her, her good
temper was somewhat restored. During Kigutikak's
stay at their house, one day as he was going out to the
privy, on getting outside he was somewhat surprised by
two big Europeans menacing him from either side with
their long swords. Greatly alarmed, he ventured to tell
his master. His master forthwith gave him a bit of a
rope with a large knob at one end, saying, " Now go
and open the door and hit away among them with all
thy might ; " and having taken the rope's end he did as
he was told, hitting right and left without ever looking at them. Having thus cleared a way for himself,
and being again ready to enter, he saw them peeping
round a corner of the house, covering their faces with a
handkerchief, for in lashing them with the rope he had
sorely hurt their eyes. His master merely said, it served
them quite right. During his stay at the captain's
house, Kigutikak sometimes went out to chase partridges. On one of these excursions he happened to
meet a great big European who wanted to kill him, but
he forestalled him and killed him instead ; and in order
that no one should find out the deed, he buried him on

the spot, and afterwards made the gravel quite smooth on the top. At home he put on an unconcerned air, as if nothing at all had happened. The next day he encountered another big Kavdlunak, who had the same bad fortune; but on meeting one on the same road the third day, whom he was just about to despatch, he suddenly in time recognised his brother. After having questioned each other about various matters, they both fell a-weeping, and then Kigutikak asked his brother where he had come to live. The brother answered him, "My present master is a very grand gentleman; in following you the other day I only turned to look about once, but from that instant losing sight of you, I was happily taken up by him, and am there in want of nothing." When Kigutikak told him what had become of the two big Kavdlunait, the brother rejoined that the other day, on a similar provocation, he had acted the same way. The brother then agreed to meet the next day after the following, whereat they parted and each returned to his place. At the next encounter Kigutikak exclaimed, "What a lot of money I have got!" and the brother replied, "The same have I." And they began to deliberate whether by adding the money together they could not buy a ship with it. The brother decided that it would not be a bad plan and should be carried out, and thus they parted. At home Kigutikak took his master into counsel, asking him, "Could we not put our money together and buy a ship, my brother and I? Pray count it over." "Why, ye have plenty to get one for," his master gave answer; and Kigutikak soon proceeded to carry out his plan, finding materials and hiring the workmen. The hull being finished in springtime, he began to talk to his master about the masts. "They are easily got," he answered; "a little south of this is a place with many straight and tall trees, just the thing for masts:" and when the time for his departure

arrived his master added, " But mark my words : when
you cut trees, have great care in looking about on all
sides and listen attentively.    If you happen to hear
any noise, then flee at once, and if you think the way
hither too long, betake yourself to a steep rock a little to
the north, and there you will find people." He promised to remember this piece of advice ; and starting
for the forest he at length reached it.   He soon found
out the highest and most beautiful trees, and very
cautiously began to cut them down ; but when he was
about to fell the second one, he fancied he saw another
tree moving, and at the same time heard a noise, but
did not take any notice of either as long as he saw
nothing (although he had been warned beforehand).
No sooner had he caught sight of a horrid beast emerging from among the trees, than he flung down his axe
and took to running with all his might.   On turning
round he plainly saw that the beast was gaining upon
him, and his master's home being too far off, he retreated towards the cave, which opened all of itself, and
closed in the same manner as soon as he had got within,
and almost instantly he heard the pursuing beast bounding against the door with a terrible roar.   Inside the
cave he found a lot of dissolute women, with whom he
remained without caring much for getting home.   As
time passed and he did not return, his master supposed
him to have been devoured by the wild beast ; but at
that very time he was preparing for his departure,
having first had his pockets filled with money by the
women as a recompense for having slept with them.   On
his way home he first repaired to the forest to cut down
the second tree and fetch off the tools, and then returned
to his master.   On seeing him enter, the latter exclaimed, " I thought the wild beast had made thee his
prey ; where hast thou been all this while ? "   He
answered him, " I was with the solitary women in the

cave ; they made themselves very pleasant towards me."
The master replied, " Oh, that's just what they always
do ; when once one gets in to them, it is no easy matter
to free one's self from them and get away."

When the ship had been masted and was ready for
sea, it was put into the water, and two men set to work
loading it ; but on going to leave port, they were only
three for the ship all told—viz., the brothers and a cook.
At this time the brother unfortunately fell ill, and,
getting worse and worse, at length died, whereupon
Kigutikak set on fire and burned his ship, and buried
all his stores in the sea. This was about the usual time
of departure for the whalers going to Greenland. His
master said, " Thou art sad and low-spirited ; a walk
would be a change and diversion for thee." They set
out, and arriving at a small lake, found a boat moored
off the shore ; in this they rowed across to the other
side, and soon reaching another lake and a small boat,
they crossed this in the same manner, and then proceeded to the next lake, where they likewise found a
boat, such being the regular means of conveyance for
travellers going this way. Having moored the last boat
and proceeded on their way, they soon arrived at a
town in the middle part of the country, where they
entered a house to get refreshments. Whilst they were
eating, they heard a cry, " The whalers are leaving !
the whalers are off ! " At this news Kigutikak started,
and leaving his meal unfinished, he sped down and
unmoored the boat, his master following at a little distance. He travelled back across the lakes all by himself, his master being continually somewhat behind.
When Kigutikak at last reached the main harbour, he
heard that the whaling ships were all gone, excepting
one, whose crew had just gone ashore to undo the
cables. Kigutikak was just in time to jump into the
boat and get on board. His master, who all this time
had been unable to keep pace with him, was now calling

to the sailors to take good care of him, and watch him closely during their stay in Greenland.

After a voyage of many days, they got sight of the southern point of the land; and from that time Kiguti-kak would no more undress himself; he wanted to make use of his time and collect as many odd bits of old iron as he could with which to stuff his pockets before leaving the Europeans. As soon as he recognised his own country, and the places where he used to live, he proposed to the sailors to land and go out partridge-shooting. To this they consented, but without leaving him alone for a single moment, fearing he would either be lost or run off for his home. Kigutikak then told them, "Ye need not fear my being lost, but just go after your game;" and so they left him for a short time. No sooner had they turned their backs upon him than he hid himself in a deep cleft; and immediately after he heard them shouting for him, and saying to each other, "We were charged to keep a good watch over him, and it will be a bad job for us if he is not found." As soon as he thought them sufficiently far off, he emerged and proceeded onwards. Having wandered a long while, he observed a steep rock, and began to descend it. Half-way down, he was somewhat perplexed at finding himself utterly unable either to advance or retreat. At length he determined to ease himself of all the things he had carried away in his pockets, and slid down the rest of the way. He proceeded still further, and came in sight of a great many tents. Seeing him approach, people came running and crying aloud, "Kigutikak is coming!" and then all the rest hastened out to have a look at him. He asked them in the Kavdlunak language, "Where is my family?" but they could not understand him. Asking them in their own language, however, their place of abode was pointed out to him. His own people had long ago given him up, and since then an old bachelor had undertaken to provide for them. Kigutikak rewarded him by allowing him to choose himself some trifles among the pieces of iron he had brought along with him.

---

## 72.

## THE MAN NOT TO BE LOOKED AT BY THE EUROPEANS.

[A tale from South Greenland.]

AT Tasiusanguak there once lived a handy and clever fellow, called Kenake (pron. Kenakee). It was in those times when the whalers used to touch on the isle of Umanak (district of Sukkertoppen), and people used to go there and fetch the rejected *matak* (whale-skin). Once Kenake went away to call on the whalers' on this errand. The natives in those times used to gather merchandise for trading with the Europeans. When he had begun dealing with them, he chanced to give some offence to the sailors ; and in a struggle that ensued Kenake was killed. The captain, however, was not made aware of this accident till later. The wife of Kenake placed his corpse in the boat, and prepared to go home, her son steering, and she herself being now the only person to row. When the boat was about to push off, the master of the ship threw a number of nice things—such as various kinds of knives, and other trifles highly prized in those days—into the boat ; but Kenake's wife flung them into the sea, all the while crying for her lost husband. At last, however, the son got hold of a knife, which he secretly put aside, thinking it rather too bad to throw away so many valuable articles. When she was about to push off in good earnest, the sailors caught hold of her boat in order to prevent her going, but biting their fingers, she obliged them to let go one after another; and after this they were allowed to return to Tasiusanguak. Although she grieved sorely, she asked her relatives and countrymen not to avenge the murder of Kenake; but nevertheless they some time afterwards began to busy themselves with the dead body for the purpose of turning (by charm) the son into one *whom the Europeans did not dare to look upon*, and also to make him proof against shaft and spear. When he was full grown, and had become a seal-hunter, and was possessed of a tolerable store of merchandise, the whalers again happened to arrive at Umanak. His relatives soon set out for the ship; and the second time they set off with their boat well loaded, the *eye-me-not* was of the party. His relatives having finished their bartering, he climbed on deck, bringing the things he had for sale, expecting the sailors to come on deck to barter with him. Finding that they did not even approach, he got his things back into the boat, but soon returned without any goods, rummaging about the deck, and taking away from the ship whatever he fancied; and though the sailors became aware of this, they turned away, pretending not to observe anything. Having brought the things into his boat, he went back on deck; and it being now meal-time on board, the visitors were now all treated to a meal, except the *eye-me-not*. But he revenged himself by going into the cabin and laying hold of whatever he chose, such as flensing-knives, and so forth. When caught in the very act of stealing these things, they quickly turned away, pretending not to see; and he only stopped of his own accord, when he had taken all he wanted. He went on this way all his life, as often as whalers came to the place. When a ship had been at Umanak for some time, and the sailors were missing

too many of their belongings, they went off in a sloop for Tasiusanguak to attack the robbers. Approaching the shore, they would call out, " Come forth, thou fellow whom no one can bear to look at ! " and while he obeyed the summons, and went down to them, his old mother would sit on the roof of the house pronouncing spells. If the charm succeeded, the token was that the nose of the first sailor who landed would begin bleeding. On seeing them land, the *eye-me-not* went down to assist them in hauling up their boat; and when the very first man set foot on shore, his nose was seen to bleed. When they had all landed, and each had his nose bleeding, the *eye-me-not* was seen running from one to another, wringing and pulling their arms to make them look at him. Then he would lift up his jacket, saying, " I am the thief ! " But they only turned away ; and he went on trying to make them aim their guns at him, still repeating, " It is I ; I am the thief ! " They hung back despite his efforts to excite them into shooting him. Such was his habit throughout his life whenever a whaler put into port there. As long as the strangers stayed at Umanak, their tormentor never left them at peace, but was always hanging about them. No one talked to them so much as he did, although he could not make out what they answered, and though they could not bear to look at him.

## 73.

## THE ANGAKOK FROM KAKORTOK.

[A tale from South Greenland.]

AN angakok, who used to have his winter station a
little north of Kakortok (Julianehaab), took a
fancy to go and discover a nice and delightful country ;
and starting for his journey, he came to Nook (Godthaab). He had a daughter called Kakamak, and a son
besides. From Nook they went farther on to Pisugfik,
and met another angakok, named Kajuernek, who was
the only person that had been far to the north. On
being questioned concerning these parts, he answered,
" Indeed all the country northwards is very fine, but no
other part of it can be compared with Ilulissat " (Jakobshavn). On hearing this, the Southlander at once started,
and after a long journey at length landed on the coast
at Ilulissat, when the earth was already becoming hard
with frost, in consequence of which they had great trouble
in getting their house built ; and being hardly able to
manage the frozen turf, they made their house very
small. During their stay at this place, a fine young
man courted Kakamak, without the knowledge of her
parents. Her brother's wife was a very modest and
timid person ; but Kakamak, on the contrary, was
proud and presumptuous, and often abused her sister-
in-law, who, however, did not mind her scolding, and her
parents likewise let her have her own way, and never
interfered. But one day another woman of the place
told Kakamak's mother that her daughter was secretly
married to the young man : the mother told it to her
husband when they had gone to rest in the evening. On
this the angakok at once had his boat put out, and every-

thing prepared for departing; and when so far ready, he ordered his daughter into the boat. People thought that he was only going on some excursion, but in reality he was quite resolved on going back to the south. The young man now stepped forward, saying, "Kakamak is mine, and I want her;" but her father replied, "No man shall ever have my daughter; and if any one should dare to take her by force, I shall be sure to fetch her back." So saying, he pushed from land; and travelling on incessantly, they at length came to a little island called Alangok, where, for the first time, they pitched their tent. In this place Kakamak secretly gave birth to a child, which she afterwards killed. Proceeding further, they came to a place just opposite Nook, where they built their house for the coming winter.

In his excursions here the angakok used to meet with a little manly kayaker, to whom he proposed to marry Kakamak. The other answered, "I am willing enough, but the women are always telling me that I am dark-skinned." The angakok did not mind that the least, but led him home to his daughter, saying, "Thou art a vain and frivolous girl, and thou hast great need of a good provider and husband, and such a one I have brought thee now." Kakamak made no reply to this, but did not reject him, and so he became her husband. One day he returned, bringing home three seals; but when he went to sit down beside her, without offering her any tobacco, she pushed him away, so that he fell down on the floor; rising quickly, he took his seat on the side ledge. Kakamak was exceedingly fond of snuff; and when he came to know of her inclination, he sometimes brought his goods to Nook to barter them for tobacco. Subsequently Kakamak got a son, whereat the grandfather rejoiced extremely; but one day, when the little one was running about and playing on the floor, he suddenly gave a loud shriek, the blood gushed out of his mouth and nostrils, and he was soon dead.

They had another son, who died about the same age, and in the same manner; and when the same misfortune befell a third, the angakok tried a conjuration. Not being able to find out anything about it, he said, " Perhaps we are too near akin: let Kajuernek be called ; " and they at once started with a boat for him. In the evening, when the conjuration was performed, he said, " When the children died the sister-in-law of Kakamak always reproached her as being guilty of a crime, and having an *anghiak* (ghost of a child) who had killed the children." The sister-in-law did not utter a word in reply. Continuing his conjurations, he farther pronounced, " I see a kayak approaching from the north ; it has the shape of a dog's head; it draws nigh ; now it is in the doorway, but it cannot get through the inner entrance." The angakok now asked, "Who was thy *sack ?* " (pôк, in the angakok language the same as mother.) All listening in silence, they heard an infant's voice replying, " Kakamak."—"Where is thy home ? " —" I was born on the island of Alangok ; it is I who have caused the death of all my younger brothers." Kajuernek ordered the anghiak to pass the threshold. It was very long in doing so ; but having at length entered, he pursued it, hoping to get it destroyed. It was now seen also by the other angakok, but slipped away through a hole near one of the roof-beams. Kajuernek said, " It is difficult to get it, because it has already killed several individuals." The conjurations having terminated, they found Kakamak sitting coiled up in the farthest corner of the ledge all tears. Seeing her thus, the sister-in-law, mindful of all the bad language she had to put up with from Kakamak, took to rebuking and scolding her in turn. The following day Kajuernek tried to catch hold of the anghiak, but in vain ; it made its escape through a small opening just as the day before, in consequence of which he was obliged to give it up. Kakamak now grew meek and more submissive ;

but her father, being greatly depressed in spirits, determined to leave for another place; and choosing Niakungunak, they went to settle there along with another family, consisting of many brothers. Towards winter they all joined company, went out deer-hunting, and killed a great many animals with bows and arrows; but his son having the greatest luck in shooting, the others got envious and killed him out of jealousy. The angakok took the loss of his son so much to heart, that he at once returned to Nook, where he remained till the day of his death.

<hr />

## 74.

## UTEREETSOK'S JOURNEY TO THE FAR NORTH.

[A tale from South Greenland.]

A MAN, named Utereetsok, once started from Ilulissat, and travelled northwards, visiting all the inhabited places he passed. He went beyond Umanak and even Upernivik, and at last came to people who had no wood for tent-poles, and merely placed the stiff dried seal-skins upon end, so as to form a tent, in which they slept on the bare ground. The first morning after their arrival, Utereetsok was standing quite unconsciously, his arms drawn out of his sleeves, when, all of a sudden, he felt some one giving him a heavy push from behind; but without hesitation he turned round and dealt the offender such a blow that he rolled along the ground, and then went off without saying a word. When this had been twice repeated, the inhabitants learned to fear him, and he was left in peace. In this place they noticed that the infants had all holes in the hoods of their jackets. Having got more familiar with the parents, they asked them about these holes, and pointing to the moon, they answered, " It is because *he on high* has been gazing at them ; whomsoever he deigns to look down on is always sure to get holes in his garments."

When Utereetsok got weary of his stay there, he travelled still farther north, following the margin of the solid ice. All along the coast there were abundance of white whales. Unable to get on shore, they pitched their tents upon the ice, sometimes spreading the skin of a white whale, without removing the blubber, as a flooring on the ground to sleep upon, and always leaving it behind on starting. At length they approached a very steep and craggy coast; and near the only place where landing was practicable they found a little house, but no people. On entering it, Utereetsok at once perceived that the ceiling-beams were made out of narwals' horn, and not a bit of wood was seen anywhere. They likewise found a head of strange appearance, consisting of tallow only, and instruments whose points were carefully wrapped up in tallow and skin. Seeing no people whatever, they began to feel uneasy, and soon left again. They managed the same way on their homeward journey, and settled for the winter at a place where the people were excellent ball-players. In the middle of winter they made an immense ball, by stuffing out an entire seal-skin with sand and various other heavy things, and finally making their old crones sit down upon it and enchant it by magic spells. On coming to the play they wore their usual dress, excepting on the feet, which they had only clothed in stockings with new soles. The ball was brought out on the ice upon a sledge, and the counter party was stationed nearer the shore. They continued playing and pushing one another until the winners succeeded in striking the ball ashore and right

through the window of their house. Then it was seized on by an old hag, who seated herself upon it. Afterwards the victorious party gave a succession of entertainments; and the general amusement continued during all the season of the increasing daylight. In spring Utereetsok returned to Ilulissat. There he met with a man called Kepigsuak, from Kangamiut (South Greenland), and it was he to whom he told his adventures in the north. During Kepigsuak's stay two sledgers also arrived from the north, who stated that they had left their far-away home at the time of full moon, and who had arrived here just at the next full moon. These visitors were total strangers to the inhabitants, and were from head to feet clothed in suits made of reindeer-skin; they reported that in their home the reindeers might be seen lying close to the houses, and on the tops of the roofs, like dogs in other places. Their object in this long journey, they said, was to barter with the Europeans for firearms, with which view they had brought fox and reindeer skins. The merchant wanted also to buy their dogs, and made a handsome bid for them, offering a tin box of powder, and a whole barrel of lead for balls, in exchange for them. The strangers, however, answered that they could not spare them.

In the spring Kepigsuak returned to Kangamiut, while Utereetsok started for another trip to the far north to revisit the house with beams of narwal-horn. This time he intended to land at a little distance and approach it cautiously from the land side, in order to find out whether it was occupied; and if so, he wanted to see what the people were like.

When Kepigsuak had been staying for some time at Kangamiut, he planned a journey southwards, and went to Kakortok. During his stay there a man named Sakak captured a *k'epokak* (fin-whale, *Balænoptera boops*). Sakak had four wives, of which the last, Igpak, was very haughty, and greedy besides. When the news of the k'epokak was spread many visitors came ; but Igpak had nothing to spare for the guests. Sakak himself invited an old man to his house, but when he was fairly seated Igpak rudely exclaimed, " Why, really, we have no lack of old men looking in upon us this time." The old man retorted, " For my part I only came because I was asked." On this reply she gave him a piece of matak, and likewise a knife for cutting it ; the latter, however, he rejected, saying he only wanted to take it home with him. Igpak, who was always eating as if she could never be satisfied, after a while went on in this style: " What ails me ? what is becoming of me ? I left my work undone because of the victuals, that always seem to be drawing me on." However, she did not give over, but ate all the more, till her tongue at length was so sore that it turned quite awry, and crying out, " Sakak, my tongue ! I am growing matak myself," she suddenly died. People say that while she lived a noxious whale-monster used to appear above the water whenever she left the house ; but after her death it was seen no more. The principal wife being gone, the others were now at liberty to share out as they liked. In the following spring Kepigsuak returned to Kangamiut. He was afterwards baptised and called Egede. He is buried at Kangamiut.

---

## 75.

## SAVANGUAK.

[A story from South Greenland.]

NEAR Kangerdlugsuatsiak there lived a man called Niumak, with his wife Kujapigak. Both were very anxious to get a suitable wife for their only son.

Niumak, from his early youth, had neither fancied nor taken any part in singing or dancing entertainments. At the dancing parties he would turn away from the performers, seeming to take no notice of them; but if a wrestling match or a trial of strength was going to come off, he was always on the alert. At last Niumak fixed upon a girl named Savanguak for the wife of his son, and he became very fond of his daughter-in-law. In summer-time he had one day gone out kayaking by himself; and on landing from a hill perceived a ship approaching. He lost no time in getting out his kayak, and rowed away to meet it. Having got alongside the vessel, he saw a rope-ladder hanging down the side, but not a single man was seen on deck; and no one answering his repeated calls, he went on board and entered the cabin. All was desolate there as elsewhere, and he concluded that the crew had recently left the ship, omitting to furl the sails. The ship having run in among the islands and grounded, he left it to fetch a boat. Returning with this, he established himself and his people on board, and they soon ascertained that the cargo was in no way injured. In the cabin they found beads like those they had been accustomed to get from the whalers, and having possessed themselves of them, they thought themselves very rich. They also overhauled the cargo, but being totally unacquainted with it, they poured into the sea such articles as peas, sugar, and molasses. Having taken from the ship all they could lay hands on, they tore down the sails in order to make use of them as an outside cover of their tents. All the finest beads were given to Savanguak.

Afterwards, when Savanguak had already got several children, some Southlanders arrived, whom Niumak invited to come and stay at his house. In the beginning of winter the younger baby of Savanguak died, and they were all very sorry. One day, when her husband was absent, a vile old crone belonging to the Southlanders went on mocking the bereaved mother, holding up her own grandchild before her in a provoking manner unobserved by the others. This roused Savanguak's suspicion against her. On the same day her husband was expected back, her mother-in-law brought all the reindeer-skins in, to have them looked over. While every one's attention was taken up with this, Savanguak ran outside to take the air. On finding she did not return, Kujapigak turned to some of the larger children and said, "Go and look after your sister-in-law." They soon came back saying, "She is standing outside the house." As she still remained out, they all ran off to fetch her back. Following her tracks, they had to cross a hill, and at length found her at the bottom of a little lake close by. Nobody was able to draw her out; but at the same time they perceived Niumak in his kayak making for the shore. No one, however, dared to call him and tell him what had happened, but getting suspicious from their silence, he put in at once, and hurried to them. On looking round for information, one of the bystanders screamed out, "Thy daughter-in-law is lying dead at the bottom of the lake." Without uttering a single word, he proceeded to draw her out, and tried every means for reviving her; but these proving all in vain, he let the others bring her to the house. On carrying her in, they brought all their things out according to custom. The husband of the deceased, who was named Taterak, also arrived, calling out that he had got a white whale. The servant-maid of the house silently went down to receive and help him. Feeling assured that something was amiss, he asked her to draw his kayak on shore. Obeying her master she pulled up the boat, but did it hurriedly without the usual care, at which he looked inquiringly at her, but got no answer. On stepping ashore his father met him and gave him the sad intelligence that his wife had drowned herself. Without undressing he quickly entered the house, and the father as well as the son went up and down the room deliberating upon how to find out the cause of her death. Meanwhile some of the others were whispering, "Now we will soon have done with the old hag," but the two men never heard them; and unable to discover any reason, they broke out into loud lamentations, joined by all the rest, the old hag only excepted, who was busy eating matak. Some time after, a baby of the place was called Savanguak in memory of the deceased; and it happened that one of Niumak's house-fellows told him that the old woman had been heard to mock and ridicule the baby's namesake. When the little one was learning to walk, the old hag one day took to scolding it; on hearing which, Niumak and his son rose up together, saying, "Now we see who is the real culprit;" and so saying, he poured out a pailful of icy water upon the naked woman, afterwards throwing the pail out of the window. Her companions quietly kept their seats in a row on the ledge; but they were soon upset by Niumak, who tore away the ledge-boards beneath them, which were likewise thrown outside, and he removed all his belongings out of the house. They departed from thence to Kassigissat, leaving their wicked house-fellows behind. During their stay at Kassigissat several other people came to encamp there, waiting for the migratory seal. About that time Haba-kuk,[1] a youth whose parents had likewise pitched their tents there, one day kayaked northwards to meet the seals; and was suddenly surprised on seeing a boat coming down upon him, rowed by a single man. Habakuk, on his part, made up to them, and rowed on alongside of them, being too modest to address them first. At last their old woman Ajugaussak began: "We are almost starving; give us a little of thy new-caught seal. We came away from Sakak, where all our house-

[1] A native, who in the year 1790 made himself a prophet and head of a Christian sect, independent of the European missionary.

fellows died of famine, and we have travelled all this way south without once taking our boat ashore for drying; our only provisions have been half-dried boat-skins." When she had ended, Habakuk went closer to them, saying, "Well, take the skin of my seal with blubber and all, and the liver besides." They forthwith tried to get the animal out of the boat, but were too weak and exhausted to do it without his help. Their old woman proceeded to cut it up, and gave each a little piece of the blubber; and having their hunger appeased for the present, they followed him home, where a meal was instantly set before them. However, they were at first only able to take a very little food, and then went off to sleep, having first asked their old woman to light a lamp. She trimmed it with blubber, accordingly; but missing the stick to stir it up with, she had to make a shift with her forefinger, at the same time exclaiming, "What a length of time I have longed for the sight of this!" However, the strange travellers began to recover by the nourishing food they were getting, but still they often fell asleep in the midst of their meal. On awaking, however, they fell to again, and at last grew so fat that they could hardly get on their boots. Soon afterwards they prepared to leave, intending to go still further to the south.

## 76.

## INUARUTLIGAK — WHOSE CHRISTIAN NAME WAS PETER RANTHOLL.

[A tale from North Greenland.]

IN times far back, the ancestors of this same Inuarut-ligak (viz., fabulous dwarf-inlander or mountain-elf) are said to have lived at the southernmost point of the country, at a place called Kutserfik; and this was before they had learned to be shy of human beings. Just about that time a lasting enmity sprang up between them on account of an Inuarutligak being killed by a man; and ever after, they say that the gnomes have resorted to desert places, making hollows in the earth for their abodes, and shunning the society of man. Thirsting for vengeance, they in return killed a man whom they chanced to meet with on one of their excursions. Being sadly in want of proper arms, they found a large willow-bush on the sunny side of the Kutserfik-mount. Its form was like a man bending down on his knees and supporting his hand against the ground. From one of its roots they made a weapon not larger in size than a closed fist, shaped like a pistol; and at the end they put a little black stone, with a little red one on the top of it. This instrument, when finished, they named the *pointing weapon*. Knowing and fearing its killing powers for their own kith and kin, they are said always to have carried it in their hand. At this time the Inuarutligak of our tale was born. His father's name was Malerke; that of the eldest son Kinavina; of the second, Kook; of the third, Asarfe; and of the fourth, Sersok, of whom we are going to tell. Being given to moving about, his parents and relatives set out on a journey to the north, and travelled on for several years successively, always passing the winter in hollows in the earth, and starting again in the early spring. It is told that they once met with some singular people, whose upper limbs were those of human beings, but below the waist they were shaped like dogs. These creatures were armed with bows, and dreadful to behold, and could catch the scent of man and beast against the wind like animals. One winter they covered the whole inside of their abode under ground with a single skin— that of the large beast called *kilivfak*, the one with six

legs. The story goes that when they had eaten the
flesh of this animal, the bones were covered anew with
flesh, but only up to the sixth time; and despite its
strength and size, they killed it with the above-men-
tioned instrument, by merely pointing at it. They also

knew how to diminish the distance from one place to
another, by drawing the various parts of the country
closer, and performed this by merely kneeling down
together and spreading their arms out towards the
mountain-tops; but finding some of them too high to
spread their arms over, the foremost crossed the already
contracted parts with one long stride, the others one by
one following in his tracks. Whenever one of them
was unfortunate enough to make a false step, several
of them were left far behind for a long time.

After a journey of several years, they arrived at
Ikerasarsuak (at the mouth of Wygat Straits), a place
where lived Inuarutligaks, as well as *Inoruseks*. There
they settled to wait till the frost should cover the ground
with ice and make it possible to join those on the other

side. Starting again in spring, and passing several
winters at different places, they at length reached
Noosak on the continent, and came to their long-
wished-for relatives, and there they lived for many
winters. People say that at the beginning of the
journey to the north the high mountains were still
without ice, and Ikerasarsuak without any glacier.

These elves had two different ways of clothing themselves—one suit they had fitting their natural size, and
the other was large enough to fit a man. During their
wandering they wore their own proper clothes, carrying
the large ones with them, ready to put on in case they
should get some heavy load to carry. They could then,
by beating themselves, reach human size. Their way of

regaining their natural appearance was by bending down
to enter their cave, and hitting the crown of their heads
against the roof, on which they dwindled down to their
ordinary smallness.

An angakok at Noosak, whose wife was childless,
wanted to buy a child from the Inuarutligaks, and offered
to pay for him with three knives, a piece of bearskin,
and some whalebones already twisted into fishing-lines.
Malerke, on seeing them, grew very desirous of these

things; and having got them, he gave the knives to his three sons, but the fourth and youngest he sold in exchange for them. His new father brought him home, and went to hide him behind the house. At night, however, he got inside, and at once slipped into the womb of his mother, on which account it was said that he was in a state of perfect consciousness while he remained in his mother's womb.

These elves were long in turning old; their youth was renewed five times over. On getting old the first time, they let themselves fall headlong down a precipice, and in this way regained the vigour and elasticity of youth. After repeating this five succeeding times, it was useless to try a sixth. This practice of letting themselves fall down they called *Inutsungnartok*. They never die young, but only after having undergone their five separate ages, excepting those who are killed by snowslips.

## 77.

## AKUTAK AND INUINAK.

SEVERAL brothers had an only sister, whom they loved dearly and were very loath to part with. To the north of them was another hamlet, where lived Akutak and Inuinak. One day when out kayaking, Akutak said, "Let us go and give the brothers yonder a call." Inuinak surmised they would only get a cold reception. However, they started, but not a man did they find at home; and the women of the place could not give them any welcome, their husbands having strictly ordered them not to receive any unmarried man whatever during their absence. The strangers nevertheless entered the house, where they found the lonely sister occupying a seat on the southern side of the ledge, where her bedding also could be seen most handsomely piled up. Though seats were offered to them at the northern end, they preferred a settle facing the unmarried sister. They now proceeded to relieve themselves of their jackets, Akutak displaying a skin as fair and soft as that of a white whale, while Inuinak on stripping himself came out as black as a raven. Thus they remained a short time; but before food had been offered to them, the men of the place were hailed returning with their prey. The women ran down to assist them in bringing up their seals; but no sooner had they re-entered the house than a voice was heard in the passage, and a man entered, and in a grumbling voice broke out, " Well, to be sure, we are having visitors." This was the middle brother, and he was soon followed by the rest of them. Akutak answered, " There thou art right; however, we were not very anxious to come at all." The middle brother then ordered some meat to be served up to them ; and, after a plenteous feast, there was a good deal of talking ; but the whole of the evening the visitors kept their seats, never turning their looks off the maiden sister. At length the brothers, longing for rest, lay down to sleep, reclining in their different places. Only the middlemost of them determined to keep watch; and, having pulled off his boots, leaned back, keeping an eye on the strangers all the while. Presently he heard Inuinak call out in a loud voice, " Young girl, make up a bed for me ! " The sister at once complied, and he lay down beside her. The brothers first thought of interfering, but soon gave up the idea, and took no further notice of them. Akutak being now left by himself, was beginning to feel rather lonely ; and, not addressing any one in particular, simply cried out, " Make up a bed for me, too ! " The brothers only glanced at

him, saying, " Why, thou art raving ; just lie down by
thyself." Somewhat abashed, he went off to sleep ; but
in the morning, when the others awoke, they found he
was gone. In his anger he had bewitched the sister, in
order to set her against her new husband.

Early in the morning, the brothers all left in their
kayaks, but the brother-in-law remained in bed till after
sunrise, when he likewise started, having first put on his
kayak-jacket. Ere long it was announced that he was
putting back, and had some spoil in tow. He had
already captured two seals ; and his young wife was
soon on the alert for flensing and cutting them up.
This done, she fell upon her husband's neck, caressing
him incessantly, and would not leave him alone a single
moment. When night set in, and the brothers had all
returned, he actually began to be afraid of her, and
removed to another corner of the room, where he seated
himself behind a lamp, always keeping her off. But
still she would not leave him at peace ; and catching
hold of him with one hand, she at last took up a
piece of a grindstone with the other, eating away at it
as if it had been a morsel of ice. At sight of this, the
brothers exclaimed, " Our sister has gone raving mad ;
let us be off from here ; " and away they fled, having
first cut asunder all the lashings of their boat ; and at
their departure, one of them said to their brother-in-law,
" If people are like this one, nothing is to be done ; and
thou hadst better come with us." But the other rejoined, " I will take my chance, and stay, if it be only
for this one night." The others all started off, while he
remained with his wife ; but she went on pursuing him
all the night, and he kept running away from her,
scarcely able to escape her clutch. At dawn of day,
however, he succeeded in making a bold leap from the
floor right down the house passage, and rushing along
to seize his kayak, he quickly got into it. But at the
very moment he was ready to push off, she again

reached him, and made an attempt to catch hold of
the kayak-point, in which, however, she did not succeed.
At first she seemed determined to follow him on the
water, but all of a sudden she turned back ; and having
looked after her a little while, the poor husband hastened
away to a small island off the coast, where he knew the
brothers had established themselves.  The middlemost
came out, inquiring how she was ; and being informed
how she was, he remarked as before, " If people are like
her, there is nothing to be done but keep away from
them."  When ten days had elapsed, one morning the
husband said, " I must go and look after her ; she may
possibly be starving for want of food."    The others
tried to dissuade him, but he insisted on going.  Having
reached the place, he only pulled his kayak half-way out
of the water, and then proceeded to the house.  For
fear of his wife, he did not venture to enter at once, but
only peeped in at the window, and there he perceived
her lying on the ledge, her hair all loose and dishevelled.
When he addressed her, she answered him back in the
blandest manner, saying, " I am quite well; come inside."
He went in at her bidding ; but no sooner had he entered
the room than she jumped up, and made a furious rush
at him, upon which he again started back, and narrowly
escaped through the doorway.  She quickly followed
him, and after vainly attempting to catch the prow of
his kayak, he suddenly observed her walking on the
water as if it had been solid ice.  Hearing her voice, he
turned round, and seeing her close by he cried, " Why
did I go and see this wicked thing ?  Probably she is
going to eat me up."  As the only way to keep her off,
he began swinging to and fro in his kayak.  Presently
her voice grew weak, and on turning round, he saw her
nearly falling ; but always giving her time to get up,
he at last brought her towards the brothers.   On
seeing her approach, they cried, " Why didst thou
bring her over ?  She will kill us all."  While they were

thus exclaiming, and the husband could not persuade
himself to leave her altogether, she saw before her a
streak of little ripples on the water; and when she came
to them, she suddenly turned, and went back wailing
and lamenting. The husband now left off visiting her
for a long time; but at last one day he said, "I must
go and see her once more; she is probably dead." On
arriving at the place, he found the house empty, and at
last discovered her sitting in a cave all shrunk together,
and stone-dead. Having buried her remains, and covered
the grave well with stones, he returned.

They now resolved upon giving up the house for good,
and settled down for the coming winter on the outermost
of the islets, soon after which the sea was frozen over.
About this time a poor orphan boy, living in the house
of Akutak, said to his house-fellows, "I am in great want
of boots, and intend to go to the brothers and offer them
my little dog in exchange for a pair of old boots." Accordingly he betook himself to their old place. On
arriving there in the morning, he wondered at seeing the
house without windows. However, he went up to it,
and found it still well provisioned; but he could neither
see a boat nor any person about the place. On entering,
he found all the skin-hangings of the walls torn down
and spread on the floor. But knowing no other inhabited house in the neighbourhood, he soon made up
his mind to stay the night over, and at dark went to
fetch some blubber, trimmed a lamp, and lighted it.
He then pulled off his ragged boots, and having put
them up above the lamp to dry, seated himself at the
south end of the ledge. At first his little dog had followed him into the house, and rolled itself up at his feet
on the floor. But while his boots were drying, the dog
began to sniff and yell; and running outside, its barking
gradually became more distant. Some time after, it
again returned, and lying down before its master, looked
at him very sharply, and then rushed out howling as

before, this time re-entering immediately. The orphan thought, "Dogs are *not unconscious of anything.*" He then put on his boots and rushed out, soon followed by the dog. Before they had made their way through the house passage, on looking out he caught sight of the ghost making towards him through the entrance, dragging its shroud behind it. The boy being in the middle part of the passage, pressed himself close up to the wall, and the dog also. At the very moment he expected to be discovered by the ghost, it passed by, on which the dog instantly jumped noiselessly out, followed by his poor master. Both now hastened down to the ice; but before they had got far, the spectre was seen emerging from the house in full pursuit of them. It did not, however, get hold of them; for at a little distance the fugitive had to pass by a large iceberg; and seeing a cave on one side of it, he stepped quickly in, and there awaited the coming day.

At dawn he issued forth again, but did not know which way to wend his steps. His first plan was to go back to his own home, when he suddenly espied a number of people on one of the outer islets. He at once turned towards them. They apparently got much excited at seeing him, thinking it might be the mad woman. Not till he was quite close did they recognise the poor orphan boy, when they all asked whether he had not slept in the haunted house, and whether he had seen anything amiss there. He answered, "No; I observed nothing particular;" and in so saying he told a lie, as he had barely escaped being devoured by the ghost. When they asked him why he had gone there at all, he made answer, "Because I wanted to barter away my little dog for a pair of boots." The middle brother now said, "Well, thou art a hearty little fellow for thy age,"—and with these words he gave him two pairs of boots without taking his dog; and when the boy was about to leave, he asked a gift of a knife with a pretty handle. All the other brothers likewise loaded him with little presents of various kinds. On reaching home, however, he exchanged all these things for a kayak of his own.

---

## 78.

## ARNARSARSUAK, THE KIVIGTOK WOMAN.

ARNARSARSUAK was a pretty girl, much courted by the best seal-hunters of the neighbourhood. Her brother being unwilling to let her get married, she at length took up with a fellow and lived with him as his concubine. Before long she was with child, but notwithstanding, her brother still continued loving her dearly. One day she had been out to fetch water, and at the very moment she was about to enter she chanced to hear her sisters-in-law within talking about her, saying to each other, " I wonder who ever will care to be troubled with the charge of that wretch Arnarsarsuak is going to give birth to." On hearing these words, she at once put down her pails in the passage, and ran off far to the inland, away from humankind. During her flight she perceived that the time had come when she should be delivered ; she fell into a deep swoon, and on recovering found she had given birth to a *kingulerak*.[1] Formerly, in the days of her prosperity, she had been kind and charitable to two orphan children, a boy and a girl, who lived among them. Many years after, when Arnarsarsuak's brothers were all dead, the two orphans took

---

[1] An *anghiak* who remained attached to the mother on account of her being *kivigtok*, until she had revenged herself.

up their abode at a solitary place out on some far away
islands. When the brother was following his trade in
his kayak the sister felt miserably lonely; to make up
for which, however, when he again returned she felt as
if the house were full of visitors. One evening when
they were sitting chatting together, the brother suddenly
said, "I think I shall try to recall the song that Arnarsarsuak used to sing." But the sister advised him rather
to desist, saying, "Remember that Arnarsarsuak now
belongs to *those of uncommon kind,* having fled from mankind during her pregnancy. I have heard that such
people have the gift of hearing their own songs a long
way off." However, the brother would not give up his
intention; but no sooner had he commenced singing
than a voice was heard outside, "On hearing my song
I could not resist coming, and here I am." The brother
and sister looked at each other in great alarm, knowing
that their house was far away from any one. However,
they soon recognised the voice to be Arnarsarsuak's, on
which the sister resumed, "Did not I tell thee she would
be sure to hear thee singing? now go and answer, thou
being the best talker of us." The brother, however,
did not stir; and the voice was again heard, "Ye need
not be afraid of me; I only want to get inside." Seeing her brothers could find no words, the sister said,
"Well, come in;" and presently a sound was heard of
something creeping along the passage, while the two
shrank back on the ledge in silence, with a sure foreboding that the next moment they would be frightened to
death. The sound rapidly approached; they only ventured a timid glance towards the entrance, and immediately after Arnarsarsuak entered, prettier than ever, and
said, "I was lately far from this place, in the interior,
whence I was suddenly lured by some voice calling
me hither." The sister now took courage to say, "It
was only for a pastime he tried to sing thy lay." Arnarsarsuak continued, "Ye know why I fled; it was be-

cause I heard my sisters-in-law observing that no one would be found willing to provide for my poor offspring. On that day I ran far off into the interior, when I was soon to give birth to a *kingulerak*, which ever since adhered to my body till a few days ago. In my present state ye have nothing to fear from me, and I would be very glad to come and stay with you." Seeing that they had no choice, and could not get rid of her, they allowed her room on the farthest end of the ledge, and themselves lay down, leaving a wide space between them; still they were quite unable to fall asleep. The following day the brother wanted to go out hunting; his sister, however, persuaded him to stay at home on account of her new housemate, whom they still considered rather a doubtful personage. On the ensuing day he went out kayaking, but kept so near to the house as not to lose sight of them for any length of time. In the evening, however, he returned, bringing with him two seals, and the sister at once ran down as usual to flense and cut up the animals, but Arnarsarsuak would not allow it, taking all the work on herself; and having quickly flensed both seals, she made up a fire, and while she did the cooking she sewed at the same time. As time went by, and their fears subsided, the brother resolved to marry her; but when she came to be pregnant the sister began to fear she would bear no human offspring, and in that case she said, " Whither am I to flee? seeing we live on an island, I can only rush down to the sea." When her time had come, the brother as well as the sister determined to run away from the house; but when the brother turned back to have a last look through the window, his wife turned towards him, saying, " It is all over, and the birth has taken place. Do not fear, but come in to me." On hearing this he hastened to bring his sister back. When they returned, Arnarsarsuak sat smiling kindly on them, and said,

"Behold the object of your fears, my two babes." She then showed them a little bear cub and a real child. Both were nursed together, and when the bear had begun to go about by himself she again bore a child and another little bear.

In due time the father gave his boys kayaks, and the bears of their own account went out for provender; and at length the father could afford to take things easy, and rest from work. Subsequently he proposed that they should all set out together in search of other people, thinking that the children ought not to live always at such a desolate place. Accordingly they started northwards, the sons following in their kayaks, while the bears kept swimming alongside the boat. Travelling on thus, they at length came in sight of a well-peopled place; on this the bears stuck closer to the boat, and out of bashfulness only popped their muzzles above water. The father remarked, "Don't be ashamed; remember ye also are of human extraction." However, on landing a little south of the settlement they were received by a number of people, who on seeing two large bears ran off for their weapons. But on the father calling to them, "What are you thinking of? they also are my children," they desisted. The new-comers took up their winter quarters at this place, where the sons both got married, and all lived happy together. When the weather was too bad for the men to go out hunting, the bears went off in their stead. After wintering there they again broke up for their old home, and were joined by several people of the place, who accompanied them thither, where their bones now rest.

## 79.

## AVATARSUAK, WHO WAS BAPTISED NATHAN.

IT is said that his grandfather, being likewise called Avatarsuak, was a wise man. It was he who took charge of his younger namesake, whose own father had been early called away from home. The grandfather admonished him not to harm the meanest dog, and never to be uncivil towards old people, not even on being reproved by them. When he came to possess a kayak of his own he remarked that his grandfather, when pushing him off the beach, was always heard to pronounce some strange words, at the same time uncovering his head by pulling the hood back behind the ears But though the youth listened carefully, he could not make out the meaning of the words.

About the time when he first commenced seal-catching his grandfather died, and being left alone he took up his winter quarters at a place where the Southlanders had to pass by when on their trading excursions to the European settlement at Pamiut (Fredrikshaab). At length two kayakers on their voyage to this place passed by his residence, whom he expected for ever so long to see return, but in vain. At length he learned from the south that both were missing, and at the same time that he was suspected of having killed them. Some time after, being in want of a skin for a hunting-bladder, he went off in search of a firth-seal. It was fine weather, and so calm that the breathing of the larger seals was plainly audible. As for the small firth-seals, however, he saw none, and was getting farther and farther into the bay. Suddenly something emerged from the water, coming up close behind him, and beating the top of his

kayak, and lo ! it was nothing less than a *tupilak* (monster made by sorcery). It accosted him, saying, " How
lucky I met thee thus alone, as I am longing for some
entrails ! " Stupefied with awe, he felt the creature creeping up on the top of the kayak behind him, constantly
repeating, " I shall soon make a feast on thy entrails ; "
at the same time pressing down the stern of the kayak
so deep as to make the prow rise in the air. Never before had he, who was wont to carry spotted seals, had
such a weight on board. Feeling his strength giving
way, and knowing nothing better, he tried to capsize his
kayak to the left, but was greatly perplexed to find his
oar striking against a hard substance below, though out
in deep water. At this he got up ; but in attempting
to turn his kayak to the right, he again hit something
hard, on which he slowly righted himself, and rowed
away, at the same time perceiving that he was regaining his strength. But though he pulled homewards with
all his strength, he found it impossible to make his kayak
go straight. It kept turning round, carrying him towards uninhabited places. The tupilak now cried,
" Thou hateful creature, I see I have made a mistake,
and climbed up to *one of uncommon kind*" (viz., a man
endowed with a certain degree of angakok power) ; and
he noticed it struggling hard to get down, but without
being able to detach itself. Thus he went on pulling
away to the sunny side of the firth. When they were
quite close to the beach, the tupilak said, " I see I shall
not get through with thee, and I think I shall be made
thy prize." Just then the man on looking round discovered a boat occupied by women, who had been
farther up the firth getting *angmagsat* (capelins). He
called out to them, " I have got something on my kayak
that is not a seal ; put ashore yonder and come round
this way quickly." When they had done as he told
them, he went on saying, " Don't attack it in front, as it
might be dangerous to you." The foremost among them

on seeing the beast fled in terror. The kayaker again
began to lose strength, but at length his repeated calls
caused the women to come back, bringing with them
oars, intending to use them as levers, the beast sticking
fast, as if glued to the kayak. At length it gave way,
and a cracking noise was heard, whereupon he was able
to get out and look at the monster, which proved to be
the size of a large firth-seal. Turning to the oldest of
the women he said, " I do not care to touch it ; ye cut it
up ; I shall repay you hereafter." In expectation of the
reward she at once fell to and cut open the tupilak,
which she found stuffed with all kinds of bones, such as
of birds, walruses, and seals. They had it entirely destroyed by sinking part of it in the sea, and hiding the
rest of it in some old tombs. This done, he prepared to
row home, but first said to the women, " Thanks to you
and your roaming thus about, without which I wonder
how I had fared. I will take care to repay you ; I am
not likely to forget you." At home he told his adventure, and all now felt sure that it must have been the
tupilak which had formerly killed the two traders. After
this all travellers were unmolested, and the women were
well paid by Avatarsuak.

Some time now elapsed without anything remarkable
happening. Towards spring, however, he found himself
in want of several necessaries, such as lead, powder, and
tobacco, and set out for the European settlement at
Pamiut. Having finished his business there, and rested
during the night, he turned homewards, rather uneasy
about a quantity of drift-ice which had accumulated at
the mouth of a firth he had to cross. Before he reached
the spot, the land wind set in, and came storming down
upon him, and the sky looked black and threatening.
Still he tried to cross the firth, winding his way through
the small passages between the broken ice. At length,
however, he found himself almost entirely stopped, and
at the same time saw a large iceberg drifting down upon

him. He tried to escape, but presently heard the roar
of its *calving* (breaking) right alongside him, and pressing
him deep under the waters. However, he rose on the
other side of the broken piece, and again sped along,
but on the shady side of the firth he was once more
overturned by a much larger iceberg, and this time he
quite lost his senses. How long he was in this state of
stupor is not known; but on reviving he noticed the
strings of his kayak-jacket rattling about, and smiting
his back with the quick motion, while he was pushed on
towards the land beneath the waves. He had no kayak,
but found himself sitting down, the loose bottom skin of
his kayak fastened round him, and having his kayak-
stick for an oar, and with one leg somewhat bent. In
front he saw some one in a large hood rushing on and
cleaving the waters for him, and behind he heard some
one talking, but without being able to make out the words.
These companions proved to be his grandparents protecting their grandson. When they came nearer to the
islets he felt exceedingly thirsty; and presently discovering an iceberg with a fine spring flowing from it
he wanted to go and quench his thirst; but at that moment he heard a warning voice behind him saying,
" Dear grandson, do not drink of the fountain designed
for those perishing at sea; if thou drinkest thou wilt
never return." At length he was carried far towards
the head of the firth, and saw light from the windows of
a very large house. Presently a woman in a white jacket
came out of the doorway, then another, and at last a
man in a reindeer cloak, followed by others, all being
dogs in shape of men, and running down on the beach
to him. When he entered the house there were people
sitting together at its southern end, keeping watch over
a dying brother. Having got inside he fell down beside
the first lamp, but still could hear one of the men say,
" An *anghiniartok* has come among us;" at that instant,
on being handled by them, and touched upon his bare

skin, he lost all consciousness, but soon after revived, hearing a sweet tune of a song from his childhood. At the very moment he revived the sick man breathed his last. The people of the house put a new skin underneath him, and let him remain perfectly quiet in his own clothes for five succeeding days, after which he began to stir about a little, and long to get home, but he had no kayak. One day, however, a woman went down along the beach to gather the red sea-weed, and returned saying, "Only fancy! I have found a complete kayak drifted ashore to us." When they had gathered on the beach, and duly inspected it, they made it out to be the kayak of their anghiniartok, in perfect order, and lying just above high-water mark, and well closed by the half-jacket. On opening this they also found his goods, not a single implement amissing. The next day he returned ; and from that time upwards he became still more of a wise man, and no witchcraft could ever work upon him.

---

## 80.

### ABOUT THE MEN FROM THE FIRTH VISITING THE PEOPLE AT THE OPEN SEA-SHORE.

THERE once lived three brothers at the head of a firth not far from Nook (Goothaab). They were born firth-people, and never thought of approaching the outer sea-coast. But on learning that great flocks of auks were to be met with at Kangek, at the mouth of the firth, they agreed to make a trip thither. When they were ready for their departure, however, the youngest changed his mind and would not be of the party; so the other two went off by themselves. Arrived at Kangek, they first intended to land at the outermost point, not being aware of the heavy surf setting in upon it. When the men of the place saw them in their trouble, they said to each other, " It is plain the firth-people yonder know nothing about surf; now we will have some fun with them." Meantime the visitors had put back, and were looking for a place nearer the habitations, where the landing was easier; but the men called out to them, " We never land anywhere but at the point yonder: it is rather an awkward thing, and cannot be done without letting the surf roll over you; however, that is the way to do it." The two poor fellows retired abashed; and paddling back to the great breakers outside the cape, they almost doubted their words. However, as the men on shore continued encouraging them, the eldest brother first paddled back, and when at the right distance from shore, he suffered himself to be carried right in upon the rocks by a monstrous wave, while he quickly made fast his oar by his kayak-strings. At the moment the wave broke over him, he had loosened his jacket from the kayak, and took a leap, jumping on shore, where he waited the next roller, which brought in his kayak, which he grasped hold of, at the right moment hauling it up. Not a word was uttered by any of the mockers, who stood in great consternation on seeing this daring act, which no one among them would have been able to accomplish. While the poor visitor was drawing up his kayak the other prepared to land in the same way, and he achieved it with even greater agility and swiftness than the brother. After this the men on shore took a sudden fancy to them, and vied with each other in inviting them to their houses. The elder, who had by this time found out their former intention of mock-ing them, replied, " Poor worthless fellows like us are little fit to come here; but our younger brother would just be the man for you. However, he had no fancy for coming. In summer, when the mighty glaciers are throwing off the icebergs into the firth, and when the spotted seals appear, we always want to get at them, but we dare not venture out on account of the dreadful surf from the glacier. We only stand watching our brother, when he, heedless of the danger, crosses the firth ; so you see that we are not at all the right ones to call in here." Still not a word escaped the others. After having put their kayaks and implements ashore, they entered the houses, and were regaled with auks, which they liked very much. However, they preferred the entrails to the flesh itself, thinking them more like the entrails of gulls, which were their usual food. The day after they went with the men auk-catching, and having loaded their kayaks, they again turned homewards.

---

## 81.

## THE DESERTED WOMAN AND HER FOSTER-DAUGHTER.

A WOMAN, who had no brothers or sisters, lived with a little foster-daughter at the house of a great seal-hunter. The daughter was very docile, and always obeyed at the least word. Once, during spring, all the people belonging to the place went away fishing. The chief hunter only lingered behind, harbouring wicked intentions. One calm morning he went outside the house and re-entered, saying, " Pack up your things ; we must be ready to start." They now made all speed, and the lonely woman was not the least busy among them — she worked away as she never did before. When she had put her own poor bundles into the boat she hurried up for her ledge-cover; but when she came outside again, she observed the foster-daughter still standing on shore watching their master closely; and when she herself came down he leaped into the boat, and shoving off, called out to them, "Ye only eat our food; we won't take you along." So saying, their house-mates turned their backs upon them, and got under way. The poor creatures, whose scanty belongings had all been put into the boat excepting the ledge-cover, on seeing the boat depart, faced each other in blank despair, and then burst into tears. However, when the boat was out of sight, the widow wiped her eyes, and said, "Never mind, my dear; we must just do without them." But the child was not so easily con-soled. When at length she stopped crying, her mother said, "Let us go and find out a house to make our home." They went through all the deserted huts, but everywhere the walls were bare and the hangings re-moved, till at length they came into one without win-dows, where the skins still hung on the walls, and the old one said, "Here, in the southern corner, we'll take up our quarters." She at once proceeded to make a room of suitable size, dividing it from the rest of the house with the skins. This done, she continued, "Let us now go outside and try to find something to eat at the flensing-place." She took the child by her hand, and they soon found some small bits of blubber and skin, which they greedily devoured, having had no food the whole day. After this meal they lay down to rest, but were unable to sleep because of the cold. The next day, after a similar search, they found the entrails of an entire seal. After this, however, they found nothing more, and had only the entrails to live upon.

It was just when the herds of seals are passing along the coast that their stock of entrails was exhausted. One morning, having taken a small morsel, they noticed that there was only a bit left for their supper at night.

Then the widow said to her daughter, " Child, thou art more strong and active than I : thou must go and dig a hole over yonder beneath the window-ledge." The daughter obeyed at once, and began to dig up the loose earth. When she had finished, the mother repeated, " Thou art more brisk and active than I : run away and fill the hole with water." The daughter continued fetching water from the sea, and before evening the hole was filled. That evening they took their last bit of food, and went to rest, but without being able to sleep. In the early morning the mother said, " I shall probably not succeed ; still I think I will try to procure something (by magic)." The daughter did not like the idea, nor did she believe in it ; but the mother rejoined, " When I commence my incantation, as I repeat it again and again, thou must listen attentively." She soon began, and as she went through it, warned her daughter to attend well. The child listened, and presently heard a splash : on which she exclaimed, " Mother dear, there is something moving in the water." When the old woman told her to see what it was, she ran off to look, and seeing a little frog-fish, called out, " Ah, mother, it is a frog-fish !" The mother told her to kill it with the old grind-stone (probably an amulet). The little girl obeyed, and the fish was boiled and cut in two, putting aside one-half for their evening meal. Next morning the mother repeated her incantation, and they got a *nepisak-fish* (*Cyclopterus lumpus*) ; the next day, in the same way, an eider-duck—and so on the following days, a firth-seal, a saddleback-seal, a small dolphin, a white whale, and at last a narwal. When she had done flensing the captured animals, the following day large quantities of different kinds of provisions were heaped up outside the house. Towards evening they went to the top of a rock sloping south to cut the flesh in thin slices for drying. While there engaged the daughter exclaimed, "I almost think I see a kayak coming in ;" and in this she was quite right. The lonely woman had one relative, a very aged man ; and this poor fellow, having lately heard of the manner in which she had been abandoned and left in an empty house, now came to see if she had not starved to death, bringing with him a frog-fish as a gift in case she was still alive. When he saw the flensing-place all red with blood he could not believe his own eyes, but thought it all a delusion. And when he observed the two women standing on the rock and slicing large pieces of flesh for drying, and when they afterwards came running down to receive him, he accosted them, " Here am I, expecting to find you starved to death : I actually came to bury you." She answered him, " Silly old thing thou art ! just get thee out of thy kayak, and partake of our good fare here." The poor old man went ashore, but tasted nothing till he had pulled his kayak properly up on the beach. The women had meanwhile boiled him a nice dish. He took his fill for once ; and when he wanted to start they stuffed his kayak with such a supply that it was almost ready to sink. On leaving he said, " As it is, there is no fear of your starving to death ; when all your provisions are ready prepared I shall come to fetch you off." When he was gone they went to rest, and the morning after she again made ready to practise her art. However, she chanted and invoked, and chanted again, and the daughter watched and listened as usual, but neither breathing nor splashing was heard. The reason was that they had taken offence at her having made the gifts over to other people ; and from that time upwards she never succeeded in calling forth anything. When her magic spell had wholly lost its effect, and she had finished drying her stock of flesh, her poor old relative came and fetched her off to his own homestead, and there she remained the rest of her days with him.

## 82.

## ISIGARSIGAK.

ISIGARSIGAK and his younger brother once set out
on a journey northwards, and did not stop till the
frost obliged them to establish themselves for the winter
before they had reached their goal. Not till the middle
of next summer did they arrive at their place of destination, where they found a number of people all friendly
and well inclined; and therefore they resolved to pass
the next winter with them. Winter went by in the
usual way; but when spring came round, some of the
people at times would say, "At midsummer-time we
shall no doubt again *see the dark stripe.*" This implied
the intention of going a trip to Akilinek (the country
beyond the ocean); but the strangers did not understand
their meaning. One day a man came up to Isigarsigak
saying, "We all of us intend to go a voyage out seawards to Akilinek; with that view thou wouldst do well
to gather skins for a double coating to thy boat." He
followed this advice; and when all had got their boats
new coverings, he noticed that every morning the inhabitants mounted the top of a hill to take a survey of
the ocean. Sometimes he joined them, and then they
used to say, "Much as we long to be off, we dare
not risk it yet." But at length the rattling noise of the
tent-poles woke him one morning, and when he saw
the others had almost finished carrying their things
down to the boats, he hastened to pull down his tent;
and being also ready, the boats started. They stood
to sea at once; and when the outer covers got
wet and began to slacken their speed, they cut their
fastenings and cast them off. Isigarsigak dropped

astern a little, and had almost given up hope of seeing
land again, when suddenly he heard land-shouts ahead
of him. As he listened again, he could make out that
they cried, " The broad *dark stripe ;* " and presently he
saw it looming out, and when he rose and stood upright
he beheld a broad expanse of land. The travellers now
broke out into exulting shouts that they had reached
the opposite shore without a gale, and on coming close
to the land they found it abounding with reindeer.
They moored their boats, and at once went off shooting,
but Isigarsigak and his brother slew the greatest number. They decided on staying at this place for a season. Some time after there was heard a cry of " Boats."
Isigarsigak went out and saw a great number coming down
from the north. These travellers also took up their quarters there ; but Isigarsigak did not care to assist them,
and remained in his tent. Before long, however, there
was a cry at the entrance, " Isigarsigak and his brother
are called upon to come out for a singing match " (*nith-
songs* or satirical songs). Although Isigarsigak had no
idea of singing, they made themselves smart and went
outside. They saw an enormous crowd of people all
going up hill, the men in front, the women following.
As soon as they were seen there was another shout,
" Let the men from East step forward." The brother of
Isigarsigak first performed a dance and retired. Isigarsigak himself was now summoned, but as he did not
know much about either singing or dancing he proposed
to his wife to advance, who was so smart and clever that
nobody could match her.

The brother of Isigarsigak being unmarried now took
a wife in this place ; but as his brothers-in-law came to
like him uncommonly well they would not allow him to
leave them. The year being far advanced, they all prepared to cross to their own land, giving their boats new
covers. Though Isigarsigak had been greatly attached
to his brother, and did not like the idea of leaving him,

he wished to die in his own country, and therefore made ready to follow his countrymen. At length they started; but a little way off land Isigarsigak said to his people, "It occurs to me that I forgot to divide our *healing remedy* (viz., amulet for health and longevity). What a pity! we shall have to go back." Accordingly they went back and unpacked the things again. Opening an old box he produced something like a small bit of coal from a fireplace—this being an amulet given to him and his brother in common. He broke it into two pieces, and gave one of them to his brother. The boat was again loaded, and steering right out to sea, he turned round to see the last of his brother, who stood watching them on the beach in his white reindeer jacket. They were never to meet again, so he did not take his eyes off him till he was quite lost to sight.

The boats safely reached their own shore without encountering any storm. Isigarsigak now began seal-hunting with his children, but in time these grew old and died successively. Then he went out in company with his grandchildren, as yet without losing strength himself. It was not till his grandchildren were getting aged that he began to feel a little less handy himself. He was much beloved by his grandchildren, and they often went with him to a craggy reddish cliff, a favourite spot of his, where a number of gulls had built their nests, and the grandchildren's children would call to him, saying, "Here we are at thy favourite cliff; do sing to us." He had a fine voice, and could also imitate the cries of birds, which delighted the urchins beyond everything. This generation also died, and their children became his companions; but his grandchildren's grandchildren had to carry him in a boat, and to treat him like a child. His strong frame had now grown thin and shrunk like that of a baby; he ate almost nothing, and to know whether he still breathed they used to hold a bit of down before his nose. In passing by the bird's-

cliff they would say, " Now we are at thy favourite spot ;
do sing a song : " and listening sharply, they could hear
a small feeble sound like the cry of a bird. At length
he began to suck his coverlet ; and one day when they
came to take him out as usual, they observed that the
feather before his mouth did not stir ; he had breathed
his last. Isigarsigak never had his like with regard to
old age in this country (Greenland) ; he got quite as old
as Nivnitak. His younger brother may even have out-
lived him, but he had never been heard of. It is through
him that we are related to the people of Akilinek.

## 83.

## ATALIANGUAK.

ATALIANGUAK was an excellent seal-hunter, and
lived as a bachelor in a large house, together
with several cousins. At spring-time he used to go out
all by himself in his boat in order to fish *angmagsat*
(Capelins). One evening when he returned to his tent,
having been out kayaking, he was much surprised at
seeing a pretty little woman standing outside of it.
She wore a pair of white boots, and her hair-tuft was
newly dressed. Atalianguak ran quickly up beside her,
and taking hold of her hand brought her into the tent,
and afterwards married her. When the fishing season
came to an end he repaired homewards in his boat, his
wife rowing, while he himself took the helm. In autumn
he again settled down in the house of his cousins. One
evening just as his wife had risen from her seat on the
ledge to go outside, one of the other people, whom she
happened to pass by, remarked, " What a very peculiar

smell I perceived ;" but his housemates told him to take great care not to offend her, as they had observed that she was not a woman of *the common kind.* The same thing, however, happened again ; this time the little woman hearing them speak of a strange smell rushed quickly out, and the moment she passed the doorway the people observed a fox-tail dangling at her back. Atalianguak pursued her to the border of a lake. In a fox-hole close by he noticed a light, and peeping in he saw his wife sitting on a ledge. He called out, " I feel so cold, let me come in." " Well, come." " But in what way am I to enter ? " " Thou hast only to breathe upon the entrance and thou wilt easily get in." Thus he entered, and sitting down beside his wife, he exclaimed, " It is dreadfully cold—do make me warm." At the same time he saw one of the walls covered with flies, dirt-flies, beetles, and all kinds of reptiles. She now raised up her head and ordered them to lull Atalianguak to sleep, and presently they all began singing, " Atalianguak, sleep, sleep ; at spring we will rouse thee again:" and he slept for ever so long. At last he awoke of his own accord, and when he rose and went outside the sun was high in the sky, while the cave itself swarmed with flies and reptiles. He went to make water, and forthwith it turned to a whole river. From that time he gave up all thought of womanhood.

## 84.

## A VISIT TO THE GIANTS.

THE orphan boy Inoosarsuk was greatly loved by his foster-mother, but not by his foster-father.

One day, when the father was out on a seal-hunt, the
mother told Inoosarsuk she was tired of seal-flesh, and
ordered him out in her husband's other kayak to catch
some frog-fish.  He remonstrated, saying that his father
had forbidden him to take the kayak ; but still she went
on desiring him to go, at the same time assuring him
she would clean and put it back all right in its place.
Notwithstanding, the father coming home observed that
it had been used, and beat Inoosarsuk till he could not
move for pain.  Another day his mother went on persuading him in the same way to take the kayak in order
to go out and get her some *quannek* (the eatable stalk
of *Angelica archangelica*), growing near the shore, a little
up the firth.  But when he had ascended the hills in
order to fetch her some, and came back to the beach, he
found, to his great alarm, that the tide had carried away
the half-jacket belonging to his foster-father's kayak.
On approaching home he got so frightened at the thought
of his foster-father that he passed it by and turned right
out to sea.  Having rowed beyond the outermost islands
he suddenly remembered his two amulets, a quannek
and an old whetstone ; and jumping out on a flake of
drift-ice, he planted one of his newly-gathered stalks,
calling out, " Thus shalt thou remain standing erect,"—
an invocation to secure him calm weather.  Like Giviok,
he passed by the ocean-lice for Akilinek, and having
first encountered the cannibals, he afterwards fell in with
the women who captured fishes by putting bladders to
them at low tide.  From the cannibals' chimney a black
smoke arose in the air, but from that of the latter a
white smoke was seen.  Among these he was very kindly
treated, but still he at last grew tired of his sojourn ; and
one day pretending to row a little in the neighbourhood,
he took himself far off, and fled to the south.  At length
he arrived at a wild firth ; but thinking it too long to
enter, he resolved merely to cross the inlet to the opposite shore.  When half-way across he saw what he fan-

cied was a rock ; but on coming closer he found it to be
an enormously big kayaker, who took hold of him and
lifted him up quite easily, kayak and all, in one hand,
and put him down before himself on his own vessel, intending to take him home as an amulet for his little
daughter. When they approached the homestead of
the giant, something like a big iceberg was standing in
front of the house ; on closer inspection it proved to
be an enormous gull, which the giant's daughter was in
the act of catching. Inoosarsuk was now brought up to
the house and put upon a shelf near the window. During the night he took a fancy to some very nice-looking
eatables lying behind the lamp. He managed to slide
down on the side ledge, but finding it quite filled up by
the giant's sleeping daughter, without any room left
where to put down his foot, he had no choice left but to
step along her one leg ; unfortunately he lost his footing
and fell down. The giant's daughter on being awakened
in this way, and unconsciously grasping him, had nearly
eaten him up, but luckily remembered that he was her
little amulet. The giant seeing Inoosarsuk's dismay
and utter dejection, at length put him down on the floor,
and covered him up with his large cloak, saying, " Thou
shalt grow as big as that, as big as that." He forthwith
commenced to grow, and was soon as tall as the daughter, after which the giant furnished him with a kayak of
suitable size. He now remembered his foster-parents ;
and longing to take revenge for the many blows he had
formerly got, he crossed the ocean, and soon found the
place where they had formerly lived. But the house
was laid waste, and the old people buried beneath its
ruins. He then returned to pass the rest of his days at
Akilinek.

## 85.

## KAGSUK.

[The story here given as having happened in the districts of Holsteinsborg and Sukkertoppen, in Greenland, is perhaps a variant of an older tale, only localised in this way. We give it here in an abridged form.]

IT is said that Kagsuk once had his wintering-place on the Karsit islands, outside of Amerdlok (Holsteinsborg), and that his son married the only sister of some men living at Satok, near Maneetsok (Sukkertoppen). Kagsuk, as well as his son, were powerful and strong men ; the former was also a man-slayer, invincible to his enemies. Once, when the son had been out during the day with his brothers-in-law, at evening, when it was growing dark, he had some talk with his wife that ended in a quarrel. Her brothers, fearing his strength, at first kept silence ; but soon after, when he gave her a kick, they all went up to him and seized him in order to protect their sister. He tried to appease their wrath, but in vain, and at last they struck him with a knife ; but every time he was wounded he only rubbed the place with his hand, and directly it healed, after which he knocked them all down, one after another. From this time, however, he did not trust his brothers-in-law ; and once, at dark night, he escaped from the house, leaving his kayak behind, and taking his way across the fast ice to the north, where he stayed a while with some other people, and at length came to the house of his father. When Kagsuk came to know how his son had been treated he got into a great rage. In vain the son tried to persuade him to delay his revenge. "If they have struck thee with a knife," he replied, "we will set out and destroy the people of Satok this very night." And off they went the same day for Satok, and slew the whole

of them, only sparing a boy and a girl. On returning to
Karsit, Kagsuk became a still more desperate murderer.
The people of Amerdlok, on becoming aware of this, did
not venture themselves far away from the shore. Kagsuk and his son, being both very suspicious, agreed on
the following mode of life : If the weather was fine, the
son went out kayaking alone, and when the father went
out, the son remained at home, unless it happened to
blow very hard, in which case, and then only, they went
out together. One winter, when the days were beginning to lengthen, two kayakers from Amerdlok, while
out seal-hunting, were overtaken by a snowstorm, and
could not make out their own land. Bewildered, they
came to Kagsuk's house ; at seeing which they got very
frightened, lest he would kill them. As soon as they
saw him come out of his house, and before he could utter
a word, they said, " Chance brought us hither, and no
intention of visiting you. We lost our way on account
of the snow, and could not advance against the storm."
Kagsuk asked them to come on shore, adding that, as
soon as the weather abated, they might set off for home.
On hearing this they were reassured, and entered the
house, which was very hot. Kagsuk talked a great deal
the whole day ; but in the evening, when it was still
blowing a gale and snowing as fast as ever, he suddenly
became silent. At length he inquired, " Which kayak
is he using to-day ? " The housemates answered, " The
narrow one." Kagsuk then remarked, " I was rather
uneasy about him ; but if he has taken that kayak I have
no fear." Later in the evening there was a cry that he
had arrived, tugging a walrus ; and when the people
whose business it was to haul it up on shore had gone
out, Kagsuk said, " They don't intend to stop, but having
lost their way, chanced to come in here much against
their will." The guests, looking round, then first discovered that he was speaking to his son, who appeared
in the entrance, and already had bent his bow and was

aiming at them, but now drew back, and directly after entered, asking if the guests had been offered something to eat. On hearing that they had as yet had nothing, he ordered different dishes to be set before them, saying he would share the repast with them. They afterwards went to rest, and slept quietly until Kagsuk roused them up, saying that now the weather was fine, they might as well start for their home. At their departure he ordered their kayaks to be filled with provisions, but at the same time added, " Take care that none of your people come hither to visit us, lest we should take their lives." They then pushed off, and arrived safely at their home. But when the people of Amerdlok saw the stores they had brought with them, they were all keen to visit Kagsuk ; and notwithstanding their being repeatedly warned by those two chance visitors of what Kagsuk had threatened, several among them would not desist from trying their chance. They went accordingly, but never returned. Among the kayakers lost in this way were the sons of two old men, who were very clever in magic spells. They prepared bows of an arm's length, and having finished these, they said to their place-fellows, " Now we will set out to punish Kagsuk : while ye approach his house from the sea-side, we will come on from behind." Kagsuk had for his amulet a *toogdlik* (the Great Northern Diver—*Colymbus glacialis*) perched on the roof of his house, and giving him notice of every impending danger. One day on hearing its cry he went out, and observing the kayakers approaching, he said, " All right; I see you." But at the same moment the two old men, having escaped observation by means of magic spells, came stealing on from behind and shot him dead on the spot. The kayakers, coming on shore, killed all his housemates, with the exception of his son, who happened not to be at home, and afterwards fled to the north.

NOTE.—Some narrators have prolonged the story of Kagsagsuk (No. 1) by making him meet with Kagsuk in the far north, the house of the latter being situated on a wide plain, the entrance to it being provided with a string leading into the inner room, and all along hung with a row of pieces of walrus - teeth, for the purpose of announcing the entrance of every stranger by the rattling sound.

---

## 86.

## THE DREAM AND CONVERSION OF AKAMALIK.

[This tradition appears to rest upon an event mentioned by Crantz in his 'Historie von Gronland,' p. 561, as having taken place in the year 1743 ; but it is given here in a very much abridged form, from two manuscripts, a great portion of which was merely copied out from the New Testament, and some other religious books.]

IN the days when missionaries had come to Nook (Goothaab with New-Herrnhut), but people in other places were still heathens, there lived in the south a clever and skilful seal-hunter, named Akamalik, who had a cousin of whom he was very fond. However, it chanced that this friend of his fell ill and died, which caused him much grief, and sorely depressed his spirits. As chance would have it, the women of the place at that time brought forth no sons, and his own wife being childless, he could get no namesake for his deceased friend. He henceforth fell into the habit of ill-treating his wife, kicking her and piercing her skin with an awl. After some time it was rumoured that a woman of a neighbouring place had borne a child and named it after his friend. On hearing this, Akamalik at once hastened thither, and was so glad at seeing the babe that he was quite unable to sleep for five succeeding nights. Having returned home, sleep at length was again restored to him, and then he dreamt as follows: Some one peeped

in at the window, and calling out for him, said that he
was to come and get his piece of blubber from a young
whale which was just being caught. He at once went
out and followed the voice, the owner of which he now
perceived was a woman. In running after her he came
across a vast plain, stretching forth like the surface of
the ocean, and gradually rising. It became brighter and
always brighter; he passed over heaps of sand, rolling
dreadfully like a mountain-river, and saw a crowd of
people playing at ball with a walrus-head. Akamalik
would fain have stopped and joined the players, but the
woman hurried him on, and, almost against his will, he
constantly followed her. However, he wondered greatly;
for in those people, on close view, he plainly recognised
men who had died a number of years ago. He then
came to three high steps, which it appeared impossible
to ascend; but merely looking at his guide, he gave a
leap and almost unwillingly mounted them. From the
top he again saw before him a great plain, and a crowd
of people in beautiful clothing; among them he recognised a man in the murder of whom he himself had
taken an active part many years ago, and could not but
be astonished at hearing people talk in answer to what
he was thinking of but had not yet spoken out. Voices
were then heard calling the crowd to divine service: the
people all sallied forth, and he followed their steps, passing over a dreadful abyss with fires burning down in the
depths; then they ascended still higher to a place so
dazzlingly bright and beautiful as he never had seen
before. Here the Saviour Himself was preaching and
leading the song of innumerable people. The Saviour
spoke to Akamalik, reproaching him with his sins, at
the same time pointing out to him the abyss, where He
told him that tornarsuk resided in the depths, and advised him, saying, "Next summer thou must repair thee
to Nook for the purpose of getting instructed." The
Saviour guided him on his way back across the abyss,

and thus going downwards, on approaching the earth again he (viz., his soul) beheld his own poor body, walking backwards and forwards all void of intellect, people believing him to be mad. It appeared very uncouth in his sight, all covered with maggots; but though he greatly abhorred it, he nevertheless entered into it, having no other abode. Having thus put on the garb of his body, he became like dead and lay in a swoon. By-and-by he recovered his reason, and was awake. He then repented his profligate life, went to Nook in the spring, and was baptised by the Moravian missionaries. He not only became a Christian by name, but also a good man and a loving husband.

---

[NOTE.—Of the following Tales only the principal parts have been selected, and are given here in a very fragmentary form.]

87. SANGIAK, OR NERNGAJORAK.— A man whose wife could beget no children was advised by an old wise man to set off in his kayak, and go out to the open sea, and when he heard a voice like that of a child crying, he was to proceed in that direction, and would then find a worm, which he was to take home and throw upon the body of his wife. Having done it, the worm disappeared in the body of his wife, who soon gave birth to a son, whom they called Sangiak. While he was yet a small child, he asked his father for a kayak ; and when following his father out to sea, he surprised him by hitting two seals, though he only threw his harpoon once. He acquired the art of always taking the whole flock of seals by only throwing at one of them. At last his father hardly knew how to bring home all the seals he captured. Once Sangiak happened to get acquainted with another seal-hunter, who could also

take two seals at a time, but only by means of two harpoons, which he threw one with each hand at once. This double-armed kayaker being much beloved by his companions, Sangiak grew envious of him; and once when he went out alone with him to sea, he picked a quarrel with him, and killed him. He then told his father what had happened, and that he would give the relatives of the double-armed notice of the murder. The relatives would fain have avenged it; but he took flight in his kayak, which, though his enemies had cut holes in its bottom, did not sink. Having filled his kayak with stones, he stopped the holes with them, and returned to his father safe and sound.

88. ATLUNGUAK was a miserable hunter, despised and mocked by his housemates, who only saw in him a poor wretch always sitting behind his mother's lamp, and feeding upon what the others brought home. But when some deed of special daring, which no one else cared to undertake, was on hand, he at length bestirred himself, and braved the danger alone. Thus, he first killed an ice-covered bear, then an amarok, and finally a kilivfak (all fabulous animals).

89. NAKASUNGNAK travelled far up north, and settled down with some people who used boats, but no kayaks. He was very presumptuous and obstinate. His new place-fellows told him that before long the ice-covered bear would make its appearance, that it was very dangerous, and for mere men a deed impracticable to slay it. But Nakasungnak, nothing heeding, set out to encounter the terrible animal; and on discovering it, he ran in upon it only armed with a knife. He instantly disappeared down its open mouth. The bear was then seen to totter, and soon after fell down dead. On approaching it, they observed a knife sticking out between its ribs; and when the hole was widened

Nakasungnak jumped out of it; but his hair, as well
as the skin of his face, had come off, and shivering with
cold and ague, he ran away to the house. In the meantime, the bear's flesh served them for food the greater
part of the winter. Afterwards they told Nakasungnak
how to behave when they were going to catch the birds
that could speak, and the little fishes with both eyes on
one side. The swarms of birds and fishes appeared;
but Nakasungnak would not follow the advice they
gave him, and consequently got none. Lastly, they
told him that gnats were soon expected, the size of
sea-fowls, and with stings like the point of an arrow;
and when the swarms were approaching, and seen to
come on like broken clouds from the south, the people
had to retreat to their tents and close them with all
care. Nakasungnak, however, again disregarded their
warnings, and took no notice of what they had said.
When the clouds appeared, and all the others sped into
their tents, he remained outside. When all was over,
and they went out to look for Nakasungnak, they found
only a skeleton lying beneath the boat.

90. THE ANGHIAK.—A company of brothers had
a single sister, and would not allow her to marry.
Nevertheless, having many suitors, she finally came to
be with child; and because of her brothers' reproaches,
she secretly had a miscarriage; but the child got intellect, and became an anghiak. It picked up the skull
of a dog, using it as a kayak, and the bone of a man's
arm for a paddle. Every night it used to creep into
the house and lie down to suckle its mother's breasts,
but during the day-time it was about pursuing her
brothers when they were kayaking, and made them
capsize and perish one after another. Having accomplished its revenge, it repented its deeds, and fled to
the north, where it slipped down in the doorway of a
house in which a conjuration was going on. The

angakok (by means of his second - sight) at once observed its approach; and when the people of the house had got a light, and went to look for it, they were all *frightened to death.* It then became still more powerful, but went back again to its mother's abode, and found a refuge in a heap of rubbish. It now happened that the angakok of the place was about to perform a conjuration for the purpose of finding out what had caused the brothers' destruction. The sister, on being examined, first denied, but finally she confessed her sin, saying, "What I brought forth was no real child." No sooner had she pronounced these words than the anghiak felt a pain in its head, and while she continued her tale, it lost its senses and died.

91. THE MOON.—Several stories are told about people travelling to the moon. The following are specimens of these myths.

*Kanak,* on fleeing from mankind, felt himself lifted up from the ground, and following the way of the dead. At length he lost his senses, and on awakening again found himself in front of the house where the spirit (or owner) of the moon resided. This man of the moon assisted him to get inside, which was a perilous undertaking, the entrance being very large, and guarded by a terrible dog. The moon-man having then breathed upon Kanak in order to ease the pain that racked his limbs, and having restored him to health, spoke thus: " By the way thou camest no man ever returned ; this is the way thou must take,"—upon which he opened a door, and pointed out to him a hole in the floor, from which he could overlook the surface of the earth, with all the dwelling-places of man. He regaled him with eating, which was served and brought in by a woman, whose back was like that of a skeleton. Kanak was getting afraid on perceiving that, on which the moon-man said, " Why, that's nothing ; but lo! soon the old woman will appear who takes out the entrails of every one she can tempt to laugh. If thou canst not withhold thy smiles, thou only needst to rub thy leg underneath the knee with the nail of thy little finger." Soon after the old hag entered dancing and whirling about, licking her own back, and putting on the most ridiculous gestures ; but when Kanak rubbed his leg with the nail of his little finger, she gave a sudden start, at which the moon-man seized her, and threw her down in the entrance. She went off, but afterwards a voice was heard, " She has left her knife and her platter, and if she does not get both, she says she will overthrow the pillars of heaven." The moon-man having thrown the knife and platter down the entrance, again opened the hatch in the floor, and blowing through a great pipe, he showed Kanak how he made it snow upon the earth. Lastly, he said to him, " Now it is time to leave me, but do not be the least afraid, lest thou never shalt come alive." He then pushed him down through the opening, on which Kanak swooned ; and on recovering, he heard the voice of his grandmother, whose spirit had followed and taken care of him ; and at length he reached the earth's surface, arose and went to his home, after which he grew a celebrated angakok.

*A Barren Wife*, who was treated badly by her husband, went off one winter night and met with the moon-man, who came driving in his sledge, and took her along with him to his home. Many days after in spring, she again appeared, and went to live with her husband. Ere long she perceived that she was with child, and gave birth to a son, who when he grew up was taken away by the moon-man.

*Manguarak*, unheeding the warnings of his father, caught a white whale which, having a black spot on one side, was known to belong to the animals of chase set apart for the spirit of the moon. On a fine winter night the moon-man was heard to call him outside and challenge him to fight. When he came down upon the ice, the moon-man said, " Well, we will presently begin, but first let us name all the animals of chase we have caught during our lifetime." They then, each in his turn, named the different sorts of birds, seals, and whales they had chased ; and beginning with the fishes, Manguarak went on to tell how he once assisted at a halibut-fishing, when they happened to haul up a ĸêraĸ (*Anarrichas lupus*). On hearing this, the moon-man exclaimed, " What art thou saying, man ? Now just wait, and listen to me." He then went on to tell how, when a child, and still living among mankind, he had once seen some people haul up a fish of that same kind, at which he was so terrified that he had never since tried to catch that fish. " And now," he continued, "that I know thou hast caught an animal which I never ventured to pursue, I will do thee no harm. I begin, in fact, rather to like thee ; so come along with me and see my place." Manguarak accordingly went up to ask his father's permission, which having gained, he returned to the ice, where he found the moon-man waiting with a sledge drawn only by a single dog. When he had taken his place on the sledge, away they drove at a great pace, and gradually rising from the ground, they seemed to fly through the air. At midnight they came to a high land, upon which they still travelled on. They went through a valley covered with snow, and had to pass by a dark-looking cliff, inside of which lived the old hag who was wont to cut out the entrails of people who could not forbear laughing. As to the rest of the adventures of Manguarak, they are much the same as those encountered by Kanak.

92. THE WOMAN WHO WANTED TO BE A MAN. —A woman named Arnarkuak would not give up scold-

ing her son on account of his want of skill in hunting
and other manly pursuits. Once in his absence, when
he had gone out kayaking, she forced her daughter-
in-law, by threatening her with death, to flee with her
to the interior of the country, where she disguised
herself like a man, and had her daghter-in-law, Ukua-
mak, for a wife. But the son found out their place of
refuge, and killed his despicable mother.

93. AN ANGAKOK FLIGHT. — A great angakok,
being once called upon to perform a conjuration, took
a thong of seal-skin, and having in one end cut a hole
for his toe, he twisted it round his body, and made
fast the other end to his head. When the lamps had
been all extinguished, he was lifted up, and soaring
about the house he made the roof lift and give way to
him. Having escaped through the opening he flew to
the inland, and came to a house inhabited only by
women, but as soon as he tried to approach any of them
the house-pillar (their enchanted husband) began to
emit sparks of fire and lead towards him. The next
time he flew to the inland he was seized hold of by the
inlanders, who essayed to play at ball with him, hurling
him backwards and forwards between them till he was
nearly dead, when he called his tornak, who quickly
rescued him. The third time he came to his sister, who
had disappeared many years before, but whom he now
found married to an inlander ; she gave him a piece of
reindeer-skin as a token to take home with him in order
to convince people of his really having been with her.

94. THE MEANS FOR GETTING CHILDREN. — A
married couple had in vain been in hope of getting
children. At length the man set out in search of
some means to attain their desire. The first summer
he travelled as far as he could get to the north, and the
next as far as possible to the south, before he succeeded

in finding an old woman who promised to help him. From the bottom of her bag she produced two small dried fishes, a male and a female, of which he was to give his wife the former to eat if he wanted a son, and the latter in case they preferred a daughter. He received the fishes, and started on his way home; but having to travel very far, and not always being able to get any victuals, he once in a great strain for something to eat began to consider, "What is the use of keeping this spawner? a son is what we desire;" on which he swallowed the one little fish. After a while he began to feel very ill at ease, at the same time growing bigger and bigger, till at length he could hardly manage to slip down in his kayak. A skilful old woman, who lived at a place where he happened to land, soon suspected what was the matter with him, and hit on a charm to deliver him of what was encumbering his inside, which soon proved to be a fine little daughter. (It is doubtful whether the rest of the tale is of genuine Eskimo origin.)

95. KANGINGUAK was a native of the south, who set forth on a journey and took up his abode near Umanarsuak (Kin of Sael, a high island of South Greenland). He had a son named Tunerak, who was such an expert rower that he used to overtake the falcons in their flight, and killed them with a blow of his paddle-oar. He went out to sea so far as to make Umanarsuak appear like a seal diving up and down among the waves. He also tried matches with celebrated kayakers, but on one of these occasions he was killed by his rival. His father afterwards went to the place where he was buried, brought out his body again and carried it along with him, till he found an angakok, who restored it to life.

96. KIGDLINARARSUK, in order to avenge the murder of his sister, went out in search of an old woman

who could assist him in getting an amulet for giving swiftness to a boat. The first one he came to replied, " I have grown rather old to no purpose (viz., without having acquired wisdom), I am only clever in —— ——,[1] but farther north I have an elder sister more cunning than I ; first try thy luck with her, and if thou dost not succeed I'll see what can be done." He then went farther, and came to another old hag, who gave him for an amulet a small bit of a dried Merganser (*Mergus serrator*). This he inserted in the prow of the boat with such care that no marks or joints were visible. Twice he tried it before the boat appeared swift enough to run down a flying Merganser, and not till then did he start to encounter his adversaries.

97. A MAN LIVING ON KARUSUK (in the firth of Goothaab) every day used to repair to Kangek (about 24 miles distant) for the purpose of hunting auks. For his companion he had an ingnersuak, who at the same time was the tornak of an angakok, living farther up the firth at Tukak. It is said that even now-adays many kayakers have an ingnersuak for their companion, and every now and then they become visible. Sometimes a kayaker observing two distinct kayaks at a distance, on coming nearer will only meet with one, who on being questioned is not aware of any other having been with him. In such cases people believe it to have been an ingnersuak, on account of their being invisible, excepting from a great distance. The said ingnersuak in the short winter days came to Karasuk, waited until he saw the man ready to start for Kangek, and then followed, and took care of him the whole day, and re-

---

[1] The original words I have not ventured to translate, sufficiently characteristic though they are of the modesty which it is considered necessary by the Eskimo to assume on such occasions as that described in the text. It would have been scarcely possible for the old woman to have claimed skill in a manufacture more lowly than that of which the words omitted would have been a translation.

turned with him to Karusuk, from whence he went on
to his home at Tukak.

98. ATARSUATSIAK and his brothers were a set of
fearful manslayers, living in the country about Upernivik (Greenland), who had their heads tattooed with a
separate mark for each murder they had committed.
On Atarsuatsiak these marks formed a whole row along
his forehead from one side to the other. At last the
people of the neighbouring places resolved upon having
him killed at a place to which he used to resort in
order to visit his concubine.

99. AMONG THE LAST ANGAKUT AT KANGER-
DLUGSUATSIAK (Greenland) was a man named Kapi-
arsuk, and a woman called Avangnanersuak, who every
day during the whole winter used to go out together
to catch partridges, but never brought any home,
and never were seen to eat anything at all. At last
a child, who was anxious as to their doings, one day
asked leave to accompany them, and soon observed that
they never looked for any partridges at all; but having
come a good way up the country, Kapiarsuak commenced to strike a flat rock with his staff, and murmuring certain words, an opening appeared in the ground,
out of which they went on angling and hauling up different kinds of food, allowing the child to partake of
the good fare. On going home they gave it a small fish
to swallow, after which it lost all remembrance of what
it had seen. Not until he was full grown, many years
after, did he suddenly recollect the event and narrate it.
    Another angakok of the same place, named Kuvat-
siak, had two brothers, Usuinak and Igpak, of whom the
former, having gone out kayaking, did not return, and
entirely disappeared. In the evening they saw the
clothes of the missing brother moving about by themselves. Kuvatsiak forthwith began to conjure, by means

of which he found out that he had been seized by the ingnersuit. Kuvatsiak had a dream somewhat like that of Akamalik; and when he began growing old he often met with his deceased brother out at sea. He observed some black thing lying on the top of his brother's kayak who laboured in vain to rid himself of it, saying that that was the only impediment hindering him from leaving the under-world people and returning to the land of the living. When the first missionary came to the country Kuvatsiak had a dream that induced him to get baptised.

100. ATUNGAK, A TALE FROM LABRADOR. — A man namd Atungak had two wives. One of them having run away, he pursued her in his sledge, and soon overtook her. They then travelled together, and came to cannibals, whose chief invited them to his house, and set before them a dish of man's and wolves' brains mixed together. When they declined eating it, another was served consisting of the flesh of a child and of a walrus; and this also being rejected, they brought in dried reindeer-flesh, which they ate with hearty appetite. Meanwhile the people got hold of some children, and feigning to pet them they killed them and sucked out their brains. A young lad was also there who carried a sling wherewith to entangle strangers; but when he approached Atungak with this design he was struck on the head with a piece of pyrites-stone, and fell to the ground. Afterwards, when his mother came from another house to look for him she only found one of his legs left, lying under the bench, with the boot still on it, by means of which she recognised it. She then exclaimed, "Ye have done very ill in taking that miserable Ajajusek, who ought to have served his younger brother for food." Atungak and his wife travelling on, came to a country the people of which were all lame. Before they reached them the chief came to receive

them, and warned them against his people as being a very ill-natured set. Nevertheless, when Atungak's wife saw their ball-playing, she could not help laughing, and said that they hopped about like so many ravens. Atungak got very much afraid when he heard the by-standers repeating this. He at once cut asunder all the lashings of the sledges belonging to the lame people, so that they could not pursue them. Hastening from there they came to two black bears engaged in a fight, and no other way being left they were obliged to pass between them ; after which they came to a pot boiling of itself, which they could not avoid crossing over. Lastly, they came to a man watching at the breathing-hole of a seal, and on speaking to him they recognised him as Atungak's son, whom they had left behind a child. They had travelled over the whole world without changing or getting old. In the north, caves and clefts in the rocks are still to be seen, in which they are said to have rested.

NOTE.—This story, and the next from East Greenland, being both imperfect fragments, received from the most widely severed Eskimo countries, will be found to contain some very curious similarities.

101. MALARSUAK, A STORY FROM EAST GREENLAND.—A man named Malarsuak started in search of his lost sister. Travelling by sledge, he came to houses inhabited by cannibals, with one of which he found his sister domesticated. A hideous-looking youth came into the house, whom Malarsuak killed by piercing his head with a bear's tooth fastened into a stick, whereupon the host threw the dead body under the bench. Some time after a woman appeared, saying, "Is this not my miserable son here—I mean the one who ought to serve as food for his brothers?" Malarsuak travelled homewards, but came back on a visit, bringing his wife and a little child with him. The cannibals robbed them of their child. When going to leave, the brother-in-law tried to persuade him first to cut all the lashings of his

place-fellows' sledges, in order to prevent their pursuing the travellers. Malarsuak took his advice, but happened to forget one of the sledges, which came speeding after him; but he killed the driver and made his escape himself.

102. A Tale from Labrador. — Sikuliarsiujuitsok, on account of his great size, was unable to walk upon new ice. He, all by himself, caught a whale from his kayak. But he was much dreaded and hated, and never ventured to sleep in strange places. He was, however, once persuaded to stay for a night in a snow-hut; and being too big to find room in it, he lay all doubled up, and allowed his feet to be tied together. In this condition he was hauled out and killed, but not before he himself had killed four men in the struggle. He had three sisters, one of whom had three sons, likewise powerful men. They had an enclosure, fenced in with stones, into which they enticed all those they intended to kill.

103. Aklaujak, a Tale from Labrador. — A man named Aklaujak was of immense strength. Once, when away on a reindeer-hunt, his brothers robbed him of his wife. But the mother, who from a high hill observed him sitting in his kayak and seizing two large reindeers by the antlers and drowning them by holding them under water, hastened down and persuaded the wife to return to him, on which the brothers took flight.

104. The Giant of Kangersuak or Cape Farewell. — The people from the south (or east) and those from the north (or west) were at war with each other. The latter had a powerful champion, who was sitting on the top of Kangersuak to watch the Southlanders passing by. A man who had been killed by him left a son, who practised angakok science, and

revenged his father by inducing the giant to walk with him over a marshy plain, where he went down, and from beneath pierced the feet of the giant, and afterwards killed him.

105. THE KIDNAPPERS.—A band of brothers tried to carry off a girl by force; but her mother, by means of a magic lay, caused them all to perish in a sudden gale. Some time after, an angakok, who had been out kayaking, stated that he had seen a shoal of dolphins; and listening to their speech, he made them out to be those brothers, who had been thus transformed.

106. THE VISITING ANIMALS.—An old man, while staying in a firth to fish for salmon, lost his son, who died at some distance up the country. In his grief he could not persuade himself to leave his son's grave, and he therefore put up his winter-house on the spot. In this lonely abode they were once surprised by seeing three men entering the house, one of them tall and long-nosed, the other smaller and with a flat nose, and the last of very small stature and white as snow. After passing the evening talking with the host, the short-nosed man, before starting, asked for a piece of sole-leather, and the white one wanted a piece of walrus-tooth. The old man saw the departing visitors out, but when they left him, stood dumfoundered at seeing them bounding off in the shape of a reindeer, a fox, and a hare. It is said that the hare had need of something for a new tooth.

107. AVIGIATSIAK was the name of a young woman who, while grinding her knife on the beach, was taken by a whale. After living for a time with the whales, she fled and was transformed into a seal, living with the seals. As such she was caught by a man, hauled upon the ice, and cut to pieces, all excepting the head,

which was thrown beneath the bench. From thence she slipped into the womb of the man's wife who had harpooned her, and was afterwards born anew, and called Avigiatsiak.

108. THE BIRD'S CLIFF. — A father and his son, while kayaking far off the land, fell in with a kayariak, who at once gave chase to them. They fortunately escaped by jumping out on a flake of ice, from which they struck their persecutor dead; but before sinking into the sea he spat repeatedly, turning round to all parts of the horizon, on which a dense fog arose, causing them to wander, and preventing their gaining their home. At last they reached land, and the father, being angakok, soon perceived a house and entered it. They found one side of it inhabited by black people, and the other by white ones. After staying a while and having some talk with the inmates on both sides, they left the house; but on looking behind them, they saw that the house was a cave in the rock, the inhabitants gulls and ravens, and a drollish visitor staying with them, a falcon.

109. KUANAK, AN ANGAKOK IN SOUTH GREENLAND, started for a flight, having previously had his feet and his head tied together. While passing along between two high rocks, an *amarsiniook* rushed out from the mountain-side and wanted to take him into his hood. He made his escape by dropping into the sea, and proceeding onwards beneath the surface of the sea and the earth, finally emerged from the floor of his own house. Another time, when he had gone off on a flight, his drum, which he had left in the house, was lifted up by itself, and soared about in the room till at length it stopped and fell down. At that same moment a voice was heard from without, and hastening to look whence it came, they found him in an almost dying state lying upon the snow, an old skin-cover from a

kayak having frightened him and caused his downfall. Kuanak was once capsized by a seal he had just harpooned ; but being an *anghiniartok*, his senses again returned, and he found himself at the bottom of the sea, in company with his grandmother.  She tied his kayak-jacket close to his body, leaving no part of it uncovered, and then supplying him with a piece of skin by way of kayak, she pushed him upwards.  When he emerged from the water he first betook himself far out to sea, and thence made the land again, but happened to touch at an inhabited place, where somebody was emptying out the urine-tub, which scared him away from the shore. He tried to land on another place, but here a woman, dressing her hair on the beach, scared him away.  If he had a third time taken fright, he would never have returned to the land of the living.  But he happened to land at Pisugfik, where a couple of old men were sitting playing at dice.  They at once knew him to be an anghiniartok ; and on merely touching his naked body, he dropped down senseless ; but on their chanting a magic lay, he revived.  They then brought him back to his homestead, where his relatives, who had already finished their days of mourning and nearly forgotten him, were gladly surprised at hearing the crew of the boat that brought him home intuning Kuanak's song.

110. An Angakok on Kekertarsuak set off in his sledge to visit his married sister.  On approaching the house his dogs suddenly stopped.  After in vain trying to urge them on with his whip, he alighted and went up to the house on foot.  But seeing no people about, he looked in at the window, and was horror-struck at seeing all the people lying or sitting about lifeless, their eyes open and staring.  His sister alone showed signs of life, and seeing her brother, began to move her mouth as if chewing, and crept towards the entrance. At sight of this he was struck with terror, and fled to his

dogs, but was again unable to make them stir. Not until the sister had come quite close, her mouth widely opened as if to devour him, did they suddenly start; and thus he escaped to his home. Afterwards he performed a conjuration, and undertook an angakok flight to examine the place. On his return he reported that those people had been frightened to death by the sight of a skin-cover from a kayak (viz., which had been used at a funeral to carry the corpse upon).

111. SINGAJUK AND HIS DESCENDANTS. — Singajuk was a celebrated hunter living in Kangek (near Godthaab). His wife miscarried, and brought forth a poor little wretch of a child, that was swaddled in the skin of an eider-duck, and had to be fostered with the utmost care to keep it alive. This child was called Mangilak, and became one of the most powerful of men. His first deed was killing an ingnersuak. Afterwards he was once caught in a gale of wind at sea, but espying a solitary spot of smooth water and a gull swimming in it, by dint of listening to its voice he learned a spell for procuring a calm; and from that time he was not to be equalled in kayaking. His mother then persuaded him to marry, and he took a wife, who, however, shortly afterwards died. Being almost a wizard, he used to visit her grave and talk with the deceased, and on one occasion she gave him a mussel-shell containing a drink to endow him with angakok wisdom. Mangilak married a second wife, and got a son, called Akajarok, whose daughter became the grandmother of the man who related this story (to the author). Akajarok died a Christian. Mangilak also was baptised, and named Moses, but was too full of angakok wisdom to become more than a nominal Christian.

112. THE COUSINS.—This tale is somewhat similar to No. 15, but in the present version the revenge is

brought on by an angakok, who assisted the cousins on a flight, and while staying with them invoked his tornak, the *toolik*, who carried a red-hot weapon, and destroyed the house and all its inhabitants by fire, while the anga-kok flew homewards. After his return to his house, while narrating the deed to his people, a laughing voice was heard from without, recognised as that of his *erkun-gasok* (the ingenious and cunning adviser, but rather powerless and boasting dweller among the tornaks), who came to give notice of his having also assisted at the destruction of his enemies.

113. MANIK was a great seal-hunter, but his mother in vain urged him to take a wife. He continued a bachelor, till one day he suddenly ordered his mother to make ready the boat for removing from the place. As soon as she had made all ready, he hastened up to the house of the chief hunter, who at the time was absent, and carried away his daughter, crying and struggling in vain to be released. Having placed her on the boat he at once pushed off, and made for the north with all speed. At the first inhabited place they came past he again carried away a woman ; and this continued until he had got a complete boat's crew of rowing girls. He con-tinued his voyage the whole season, till at length, having reached the far north, the frost set in, and for the time obliged him to take up his quarters there. While win-tering here, and making excursions into the country, he once came to a solitary house, where he had an ad-venturous meeting with the ghost of a deceased woman ; and from there he came to another, where he found the people feasting upon various meats, which they kept hauling from the ground by help of magic lays. The next year he set out for his own country, returning to their relatives all the women, excepting only the first one, whom he kept for his wife.

114. The Land of the Isarukitsok Bird (*Alca impennis*), a story from South Greenland.—Two young men with one elder companion lost their way when kayaking in foggy weather, and having roamed about without being able to sight any land, they came to a high promontory, showing one continuous steep and inaccessible cliff, inhabited by crowds of isarukit-soks. By following the coast they at last came to a landing-place, and found a nice situation, where they rested themselves, and had their strength restored by eating birds. Having also filled their kayaks with them, they put off to sea again, and happened to pass by one of the monstrous gulls which are in the habit of picking up the kayakers and giving them as food to their young ones ; but they reached their home in safety. It is told that before the land of the isarukitsok sank there were plenty of these birds about Nook (Godthaab).

115. Kakortuliak was at a reindeer-hunt, when they only succeeded in hitting one large deer, which made its escape by jumping into a lake. Kakortuliak, however, pursued it by swimming, and fastened a line to its antlers, by which it was hauled on land. He got a large piece of the tallow, and leaving the party, went off by himself in search of further game. He saw two ravens pursuing one another ; but on viewing them more closely they had the features of man. At the same moment a reindeer suddenly bounded forth, apparently from his own bag ; and he found the tallow at the same time had disappeared, a little morsel only remaining. He then felt himself lifted off his feet and carried away through the air ; but by rubbing his skin with the bit of tallow he again quickly descended towards the earth ; yet without touching it he gained his home. On arriving, however, he had lost the use of his senses, and lay down almost lifeless, though unable to die. Such was,

as has been told, the condition of the heathen when the ruler of the moon had taken the souls out of their body. From this time Kakortuliak gave up hunting, and turned a clairvoyant. His soul used to leave the body and roam about the inland and along the east coast; and on returning he related what he had seen, and how he had lived with the inlanders.

116. THE KUINASARINOOK.—Uvnek, one of the last angakut at the firth of Godthaab, on one of his spirit-flights narrowly escaped being taken by an *amarsiniook*. After his return he once performed a conjuration and summoned the *amarsiniook*. A brightness was observed, and a voice was heard from above the house saying, " If thou hadst not happened to be an angakok thou wouldst never have escaped; it was I who killed the *kuinasarinook* (another monster, dwelling in certain mountains), because it had torn a man to pieces." The auditors then remembered how some time ago a man had been found dead, and his body terribly mutilated; but nobody had been able to make out how the murder was committed, till it was thus explained by Uvnek.

117. AN OLD MAN, WHO WAS ALWAYS ANXIOUS TO OUTDO OTHER PEOPLE, had laid a bet with his friend as to whose wife should first get a son; and afterwards, as to which of their sons should in course of time become the greatest angakok. One of them, Ajagutarsuk, attained angakok wisdom in a cave; and the other, named Ularpana, acquired it in a dried-up lake. The latter went on an angakok flight to the first, and while staying with him Ajagutarsuk called forth his tornaks, which belonged to the inlanders, and instantly appeared. But Ularpana invoked his tornaks, being the upper ingnersuit, who totally defeated the inlanders.

118. THE REVENGING ANIMALS.—A great angakok, while kayaking about at midsummer, suddenly took a

longing for eggs; and landing upon an island, he found a merganser's nest with plenty of eggs, all of which he carried away. On his way home he met with a flock of seals, of which he harpooned one; but after having taken it, he heard voices from among the rest encouraging each other to go and get hold of a piece of ice, and return as *umiarissat*. On getting home he walked up to his house, forgetting the eggs in his kayak; but he ordered his housemates to throw down on the beach all manner of filthy stuff to frighten away the umiarissat. In the evening a boat was seen to arrive manned with seals, but as soon as they scented the filth they all jumped into the water, and the boat appeared as a piece of ice. Later in the evening a voice was heard outside, and the head of the gooseander emerged from the entrance with dreadfully enlarged eyes. Addressing itself to the angakok, it scolded him for having robbed it of its descendants, but now it had come to fetch its eggs back, having by help of a charm caused him to forget them and leave them in his kayak. If he had not left them it certainly would have frightened them all to death. Another angakok in a similar case was bereft of his angakok power by the merganser.

119. THE IGDLOKOK.—A man had lost his beloved cousin and friend, who in his sight had been torn to pieces by one of those bears that are made by sorcery. In his despair he went out to encounter and brave all kinds of danger by way of excitement; and he first killed an amarok. One evening, when staying at home, he was surprised in his lonely house by a stranger dropping in, who explained that he also having lost his brother was roaming about for excitement. Being very talkative, he spent the evening there very pleasantly, until the hostess, who had boiled some flesh of the amarok, came and served it before the men. The guest then burst out in loud praises of its delicious

flavour and tempting appearance ; but before he had taken a morsel he went on, "But I see the dish is all aslope," and the same instant arose and vanished through the entrance. The host immediately followed him ; and on examining his footsteps in the snow, he found them to be made by only one foot, so that the guest must have been an *igdlokok* (whose body is only the one half of the human body cut in twain).

NOTE.—In another similar story there are two guests, who at their sudden disappearance manifest themselves as certain *stars* (**siagtut** or **kilugtûssat**). The mysterious words about the sloping dish are the same.

120. IVIANGERSOOK TRAVELLED ALL AROUND THE COAST OF GREENLAND.—He started for the south, and having passed Cape Farewell, he came on the eastward to some light-haired people of European complexion ; and lastly he returned through the Sound, which was formerly open from east to west, near Ilulissat (Jakobshavn). When approaching his home near Godthaab he lost his brother, who was buried upon a small island, after them named Uviarniak (one who travelled all around).

121. A MARRIED COUPLE REMAINED CHILDLESS ON ACCOUNT OF THEIR BOTH BEING ANGAKOK.— The husband and wife always used to go out kayaking together. Once they happened to come to a foreign place, where a young man was found in an almost dying state. The angakok-man began a conjuration, summoning the witch who had caused his sickness. He detected the ghost of the witch approaching the sick youth in order to touch him with her black hands. But the angakok thrust his harpoon at her, hitting her heel ; and almost at the same moment the aunt of the sick youth died in the next house, and proved to have been the witch. While spending the rest of the evening there, eating and talking in a pleasant way, the visitors noticed

the children playing on the floor ; and thinking of their own childless state burst out, " That crowd of boys might almost make people envious." They were answered, " The boys yonder are the namesakes of those whom the monster-gulls carried off as food for their young ones " (viz., who perished in kayaks); whereupon the whole assembly at once became silent.

122. AN OLD MAN LOST HIS ONLY SON when they were both reindeer-hunting up the country. After returning home he often used to visit his son's grave. Kayaking up the firth with this view, he once right before him saw an inlander pulling himself through the water without any kayak ("using the fog as kayak"), and after some angry words, he killed the inlander. Another time, when he was again visiting the grave, he was surprised at the sight of an inlander, who questioned him as to the cause of his grief. " Yonder wretched heap of stones is the only object of my distress," he answered. The inlander then told him how he also had, some time ago, lost a son who had been seal-hunting. The old man made out that it must have been the one he had killed; on which he pretended to be expected home, pushed off in his skiff, and never more visited the grave of his son.

123. ANGAKORSIAK WAS VERY PROUD OF HIS ANGAKOK WISDOM, and always roamed about seeking opportunities of emulating other angakut. When he happened to surpass them, he used to mock and ridicule them in a most overbearing manner. Once he visited an angakok far up north, and challenged him to a match, at which, in broad daylight, they were to contend in working the wonders of their art before an assembly. Angakorsiak began his performance by cutting off his arm near the shoulder, inserting it again and drinking the blood from the wound; after which he

swallowed an arrow-point and made it appear again, opened his stomach with a knife, and so on. When he had finished, the other angakok repeated the same feats with the utmost perfection, and then remarked, " Well, what we have yet done amounts to nothing; but I should now like to try a kayak-race with thee." They went down in their kayaks, and the angakok of the place, taking his way to an island, threw his harpoon at a rock with such force as to make it enter the stone and blood to spring from it. Angakorsiak on trying this entirely failed, his harpoon being broken and lost. On their way back to the shore he bent down his head from shame, capsized his kayak, and sank. But directly afterwards a reindeer emerged from the water, and ran up on the beach. Shame having thus transformed him into a reindeer, he afterwards turned a man again, and hastened away, resolved to give up all kind of emulation in future.

NOTE.— Of this tale several variants exist, the traditions about the deeds of angakut, on the whole, being numerous.

124. A GIRL NAMED TUAGTUANGUAK fled from her brother-in-law, who persecuted her. Running across the ice, she fell through; but having again got up, she ran on and on to the north constantly, viewing a black spot before her. Swooning several times, and again seeing the black spot on awaking, she meanwhile acquired angakok power. Going on in this way for five successive days, she came to a precipice, and setting out from its edge, she leaped across, but was somehow wafted back through the air to the same spot. This process she continued for five days. She then pursued her journey north, and came to an inhabited place, where she took up her abode, and afterwards got married. She visited the ingnersuit, and received presents from them; but while carrying them homewards the gifts were wafted out of her hands, and flew back to their first owners.

125. THE GIFTS FROM THE UNDER-WORLD.—An old bachelor, feeling envious of a younger one because of his better luck in hunting and his finding more favour with women, applied to his mother for counsel and aid. She pointed out to him a certain spot where he would find a large stone, and moving it aside, an opening would appear leading straight to the under-world, where he would come to a lake; and on seeing two boats, he was to let the first one pass, but was to apply to the second. Acting upon her advice, he received a piece of *matak* (whale-skin) from the second boat, by eating which he acquired astonishing good-luck in hunting. The young man, noticing this change of fortune, questioned him as to the cause of his recent success, when he imparted to him the information he had gained from his mother, only substituting the first boat for the second. The young man in this way also got a piece of matak, by eating which he only secured the worst luck in his hunting. Meanwhile the old man had consumed his piece, and went to fetch more; but when he came to the spot the second time, he found himself quite unable to move the stone.

126. THE TUPILAK.—An old man named Nikook, who had given up seal-hunting, once, entirely by chance, brought home a walrus. The middle one of some brothers with whom he lived grew jealous of him at this, and every morning repaired to the opposite shore of an island, where he secretly worked at a tupilak. Nikook got a suspicion of this, and following him, he surprised the wretch in the act of allowing his own body to be sucked by the monster, at the same time repeating the words, "Thou shalt take Nikook." But Nikook hurried down, and seized him, crying, "What art thou doing there?" At that moment the man fell down lifeless. Meanwhile the brothers had also reached the island, and on being guided to the place by Nikook, they found

the tupilak still sucking the dead. They then killed it with stones, sinking it, as well as the maker of it, into the sea. During five nights Nikook was disturbed by a bubbling sound, but afterwards nothing more was perceived.

127. THE GRATEFUL BEAR.—A married couple lived on a lonely spot far from other people. When the man was out on his hunting-ground his place of refuge used to be a snow-hut. Once, when he was stopping in it, he saw his wife running about quite naked. Greatly excited, he hastened home, but found his wife inside the house, sitting quietly with her baby, without having stirred. The man now went raving mad; and the wife, frightened at seeing him in such a state, fled from the house with her child. When at the very point of starvation she chanced to catch a partridge, but seeing a terrible bald-headed bear approaching, she threw the bird to him and made her escape. Afterwards, when she had built herself a hut on the shore, she always got an ample supply of newly-killed seals, which used to come drifting in, being gifts from the grateful bear.

128. THE INHABITANTS OF AKILINEK.—Iviangersook, while travelling far and wide for some time, settled down in Akilinek, leaving descendants there. Many years after, some people from the farthest north, in crossing the ice, came to a crevice far off the coast, and had some talk with people who appeared on the opposite side and announced themselves as Iviangersook's descendants in Akilinek. The countrymen from each side alternately enumerated all the products of their homesteads.

129. THE MOTHER AND SON AS KIVIGTUT.—A widow, greatly harassed by the persecutions of a man who wanted to marry her, fled to the inland with her

little son, whom she educated with the view of making him a hater of the male sex. She built her hut near the border of the inland glacier, and made the acquaintance of another woman, who led the same solitary life on a bare hillock emerging from the glacier. When the son had grown up, his reindeer-hunting secured them ample subsistence. Once they were surprised by the visit of one of her brothers, who told them that, from the time they had disappeared, he had devoted himself to the study of angakok science in order to find out her place of retreat; and having attained the powers of an angakok, he instantly discovered her trace, by means of which he had found her out. He henceforth remained with them. The sister died from old age, and, later on, her son fell sick and died, but revived three times after his mother's brother had buried him. The fourth time, however, the latter pulled down the house on the top of him, and then left the place. While passing the night in a cave on his way towards the coast, he was overtaken by the ghost of the deceased appearing in the shape of a fire, with a voice saying, that from childhood he had been fostered up to hate the whole male sex, and had the other not been his mother's brother, he would certainly have killed him.

130. THE HELP FROM INGNERSUIT.—An old man once met with an ingnersuak, who invited him to his house, and told him that he had watched in order to have some talk with him that no one else might hear. He wanted to let him know that, if ever he was in want, he only had to apply to him for help—the ingnersuak would at any time provide him with food. The old man from this time had a comfortable life, being always supplied with what he required. But at last he began to hint at the source of his riches to other people, and henceforth the ingnersuak declined to assist him further.

131. THE REMOVAL OF DISCO ISLAND.— Off the southernmost part of Greenland an island was situated which some of the inhabitants of the mainland took a dislike to, because it cut them off from the open sea. Two old men got the idea of removing it by help of some magic lay. Their names were Nevingasilernak and Nivfigfarsuk; but another oldster, called Kiviaritajak, rather inclined to retain the island. The first two went in their kayaks to fasten a hair from the head of a little child to the outside, while the last from shore tried to keep it back by means of a thong of sealskin made fast to it. The two old kayakers then pushed off, chanting their spells and tugging the hair. At length the thong burst, and the island got afloat; and continually singing, they pulled away to the north, and placed it in front of Ilulissat. It is now Disco Island. The translation caused the bottom of the sea to rise all along where they travelled.

132. THE AMAROK.—A man who mourned the death of a relative went out in hopes of finding some means of excitement; and being told that an amarok had been heard roaring in the firth of Nook (Godthaab), he could not be kept from going off to encounter the beast. Accompanied by a relative, he went up the country, and finding the young ones of the amarok, the mourner instantly killed the whole. But his companion, getting terribly frightened, betook himself to a cave for refuge, accompanied by the mourner. From their retreat the relative soon saw how the old amarok came running, holding a whole reindeer between its jaws; and having looked in vain for its young ones, it rushed down to the lake, where it appeared to be hauling out something of a human shape. At the same moment, turning round to his companion, he saw him falling helpless to the ground. The amarok, from which nothing remains concealed, had discovered him and taken the soul out of his body.

133. AN OLD BACHELOR, being a very successful hunter, was always worried by his place-fellows about taking to himself a wife.  At last he consented; but when about to make a choice, none of the women at the place appeared good enough for him.  Starting in his boat for the neighbouring hamlet, he declared he was going to fetch the only sister of some men living there. On his way thither he met with another kayaker, and addressed him, "Art not thou one of the many brothers?"  "Yes, I am the middle one of them."  "I come to demand thy only sister in marriage, and if I may have her I will give thee my boat and a new tent." "We will allow no one to get her, because she is the only woman in our house."  Having got this information the old bachelor instantly made about, went home, and gave up all thoughts of marrying.  Being once in his kayak, and suffering from thirst, he observed a small stream of water running down a rock.  Remaining in his kayak, he merely turned his face upwards, so as to let the water run into his open mouth.  When his thirst had been quenched, and he wanted to push off, his mouth clung to the rock, being at the same time gradually prolonged, because the tide was falling; and thus he had to remain hanging until the next tide should float him off again.

NOTE.—A number of stories are found ridiculing bachelors, and all more or less trifling, like this one.  Generally their passions are represented as being excited at the sight of a fine woman ; but on approaching her, and perhaps even getting hold of her, she proves to be a gull, or perhaps a stone. Others will marry none but a dwarf, or a woman without breasts.  One of them out of a piece of ice makes a little island to live upon by himself.

134. A GIRL NAMED ISSERFIK preferred animals to men.  Lastly, she fell in love with an eagle, that carried her off further inland.  A man went after them to fetch her back ; but she excited the eagle against him.  The man sought refuge beneath a stone.  The eagle began to peck at it with its beak to make a hole in it ; but the

man sent out his amulet, killed the eagle, and carried Isserfik back to her home, where she gave birth to a child, half man, half eagle. Finally, she lost her mind and died.

135. THE SUNRISE.—A man from the east coast of Greenland from love for his home never left it even during the summer-time; and among his principal enjoyments was that of gazing at the sun rising out of the ocean. But when his son grew up he became desirous of seeing other countries, and, above all, accompanying his countrymen to the west coast. At length he persuaded his father to go with him. No sooner, however, had he passed Cape Farewell, and saw the sun about to rise behind the land, than he insisted upon returning immediately. Having again reached their home island, he went out from his tent early next morning, and when his people had in vain waited for his return, they went out and found him dead. His delight at again seeing the sunrise had overpowered and killed him.

136. THE ARNARKUAGSAK.—An angakok performed a conjuration in order to procure good seal-hunting. He went down to the old hag, the arnarkuagsak, at the bottom of the sea, and found her in a great rage. Having entered her abode, she seized hold of her hair behind one ear, grasping some bloody clothes, and afterwards from behind the other one she fetched down a crying baby, flinging both upon the floor. The angakok then succeeded in propitiating her.

137. SAUGAK had a quarrel with his brother and fled. He came to a house of such length that a man could wear out the soles of his boots wandering from one end to the other. The master of the house had a crowd of daughters, and an immense stock of provisions. He ordered meat to be served up for Saugak, and forced

him to eat. When Saugak declared that he was sati-
ated, his host went on to point his knife at his eyes, saying that as long as he could twinkle them he could also
eat. When he finally left off twinkling they served up
dried human flesh before him.

138. THE BLOODY ROCK.—At a certain wintering-
place all the men successively disappeared on going out.
Two young lads who were still left, while roaming about
came to a mountain continually turning round, and on
one side all bloody. One youth tried the bloody path,
but fell down and perished. The other waited till the
bloody side turned away from him, and climbing gained
the summit, when he found· a house, and a man who
lived by hunting eider-ducks in a lake. After having
stayed some time, and rendered assistance to this man,
he returned home safely.

139. ISIGARSIGAK AND HIS SISTER were frightened
from home by the angakok tricks of their mother, and
fled to the south, travelling on for three years in order
to reach the end (of the land ?). Meanwhile, Isigarsigak
perceived his stomach to swell up, so as to make him
unfit for kayaking. In crossing a frozen firth, he once
saw two ravens coming from the interior, which as they
came nearer looked like women hurrying towards the sea;
and having caught two seals, they took them on their
shoulders and hastened back to the inland. Guided by
them, Isigarsigak came to a house, where an old woman
offered to cure his stomach. She then examined him by
*head-lifting*, and found out that on leaving his mother
he had forgotten some hunting - bladders. Cutting
open his stomach she brought forth the bladders, which
would otherwise have made him burst, she said, if they
had been allowed to remain much longer. At that instant a woman appeared at the entrance, armed with a
knife ; and they warned him to make haste if he would

escape her, because it was she who had killed the men
of the house.  Having returned safely to his sister, he
took a fancy to trace the passage of the birds in autumn.
He travelled in his kayak until the sky became so low
that he could reach it with his paddle-oar.  It had two
large holes, beyond which he discovered a sea, and was
obliged to turn back.

140. A WOMAN NAMED ARNASUGAUSSAK, on being
scolded by her parents for having broken her mother's
precious needle, fled with her daughter to the inland,
where they lived with people, who after a while were
transformed into partridges, and afterwards with others
who changed into reindeers.  Finally, they returned to
the sea - coast, and saw some men flensing a whale.
While standing calling out to them they were converted
into stones.

141. A TALE FROM EAST GREENLAND.—Two cousins
loved each other, but one of them having a passion for
outdoing other people, grew irritated at seeing the other
not only getting first married, but also having the first
son, and that one catching seals before his own son had
got a bird.  He then removed to another place, and his
son trained a dog to tear men to pieces, by feeding it
with food that had been in contact with human bones.
It had already devoured several travellers when the
cousin and his son came and attacked the dangerous
animal, and killed it between them.

142. ANOTHER TALE FROM EAST GREENLAND.—A
widow and her son were despised by their housemates,
and suffered want of food.  At last she died, and the
child, named Kongajuk, being very sick, was left alone
in the house.  There it heard the bones of the graves
rattling, and in came its mother, leading another child
in her hand, and afterwards its father, accompanied by

other deceased people, who took Kongajuk along with them to their abodes.

143. THE SWIMMER, A TALE FROM LABRADOR.—
A mother, who lived at a solitary place, successively lost all her children, who were killed by enemies. Finally, she got a son, whom from his babyhood she brought up with the aim of making him fit for dwelling in the water like a seal. The enemies once went to the place with the intention of killing him also. But the mother, seeing the kayakers approach, told him to make his escape through the water. The enemies, who observed him jumping into the water, had no doubt they would get hold of him ; but, swimming like a seal, he seduced them far out to sea, when the mother whipped the surface of the water with a string, causing a storm, by which they all perished, her son being the only one saved.

NOTE.—From East Greenland there is a somewhat similar tale about a man having three sons, who would not grow properly, and were brought up as swimmers.

144. THE NATIVES OF LABRADOR tell how our ancestors and the *tunneks* (or *tunnit*, in Greenlandish **tornit**, plural of **tunek**) in days of yore lived together ; but the tunneks fled from fear of our people, who used to drill holes in their foreheads while yet alive. With this view they removed from here to the north, crossing over to Killinek (Cape Chudleigh). While dwelling among us they had sealskins with the blubber attached for bed-robes. Their clothes were made in the same way. Their weapons were formed of slate and hornstone, and their drills of crystal. They were strong and formidable, especially one of them, called by the name of Jauranat, from which is formed *javianarpok* (Greenlandish, **navianarpok**). Huge blocks of stone are still to be seen which they were able to move. Some ruins of their houses are also to be found here and there in our coun-

try, chiefly upon the islands, having been built of stones, and differing from the abodes of our people. One of our ancestors when kayaking had a tunnek for his companion, who had a bird-spear, the points of which were made of walrus-tooth.

NOTE.—This tradition is compiled from several manuscripts in German from the missionaries in Labrador, in which the alien nation, expelled by the present inhabitants, are called partly "Die Tunnit," and partly "Die Grönlaender." Very probably these denominations have arisen from a misunderstanding, induced by inquiries put to the natives as to their knowing anything about the Greenlanders. The tunnit are almost certainly identical with the tornit or inlanders of the Greenland tales. The Eskimo of Cumberland Inlet speak about the *tunudlermiut*, which signifies people living in the inland. The present Indians of Labrador are called by the Eskimo of the same country *aullak;* but it is possible they distinguish between these and the traditional or fabulous inlanders. However, the most striking incongruity is that of the tunnit having had their abodes on the islands, which looks as if ancient settlers of European race are hinted at. Be this as it may, the tradition of the Labradorans should be more closely examined.

145. THE SHARK AS PROVIDER.—A mother with her daughter being abandoned by their relatives, and helpless, were saved from starvation by a dead seal which drifted to the shore. After a time they found another, and a shark appeared to them, rising out of the sea, and saying that now he would supply all their wants. He took up his abode with them; and afterwards, when some inuarutligaks were approaching, he took the two women on his back, along with all their implements, and brought them away to an island.

146. A WOMAN NAMED ALEKAKUKIAK had been allied to her enemies by the bands of marriage. A poor old wife, to whom she had shown much kindness, once informed her of her brothers-in-law intending to kill her. On hearing this she fled to the inland, where she first met with a bear. Having no sort of weapon whatever, she took a string from her hood, and cracking it like a whip in the front of the animal, she made it fall to the

ground. She proceeded in the same manner with an amarok, and at length she reached the sea on the other side, and came to her relatives.

NOTE.—A very similar, but equally trifling and insignificant fragment, has been received from Labrador.

147. THE OCEAN-SPIDER.—A kayaker in the firth of Godthaab once, at a place where no shoal was known to exist, saw the bottom quite close to him. He then suddenly recollected to have heard old people talking of the ocean-spider, a most dangerous animal to the kayakers. Presently he discovered a monstrous eye, and at the distance of about a kayak-paddle's length from it a similar one, and on tearing away from the spot a terrible gap made its appearance. Indeed, if he had been a less skilled kayaker, he would never have got off alive.

148. A WOMAN WHO WAS MATED WITH A DOG [1] got ten children. When they had grown larger, she ordered them to devour her father, whereupon she divided them into two parties and sent them off from home to seek their subsistence henceforth by themselves. Five of them, who were sent up the country, grew erkileks ; and to the other five she gave the sole of an old boot, and put it in the sea, where it rapidly expanded and grew a ship, in which they went off, turning into kavdlunaks (Europeans).

149. KATIGAGSE [2] had no faith in the angakut, and sometimes, when attending their conjurations, he tore

[1] This is an abstract of the tale mentioned in the note to No. 11 (p. 143), which for obvious reasons cannot be given in its original form. It seems to exhibit an analogy to several traditions of other nations—the idea about the origin of the Europeans, for instance, corresponding, as far as we know, to the origin attributed by a Japanese popular tradition to the Ainos of the Kurile Islands.

[2] This and the following tale are only interesting as showing the deeply-seated fear of, and belief in, the angakut.

away the window-curtain, and thereby dispelled all their doings. But once when an angakok had begun his conjuration, and announced his tornak to be approaching in the shape of a fire, Katigagse tore away the curtain which covered the entrance, and ran outside. Suddenly he discovered a great flame rushing through the air, which struck him with terror, and made him re-enter the house, and trembling from head to foot cling to the rafters of the hut, from whence fatigue soon made him fall to the ground. When the conjuration had been finished, and the fire kept off, Katigagse was missed. At length they brought him forth from underneath the ledge, all covered with filth, in which state he left the house, never to attend angakok service any more.

150. ORDLAVARSUK despised the angakut, and never used to attend their conjurations. But once spending an evening at another place, in a house where an angakok went on performing his art, he became so fond of the women's song, that suddenly he took a fancy to become an angakok himself. Imitating the angakut's fashion, he betook himself to lonely places, and called for a tornak. At length a giant-like man appeared, armed with a long staff, with which he would touch him. But Ordlavarsuk got terrified, and turning round to the beach walked through some shallow water to an island, whither the demon was unable to follow him. The tornak having in vain offered himself to his disposal, turned back and disappeared. Ordlavarsuk then repenting his foolishness, called out for him again, but received no answer, and never more succeeded in calling forth a tornak.

# ERRATA.

Page 2, line 5, *for* " only an " *read* " the only."

" 2, line 27, *for* " southernmost " *read* " south-eastern."

" 3, line 16, *for* " North and South " *read* " South and North."

" 5, line 13, *for* " these introductory remarks " *read* " the following introduction (page 83.)"

" 15, line 3, *read* " r'." The letter r is sometimes, but not necessarily, marked with an apostrophe, or headed by a comma, to make it sound like a very guttural German *ch*.

" 15, line 16, *for* " is allowed " *read* " is not allowed."

" 15, line 30, *for* " igdlorssualiκ " *read* " igdlorssualik."

" 17, line 23, *for* " sentence " *read* " subject."

" 19, line 30, *for* " idglorssuaκ " *read* " igdlorssuaκ."

" 20, line 8, *for* " —as " *read* " as—"

" 20, line 10, *for* " saaveκarpoκ " *read* " saveκarpoκ."

" 22, line 12, *for* " takugivκit, &c., nalugavκit," *read* " takugivkit, &c., nalugavkit."

" 23, line 35, *for* " barbarous and " *read* " so-called."

" 35, line 15, in " persons; threatening," omit the semicolon.

" 48, line 4, *for* " kiliopak, &c., kukiopâgâκ," *read* " kilivfak, &c., kukivfâgâκ."

" 49, line 24, *for* " sorcery " *read* " witchcraft."

" 62, line 7, *for* " arnarkuagsa " *read* " arnarkuagsak."

" 66, line 19, *for* " haijâ " *read* " ha."

" 69, line 21, *for* " breaks " *read* " dotted lines."

" 72, line 6, *for* " has been above stated " *read* " will be explained in the following introduction."

" 73, line 26, *for* " on the coast (Tschoukschees) " *read* " or the Coast-Tschoukschees."

" 84, line 36, *for* " were astonished " *read* " were apparently astonished."

" 85, line 17, *for* " shorter " *read* " other."

" 90, line 24, *for* " means " *read* " mean."

" 90, line 36, *for* " a barbarous " *read* " a so-called barbarous."

" 94, line 12, *for* " beard-spear " *read* " bird-spéar."

" 179, line 5, *for* " lanced " *read* " landed."

" 179, line 7, *for* " half " *read* " hold."

" 277, line 31, the words " thereby, &c., rulers," to be put in parentheses.

" 344, line 24, *for* " brothers " *read* " brother."

" 356, line 20, *for* " frog-fishing " *read* " fishing frog-fish."

" 410, lines 8 and 11, *for* " brother " *read* " brothers."

" 411, line 25, *for* " brothers " *read* " brother."

" 429, line 35, *for* " wild " *read* " wide."

" 443, line 20, *for* " lead " *read* " lean."

" 445, line 29, *for* " Karasuk " *read* " Karusuk."

" 453, line 24, *for* " a wizard " *read* " an angakok."

A CATALOG OF SELECTED
# DOVER BOOKS
IN ALL FIELDS OF INTEREST

# A CATALOG OF SELECTED DOVER
# BOOKS IN ALL FIELDS OF INTEREST

CONCERNING THE SPIRITUAL IN ART, Wassily Kandinsky. Pioneering work by father of abstract art. Thoughts on color theory, nature of art. Analysis of earlier masters. 12 illustrations. 80pp. of text. 5⅜ x 8½.                          23411-8 Pa. $3.95

ANIMALS: 1,419 Copyright-Free Illustrations of Mammals, Birds, Fish, Insects, etc., Jim Harter (ed.). Clear wood engravings present, in extremely lifelike poses, over 1,000 species of animals. One of the most extensive pictorial sourcebooks of its kind. Captions. Index. 284pp. 9 x 12.                          23766-4 Pa. $12.95

CELTIC ART: The Methods of Construction, George Bain. Simple geometric techniques for making Celtic interlacements, spirals, Kells-type initials, animals, humans, etc. Over 500 illustrations. 160pp. 9 x 12. (USO)          22923-8 Pa. $9.95

AN ATLAS OF ANATOMY FOR ARTISTS, Fritz Schider. Most thorough reference work on art anatomy in the world. Hundreds of illustrations, including selections from works by Vesalius, Leonardo, Goya, Ingres, Michelangelo, others. 593 illustrations. 192pp. 7⅛ x 10¼.                          20241-0 Pa. $9.95

CELTIC HAND STROKE-BY-STROKE (Irish Half-Uncial from "The Book of Kells"): An Arthur Baker Calligraphy Manual, Arthur Baker. Complete guide to creating each letter of the alphabet in distinctive Celtic manner. Covers hand position, strokes, pens, inks, paper, more. Illustrated. 48pp. 8¼ x 11.     24336-2 Pa. $3.95

EASY ORIGAMI, John Montroll. Charming collection of 32 projects (hat, cup, pelican, piano, swan, many more) specially designed for the novice origami hobbyist. Clearly illustrated easy-to-follow instructions insure that even beginning papercrafters will achieve successful results. 48pp. 8¼ x 11.     27298-2 Pa. $3.50

THE COMPLETE BOOK OF BIRDHOUSE CONSTRUCTION FOR WOODWORKERS, Scott D. Campbell. Detailed instructions, illustrations, tables. Also data on bird habitat and instinct patterns. Bibliography. 3 tables. 63 illustrations in 15 figures. 48pp. 5¼ x 8½.                          24407-5 Pa. $2.50

BLOOMINGDALE'S ILLUSTRATED 1886 CATALOG: Fashions, Dry Goods and Housewares, Bloomingdale Brothers. Famed merchants' extremely rare catalog depicting about 1,700 products: clothing, housewares, firearms, dry goods, jewelry, more. Invaluable for dating, identifying vintage items. Also, copyright-free graphics for artists, designers. Co-published with Henry Ford Museum & Greenfield Village. 160pp. 8¼ x 11.                          25780-0 Pa. $10.95

HISTORIC COSTUME IN PICTURES, Braun & Schneider. Over 1,450 costumed figures in clearly detailed engravings–from dawn of civilization to end of 19th century. Captions. Many folk costumes. 256pp. 8⅜ x 11¾.          23150-X Pa. $12.95

# CATALOG OF DOVER BOOKS

STICKLEY CRAFTSMAN FURNITURE CATALOGS, Gustav Stickley and L. & J. G. Stickley. Beautiful, functional furniture in two authentic catalogs from 1910. 594 illustrations, including 277 photos, show settles, rockers, armchairs, reclining chairs, bookcases, desks, tables. 183pp. 6½ x 9¼. 23838-5 Pa. $9.95

AMERICAN LOCOMOTIVES IN HISTORIC PHOTOGRAPHS: 1858 to 1949, Ron Ziel (ed.). A rare collection of 126 meticulously detailed official photographs, called "builder portraits," of American locomotives that majestically chronicle the rise of steam locomotive power in America. Introduction. Detailed captions. xi + 129pp. 9 x 12. 27393-8 Pa. $12.95

AMERICA'S LIGHTHOUSES: An Illustrated History, Francis Ross Holland, Jr. Delightfully written, profusely illustrated fact-filled survey of over 200 American lighthouses since 1716. History, anecdotes, technological advances, more. 240pp. 8 x 10¾. 25576-X Pa. $12.95

TOWARDS A NEW ARCHITECTURE, Le Corbusier. Pioneering manifesto by founder of "International School." Technical and aesthetic theories, views of industry, economics, relation of form to function, "mass-production split" and much more. Profusely illustrated. 320pp. 6⅛ x 9¼. (USO) 25023-7 Pa. $9.95

HOW THE OTHER HALF LIVES, Jacob Riis. Famous journalistic record, exposing poverty and degradation of New York slums around 1900, by major social reformer. 100 striking and influential photographs. 233pp. 10 x 7⅞. 22012-5 Pa. $10.95

FRUIT KEY AND TWIG KEY TO TREES AND SHRUBS, William M. Harlow. One of the handiest and most widely used identification aids. Fruit key covers 120 deciduous and evergreen species; twig key 160 deciduous species. Easily used. Over 300 photographs. 126pp. 5⅜ x 8½. 20511-8 Pa. $3.95

COMMON BIRD SONGS, Dr. Donald J. Borror. Songs of 60 most common U.S. birds: robins, sparrows, cardinals, bluejays, finches, more–arranged in order of increasing complexity. Up to 9 variations of songs of each species.
Cassette and manual 99911-4 $8.95

ORCHIDS AS HOUSE PLANTS, Rebecca Tyson Northen. Grow cattleyas and many other kinds of orchids–in a window, in a case, or under artificial light. 63 illustrations. 148pp. 5⅜ x 8½. 23261-1 Pa. $4.95

MONSTER MAZES, Dave Phillips. Masterful mazes at four levels of difficulty. Avoid deadly perils and evil creatures to find magical treasures. Solutions for all 32 exciting illustrated puzzles. 48pp. 8¼ x 11. 26005-4 Pa. $2.95

MOZART'S DON GIOVANNI (DOVER OPERA LIBRETTO SERIES), Wolfgang Amadeus Mozart. Introduced and translated by Ellen H. Bleiler. Standard Italian libretto, with complete English translation. Convenient and thoroughly portable–an ideal companion for reading along with a recording or the performance itself. Introduction. List of characters. Plot summary. 121pp. 5¼ x 8½. 24944-1 Pa. $2.95

TECHNICAL MANUAL AND DICTIONARY OF CLASSICAL BALLET, Gail Grant. Defines, explains, comments on steps, movements, poses and concepts. 15-page pictorial section. Basic book for student, viewer. 127pp. 5⅜ x 8½. 21843-0 Pa. $4.95

BRASS INSTRUMENTS: Their History and Development, Anthony Baines. Authoritative, updated survey of the evolution of trumpets, trombones, bugles, cornets, French horns, tubas and other brass wind instruments. Over 140 illustrations and 48 music examples. Corrected and updated by author. New preface. Bibliography. 320pp. 5⅜ x 8½. 27574-4 Pa. $9.95

HOLLYWOOD GLAMOR PORTRAITS, John Kobal (ed.). 145 photos from 1926-49. Harlow, Gable, Bogart, Bacall; 94 stars in all. Full background on photographers, technical aspects. 160pp. 8⅜ x 11¼. 23352-9 Pa. $12.95

MAX AND MORITZ, Wilhelm Busch. Great humor classic in both German and English. Also 10 other works: "Cat and Mouse," "Plisch and Plumm," etc. 216pp. 5⅜ x 8½. 20181-3 Pa. $6.95

THE RAVEN AND OTHER FAVORITE POEMS, Edgar Allan Poe. Over 40 of the author's most memorable poems: "The Bells," "Ulalume," "Israfel," "To Helen," "The Conqueror Worm," "Eldorado," "Annabel Lee," many more. Alphabetic lists of titles and first lines. 64pp. 5$\frac{3}{16}$ x 8¼. 26685-0 Pa. $1.00

PERSONAL MEMOIRS OF U. S. GRANT, Ulysses Simpson Grant. Intelligent, deeply moving firsthand account of Civil War campaigns, considered by many the finest military memoirs ever written. Includes letters, historic photographs, maps and more. 528pp. 6⅛ x 9¼. 28587-1 Pa. $11.95

AMULETS AND SUPERSTITIONS, E. A. Wallis Budge. Comprehensive discourse on origin, powers of amulets in many ancient cultures: Arab, Persian Babylonian, Assyrian, Egyptian, Gnostic, Hebrew, Phoenician, Syriac, etc. Covers cross, swastika, crucifix, seals, rings, stones, etc. 584pp. 5⅜ x 8½. 23573-4 Pa. $12.95

RUSSIAN STORIES/PYCCKNE PACCKA3bl: A Dual-Language Book, edited by Gleb Struve. Twelve tales by such masters as Chekhov, Tolstoy, Dostoevsky, Pushkin, others. Excellent word-for-word English translations on facing pages, plus teaching and study aids, Russian/English vocabulary, biographical/critical introductions, more. 416pp. 5⅜ x 8½. 26244-8 Pa. $8.95

PHILADELPHIA THEN AND NOW: 60 Sites Photographed in the Past and Present, Kenneth Finkel and Susan Oyama. Rare photographs of City Hall, Logan Square, Independence Hall, Betsy Ross House, other landmarks juxtaposed with contemporary views. Captures changing face of historic city. Introduction. Captions. 128pp. 8¼ x 11. 25790-8 Pa. $9.95

AIA ARCHITECTURAL GUIDE TO NASSAU AND SUFFOLK COUNTIES, LONG ISLAND, The American Institute of Architects, Long Island Chapter, and the Society for the Preservation of Long Island Antiquities. Comprehensive, well-researched and generously illustrated volume brings to life over three centuries of Long Island's great architectural heritage. More than 240 photographs with authoritative, extensively detailed captions. 176pp. 8¼ x 11. 26946-9 Pa. $14.95

NORTH AMERICAN INDIAN LIFE: Customs and Traditions of 23 Tribes, Elsie Clews Parsons (ed.). 27 fictionalized essays by noted anthropologists examine religion, customs, government, additional facets of life among the Winnebago, Crow, Zuni, Eskimo, other tribes. 480pp. 6⅛ x 9¼. 27377-6 Pa. $10.95

FRANK LLOYD WRIGHT'S HOLLYHOCK HOUSE, Donald Hoffmann. Lavishly illustrated, carefully documented study of one of Wright's most controversial residential designs. Over 120 photographs, floor plans, elevations, etc. Detailed perceptive text by noted Wright scholar. Index. 128pp. 9¼ x 10¾. 27133-1 Pa. $11.95

THE MALE AND FEMALE FIGURE IN MOTION: 60 Classic Photographic Sequences, Eadweard Muybridge. 60 true-action photographs of men and women walking, running, climbing, bending, turning, etc., reproduced from rare 19th-century masterpiece. vi + 121pp. 9 x 12. 24745-7 Pa. $10.95

1001 QUESTIONS ANSWERED ABOUT THE SEASHORE, N. J. Berrill and Jacquelyn Berrill. Queries answered about dolphins, sea snails, sponges, starfish, fishes, shore birds, many others. Covers appearance, breeding, growth, feeding, much more. 305pp. 5¼ x 8¼. 23366-9 Pa. $8.95

GUIDE TO OWL WATCHING IN NORTH AMERICA, Donald S. Heintzelman. Superb guide offers complete data and descriptions of 19 species: barn owl, screech owl, snowy owl, many more. Expert coverage of owl-watching equipment, conservation, migrations and invasions, etc. Guide to observing sites. 84 illustrations. xiii + 193pp. 5⅜ x 8½. 27344-X Pa. $8.95

MEDICINAL AND OTHER USES OF NORTH AMERICAN PLANTS: A Historical Survey with Special Reference to the Eastern Indian Tribes, Charlotte Erichsen-Brown. Chronological historical citations document 500 years of usage of plants, trees, shrubs native to eastern Canada, northeastern U.S. Also complete identifying information. 343 illustrations. 544pp. 6½ x 9¼. 25951-X Pa. $12.95

STORYBOOK MAZES, Dave Phillips. 23 stories and mazes on two-page spreads: Wizard of Oz, Treasure Island, Robin Hood, etc. Solutions. 64pp. 8¼ x 11. 23628-5 Pa. $2.95

NEGRO FOLK MUSIC, U.S.A., Harold Courlander. Noted folklorist's scholarly yet readable analysis of rich and varied musical tradition. Includes authentic versions of over 40 folk songs. Valuable bibliography and discography. xi + 324pp. 5⅜ x 8½. 27350-4 Pa. $9.95

MOVIE-STAR PORTRAITS OF THE FORTIES, John Kobal (ed.). 163 glamor, studio photos of 106 stars of the 1940s: Rita Hayworth, Ava Gardner, Marlon Brando, Clark Gable, many more. 176pp. 8⅜ x 11¼. 23546-7 Pa. $12.95

BENCHLEY LOST AND FOUND, Robert Benchley. Finest humor from early 30s, about pet peeves, child psychologists, post office and others. Mostly unavailable elsewhere. 73 illustrations by Peter Arno and others. 183pp. 5⅜ x 8½. 22410-4 Pa. $6.95

YEKL and THE IMPORTED BRIDEGROOM AND OTHER STORIES OF YIDDISH NEW YORK, Abraham Cahan. Film Hester Street based on Yekl (1896). Novel, other stories among first about Jewish immigrants on N.Y.'s East Side. 240pp. 5⅜ x 8½. 22427-9 Pa. $6.95

SELECTED POEMS, Walt Whitman. Generous sampling from *Leaves of Grass.* Twenty-four poems include "I Hear America Singing," "Song of the Open Road," "I Sing the Body Electric," "When Lilacs Last in the Dooryard Bloom'd," "O Captain! My Captain!"–all reprinted from an authoritative edition. Lists of titles and first lines. 128pp. 5³⁄₁₆ x 8¼. 26878-0 Pa. $1.00

THE BEST TALES OF HOFFMANN, E. T. A. Hoffmann. 10 of Hoffmann's most important stories: "Nutcracker and the King of Mice," "The Golden Flowerpot," etc. 458pp. 5⅜ x 8½. 21793-0 Pa. $9.95

FROM FETISH TO GOD IN ANCIENT EGYPT, E. A. Wallis Budge. Rich detailed survey of Egyptian conception of "God" and gods, magic, cult of animals, Osiris, more. Also, superb English translations of hymns and legends. 240 illustrations. 545pp. 5⅜ x 8½. 25803-3 Pa. $13.95

FRENCH STORIES/CONTES FRANÇAIS: A Dual-Language Book, Wallace Fowlie. Ten stories by French masters, Voltaire to Camus: "Micromegas" by Voltaire; "The Atheist's Mass" by Balzac; "Minuet" by de Maupassant; "The Guest" by Camus, six more. Excellent English translations on facing pages. Also French-English vocabulary list, exercises, more. 352pp. 5⅜ x 8½. 26443-2 Pa. $8.95

CHICAGO AT THE TURN OF THE CENTURY IN PHOTOGRAPHS: 122 Historic Views from the Collections of the Chicago Historical Society, Larry A. Viskochil. Rare large-format prints offer detailed views of City Hall, State Street, the Loop, Hull House, Union Station, many other landmarks, circa 1904-1913. Introduction. Captions. Maps. 144pp. 9⅜ x 12¼. 24656-6 Pa. $12.95

OLD BROOKLYN IN EARLY PHOTOGRAPHS, 1865-1929, William Lee Younger. Luna Park, Gravesend race track, construction of Grand Army Plaza, moving of Hotel Brighton, etc. 157 previously unpublished photographs. 165pp. 8⅞ x 11¾. 23587-4 Pa. $13.95

THE MYTHS OF THE NORTH AMERICAN INDIANS, Lewis Spence. Rich anthology of the myths and legends of the Algonquins, Iroquois, Pawnees and Sioux, prefaced by an extensive historical and ethnological commentary. 36 illustrations. 480pp. 5⅜ x 8½. 25967-6 Pa. $8.95

AN ENCYCLOPEDIA OF BATTLES: Accounts of Over 1,560 Battles from 1479 B.C. to the Present, David Eggenberger. Essential details of every major battle in recorded history from the first battle of Megiddo in 1479 B.C. to Grenada in 1984. List of Battle Maps. New Appendix covering the years 1967-1984. Index. 99 illustrations. 544pp. 6½ x 9¼. 24913-1 Pa. $14.95

SAILING ALONE AROUND THE WORLD, Captain Joshua Slocum. First man to sail around the world, alone, in small boat. One of great feats of seamanship told in delightful manner. 67 illustrations. 294pp. 5⅜ x 8½. 20326-3 Pa. $5.95

ANARCHISM AND OTHER ESSAYS, Emma Goldman. Powerful, penetrating, prophetic essays on direct action, role of minorities, prison reform, puritan hypocrisy, violence, etc. 271pp. 5⅜ x 8½. 22484-8 Pa. $6.95

MYTHS OF THE HINDUS AND BUDDHISTS, Ananda K. Coomaraswamy and Sister Nivedita. Great stories of the epics; deeds of Krishna, Shiva, taken from puranas, Vedas, folk tales; etc. 32 illustrations. 400pp. 5⅜ x 8½. 21759-0 Pa. $10.95

BEYOND PSYCHOLOGY, Otto Rank. Fear of death, desire of immortality, nature of sexuality, social organization, creativity, according to Rankian system. 291pp. 5⅜ x 8½. 20485-5 Pa. $8.95

A THEOLOGICO-POLITICAL TREATISE, Benedict Spinoza. Also contains unfinished Political Treatise. Great classic on religious liberty, theory of government on common consent. R. Elwes translation. Total of 421pp. 5⅜ x 8½. 20249-6 Pa. $9.95

MY BONDAGE AND MY FREEDOM, Frederick Douglass. Born a slave, Douglass became outspoken force in antislavery movement. The best of Douglass' autobiographies. Graphic description of slave life. 464pp. 5⅜ x 8½. 22457-0 Pa. $8.95

FOLLOWING THE EQUATOR: A Journey Around the World, Mark Twain. Fascinating humorous account of 1897 voyage to Hawaii, Australia, India, New Zealand, etc. Ironic, bemused reports on peoples, customs, climate, flora and fauna, politics, much more. 197 illustrations. 720pp. 5⅜ x 8½. 26113-1 Pa. $15.95

THE PEOPLE CALLED SHAKERS, Edward D. Andrews. Definitive study of Shakers: origins, beliefs, practices, dances, social organization, furniture and crafts, etc. 33 illustrations. 351pp. 5⅜ x 8½. 21081-2 Pa. $8.95

THE MYTHS OF GREECE AND ROME, H. A. Guerber. A classic of mythology, generously illustrated, long prized for its simple, graphic, accurate retelling of the principal myths of Greece and Rome, and for its commentary on their origins and significance. With 64 illustrations by Michelangelo, Raphael, Titian, Rubens, Canova, Bernini and others. 480pp. 5⅜ x 8½. 27584-1 Pa. $9.95

PSYCHOLOGY OF MUSIC, Carl E. Seashore. Classic work discusses music as a medium from psychological viewpoint. Clear treatment of physical acoustics, auditory apparatus, sound perception, development of musical skills, nature of musical feeling, host of other topics. 88 figures. 408pp. 5⅜ x 8½. 21851-1 Pa. $10.95

THE PHILOSOPHY OF HISTORY, Georg W. Hegel. Great classic of Western thought develops concept that history is not chance but rational process, the evolution of freedom. 457pp. 5⅜ x 8½. 20112-0 Pa. $9.95

THE BOOK OF TEA, Kakuzo Okakura. Minor classic of the Orient: entertaining, charming explanation, interpretation of traditional Japanese culture in terms of tea ceremony. 94pp. 5⅜ x 8½. 20070-1 Pa. $3.95

LIFE IN ANCIENT EGYPT, Adolf Erman. Fullest, most thorough, detailed older account with much not in more recent books, domestic life, religion, magic, medicine, commerce, much more. Many illustrations reproduce tomb paintings, carvings, hieroglyphs, etc. 597pp. 5⅜ x 8½. 22632-8 Pa. $11.95

SUNDIALS, Their Theory and Construction, Albert Waugh. Far and away the best, most thorough coverage of ideas, mathematics concerned, types, construction, adjusting anywhere. Simple, nontechnical treatment allows even children to build several of these dials. Over 100 illustrations. 230pp. 5⅜ x 8½. 22947-5 Pa. $7.95

DYNAMICS OF FLUIDS IN POROUS MEDIA, Jacob Bear. For advanced students of ground water hydrology, soil mechanics and physics, drainage and irrigation engineering, and more. 335 illustrations. Exercises, with answers. 784pp. 6⅛ x 9¼. 65675-6 Pa. $19.95

SONGS OF EXPERIENCE: Facsimile Reproduction with 26 Plates in Full Color, William Blake. 26 full-color plates from a rare 1826 edition. Includes "The Tyger," "London," "Holy Thursday," and other poems. Printed text of poems. 48pp. 5¼ x 7. 24636-1 Pa. $4.95

OLD-TIME VIGNETTES IN FULL COLOR, Carol Belanger Grafton (ed.). Over 390 charming, often sentimental illustrations, selected from archives of Victorian graphics—pretty women posing, children playing, food, flowers, kittens and puppies, smiling cherubs, birds and butterflies, much more. All copyright-free. 48pp. 9¼ x 12¼. 27269-9 Pa. $7.95

PERSPECTIVE FOR ARTISTS, Rex Vicat Cole. Depth, perspective of sky and sea, shadows, much more, not usually covered. 391 diagrams, 81 reproductions of drawings and paintings. 279pp. 5⅜ x 8½. 22487-2 Pa. $7.95

DRAWING THE LIVING FIGURE, Joseph Sheppard. Innovative approach to artistic anatomy focuses on specifics of surface anatomy, rather than muscles and bones. Over 170 drawings of live models in front, back and side views, and in widely varying poses. Accompanying diagrams. 177 illustrations. Introduction. Index. 144pp. 8⅜ x11¼. 26723-7 Pa. $8.95

GOTHIC AND OLD ENGLISH ALPHABETS: 100 Complete Fonts, Dan X. Solo. Add power, elegance to posters, signs, other graphics with 100 stunning copyright-free alphabets: Blackstone, Dolbey, Germania, 97 more–including many lower-case, numerals, punctuation marks. 104pp. 8⅛ x 11. 24695-7 Pa. $8.95

HOW TO DO BEADWORK, Mary White. Fundamental book on craft from simple projects to five-bead chains and woven works. 106 illustrations. 142pp. 5⅜ x 8. 20697-1 Pa. $4.95

THE BOOK OF WOOD CARVING, Charles Marshall Sayers. Finest book for beginners discusses fundamentals and offers 34 designs. "Absolutely first rate . . . well thought out and well executed."–E. J. Tangerman. 118pp. 7¾ x 10⅝. 23654-4 Pa. $6.95

ILLUSTRATED CATALOG OF CIVIL WAR MILITARY GOODS: Union Army Weapons, Insignia, Uniform Accessories, and Other Equipment, Schuyler, Hartley, and Graham. Rare, profusely illustrated 1846 catalog includes Union Army uniform and dress regulations, arms and ammunition, coats, insignia, flags, swords, rifles, etc. 226 illustrations. 160pp. 9 x 12. 24939-5 Pa. $10.95

WOMEN'S FASHIONS OF THE EARLY 1900s: An Unabridged Republication of "New York Fashions, 1909," National Cloak & Suit Co. Rare catalog of mail-order fashions documents women's and children's clothing styles shortly after the turn of the century. Captions offer full descriptions, prices. Invaluable resource for fashion, costume historians. Approximately 725 illustrations. 128pp. 8⅜ x 11¼. 27276-1 Pa. $11.95

THE 1912 AND 1915 GUSTAV STICKLEY FURNITURE CATALOGS, Gustav Stickley. With over 200 detailed illustrations and descriptions, these two catalogs are essential reading and reference materials and identification guides for Stickley furniture. Captions cite materials, dimensions and prices. 112pp. 6½ x 9¼. 26676-1 Pa. $9.95

EARLY AMERICAN LOCOMOTIVES, John H. White, Jr. Finest locomotive engravings from early 19th century: historical (1804–74), main-line (after 1870), special, foreign, etc. 147 plates. 142pp. 11⅜ x 8¼. 22772-3 Pa. $10.95

THE TALL SHIPS OF TODAY IN PHOTOGRAPHS, Frank O. Braynard. Lavishly illustrated tribute to nearly 100 majestic contemporary sailing vessels: Amerigo Vespucci, Clearwater, Constitution, Eagle, Mayflower, Sea Cloud, Victory, many more. Authoritative captions provide statistics, background on each ship. 190 black-and-white photographs and illustrations. Introduction. 128pp. 8⅞ x 11¾. 27163-3 Pa. $13.95

EARLY NINETEENTH-CENTURY CRAFTS AND TRADES, Peter Stockham (ed.). Extremely rare 1807 volume describes to youngsters the crafts and trades of the day: brickmaker, weaver, dressmaker, bookbinder, ropemaker, saddler, many more. Quaint prose, charming illustrations for each craft. 20 black-and-white line illustrations. 192pp. 4⅝ x 6. 27293-1 Pa. $4.95

VICTORIAN FASHIONS AND COSTUMES FROM HARPER'S BAZAR, 1867–1898, Stella Blum (ed.). Day costumes, evening wear, sports clothes, shoes, hats, other accessories in over 1,000 detailed engravings. 320pp. 9⅜ x 12¼.
22990-4 Pa. $14.95

GUSTAV STICKLEY, THE CRAFTSMAN, Mary Ann Smith. Superb study surveys broad scope of Stickley's achievement, especially in architecture. Design philosophy, rise and fall of the Craftsman empire, descriptions and floor plans for many Craftsman houses, more. 86 black-and-white halftones. 31 line illustrations. Introduction 208pp. 6½ x 9¼. 27210-9 Pa. $9.95

THE LONG ISLAND RAIL ROAD IN EARLY PHOTOGRAPHS, Ron Ziel. Over 220 rare photos, informative text document origin ( 1844) and development of rail service on Long Island. Vintage views of early trains, locomotives, stations, passengers, crews, much more. Captions. 8⅞ x 11¾. 26301-0 Pa. $13.95

THE BOOK OF OLD SHIPS: From Egyptian Galleys to Clipper Ships, Henry B. Culver. Superb, authoritative history of sailing vessels, with 80 magnificent line illustrations. Galley, bark, caravel, longship, whaler, many more. Detailed, informative text on each vessel by noted naval historian. Introduction. 256pp. 5⅜ x 8½. 27332-6 Pa. $7.95

TEN BOOKS ON ARCHITECTURE, Vitruvius. The most important book ever written on architecture. Early Roman aesthetics, technology, classical orders, site selection, all other aspects. Morgan translation. 331pp. 5⅜ x 8½. 20645-9 Pa. $8.95

THE HUMAN FIGURE IN MOTION, Eadweard Muybridge. More than 4,500 stopped-action photos, in action series, showing undraped men, women, children jumping, lying down, throwing, sitting, wrestling, carrying, etc. 390pp. 7⅞ x 10⅝.
20204-6 Clothbd. $25.95

TREES OF THE EASTERN AND CENTRAL UNITED STATES AND CANADA, William M. Harlow. Best one-volume guide to 140 trees. Full descriptions, woodlore, range, etc. Over 600 illustrations. Handy size. 288pp. 4½ x 6⅜.
20395-6 Pa. $6.95

SONGS OF WESTERN BIRDS, Dr. Donald J. Borror. Complete song and call repertoire of 60 western species, including flycatchers, juncoes, cactus wrens, many more—includes fully illustrated booklet.        Cassette and manual 99913-0 $8.95

GROWING AND USING HERBS AND SPICES, Milo Miloradovich. Versatile handbook provides all the information needed for cultivation and use of all the herbs and spices available in North America. 4 illustrations. Index. Glossary. 236pp. 5⅜ x 8½.
25058-X Pa. $6.95

BIG BOOK OF MAZES AND LABYRINTHS, Walter Shepherd. 50 mazes and labyrinths in all—classical, solid, ripple, and more—in one great volume. Perfect inexpensive puzzler for clever youngsters. Full solutions. 112pp. 8⅛ x 11.
22951-3 Pa. $4.95

PIANO TUNING, J. Cree Fischer. Clearest, best book for beginner, amateur. Simple repairs, raising dropped notes, tuning by easy method of flattened fifths. No previous skills needed. 4 illustrations. 201pp. 5⅜ x 8½. 23267-0 Pa. $6.95

A SOURCE BOOK IN THEATRICAL HISTORY, A. M. Nagler. Contemporary observers on acting, directing, make-up, costuming, stage props, machinery, scene design, from Ancient Greece to Chekhov. 611pp. 5⅜ x 8½. 20515-0 Pa. $12.95

THE COMPLETE NONSENSE OF EDWARD LEAR, Edward Lear. All nonsense limericks, zany alphabets, Owl and Pussycat, songs, nonsense botany, etc., illustrated by Lear. Total of 320pp. 5⅜ x 8½. (USO) 20167-8 Pa. $6.95

VICTORIAN PARLOUR POETRY: An Annotated Anthology, Michael R. Turner. 117 gems by Longfellow, Tennyson, Browning, many lesser-known poets. "The Village Blacksmith," "Curfew Must Not Ring Tonight," "Only a Baby Small," dozens more, often difficult to find elsewhere. Index of poets, titles, first lines. xxiii + 325pp. 5⅜ x 8¼. 27044-0 Pa. $8.95

DUBLINERS, James Joyce. Fifteen stories offer vivid, tightly focused observations of the lives of Dublin's poorer classes. At least one, "The Dead," is considered a masterpiece. Reprinted complete and unabridged from standard edition. 160pp. 5³⁄₁₆ x 8¼. 26870-5 Pa. $1.00

THE HAUNTED MONASTERY and THE CHINESE MAZE MURDERS, Robert van Gulik. Two full novels by van Gulik, set in 7th-century China, continue adventures of Judge Dee and his companions. An evil Taoist monastery, seemingly supernatural events; overgrown topiary maze hides strange crimes. 27 illustrations. 328pp. 5⅜ x 8½. 23502-5 Pa. $8.95

THE BOOK OF THE SACRED MAGIC OF ABRAMELIN THE MAGE, translated by S. MacGregor Mathers. Medieval manuscript of ceremonial magic. Basic document in Aleister Crowley, Golden Dawn groups. 268pp. 5⅜ x 8½. 23211-5 Pa. $8.95

NEW RUSSIAN-ENGLISH AND ENGLISH-RUSSIAN DICTIONARY, M. A. O'Brien. This is a remarkably handy Russian dictionary, containing a surprising amount of information, including over 70,000 entries. 366pp. 4½ x 6⅛. 20208-9 Pa. $9.95

HISTORIC HOMES OF THE AMERICAN PRESIDENTS, Second, Revised Edition, Irvin Haas. A traveler's guide to American Presidential homes, most open to the public, depicting and describing homes occupied by every American President from George Washington to George Bush. With visiting hours, admission charges, travel routes. 175 photographs. Index. 160pp. 8¼ x 11. 26751-2 Pa. $11.95

NEW YORK IN THE FORTIES, Andreas Feininger. 162 brilliant photographs by the well-known photographer, formerly with *Life* magazine. Commuters, shoppers, Times Square at night, much else from city at its peak. Captions by John von Hartz. 181pp. 9¼ x 10¾. 23585-8 Pa. $12.95

INDIAN SIGN LANGUAGE, William Tomkins. Over 525 signs developed by Sioux and other tribes. Written instructions and diagrams. Also 290 pictographs. 111pp. 6⅛ x 9¼. 22029-X Pa. $3.95

## *CATALOG OF DOVER BOOKS*

ANATOMY: A Complete Guide for Artists, Joseph Sheppard. A master of figure drawing shows artists how to render human anatomy convincingly. Over 460 illustrations. 224pp. 8⅜ x 11¼. 27279-6 Pa. $10.95

MEDIEVAL CALLIGRAPHY: Its History and Technique, Marc Drogin. Spirited history, comprehensive instruction manual covers 13 styles (ca. 4th century thru 15th). Excellent photographs; directions for duplicating medieval techniques with modern tools. 224pp. 8⅜ x 11¼. 26142-5 Pa. $12.95

DRIED FLOWERS: How to Prepare Them, Sarah Whitlock and Martha Rankin. Complete instructions on how to use silica gel, meal and borax, perlite aggregate, sand and borax, glycerine and water to create attractive permanent flower arrangements. 12 illustrations. 32pp. 5⅜ x 8½. 21802-3 Pa. $1.00

EASY-TO-MAKE BIRD FEEDERS FOR WOODWORKERS, Scott D. Campbell. Detailed, simple-to-use guide for designing, constructing, caring for and using feeders. Text, illustrations for 12 classic and contemporary designs. 96pp. 5⅜ x 8½. 25847-5 Pa. $2.95

SCOTTISH WONDER TALES FROM MYTH AND LEGEND, Donald A. Mackenzie. 16 lively tales tell of giants rumbling down mountainsides, of a magic wand that turns stone pillars into warriors, of gods and goddesses, evil hags, powerful forces and more. 240pp. 5⅜ x 8½. 29677-6 Pa. $6.95

THE HISTORY OF UNDERCLOTHES, C. Willett Cunnington and Phyllis Cunnington. Fascinating, well-documented survey covering six centuries of English undergarments, enhanced with over 100 illustrations: 12th-century laced-up bodice, footed long drawers (1795), 19th-century bustles, 19th-century corsets for men, Victorian "bust improvers," much more. 272pp. 5⅝ x 8¼. 27124-2 Pa. $9.95

ARTS AND CRAFTS FURNITURE: The Complete Brooks Catalog of 1912, Brooks Manufacturing Co. Photos and detailed descriptions of more than 150 now very collectible furniture designs from the Arts and Crafts movement depict davenports, settees, buffets, desks, tables, chairs, bedsteads, dressers and more, all built of solid, quarter-sawed oak. Invaluable for students and enthusiasts of antiques, Americana and the decorative arts. 80pp. 6½ x 9¼. 27471-3 Pa. $8.95

HOW WE INVENTED THE AIRPLANE: An Illustrated History, Orville Wright. Fascinating firsthand account covers early experiments, construction of planes and motors, first flights, much more. Introduction and commentary by Fred C. Kelly. 76 photographs. 96pp. 8¼ x 11. 25662-6 Pa. $8.95

THE ARTS OF THE SAILOR: Knotting, Splicing and Ropework, Hervey Garrett Smith. Indispensable shipboard reference covers tools, basic knots and useful hitches; handsewing and canvas work, more. Over 100 illustrations. Delightful reading for sea lovers. 256pp. 5⅜ x 8½. 26440-8 Pa. $7.95

FRANK LLOYD WRIGHT'S FALLINGWATER: The House and Its History, Second, Revised Edition, Donald Hoffmann. A total revision–both in text and illustrations–of the standard document on Fallingwater, the boldest, most personal architectural statement of Wright's mature years, updated with valuable new material from the recently opened Frank Lloyd Wright Archives. "Fascinating"–*The New York Times*. 116 illustrations. 128pp. 9¼ x 10¾. 27430-6 Pa. $11.95

PHOTOGRAPHIC SKETCHBOOK OF THE CIVIL WAR, Alexander Gardner. 100 photos taken on field during the Civil War. Famous shots of Manassas Harper's Ferry, Lincoln, Richmond, slave pens, etc. 244pp. 10⅝ x 8¼.          22731-6 Pa. $9.95

FIVE ACRES AND INDEPENDENCE, Maurice G. Kains. Great back-to-the-land classic explains basics of self-sufficient farming. The one book to get. 95 illustrations. 397pp. 5⅜ x 8½.          20974-1 Pa. $7.95

SONGS OF EASTERN BIRDS, Dr. Donald J. Borror. Songs and calls of 60 species most common to eastern U.S.: warblers, woodpeckers, flycatchers, thrushes, larks, many more in high-quality recording.          Cassette and manual 99912-2 $9.95

A MODERN HERBAL, Margaret Grieve. Much the fullest, most exact, most useful compilation of herbal material. Gigantic alphabetical encyclopedia, from aconite to zedoary, gives botanical information, medical properties, folklore, economic uses, much else. Indispensable to serious reader. 161 illustrations. 888pp. 6½ x 9¼. 2-vol. set. (USO)          Vol. I: 22798-7 Pa. $9.95
Vol. II: 22799-5 Pa. $9.95

HIDDEN TREASURE MAZE BOOK, Dave Phillips. Solve 34 challenging mazes accompanied by heroic tales of adventure. Evil dragons, people-eating plants, blood-thirsty giants, many more dangerous adversaries lurk at every twist and turn. 34 mazes, stories, solutions. 48pp. 8¼ x 11.          24566-7 Pa. $2.95

LETTERS OF W. A. MOZART, Wolfgang A. Mozart. Remarkable letters show bawdy wit, humor, imagination, musical insights, contemporary musical world; includes some letters from Leopold Mozart. 276pp. 5⅜ x 8½.          22859-2 Pa. $7.95

BASIC PRINCIPLES OF CLASSICAL BALLET, Agrippina Vaganova. Great Russian theoretician, teacher explains methods for teaching classical ballet. 118 illustrations. 175pp. 5⅜ x 8½.          22036-2 Pa. $5.95

THE JUMPING FROG, Mark Twain. Revenge edition. The original story of The Celebrated Jumping Frog of Calaveras County, a hapless French translation, and Twain's hilarious "retranslation" from the French. 12 illustrations. 66pp. 5⅜ x 8½.
22686-7 Pa. $3.95

BEST REMEMBERED POEMS, Martin Gardner (ed.). The 126 poems in this superb collection of 19th- and 20th-century British and American verse range from Shelley's "To a Skylark" to the impassioned "Renascence" of Edna St. Vincent Millay and to Edward Lear's whimsical "The Owl and the Pussycat." 224pp. 5⅜ x 8½.
27165-X Pa. $4.95

COMPLETE SONNETS, William Shakespeare. Over 150 exquisite poems deal with love, friendship, the tyranny of time, beauty's evanescence, death and other themes in language of remarkable power, precision and beauty. Glossary of archaic terms. 80pp. 5³⁄₁₆ x 8¼.          26686-9 Pa. $1.00

BODIES IN A BOOKSHOP, R. T. Campbell. Challenging mystery of blackmail and murder with ingenious plot and superbly drawn characters. In the best tradition of British suspense fiction. 192pp. 5⅜ x 8½.          24720-1 Pa. $6.95

CATALOG OF DOVER BOOKS

THE WIT AND HUMOR OF OSCAR WILDE, Alvin Redman (ed.). More than 1,000 ripostes, paradoxes, wisecracks: Work is the curse of the drinking classes; I can resist everything except temptation; etc. 258pp. 5⅜ x 8½. 20602-5 Pa. $5.95

SHAKESPEARE LEXICON AND QUOTATION DICTIONARY, Alexander Schmidt. Full definitions, locations, shades of meaning in every word in plays and poems. More than 50,000 exact quotations. 1,485pp. 6½ x 9¼. 2-vol. set.
Vol. 1: 22726-X Pa. $16.95
Vol. 2: 22727-8 Pa. $16.95

SELECTED POEMS, Emily Dickinson. Over 100 best-known, best-loved poems by one of America's foremost poets, reprinted from authoritative early editions. No comparable edition at this price. Index of first lines. 64pp. 5³⁄₁₆ x 8¼.
26466-1 Pa. $1.00

CELEBRATED CASES OF JUDGE DEE (DEE GOONG AN), translated by Robert van Gulik. Authentic 18th-century Chinese detective novel; Dee and associates solve three interlocked cases. Led to van Gulik's own stories with same characters. Extensive introduction. 9 illustrations. 237pp. 5⅜ x 8½. 23337-5 Pa. $6.95

THE MALLEUS MALEFICARUM OF KRAMER AND SPRENGER, translated by Montague Summers. Full text of most important witchhunter's "bible," used by both Catholics and Protestants. 278pp. 6⅝ x 10. 22802-9 Pa. $12.95

SPANISH STORIES/CUENTOS ESPAÑOLES: A Dual-Language Book, Angel Flores (ed.). Unique format offers 13 great stories in Spanish by Cervantes, Borges, others. Faithful English translations on facing pages. 352pp. 5⅜ x 8½.
25399-6 Pa. $8.95

THE CHICAGO WORLD'S FAIR OF 1893: A Photographic Record, Stanley Appelbaum (ed.). 128 rare photos show 200 buildings, Beaux-Arts architecture, Midway, original Ferris Wheel, Edison's kinetoscope, more. Architectural emphasis; full text. 116pp. 8¼ x 11. 23990-X Pa. $9.95

OLD QUEENS, N.Y., IN EARLY PHOTOGRAPHS, Vincent F. Seyfried and William Asadorian. Over 160 rare photographs of Maspeth, Jamaica, Jackson Heights, and other areas. Vintage views of DeWitt Clinton mansion, 1939 World's Fair and more. Captions. 192pp. 8⅞ x 11. 26358-4 Pa. $12.95

CAPTURED BY THE INDIANS: 15 Firsthand Accounts, 1750-1870, Frederick Drimmer. Astounding true historical accounts of grisly torture, bloody conflicts, relentless pursuits, miraculous escapes and more, by people who lived to tell the tale. 384pp. 5⅜ x 8½. 24901-8 Pa. $8.95

THE WORLD'S GREAT SPEECHES, Lewis Copeland and Lawrence W. Lamm (eds.). Vast collection of 278 speeches of Greeks to 1970. Powerful and effective models; unique look at history. 842pp. 5⅜ x 8½. 20468-5 Pa. $14.95

THE BOOK OF THE SWORD, Sir Richard F. Burton. Great Victorian scholar/adventurer's eloquent, erudite history of the "queen of weapons"–from prehistory to early Roman Empire. Evolution and development of early swords, variations (sabre, broadsword, cutlass, scimitar, etc.), much more. 336pp. 6⅛ x 9¼.
25434-8 Pa. $9.95

AUTOBIOGRAPHY: The Story of My Experiments with Truth, Mohandas K. Gandhi. Boyhood, legal studies, purification, the growth of the Satyagraha (nonviolent protest) movement. Critical, inspiring work of the man responsible for the freedom of India. 480pp. 5⅜ x 8½. (USO) 24593-4 Pa. $8.95

CELTIC MYTHS AND LEGENDS, T. W. Rolleston. Masterful retelling of Irish and Welsh stories and tales. Cuchulain, King Arthur, Deirdre, the Grail, many more. First paperback edition. 58 full-page illustrations. 512pp. 5⅜ x 8½. 26507-2 Pa. $9.95

THE PRINCIPLES OF PSYCHOLOGY, William James. Famous long course complete, unabridged. Stream of thought, time perception, memory, experimental methods; great work decades ahead of its time. 94 figures. 1,391pp. 5⅜ x 8½. 2-vol. set.
Vol. I: 20381-6 Pa. $12.95
Vol. II: 20382-4 Pa. $12.95

THE WORLD AS WILL AND REPRESENTATION, Arthur Schopenhauer. Definitive English translation of Schopenhauer's life work, correcting more than 1,000 errors, omissions in earlier translations. Translated by E. F. J. Payne. Total of 1,269pp. 5⅜ x 8½. 2-vol. set. Vol. 1: 21761-2 Pa. $11.95
Vol. 2: 21762-0 Pa. $12.95

MAGIC AND MYSTERY IN TIBET, Madame Alexandra David-Neel. Experiences among lamas, magicians, sages, sorcerers, Bonpa wizards. A true psychic discovery. 32 illustrations. 321pp. 5⅜ x 8½. (USO) 22682-4 Pa. $8.95

THE EGYPTIAN BOOK OF THE DEAD, E. A. Wallis Budge. Complete reproduction of Ani's papyrus, finest ever found. Full hieroglyphic text, interlinear transliteration, word-for-word translation, smooth translation. 533pp. 6½ x 9¼.
21866-X Pa. $10.95

MATHEMATICS FOR THE NONMATHEMATICIAN, Morris Kline. Detailed, college-level treatment of mathematics in cultural and historical context, with numerous exercises. Recommended Reading Lists. Tables. Numerous figures. 641pp. 5⅜ x 8½.
24823-2 Pa. $11.95

THEORY OF WING SECTIONS: Including a Summary of Airfoil Data, Ira H. Abbott and A. E. von Doenhoff. Concise compilation of subsonic aerodynamic characteristics of NACA wing sections, plus description of theory. 350pp. of tables. 693pp. 5⅜ x 8½. 60586-8 Pa. $14.95

THE RIME OF THE ANCIENT MARINER, Gustave Doré, S. T. Coleridge. Doré's finest work; 34 plates capture moods, subtleties of poem. Flawless full-size reproductions printed on facing pages with authoritative text of poem. "Beautiful. Simply beautiful."–*Publisher's Weekly.* 77pp. 9¼ x 12. 22305-1 Pa. $6.95

NORTH AMERICAN INDIAN DESIGNS FOR ARTISTS AND CRAFTSPEOPLE, Eva Wilson. Over 360 authentic copyright-free designs adapted from Navajo blankets, Hopi pottery, Sioux buffalo hides, more. Geometrics, symbolic figures, plant and animal motifs, etc. 128pp. 8⅜ x 11. (EUK) 25341-4 Pa. $8.95

SCULPTURE: Principles and Practice, Louis Slobodkin. Step-by-step approach to clay, plaster, metals, stone; classical and modern. 253 drawings, photos. 255pp. 8⅛ x 11.
22960-2 Pa. $11.95

# CATALOG OF DOVER BOOKS

THE INFLUENCE OF SEA POWER UPON HISTORY, 1660–1783, A. T. Mahan. Influential classic of naval history and tactics still used as text in war colleges. First paperback edition. 4 maps. 24 battle plans. 640pp. 5⅜ x 8½.       25509-3 Pa. $12.95

THE STORY OF THE TITANIC AS TOLD BY ITS SURVIVORS, Jack Winocour (ed.). What it was really like. Panic, despair, shocking inefficiency, and a little heroism. More thrilling than any fictional account. 26 illustrations. 320pp. 5⅜ x 8½.
20610-6 Pa. $8.95

FAIRY AND FOLK TALES OF THE IRISH PEASANTRY, William Butler Yeats (ed.). Treasury of 64 tales from the twilight world of Celtic myth and legend: "The Soul Cages," "The Kildare Pooka," "King O'Toole and his Goose," many more. Introduction and Notes by W. B. Yeats. 352pp. 5⅜ x 8½.       26941-8 Pa. $8.95

BUDDHIST MAHAYANA TEXTS, E. B. Cowell and Others (eds.). Superb, accurate translations of basic documents in Mahayana Buddhism, highly important in history of religions. The Buddha-karita of Asvaghosha, Larger Sukhavativyuha, more. 448pp. 5⅜ x 8½.       25552-2 Pa. $12.95

ONE TWO THREE . . . INFINITY: Facts and Speculations of Science, George Gamow. Great physicist's fascinating, readable overview of contemporary science: number theory, relativity, fourth dimension, entropy, genes, atomic structure, much more. 128 illustrations. Index. 352pp. 5⅜ x 8½.       25664-2 Pa. $8.95

ENGINEERING IN HISTORY, Richard Shelton Kirby, et al. Broad, nontechnical survey of history's major technological advances: birth of Greek science, industrial revolution, electricity and applied science, 20th-century automation, much more. 181 illustrations. ". . . excellent . . ."—*Isis.* Bibliography. vii + 530pp. 5⅜ x 8¼.
26412-2 Pa. $14.95

DALÍ ON MODERN ART: The Cuckolds of Antiquated Modern Art, Salvador Dalí. Influential painter skewers modern art and its practitioners. Outrageous evaluations of Picasso, Cézanne, Turner, more. 15 renderings of paintings discussed. 44 calligraphic decorations by Dalí. 96pp. 5⅜ x 8½. (USO)       29220-7 Pa. $4.95

ANTIQUE PLAYING CARDS: A Pictorial History, Henry René D'Allemagne. Over 900 elaborate, decorative images from rare playing cards (14th–20th centuries): Bacchus, death, dancing dogs, hunting scenes, royal coats of arms, players cheating, much more. 96pp. 9¼ x 12¼.       29265-7 Pa. $11.95

MAKING FURNITURE MASTERPIECES: 30 Projects with Measured Drawings, Franklin H. Gottshall. Step-by-step instructions, illustrations for constructing handsome, useful pieces, among them a Sheraton desk, Chippendale chair, Spanish desk, Queen Anne table and a William and Mary dressing mirror. 224pp. 8⅛ x 11¼.
29338-6 Pa. $13.95

THE FOSSIL BOOK: A Record of Prehistoric Life, Patricia V. Rich et al. Profusely illustrated definitive guide covers everything from single-celled organisms and dinosaurs to birds and mammals and the interplay between climate and man. Over 1,500 illustrations. 760pp. 7½ x 10⅛.       29371-8 Pa. $29.95

*Prices subject to change without notice.*

Available at your book dealer or write for free catalog to Dept. GI, Dover Publications, Inc., 31 East 2nd St., Mineola, N.Y. 11501. Dover publishes more than 500 books each year on science, elementary and advanced mathematics, biology, music, art, literary history, social sciences and other areas.